Conflict & Diplomacy from the Great War to the Cold War

STUDIES IN MODERN EUROPEAN HISTORY

Frank J. Coppa
General Editor

Vol. 34

PETER LANG
New York • Washington, D.C./Baltimore • Boston • Bern
Frankfurt am Main • Berlin • Brussels • Vienna • Canterbury

Donald E. Shepardson

CONFLICT & DIPLOMACY FROM THE GREAT WAR TO THE COLD WAR

PETER LANG
New York • Washington, D.C./Baltimore • Boston • Bern
Frankfurt am Main • Berlin • Brussels • Vienna • Canterbury

LIBRARY OF CONGRESS CATALOGING-IN-PUBLICATION DATA
Shepardson, Donald E.
Conflict and diplomacy from the Great War
to the Cold War / Donald E. Shepardson.
p. cm. — (Studies in modern European history; vol. 34)
Includes bibliographical references and index.
1. History, Modern—20th century. I. Title. II. Series.
D421.S513   909.82—dc21   98-36825
ISBN 0-8204-4194-5
ISSN 0893-6897

DIE DEUTSCHE BIBLIOTHEK-CIP-EINHEITSAUFNAHME
Shepardson, Donald E.:
Conflict and diplomacy from the great war
to the cold war / Donald E. Shepardson.
–New York; Washington, D.C./Baltimore; Boston; Bern;
Frankfurt am Main; Berlin; Brussels; Vienna; Canterbury: Lang.
(Studies in modern European history; Vol. 34)
ISBN 0-8204-4194-5

Cover design by Lisa Dillon

The paper in this book meets the guidelines for permanence and durability
of the Committee on Production Guidelines for Book Longevity
of the Council of Library Resources.

© 1999 Peter Lang Publishing, Inc., New York

All rights reserved.
Reprint or reproduction, even partially, in all forms such as microfilm,
xerography, microfiche, microcard, and offset strictly prohibited.

Printed in the United States of America

To Those Wonderful People

In the

Donald O. Rod Library

Who Have Helped Me in So Many Ways

for So Many Years

ACKNOWLEDGEMENTS

I have benfited greatly from the help of others. The Graduate College at the University of Northern Iowa provided financial support for the project with a Professional Development Leave. The staff of the Donald O. Rod Library contributed to the completion of the book by securing quantities of material through interlibrary loan and by providing a faculty study where much of the research and writing was done. A note of appreciation must go to my two department heads, Dr. John Johnson and Dr. Donald Whitnah for their encouragement. I send a heartfelt thanks to my colleagues in the History Department, and especially to Dr. Robert Martin whose counsel on numerous occasions helped me to complete the manuscript.

TABLE OF CONTENTS

List of Maps viii
1. On These Battlefields 1
2. The Future Belongs to Us 16
3. The Decline of the West 37
4. A Spectacle of Miserable Disagreement.............. 48
5. A New Axis of Power 68
6. A Faraway Country 81
7. Speak for England! 98
8. We Would Have Been Invincible 119
9. Hitler Looks East 143
10. The World Will Hold Its Breath 158
11. The End of the Beginning.................................... 177
12. The Road to Teheran.. 197
13. The Beginning of the End.................................... 219
14. Victory Disease 232
15. Yalta 247
16. Twilight of the Gods 262
17. Hell From the Top... 277
Bibliography 297
Index 317

MAPS

World War I in Europe 15

World War I Peace Settlement 36
  in Europe and the Middle East

Axis Europe, 1941..118

North African Campaigns, 1942 - 1945 196

Defeat of the Axis in Europe, 1942 - 1945..231

World War II in the Pacific 276

Chapter One

On These Battlefields

On the battlefields of the Western Front, said Scott Fitzgerald's Dick Diver, "All my beautiful lovely safe world blew itself up."[1] It had begun on a wave of patriotism buoyed by optimism. Most Europeans saw the wars of Bismarck as the model for the future with high rewards being won at low cost. Only a few, such as the elder Helmuth von Moltke, the architect of the Prussian victory in 1871, realized that the coming war would be a battle of attrition more like the Seven Years War or even the Thirty Years War. When the Germans approached the Belgian fortifications at Liège in early August of 1914, they and the entire world had a grisly glimpse of what this war would be as the machine gun and a new generation of artillery set a pattern of butchery that became so common on the Western Front.

The first phase of the war came to an end with the Battle of the Marne. Lasting from September 5 to September 12, the battle was in reality a collection of several skirmishes over a wide front with no clear winner. Throughout September and October each side attempted to outflank the other, causing the front to gradually extend to the North Sea. Although the sea was not the original target, control of the channel ports offered increasing advantages as it came to be realized that a long war was in store. By Christmas the Western Front had stabilized. From Switzerland to the sea, armies faced each other across No Man's Land.

The first month of war in the East also provided a glimpse into the future. Responding to a plea from their French ally, the Russians launched an attack on August 13, with an army badly led and ill equipped. Initially, under the command of the aged General Max von Pritwitz, the Germans were surprised, since they had expected it would take the Russians at least six weeks to mobilize. But at Tannenberg (August 26-29) and then at the Masurian Lakes (September 6-15) the Russians were annihilated as much by their own incompetence as by German strength. Tannenberg altered the course of history for decades to come when Paul von Hindenburg was called out of retirement to replace the faltering General Max von Pritzwitz. Erich Ludendorff, who had just distinguished himself at Liège, was then assigned to aid Hindenburg. They met in Hanover and arrived at the front in time to receive credit for the victories that would eventually elevate them to national heroes and de facto rulers of Germany.

Within a month the war had spread from Europe to the colonial empires of the belligerents. The Western Front encompassed only a small part of the global action, but here the great Western powers of the old order faced each other in the lingering throes of death. Even when there was a lull, the killing continued from haphazard shelling, the sudden sweep of machine gun fire, or just the lone sniper waiting for someone to be careless. The mental wounds were more subtle, but also devastating. Fear and tension combined with suffering and death to produce a group of brutalized men who had lost the veneer of civilization. Death and pain began to lose all meaning in a world where many found their only solace in a strange kind of fatalism that said when the time came it would simply come and there was nothing to be done about it save to greet it with relief.

After fruitless attacks and counterattacks throughout 1915 both sides abandoned attempts for a victorious breakthrough. They now would bleed the enemy on the battlefield while breaking morale at home. On February 21, 1916, "the year of the killing" began with the German attack on Verdun. Field Marshal Erich von Falkenhayn and the Supreme Command believed the French would defend it at all cost. They were right. The Verdun commander, General Henri-Philippe Pétain, promised that the Germans "shall not pass." The French held, but at a terrible price that haunted the country long after the war had ended.

British forces aided the French with an offensive on the Somme in July. By 1916 the small professional British army had virtually disappeared in the wake of many battles. In its place there stood "Kitchener's Army" of volunteers who had answered the call for king and country. They were the flower of British youth, and their fate at the Somme inflicted a wound upon the British psyche equal to that suffered by the French at Verdun. At 0730 on July 1, the new army went over the top and into the greatest slaughter ever witnessed in one day of combat. With the end of the Somme offensive in November and the coming of winter, the year of the killing came to an end. The number of men lost will never be known. During the five months of Verdun and the Somme, wrote Martin Gilbert, nearly one million men were killed, an average of more than 6,600 men killed every day, more than 277 every minute, nearly five men every second."[2] For that sacrifice the Western Front remained virtually unchanged and little was accomplished except to further the destruction of a generation.

Millions of casualties produced their own imperative. The entire political and social structure of Europe was transformed by the war and then torn asunder. At home, the failure in war and the losses suffered produced a dual effect of gloom and optimism. The belligerents had entered the war with little in the way of goals beyond survival. But within a short time, appetites were whetted for new territories and increased power. With high casualties, even more grandiose conquests were deemed necessary to justify them.

Throughout the war and indeed up to the armistice, the Germans appeared to be stronger, since their soldiers occupied enemy land. For the French and the Russians the situation was the opposite. There could be no peace without a German withdrawal or an Allied victory. Until one side or the other managed to alter the status quo of battle there was little chance for any peace without victory. Both sides had gone too far down the road of war. Reason, compassion, and truth had been among the first to fall at Liège and Tannenberg.

No one wished to end the war more than the American President Woodrow Wilson. Wilson's "every action and policy," wrote Arthur Link, "was ultimately informed and molded by his Christian faith," and this faith in God and in a moral universe became his main guide both in politics and diplomacy.[3] Added to this belief in God as the supreme arbiter of history and purpose, Wilson believed Anglo-American democracy was the most Christian form of government. America was uniquely qualified and destined to lead in establishing democracy throughout the world along with the extension of American capitalism. Democracy and political liberty could exist only within a system of economic liberty; and economic liberty was a requisite for political liberty. Wilson believed the President must be sovereign in foreign policy to carry out this mission. "Our President," he wrote in 1907, ". . . must stand always at the front of our affairs, and the office will be as big and as influential as the man who occupies it."[4]

By the middle of 1915 the man who occupied the White House saw America headed for war. The sinking of the *Lusitania* in May had inflamed American opinion and intensified agitation for intervention. Wilson wanted to avoid war, but he feared that someday the United States might have to fight for its rights at sea. He sought peace in Europe without victory, but to the belligerents, victory at the cost of additional millions was preferable to peace without conquest and vengeance.

Wilson saw his reelection in 1916 as a mandate from the American people to continue his efforts for peace and to keep the country out of war. He went before Congress on January 22, 1917 to speak for the "silent mass of mankind everywhere." He asked for a peace without victory as the basis for building a community of nations free to from the alliances and rivalries of the past. This new community of democratic nations would be based on "American principles, American policies. They are the principles of mankind and must prevail." The new world order would be created in the American image. "The President," noted one critic, "thinks he is President of the whole world."[5]

Nearly two weeks before Wilson's speech Hindenburg and Ludendorff, who now had transformed Germany into their military dictatorship, secured the Kaiser's permission to resume unrestricted submarine warfare. Pleading military necessity, the Supreme Command argued that time was running against them. A concentrated submarine campaign would starve Britain out of the war in six months, long before the United States could intervene in any meaningful way.[6]

Resumption of submarine warfare along with the offer of an alliance with Mexico via the Zimmermann note convinced Wilson that Germany was governed by men gone mad in their lust for conquest and domination of Europe. Whatever his reservations about Britain and France, they were democracies upon which to build a new world community, a goal recently furthered by the fall of Tsardom in Russia and the establishment of a liberal Provisional Government. Wilson went before Congress on April 2, 1917 to ask for war against Germany, not merely to secure neutral rights, but "to vindicate the principle of peace and justice in the life of the world as against selfish autocratic power and to set up amongst the really free and self-governed peoples of the world such a concert of purpose and of action as will henceforth ensure the observance of those principles." To this group he noted the addition of Russia, "a fit partner for a League of

Honor." "To such a task," he closed, "we can dedicate our lives and our fortune . . . with the pride of those who know that the day has come when America is privileged to spend her blood and her might for the principles that gave her birth."[7]

Russia provided the cause for much of Wilson's optimism. The hope for a strong and unified democratic Russia was perhaps illusory for several reasons, not the least among them being that the Provisional Government had little to govern and even less authority. By early 1917 the Romanov Empire had virtually disintegrated. The harsh winter of 1916-1917 had added to the anger, frustration, and misery so pervasive in Petrograd. On March 8, a group of demonstrators celebrating International Women's Day merged with another group of women protesting the shortage of bread.[8] Together they turned more violent, replacing the demand for bread with "Down with the Autocracy" and "Down with the War." The war had magnified the brutality, incompetence, and inefficiency of the government, and in the end the upheaval "happened." The people of Petrograd had suffered enough. When it became obvious that no one wished him to remain, Nicholas II abdicated for himself and his hemophilic son. The Romanov dynasty itself came to an end when the tsar's brother, Grand Duke Michael, waved all claim to the throne.

Under the direction of Prime Minister Prince George Lvov the new Provisional Government proclaimed civil liberties, acknowledged the autonomy and independence of border areas and promised extensive social reforms for the future under a new government to be organized by an elected Constituent Assembly. The success of the government depended on whether it was willing to end the war with Germany and devote its full energies to rebuilding the country. To do so meant abandoning allies who feared destruction unless the eastern front were continued. It also meant abandoning promised war gains in the Balkans and even the age old dream of ruling Constantinople. The Provisional Government refused to do either and thereby gradually lost what little power and prestige it had to the Petrograd Soviet.

The Petrograd Soviet of Workers' and Soldiers' Deputies remained aloof from the Provisional Government. Its leadership believed the Soviet should remain so during this bourgeois phase of history. The attitude of the Soviet changed, however, with the return of Vladimir Ilyich Lenin to Russia. In 1903 Lenin had challenged the leadership of the Russian Social Democratic Labor Party on philosophical grounds and party organization. He rejected the orthodox view that the middle class must topple the monarchy and lead Russia through a capitalist stage before there could be a socialist revolution. He believed the middle class was too weak in body and spirit to lead in much of anything; that it would have to be pushed by a Dictatorship of the Proletariat. He saw revolution in Russia as a spark for a general European revolution that would in turn ensure success of the socialist revolution in Russia.

To carry out the revolution Lenin believed the party must be ever vigilant against opportunists who would compromise revolution with reform. Lenin merged the ideological goals of Marxism with the conspiratorial traditions of former Russian revolutionaries. The party must be small and well-disciplined, operating on the principle of "democratic centralism," with emphasis on the latter. There would be debate among the party leadership, but once the decision was made, it was to be obeyed by all lower echelons.

Lenin's challenge split the party. Taking advantage of a temporary majority, Lenin designated his faction Bolshevik, or a majority faction, and opponents the Menshevik, or minority faction. Within each faction there were shades of opinion. Generally, however, Lenin's faction remained a minority within the Russian Social Democratic Party until 1912 when he formed his own Bolshevik Party.

Lenin thundered against the opportunists of the Second International who supported their governments when war came. Instead, he argued they must convert this imperialist war into a class war to destroy the old order.[9] To advance his cause Lenin attended conferences at Zimmerwald, Switzerland, in 1915 and at Kienthal the following year where he told other delegates that the war was the signal for mobilizing the working class in a final assault against the bourgeoisie and the transition to socialism.[10] Lenin did not believe he would see the coming revolution until the Germans offered to send him back to Russia like a fire ship into an enemy harbor. On April 16, 1917, six days after his forty-seventh birthday, he arrived in Petrograd.

Lenin dazed his followers by calling for an alliance of the proletariat and the poor peasantry to overthrow the Provisional Government as the first step toward the socialist revolution in Europe. He also said the Bolsheviks must establish a new Communist Party and form a Third, or Communist, International under Russian leadership.

Lenin and the Bolsheviks blended into the kaleidoscope of shifting personalities and parties for several weeks while the government continued to weaken. War Minister Alexander Kerensky, believed a successful offensive would impress the Germans and allow the government to make an honorable peace. On July 1, the Russian army launched an offensive against the Austrians in Galicia. After some initial success, the drive was stopped and then turned into a defeat when the Germans came to the aid of their Austrian ally.

Failure of the offensive led to violent protests in Petrograd that were eased somewhat when rumors began to spread that Lenin was a German agent. On July 18, government forces moved against the Bolsheviks and forced Lenin to flee to Finland. Despite the show of force, the government continued to lose authority while the Bolsheviks gained support. Kerensky became prime minister on July 20 and reorganized the government. Caught between the Left and the Right, the Provisional Government attempted to govern a country that had become little more than a geographic expression with little authority outside of Petrograd and less each day within the city itself.

By October the Bolsheviks had gained control of the Petrograd Soviet, making it possible for Lenin to speak with conviction when he demanded "All Power to the Soviet." Lenin believed that the time was right for a final blow that would give power to the Soviet. The assault began on the night of November 6 with Leon Trotsky coordinating the Bolshevik forces. Except for a minor skirmish at the Winter Palace, there was little resistance, and hardly a second look when Kerensky fled the city.

In a Decree of Peace of November 8, the new Soviet Government called for "negotiations for a just, democratic peace" based on "peace without annexations," but the Allied government were no more receptive than they had been about Wilson's peace without victory.[11] They were more unhappy when the Soviets published secret treaties made with the Tsarist and Provisional Governments giving substance to the charge that this was indeed a war of imperialism. In addition, the Bolshevik call for European revolution, and repudiation of foreign debts made any kind of peace nearly impossible.

The Germans and their Austrian allies now had the best of all possible worlds: victory with annexations. Berlin accepted the Soviet offer for a cease fire. The two sides reached a preliminary armistice agreement at Brest Litovsk on December 5, and negotiations for a final peace began on December 22. It was quickly apparent that Germans intended the conference to be one of ratification more than negotiation. The Bolsheviks were ambivalent on whether the road to peace lay through revolution or the reverse. Their primary objective was simply to delay as long as possible in order to gauge shifting events and propagate the coming European revolution.

The German military representative, General Max von Hoffmann, presented War Commissar Trotsky with an ultimatum in the form of a large map designating the new borders of Russia on January 24, 1918. Trotsky's "no war — no peace" response seemed like a brilliant ploy to avoid the harsh terms until the Germans launched an attack. Even then many of the Bolsheviks, including the normally realistic Deputy Commissar for Foreign Affairs, George Chicherin, urged a new revolutionary war. Lenin knew better. Continuing the war had destroyed the Provisional Government more than he or any other revolutionary. His government needed a "breathing space" until the coming revolution nullified all treaties along with the old order. On March 3, the Soviet government signed the treaty of Brest Litovsk. Two days later they moved their capital to Moscow.

Moving to Moscow gave Lenin greater distance from the Germans. It also gave him a more strategic location for fighting a civil war his coup had begun. Opposition to Lenin had formed immediately after the Petrograd coup and grew rapidly following his dispersal of the Constituent Assembly. The November 25 elections had given the Bolsheviks only 168 of 703 deputies. But Lenin had no intention of turning power over to the Assembly, regardless of public opinion. It met on January 18, 1918, and was quickly dispersed by Bolshevik troops in what Lenin called the "open liquidation of formal democracy in the name of revolutionary dictatorship."[12]

By the summer of 1918 there were as many as eighteen insurgent groups in addition to various national movements. Lenin's opponents were known collectively as the Whites, although they included moderates and even radicals. As civil war increased, however, leadership fell to former tsarist officers who had as little appreciation for political propaganda as they did for military coordination. The Bolsheviks, on the other hand, were well coordinated, adept at propaganda, and able to gain many adherents by associating the Whites with forces of reaction and foreign domination.

Lenin's revolution sought to destroy the established order as the French Revolution had sought to destroy the *ancien régime*.[13] Throughout the civil war, Lenin was concerned as much with sparking a European revolution as with securing a Bolshevik victory in Russia. His hope was more plausible than it might seem in retrospect. Throughout central Europe the old empires collapsed, while in Germany the morale of the populace ebbed further in the wake of defeat and malnutrition. Lenin and the Bolsheviks attempted to use the upheaval in the West to "overthrow the rule of capital . . . in order to reconstruct Europe and the whole world on democratic and socialist lines."[14]

The Bolsheviks were themselves being besieged while carrying out their offensive against the West. The Germans remained the primary threat during the first months of the revolution. In August of 1918 they forced the Soviets to sign a supplementary treaty ceding Livonia and Estonia in addition to payment of an indemnity of six billion marks. Berlin might have put an end to the Soviet government altogether, but that could have led to a White victory and a reopening of the Eastern Front.

The immediate concern for the Allies was military. Closure of the Eastern Front threatened to bring defeat in the West. Allied leaders first discussed the new Russian situation in late November, 1917. Their concerns were more military than ideological. Intervention was considered but rejected until the situation became clearer. It became apparent that the Bolsheviks were becoming stronger each day, and that their control was greater than previously thought. The loss of the Eastern Front was already having grave repercussions as the German transferred troops westward for the offensive in the spring of 1918.

German penetration into the Ukraine and the Caucasus also endangered the Balkans and the Middle East. The Allies were also concerned about the war material they had sent to Russia prior to the Bolshevik coup. The Bolsheviks refused to pay for it, and their general hostility opened the possibility it might fall to the Germans. The German offensive following Trotsky's "no war, no peace" ploy, alarmed the Allies and increased open sentiment for intervention.[15] Lenin's decision to sign what Clemenceau called "the shameful peace" of Brest Litovsk coincided with the surrender of Romania, removing Allied pressure in southeastern Europe.[16]

Western leaders were bitter toward the Bolsheviks and saw intervention as necessary for their survival. By late spring 1918 each of the Allied leaders were leaning to intervention in the face of what they perceived as military necessity. Wilson remained the most reluctant. He disliked the Bolsheviks because they had overthrown the Provisional Government, which he had seen as something of an American protégé, and he opposed it as a threat to his own vision of the future. If he must choose, however, he preferred the Bolsheviks to any Romanov restoration.[17] Japanese penetration into Siberia concerned him also, but not yet enough to warrant American military intervention.

As the situation worsened, however, Wilson approved limited Allied intervention, but continued to withhold American forces. On June 27, Wilson received a telegram from Field Marshal Ferdinand Foch, the Allied commander in chief, linking intervention in Russia to "success in Europe."[18] At the same time the situation in Russia worsened as a result of warfare between the Czech Legion and the Bolsheviks. Prior to the March revolution the legion had been a contingent of approximately 70,000 men within the Russian army fighting against the Austro-Hungarian Empire in return for independence following the war.

With the collapse in the east the Allies intended to transport the Legion to the west as a contingent under French command, and it appeared the Soviets were agreeable to transporting it across the Trans-Siberian railway for eventual passage to France. As they traveled, however, the Czechs became strung out in pockets from the Ukraine to Vladivostok and then found themselves fighting the Bolsheviks.

Foch's letter combined with the Czech situation made Wilson receptive to the appeal of the Supreme War Council on July 3. The Council argued that intervention should bring "control of Siberia to the Urals" and even an eventual "advance to the center of Russia," while failure to intervene would prolong the war and discredit the Allies in the Slavic world. Wilson agreed to intervention, but solely to save the Czechs. He opposed any attempt to reopen the eastern front, he had no intention of adding to the "present sad confusion in Russia" with military intervention.[19] The Allies were dissatisfied with Wilson's reply, but used the promise of American support to extend their control in northern Russia as well as in Siberia.

Although Wilson knew relatively little about Lenin and his Bolsheviks, he believed Lenin represented a genuine desire by the Russian people for peace without annexations and indemnities. Lenin also represented a new and potentially successful challenge to the old diplomacy that had brought on the war. On January 8, 1918, Wilson had gone before Congress to announced democracy's answer to the Soviet Peace Decree of November 8, 1917, as well as an appeal to inhabitants of all the belligerent countries. He presented his famous Fourteen Points as a foundation for ending the war and constructing a new global order. Wilson repeated his desire for a peace that would preserve the legitimate interests and institutions of Germany, but added the condition that "we should know who her spokesmen speak for when they speak to us, whether for the Reichstag majority or for the military party and the men whose creed is imperial domination."[20]

Wilson knew that peace without victory was unlikely while Hindenburg and Ludendorff controlled Germany. In the spring of 1918 Germany held much of what expansionist had dreamed of for decades. The time would have been right to go on the defensive in the West while securing an empire in central Europe as a barrier to the Bolshevik threat. But Austria was staggering, and its collapse would leave southern Germany open to attack while cutting off resources from the Balkans.

Prior to Brest Litovsk, Hindenburg and Ludendorff had decided on a massive assault in the west to end the war before the Americans could enter in force. On March 21, 1918 the Ludendorff Offensive began with an attack reminiscent of 1914. Led by shock troops and employing new methods of artillery, the Germans gained almost forty miles in five days and appeared to be on the way to splitting Anglo-French lines. Faced with defeat, the Allies agreed to a unified command under Field Marshal Ferdinand Foch in late March. Foch improved military coordination, but the Germans continued to advance. By late May they had again reached the Marne River. But again the Allies held, bolstered now by impressive American showings at Cantigny and Château-Thierry.

The German army of 1914 had been able to absorb defeat. The army of 1918 had grown weak in body and spirit. It fell back on July 17, when Foch unexpectedly ordered a counterattack. Foch pressed the attack relentlessly, and by mid-August Ludendorff was forced to admit that Germany's only chance lay in strategic defense. In September the pace of collapse accelerated when Germany's allies faltered. By the end of the month Bulgaria was out of the war while Austria-Hungary and Turkey staggered toward surrender.

Ludendorff himself suffered a complete emotional and physical breakdown on the twenty-eighth. The next day he and Hindenburg met with Kaiser William II at Spa in Belgium to recommend an armistice based on Wilson's Fourteen Points. When the army admitted defeat to the Reichstag on October 2, a storm of protest broke loose filled with charges of betrayal and deception. The Supreme Command could no longer block long awaited democratic reforms after losing its credibility. On the following day the new government of Prince Max of Baden asked Wilson for an armistice based on the Fourteen Points.[21]

Allied response to the note was divided. Some saw it as a ploy to buy time, and there was substance to the suspicion. Ludendorff had recovered enough to oppose ending the war until he was dismissed by the kaiser on

October 27. London and Paris resented the unilateral negotiations between Berlin and Washington, and they had no sympathy for an armistice based on the Fourteen Points. Foch believed that any armistice should deal with immediate terms on the field that would leave Germany unable to continue the war. He was supported by the American Army commander, General John J. Pershing, and to a lesser extent by the British commander, Sir Douglas Haig. Under pressure from his allies, the military, and politicians at home, Wilson gave the Germans a choice between continuation of the Allied attack or an armistice that included "destruction of the arbitrary power . . . which had hitherto controlled the German nation."[22]

The Germans would have to change their political system as well as lay down their arms to receive an armistice. When Prince Max stated that the government had already "undergone a fundamental change" it was not enough. The United States would not deal with "monarchical autocrats" of Germany now or later.[23] There must be an end to the monarchy of William II. William II had been *Deutscher Kaiser* for thirty years and the Hohenzollerns had ruled Prussia for centuries. But by late October most Germans wanted peace more than William II, and the country itself was beginning to disintegrate in the wake of war and the ominous shadow of Soviet Bolshevism. On November 2, the kaiser fled the chaos of Berlin and traveled to Spa where the news was worse. The Allies had again broken through while German soldiers and sailors mutinied when ordered to fight. William refused to abdicate in the belief that the army was still loyal to him. That illusion ended on the night of November 9. Ludendorff's replacement, General William Gröner, did what Hindenburg had not the courage to do. "The army," he said, "will march home in good order under its generals, but not under Your Majesty."[24]

Prince Max believed abdication was imminent and announced it in the hope of buying time and saving the monarchy. He then turned the government over to the Social Democratic leaders Frederick Ebert and Philipp Scheidemann. Feeling pressures from radicals, Scheidemann took it upon himself to proclaim a republic, to the consternation of Ebert and the Reichstag. Upon hearing the news, Hindenburg convinced the kaiser to seek refuge in Holland for his own safety and to avoid civil war.

Before leaving the government, Prince Max had dispatched a delegation led by Matthias Erzberger of the Catholic Center Party to seek an armistice. At the first meeting on November 8, Marshal Foch presented them with terms calling for virtual demilitarization, repatriation of Allied prisoners, and plans to impose reparations on Germany for damages done during the war. The terms were harsher than expected, but the desperate Germans had to accept. At 1100 hours on Monday, November 11, the armistice went into effect.

The Great War was over, but the fire of another conflict lay in the smoking ashes of the old order. Britain and France, and the spirit of liberal democracy they represented, had been wounded and weakened. They had survived the war more than they had won it. The great empires of Germany, Austria-Hungary, and Russia had fallen. The new states of central Europe now faced the insecurities of independence, while to the east Lenin's revolution sought to destroy what remained of the old order with international revolution. Within a year, seething discontents of returning veterans would help Benito Mussolini to forge a new ideology and movement to challenge Lenin's Communism as well as Western Liberalism for political control of the future.

NOTES

1. F. Scott Fitzgerald, *Tender is the Night* (New York: Charles Scribner's Sons, 1980), 57.
2. Martin Gilbert, *The First World War: A Complete History* (New York: Henry Holt, 1994), 300.
3. *Wilson's Diplomacy: An International Symposium,* ed. J. Joseph Huthmacher and Warren I. Susman (Cambridge, Mass: Schenk Publishing Company, 1973), 7.
4. *The Papers of Woodrow Wilson,* ed. Arthur S. Link. vol. 18 (Princeton: Princeton University Press, 1971), 121.
5. *Congressional Record,* 64th Congress, 2nd Session, pt. 2. (Washington: U.S. Government Printing Office, 1917), 1741-1743. *New York Times,* January 22, 1917, 1.
6. Robert H. Ferrell, *Woodrow Wilson and World War I* (New York: Harper and Row, 1985), 15.
7. *Congressional Record,* 65th Congress, 1st Session (Washington: U.S. Government Printing Office, 1917), 102-104.
8. All dates used are according to the Gregorian calendar.
9. V.I. Lenin, *Collected Works,* vol. 21. trans. Julius Katzer (Moscow: Progress Publishers, 1964), 27-34.
10. Ibid., vol. 22, 144.
11. Lenin, *Collected Works,* vol. 26, 149-153.

12. Richard Pipes, *The Russian Revolution* (New York: Alfred A. Knopf), 556.
13. Henry Kissinger, *Diplomacy* (New York: Simon and Schuster, 1994), 258. John L. Gaddis, *We Now Know: Rethinking Cold War History* (New York: Oxford University Press, 1997), 5.
14. Jane Degras, ed., *Soviet Documents on Foreign Policy*, vol. 1 (New York: Oxford University Press, 1951), 19.
15. *Papers Relating to the Foreign Relations of the United States: 1918: Russia*, vol. 1 (Washington: U.S. Government Printing Office, 1931), 384.
16. George Clemenceau, *Grandeur and Misery of Victory* (New York: Harcourt, Brace, and Company, 1930), 191.
17. Edward M. Bennett, *Recognition of Russia: An American Foreign Policy Dilemma* (Waltham, Mass., Blaisdell Publishing Company, 1970), 24.
18. *The Papers of Woodrow Wilson*, vol. 48, 446.
19. *FRUS: 1918: Russia*, vol. 2 (Washington, 1931), 241-246, 262-263. Richard K. Debo, *Survival and Consolidation: The Foreign Policy of Soviet Russia, 1918-1921* (Montreal: McGill-Queens University Press, 1992), 6.
20. *Congressional Record*, 65th Congress, 2nd Session (Washington: U.S. Government Printing Office, 1918), 680-681.
21. *FRUS: 1918,* Supplement 1 (Washington, 1930), 338.
22. Ibid., 359
23. Ibid., 381-382.
24. Michael Balfour, *The Kaiser and His Times* (New York: W.W. Norton and Company, 1972), 407.

World War I in Europe

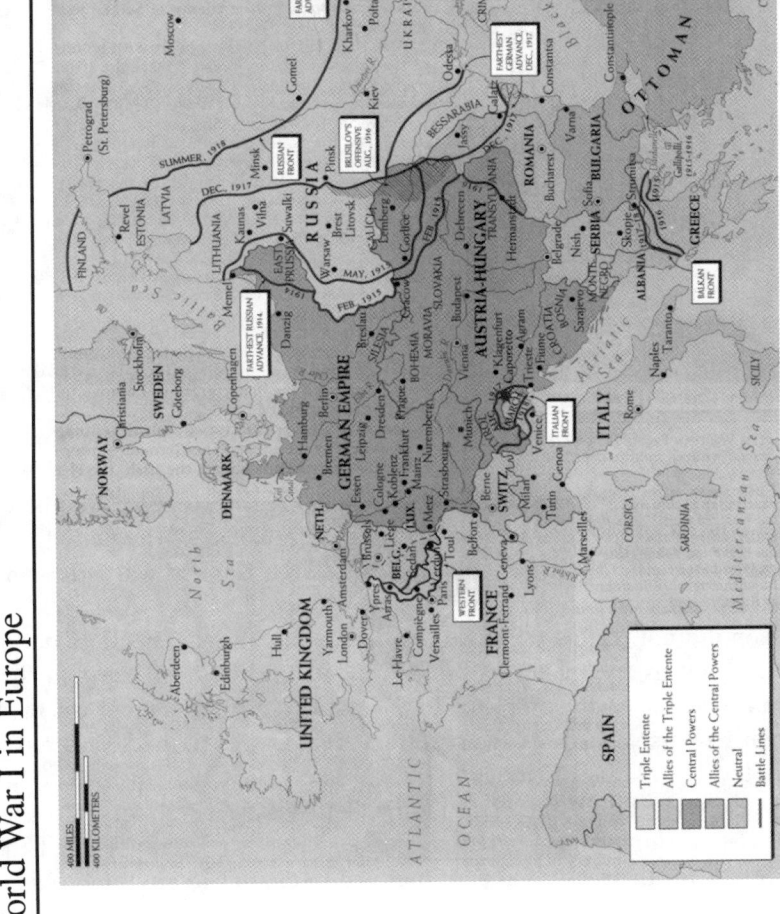

WESTERN HERITAGE VOL. 2 SINCE 1648 6/E. by KAGAN/OZMENT/TURNER, © 1998. Reprinted by permission of Prentice-Hall, Inc., Upper Saddle River, NJ.

Chapter Two

The Future Belongs To Us

"Never," wrote Frank Dilnot for the *New York Times,* "has a Continent received an individual with the expectation and interest that Europe will receive President Wilson. . . ."[1] Wilson came as the savior of Europe when he arrived in France on December 13, 1918. The joyous reception reinforced his own belief that he did indeed speak for the common people of all nations. In their interest he would lead the goodness of the new diplomacy against the old diplomacy that had caused the war and was still being practiced by European leaders.

Wilson did not realize that the crowds cheered him as the architect of victory and not as the maker of the peace, nor did he heed the fact that European leaders had come to Paris with the confidence of their Parliaments. Wilson's own Democratic Party, however, had suffered a defeat in the 1918 Congressional elections. The Allies had never liked the Fourteen Points and only agreed to them when Wilson's emissary, Colonel Edward House, hinted at a separate peace. They no longer needed the United States for their survival and intended to challenge anything inconsistent with their national interests.

David Lloyd George came to Paris to maintain or strengthen the British Empire. Georges Clemenceau intended to make Germany pay for the war and guarantee French security in the future. Vittorio Orlando expected a payoff in the Adriatic Balkans for Italy's entrance into the war against its former allies in 1915. All of these goals belonged to the Old

Diplomacy and, for Wilson, they were overshadowed by the need to create a League of Nations. To do this, Wilson was willing to sacrifice his other points. He knew others opposed him, but his new system must be implemented to satisfy a demand among the peoples of the world to purge the ways of the old order and meet the challenge of Bolshevism.

The Paris Peace Conference opened at Versailles on January 18, 1919, forty-eight years to the day after Bismarck had proclaimed the new German Empire in the same place. When Wilson presented his plan for the League to the second plenary session on the twenty-fifth, his lofty — and self-righteous — manner brought "decorous diplomatic silence" among the delegates.[2] Some were already questioning his genuineness and that of the peace conference itself. Despite talk about a new era in global diplomacy, the main business was done by the old method of a Council of Ten, consisting of the American, British, French, Italian, and Japanese delegates along with their chief advisor on foreign affairs. Resentment among the smaller nations lingered and deepened when it became apparent that the needs of the Old Diplomacy had conquered the dreams of the New, adding an odor of hypocrisy to the conference that caused some to reject the West in favor of Soviet Communism.

For Wilson the opening weeks were the most hopeful. As chair for the commission in charge of drafting a League covenant, he pursued his goal with dogged determination, and on February 14, he presented the proposed covenant to the conference. It marked, perhaps, the greatest day of his life: according to his biographer Arthur Walworth, he gave "a constitution to the twentieth century world."[3] He left for the United States the next day carrying the promise of lasting peace and justice and the plan for realizing them. "Not for an instant, " wrote John Baptiste Duroselle, "did he dream the Senate would refuse this pact that he had put through so masterfully."[4]

But Wilson's assumption of obedience was shattered when Henry Cabot Lodge, upcoming chair of the Senate Committee on Foreign Relations, publicly questioned whether the League would diminish the Monroe Doctrine and American sovereignty as well as increase the chance for American involvement in foreign quarrels. He suggested that debate on the League be separated from the Versailles Treaty itself. On March 2, thirty-nine Republican senators joined Lodge in opposing the present covenant.[5] Wilson believed senators should ratify all treaties negotiated by the president. He was bitter at the opposition and determined that there would be no treaty without the League when he left for Paris on March 5.

He was even more bitter when he found out that Colonel House had agreed to a preliminary treaty without the Covenant. The angry and tired president vowed to restore it.[6] Except for minor amendments, Wilson won his fight for the League, but during negotiations on the peace treaties his influence and idealism waned. He was simply worn down by the reality of the old diplomacy and declining health. Shortly after his return, the Great Powers decided to replace the awkward Council of Ten in favor of the Council of Four, with Japan being added whenever Far Eastern matters were discussed. Clemenceau and Lloyd George saw Wilson's objections as petty at times. On one occasion the Old Tiger said, "The President of the United States does not understand the basic workings of human nature."[7] Conflict between the two men nearly ended the conference in early April when Clemenceau and Foch proposed to detach the Rhineland from Germany and to occupy it with Allied troops. Eventually Clemenceau consented to demilitarization, occupation for fifteen years, and a British and American guarantee against future German aggression.[8]

On May 7, Count Ulrich von Brockdorff-Rantzau led the German delegation to Versailles to "receive" the treaty. Essentially they received an ultimatum calling for reparations, loss of territory, continued demilitarization, and most galling of all, accepting sole guilt for the war. Most Germans were willing to accept some responsibility for the war, but not all of it. They also believed they had agreed to an armistice in exchange for a negotiated treaty based on the Fourteen Points. They recoiled in anger against this *Diktat* of Versailles and the Allies. Wilson was seen as the supreme hypocrite hiding his intention to destroy Germany behind lofty principles.[9]

The rage in Germany threatened to provoke civil war, but there was little recourse but to accept the treaty. On June 28, German representatives Johannes Bell and Hermann Müller went to Versailles to sign the treaty in a tense ceremony. The peace treaty was signed, but for many Germans the armistice would continue only until they were strong enough to fight again.[10]

A confident Wilson presented the treaty to Congress on July 10 as "nothing less than a world settlement." The League of Nations, he said, was "the only hope of mankind. . . . We can only go forward. . . ." America, he concluded, "shall in truth show the way. The light streams upon the path ahead, and nowhere else."[11]

But many Americans feared Wilson's path for the dangers it might bring. In the face of Senate opposition, Wilson decided to appeal directly to the American people. On September 3, he launched an exhausting campaign consisting of forty-two speeches in three weeks while covering eight thousand miles. In some respects his opponents had an easier time appealing to an assortment of prejudices and fears — and above, all the fear of another foreign war. The president made his last speech on September 25, at Pueblo, Colorado, in which he pledged that the children of those he had sent to war "shall not be sent on a similar errand."[12]

Wilson finished the speech with difficulty and collapsed shortly after. His doctor convinced him to cancel the tour and return to Washington, where he suffered a paralytic stroke. His illness crippled supporters of the League as well as the entire process of government. He improved, but questions remained about his mental and physical health. He seemed more stubborn and righteous. There would be no compromise on the treaty. It would be either victory or defeat. After three attempts it was defeat, falling seven votes short of the needed two-thirds majority.[13] Congress eventually ended the technical state of war with Germany on July 2, 1921, and the following August the United States signed the Treaty of Berlin confirming all the rights previously granted by the Versailles Treaty. Similar treaties were signed with Austria, Hungary, and Turkey, as well as the new countries of Eastern Europe.

Many saw the Versailles Treaty as an armistice for twenty years. The Paris peacemakers found even an armistice to be elusive in dealing with the Lenin's Bolshevik revolution. Lenin had seen revolution in Russia as a prelude to a European upheaval with Germany as the key. In Berlin Friedrich Ebert faced the prospect of becoming a German Kerensky until receiving the famous phone call from General Gröner at Spa. Ebert agreed to defend Germany from Bolshevism and in return Gröner promised support from the army. In contrast to Russia a year earlier, the German army held, while the country, though stunned, remained loyal to the existing system.

Lenin's hope for revolution in Germany lay with the *Spartakusbund* of Karl Liebknecht and Rosa Luxemburg. On December 30, Liebnecht and Luxemburg led in forming the *Kommunistische Partei Deutschlands (Spartakusbund)* with the avowed intent to overthrow Ebert. The new party was overconfident and eager to seize power. It launched a putsch on January 5, 1919, and paid dearly for it. Ebert launched an assault against the Communists with the aid of loyal Free Corps. The attempted coup was broken in a few days. Liebknecht and Luxemburg were murdered by their captors on January 15.

The Paris peacemakers attempted to deal with the Bolshevik threat during the spring of 1919. Wilson believed the Russian problem could best be handled by the League, if not by the conference itself. He was most opposed to further military intervention in support of the Whites whom he suspected of being reactionaries behind a democratic facade. In contrast, Clemenceau and Marshal Foch urged a "crusade" to destroy the Soviet government. When discussing such plans, however, those urging intervention could not ignore reality. Neither their soldiers nor civilians would support war in Russia after four years of suffering. The cost of supporting the Whites was also becoming a burden with little to show for it. Lloyd George, who was plagued by labor unrest at home, realized that military intervention was not the answer to the Bolshevik threat. He stated his position to the Council of Four on March 25, and later reminded Parliament of the disasters that had befallen previous invaders of Russia.

There was never an Allied policy throughout the conference because each member had its own aspirations and needs. The Allied coalition had been formed by rival powers against a greater threat that had been removed by the defeat of Germany. But even the strongest and most dedicated coalition would have had difficulty exercising its will in a civil war thousands of miles away, especially when most of the Russian population wished only for peace and time to heal the wounds of war.

The confusion and cross purpose characterizing Allied policy was compounded by the various White groups. In the late spring of 1919 it appeared as though Admiral Alexander Kolchak had the best chance to form a single White government from his capital in Omsk. But Kolchak's strength was more apparent than real, and by July the Bolsheviks had him reeling eastward. By October the Red Army approached Omsk almost without opposition and took it on November 19. As the Bolsheviks advanced toward the Pacific all semblance of chivalry and honor gave way to panic. In January of 1920 Kolchak abdicated in favor of General Anton Deniken and placed himself under Allied protection. For his protectors he was a valuable commodity to be exchanged for free transit to Vladivostok. He was turned over to the Bolsheviks at Irkutsk on January 14, 1920, and executed on the morning of February 7, 1920, on Lenin's orders.[14]

Trotsky's Red Army also won in the West. In October both Moscow and Petrograd were in danger of falling to Deniken's forces moving from the south and those of Nicholas Yudenich from Estonia. In face of defeat Trotsky rallied his forces and within days the situation changed. Both Deniken and Yudenich were overextended and lacked a political support to draw upon once their armies collapsed.[15] Defeat of the Whites was accelerated by the Allied withdrawal. Most Allied forces were gone by the end of 1919. The British, ever mindful of oil, remained in Georgia until the summer of 1922, while the Japanese continued to case Siberia until withdrawing under American pressure the following October.

In many respects the Allied intervention and support of the Whites was but one front in a more general conflict. The Allied governments were justified in believing that they were fighting a defensive war against the Bolsheviks. The violence of Soviet rhetoric and attempts at revolution in central Europe gave ample cause to fear Lenin's new government. Lenin's movement was based on hostility to capitalism and the overthrow of its governments from its inception, and would have remained so if the Allied intervention had never happened.[16]

The Bolsheviks continued to believe a European revolution was imminent as late as the spring of 1920. On April 25, Jozef Pilsudski sent his army into Russia in a foolish attempt to recreate eighteenth century Poland. At first the Poles advanced rapidly and took Kiev on May 6. The Poles were overextended and faced increasing opposition from Ukrainians who liked them less than they liked the Bolsheviks. Many Russians who opposed or were indifferent to the Soviets volunteered to fight the Poles. A Russian counterattack in June drove the Poles back and within a month the Red Army was advancing on Warsaw. The Allies now decided to intervene, lest Poland and parts of Germany fall to Soviet control. On July 12, British Foreign Secretary Lord George Curzon proposed a truce to his Soviet counterpart, George Chicherin. He closed with a warning of Allied military aid to Poland should the Soviet advance continued.[17] On July 17, Chicherin scornfully rejected "any interference . . . in the matter of peace between Russia and Poland."[18]

Many in Moscow were carried away by the prospect of the Red Army becoming the vanguard of the long awaited European revolution. Pilsudski and his French advisor, General Maxime Weygand, struck back in August. The Poles were again advancing into Russia territory by the end of the month. Pilsudski had now abandoned his fantasy of a great Polish state, and the Soviets needed peace to eliminate the last of the Whites and to consolidate their power.

The two parties agreed to negotiate and completed a preliminary peace of Riga on October 12. In his note to Chicherin of July 12, Curzon had suggested a settlement based on the recommendations of the Paris Conference. The "Curzon Line," as it came to be called, ran from Lithuania to Czechoslovakia just east of Brest Litovsk. Because of late

Polish military success, and the desire of Moscow to secure peace, the settlement of March 1921 set the boundary roughly one hundred miles east of the proposed Curzon Line where it remained until the fourth partition of Poland in August of 1939.[19]

The end of the Polish war was followed by a transition in Soviet foreign policy. Lenin had formed the Third or Communist International in March of 1919 to accelerate the drive for international revolution. The first congress had consisted of only nineteen delegations, mainly from countries of central and eastern Europe. The real founding of the Comintern, as it came to be called, occurred in July of 1920 when delegations from thirty-seven countries met in Moscow. To implement his program Lenin formulated the Twenty-One Conditions of Admission to the International requiring foreign Communist parties to purge all "reformists" and "centrists" and to obey the Central Committee in Moscow.[20]

By the fall of 1921 it had become apparent that the European revolution would not happen. This did not mean abandoning the hope of revolution nor slackening the effort to bring it about. The Soviet Union must now enter the family of nations, but only as a tactical and temporary retreat. "We must limit ourselves to a defensive posture . . . ," Lenin said following the defeat in Poland. "We will keep shifting from a defensive to an offensive policy over and over again until we finish all of them off for good."[21] In the meantime, the Comintern was to pursue its historical mission as "the grave-digger of bourgeois society."[22]

The Soviets signed an economic agreement with Britain in March of 1921 as the first step toward diplomatic recognition. In January of 1922 they agreed to attend an economic conference scheduled for April in Genoa. Lenin believed he could use the conference to secure diplomatic recognition and forestall any further Allied military intervention. Lloyd George hoped to grasp the mantel of world leadership at Genoa while drawing the United States into global affairs. The former Allies, however, were already bickering among themselves, and the Americans decided to stay home. Chicherin used the Genoa meeting to prevent any rapprochement between Germany and the Western powers by proposing a bilateral treaty with Germany in which both countries renounced fiancial claims against the other. German Foreign Minister Walter Rathenau had come to Genoa hoping to improve relations with the Allies, but became angry with British evasiveness and French intransigence. He decided to sign with the Soviets to at least rid Germany of one financial threat, and on April 16, the two countries met at the nearby resort of Rapallo to sign the agreement.

The "rapprochement of the pariahs," as Carole Fink described it, jolted the conference and sent shock waves across Europe.[23] Diplomatic recognition from Germany helped to forestall any united front against the Soviet Union, although it did not deter the Comintern from promoting revolution in Germany during the Ruhr crisis a year later. Rapallo also laid the foundation for future German-Soviet cooperation. In 1925 and 1926 the two most powerful revisionist countries in Europe supplemented Rapallo with treaties of nonaggression and friendship. In addition to the treaties, the new German army, the Reichswehr, cooperated with the Red Army to undermine restrictions imposed by the Versailles Treaty. Soviet relations with other states continued to expand during the next two years, and by January of 1924 full diplomatic recognition had been received from all the great powers except the United States. "We cannot recognize," the American Secretary of State Bainbridge Colby said in August of 1920, "any official relations with . . . the agents of a government which is determined and bound to conspire against our institutions."[24]

For the moment, the Soviet Union had made its truce with the West. From Poland to the Pacific the country lay exhausted by years of war. "I have been over into the future," said Lincoln Steffens upon returning from Moscow in 1919, "and it works."[25] Not really. Lenin's initial drive for socialism had accelerated an economic collapse that threatened Bolshevik survival. To avoid being overthrown, Lenin decreed the "peasant's Brest Litovsk," the New Economic Policy of limited capitalism.

But the myth of the future remained as part of the opiate that would sustain many believers through the excesses of Stalinism and into the years of the Cold War. The collapse of Soviet Communism makes it difficult to remember what a powerful ideology Leninism, and indeed, Stalinism once was, and what an important part it played in global diplomacy before becoming the grand failure of the twentieth century.[26]

Lenin's death in January of 1924 had brought a vacuum to the Soviet Union. Temporary power lay with a Triumvirate of Gregory Zinoviev, head of the Comintern; Lev Kamenev, vice-chairman of the council of peoples' commissars, and Joseph Stalin, general secretary of the Communist Party. Stalin had made a virtue of mediocrity by accepting other governmental positions spurned by his more intellectual and snobby colleagues. Above all, he knew that whoever controlled the party controlled the Soviet Union. He was generally viewed as the junior member of the triumvirate by far, and he used that misjudgment to lull rivals into carelessness while outmaneuvering them.

The triumvirs had begun plotting against Trotsky before Lenin died. Many disliked Trotsky for his arrogance, resented him as a newcomer to the party, and feared him as a Bonaparte. Trotsky had also become a man whose time had passed. At forty-five, he was declining both physically and psychologically. The strains of revolution and war may have had a cumulative effect, causing the bold and daring commander of the Red Army to sit passively in the face of defeat, as though he himself believed, as his biographer, Isaac Deutscher stated, that "the triumphant part of himself had together with Lenin gone down to the grave."[27]

The triumvirate disintegrated with Trotsky's fall. Zinoviev and Kamenev realized that victory belonged to Stalin and not to them. By 1925 Stalin controlled the party. He had also done something they and others thought beyond him: Stalin became a theorist. In the autumn of 1924 Stalin wrote *Questions of Leninism,* advancing the theory of "socialism in one country." Stalin originally had formulated his theory to discredit Trotsky's "permanent revolution" and its stress on revolution abroad as necessary for the survival of socialism in Russia. He now became the champion of an idea whose time had come. The "one country" aspect appealed to his own sense of "red patriotism" and to the Russian and Communist ego of others within the party. The Soviet Union, he maintained, could move on to socialism without foreign help.[28]

Ideologically Zinoviev and Kamenev were much closer to Trotsky in wishing to continue the primacy of international revolution, but they withheld their opposition in order to maintain a united front. By the time they tried to challenge Stalin in the summer of 1925, he had already allied himself with the conservative wing of the party led by Nicholas Bukharin, whom Lenin had described in his testament as "a most valuable and major theorist of the party."[29] Bukharin favored continuation of Lenin's New Economic Policy (NEP) of limited capitalism and the eventual achievement of socialism at a "snail's pace." His support for the NEP and his admonition to the relatively wealthy peasant class, the Kulak, to "enrich yourselves" caused consternation among many in the party who viewed such a policy as a betrayal of the revolution and a threat to the Soviet system.

When Zinoviev and Kamenev tried to stop Stalin by allying with Trotsky, it was simply too little too late. Stalin welcomed the opportunity to eliminate this "block of political eunuchs" once and for all. He had removed Zinoviev and Trotsky from the Politburo by the fall of 1926, and then stripped Zinoviev of his last vestige of power by appointing Bukharin as head of the Comintern. In early 1927 the trio tried to take advantage of a Comintern defeat in China. Trotsky entered the debate with his "Clemenceau" statement, claiming he would adopt a policy similar to that of Clemenceau during the Great War. He would criticize until he had forced a change in the Soviet government. Stalin retaliated by adding treason to the charges against the opposition. Zinoviev and Kamenev recanted, but Trotsky refused. On January 17, 1927 he was exiled to Alma Ata in Turkestan to begin a long odyssey ending with his murder in Mexico in the August of 1940.

Stalin then crushed Bukharin's faction with little more than a whimper. Once the Left Opposition had been defeated, Stalin moved quickly against the Right. By April of 1929 he was confident enough to publicly label Bukharin as the leader of the Right Opposition and to secure his removal from the Comintern and the Politburo. Stalin was now master of Russia and the Comintern. When festivities were held to celebrate his fiftieth birthday in December, he stood atop Lenin's mausoleum as a prophet upon whom responsibility had fallen to complete the work begun in 1917.

As "the Lenin of today" Stalin began the drive to achieve socialism in the Soviet Union. Through a series of five-year plans he was determined to achieve in ten years what would normally require fifty. Progress itself seemed to impel Stalin toward goals far exceeding those originally planned as he came to see himself as "a new Moses leading a chosen nation in the desert."[30] He began to speak of eliminating the Kulak as a class while applying the term to any peasant who resisted collectivization. In pursuit of "Dekulakization," Stalin made war against his own people in a terrible harvest of sorrow costing the lives of 10 million people, 20 million horses, and 30 million cattle, and leaving a bitterness among many who welcomed the German invader in 1941.[31]

The strains of Stalin's terror reached into his own family when his despondent wife, Nadezhda Alliluyeva, killed herself in November of 1932. Years later his daughter recounted that Stalin was always trying to find those "guilty" of her death.[32] The death of his wife, whose suicide was caused in part by his verbal abuse, may have intensified the streak of paranoia that had long been part of his personality.

Stalin then launched his Third Revolution. "He contrived," wrote George Kennan, "to conduct a veritable revolution from above . . . killing people by the thousands, . . . throwing the whole structure of power into a state of babbling terror and hysteria, casting a tremendous cloud of bewilderment and despair over all that was left of educated Soviet society."[33]

Sergei Kirov had been a rising star in the party for some time. At forty-six he possessed the physical presence and oratorical ability that Stalin did not, and he was the leading prospect for those who wanted to remove Stalin as party leader. Signs of an "inside job" were present when an assassin penetrated Kirov's Leningrad headquarters on the night of December 31, 1934. Stalin then used the murder to launch the *Yezhovshchina* (wicked deeds of Yezhov), so named for Nicholas Yezhov, head of People's Commissariat of Internal Affairs (NKVD).[34] Yezhov accused the Left Opposition, those led by Trotsky and Zinoviev, of Kirov's murder and plotting to kill Stalin. The Left Opposition was in turn linked to the Right Opposition, that is, to Bukharin and his followers. Fear now prevailed over friendship and conscience. Millions of party members fell to public humiliation, imprisonment, and secret execution.

In June of 1937 Stalin struck at the Red Army, purging three of the five marshals, thirteen army commanders, and one half of the officer corp, with similar action taken against the Air Force and the Navy.[35] To purge the military at a time when real enemies lurked in Europe and Asia required a special madness. In strengthening his own power within the Soviet Union Stalin had damaged the defenses of his country while encouraging aggression against it. He also had caused many in the West to recoil at his barbarity and to question the reliability of the Red Army in any war with Hitler. Stalin's terror cost the lives of between 17 and 22 million people by the time war came in 1941.[36] For some, however, the enduring vision of the omelet justified the broken eggs.

Fascism proved more difficult to comprehend as an ideology. It seemed difficult at times to determine just what fascism meant and how it differed from conservative nationalism. Benito Mussolini hoped to harness Italian anger and fear to destroy the old order when he formed the *Fasci di Combattimento* (Bands of Combat) in Milan on March 22, 1919. Mussolini later linked the movement to the fasces, the bundle of elm rods bound to an axe that had been the symbol of Roman lictors. [37]

Because of World War II and his ignoble death, Mussolini is remembered more as Hitler's lackey than as the popular and successful ruler of Italy for twenty years. Born in 1883, he had been a hero in search of a faith as much as a role for much of his life. He first opposed the Italian entrance into World War I as a Socialist, but then broke with the party in favor of intervention. By combining heretical Marxism with activism and strident nationalism, he saw the proletariat embodied in the Italian nation in opposition to the bourgeois or "plutocratic" democracies of the West. Above all,

Italy must enter the war against Austria-Hungary, the decadent oppressor of Italian nationalism. Mussolini drew upon Italian discontent following the war to form a basis for his movement. Many Italians believed the Paris Peace Conference had cheated them out of their just demands. Returning soldiers, brutalized and embittered by the war, added to economic dislocation and political unrest, while the shadow of Bolshevism alarmed the aristocratic and business classes.

Fascist squadra went into open combat against Communist, Socialist, and Republican organizations, and from 1920 to 1922 they gained strength in the towns of northern Italy. By 1922 Mussolini's Fascists had attained a measure of respectability as well as strength while the liberal opposition seemed to become more inept and weak. In a monumental bluff Mussolini threatened to march on Rome on October 24. The government of Prime Minister Luigi Facta urged King Victor Emmanuel III to declare a state of siege, but the king chose Mussolini and fascism over civil war. On October 28, the Facta government resigned, and on the following day Mussolini agreed to head a coalition government.[38]

Mussolini's Italy remained a relatively benign form of authoritarianism. Ideology was used to rally and vitalize the populace as parades entertained them. Until Mussolini became identified with Hitler he was regarded by many far differently than it might seem today. The standard expression about the trains running on time spoke of the admiration accorded to the efficiency given to Italy by fascism through public works programs and imposed stability.

Mussolini pursued many of the traditional goals of Italian foreign policy. Italy had arrived late as an imperialist power, and its efforts in conquest had been less than stunning. Italian imperialism was supplemented by the ideology of fascism stressing will and the glorification of war. Mussolini was captivated by the Roman Empire and the dream of its resurrection. But like his domestic policy Mussolini's ambitions were more bluster than action. He had no intention of directly challenging British or French domination of the Mediterranean or enlarging Italy's African empire without their consent. The Duce increased military spending, but the economic and strategic strength of Italy remained weak while much of the military lacked organization and modern technology.

The Great Depression caused many in the Western democracies to question whether liberal democracy could cope with the problems of the modern world. Weakness and uncertainty in the West gave more credence to the illusion of fascist power while offering opportunity for conquest and glory. Mussolini remained cautious, lest the world learn the truth: that behind the bluster neither Fascist Italy nor its leader possessed the strength attributed to them. With the rise of Hitler in Germany the pressure for action became acute, for now there had appeared a Fascist ruler who intended to put his words into action with the military power to do so.

Adolf Hitler was a man possessed of a malignant soul whose very presence on the planet challenged the concept of a just universe. At the same time, he may have been one of the most important figures of the twentieth century, if only because of the consequences inherent in the destruction he wrought. His rise to power in Germany alone was a remarkable achievement. He was not a citizen until shortly before attaining power. Respectable society held him and his movement in contempt, and many continued to do so even after he ruled most of Europe.

Historians have been analyzing Hitler's impact on German history, the Holocaust, and World War II from Friedrich Meinecke's *Die Deutsche Katastrophe* of 1946 to the present. Much of the analysis and soul-searching carries an implicit question of "what went wrong?" Most likely the answer is "nothing" and "everything." Hitler was propelled to power by no one thing, but rather by the conjunction of his political genius with his era. Had one of the variables in that conjunction differed on only one of numerous occasions, he might well have remained an inconsequential figure in history, and the world would have been far better for it.

Hitler was a twenty-five-year-old social reject living in Munich in August of 1914. Before fleeing his native Austria-Hungary a year earlier, he had lived in Vienna where he formulated a worldview that lasted to the end of his life.[39] Hitler saw the human arena as a place of struggle similar to the jungle for animals, with the same result: the stronger triumphed over the weak with no apology and no guilt. He extended the concept of the human jungle to include conflict among the various races for territory. Hitler had also embraced a particularly virulent form of anti-Semitism that placed Jews at the bottom of the *untermenshen* to be defeated in a coming struggle.

Hitler's views were reinforced by combat. Like many others who fought on the Western Front, he became hardened by brutality and suffering. He also developed a fatalism not uncommon to combat, a belief that life is beyond human control, that all human endeavor must bow to the will of the gods. Because he had survived when so many others had not, Hitler came to believe it was for a purpose, that a mission lay before him known only to a Providence whose will he must execute.

The Armistice was more traumatic for Hitler than for most Germans. He eagerly embraced the myth of *Dolchstoss*, the "stab in the back" of betrayal at home by the "November Criminals." Peace also forced him to again find a job as well as a place in civilian life. He avoided it as long as possible by remaining in the army and then by going into politics. The *Deutsche Arbeiter Partei* Hitler encountered in Munich was similar to organizations present in Vienna prior to the war. By developing his organizational and theatrical talents, Hitler was able to put his stamp on the party. The name was changed to The National Socialist German Worker's Party (Nationalsozialistische Deutsche Arbeiterpartei), and adopted the Hakenkreuz, or Swastika, an ancient Hindu symbol used formerly by radical groups within the Austro-Hungarian Empire.

Hitler remained a regional politician until he attempted to emulate Mussolini by seizing power in Munich in November of 1923. Failure of the "Beer Hall Putsch" brought a trial giving him national exposure, and he skillfully used it to appeal to German nationalism. His five-year sentence to Landsberg prison offered the opportunity for more publicity when he dictated *Mein Kampf.*

In *Mein Kampf* and his *Second Book* of 1928 Hitler laid out his plans for German expansion into eastern Europe and eventual domination of the continent. What lay beyond that and beyond his own lifetime is still debated as is the nature of his personality itself. The dynamic nature of National Socialism suggests continual expansion of some kind, especially since there was no lacking for sympathizers in foreign countries. The continuing debate over Hitler's goals, in addition to questions of his sanity, part sanity, or insanity, remains elusive for eminent scholars. We may forgive his contemporaries for their own imperfections in the pressure of the moment.

Hitler believed Imperial Germany had failed because it had followed the wrong path to expansion, tied itself to feeble allies, and lacked the toughness to enforce its will at home. The imperial government had blundered by challenging Britain on the seas and had relied too much on Austria-Hungary. There was a good chance Britain would allow German hegemony on the continent in the future as long as there was no threat to its empire. If Britain opposed him, however, it would have to defeated.[40] In securing hegemony he must first gain Fascist Italy as an ally and destroy France. Once he had gained control of central and western Europe, he then would pursue Lebensraum into "Russia and her vassal states." "Nature," he said, "has not reserved this area for any particular nation or race . . . [but] for the people who possess the force to take it . . . ." In setting out his goals Hitler clearly broke with those advocating cooperation with the Soviet Union in revising the Paris settlements. "The struggle against Jewish Bolshevism requires a clear attitude toward Soviet Russia. You can not drive out the Devil with Beelzebub *(Man kann nicht den Teufel mit Beelzebub austreiben.)*" In August of 1939 he would make his pact with Beelzebub to defeat the Devil.[41]

Hitler appeared to be a man whose time had passed when he was released on December 20, 1924. The discontent so needed for success had been replaced by economic prosperity and national pride under the leadership of Gustav Stresemann. As foreign minister from November of 1923 to his death in October of 1929, Stresemann adopted a policy of "national realism" to regain German power behind the guise of reconciliation and the pursuit of European unity. His most successful achievement came at the Locarno conference in October of 1925. The conference produced a series of treaties guaranteeing the Belgian-German and Franco-German borders, as well as arbitration treaties between Germany and Poland, Czechoslovakia, and France.

The "spirit of Locarno" began what Sally Marks called "the years of illusion" in which many hoped and some believed that the era of old animosities had been replaced by a new era of international cooperation. But despite Locarno and the Kellogg-Briand pact of 1928 outlawing war, neither Stresemann nor his successors would sign an "Eastern Locarno" recognizing the eastern boundaries of Germany as permanent. Stresemann and others also continued to subvert the disarmament clauses of the Versailles Treaty while preparing to extend German control eastward at the first opportunity. Stresemann's last victory came at the Hague Conference in August of 1929. Allied leaders consented to the Young Plan reducing the scale of reparations payments stipulated by the Dawes Plan of 1924 while gaining a French promise to withdraw from the Rhineland.[42]

The tranquility of the Stresemann era was aided by the election of Hindenburg as president in 1925. The old field marshal provided a link to the monarchy many Germans still revered. Tranquility also aided Hitler by providing a respite to regain control of the party and to prepare for the calamity he believed would come, and he was ready when it did. The German economy depended on foreign loans, mainly from the United States. In the interlocking world economy of 1930 the American collapse jolted everyone, and especially Germany. Behind unemployment statistics fearful people looked to a host of charlatans and soothsayers. Hitler perceived that the crisis was one of spirit as well as economics that only the voice of authority could cure.[43]

Economic and political disarray fed on each other to help prolong the Depression and increase Nazi strength. In two years the Nazi vote went from 810,000 to 6.4 million while its strength in the Reichstag rose from 12 to 104. The Nazi party became the second largest party in the Reichstag after the election of September 1930, and closing in on the Social Democrats. Nazi victories produced a bandwagon effect by drawing members who wanted to be part of a winner. Larger membership also enhanced the Nazi financial position by enabling local districts to pay bills without tapping the national treasury and using volunteers for services other parties paid for.[44]

Weimar politics now descended into a maelstrom of elections, street fighting, and political intrigue. Despite advanced campaign tactics and storm trooper intimidation, Hitler could not win a majority. But he remained the master of intrigue. By 1933 the country was weary of the chaos and anxiety as well as the slow economic recovery they caused. In late January the perennial schemer Franz von Papen and Hindenburg's son Oskar convinced the old man to appoint Hitler as chancellor in a cabinet controlled by Papen and other conservatives. On the night of January 30, a jubilant crowd paraded before Hitler as though he had already achieved his goal of unlimited power. For the moment he had not, but the future of Germany belonged to him, and the hopes of those who hailed him were soon justified.

Within two years Hitler brought nearly all of Germany under his control. He was aided by the burning of the Reichstag building on February 23. The true story of the fire may never be known, but Hitler used it to crush opposing parties. Hindenburg signed a decree "For the Protection of the People and the State" suspending what remained of civil liberties in Germany while giving Hitler a virtual blank check to maintain order. Despite the advantages of power and intimidation, Hitler still could not win a majority vote in the March 5 elections. With a skillful blend of cajolery and intimidation, however, he secured passage of the Enabling Act (Law for Removing the Distress of People and Reich) on March 24.[45]

Passage of the bill began the process of *Gleichschaltung,* or coordination, as the Nazi party wrapped itself around Germany like a belt, with Hitler as its buckle. State's rights, artistic freedom, and educational integrity either ended or Nazified themselves. German industry and labor were not socialized as much as they were conscripted. In June of 1934 Hitler removed the last challenge from within the Nazi party. In the Blood Purge of the Sturmabteilungen, the party army that had helped bring him to power, Hitler also eliminated other rivals past and present. In August the mantel of full leadership passed to him with the death of Hindenburg. The offices of chancellor and president were combined in Hitler as Führer and the Army was required to take an oath of personal allegiance. What the army pleged and conceded in August of 1934 was written into law the following spring. In March of 1935 Hitler announced German rearmament and a reorganization of the armed forces. The Reichswehr of Weimar Germany was replaced by the Wehrmacht headed by Oberkommndo de Wehrmacht (OKW) or Supreme Command of the Armed Forces. The Wehrmacht Law of May 21, 1935 declared that "The Supreme Commander of the Wehrmacht is the Führer and Chancellor of the Reich." The Army became the last institution in Germany to believe it could use Hitler, only to be used by him.[46]

Hitler benefited from a general recovery of the world economy. He also accelerated recovery by a combination of rearmament and public works programs that virtually eliminated unemployment while impressing foreigners as well as Germans. Behind the economic miracle lay the Nazi police state. But, as with many who visited Stalin's Russia, foreigners found it easy to see what they wanted to see while convincing themselves that the unpleasantness of Nazi rule would pass with time. The most blatant unpleasantness became legal in September of 1935 with the first of the Nuremberg Laws depriving Jews of all civil rights. Despite treatment of the Jews and other dissidents, visitors saw much to admire. Former British Prime Minister David Lloyd George saw in Germany many of the social welfare programs he had advocated for decades. He returned from Germany in 1936 to proclaim Hitler a great man.[47] And to be sure, there seemed much to admire when a vibrant Germany hosted the Olympic Games. By submitting themselves to Hitler and National Socialism the country had gone from depression to prosperity, and the young had reason to be confident in singing "Tomorrow Belongs to Me."

NOTES

1. Frank Dilnot, "What Will The Europeans Think of Wilson?" *New York Times* (Supplement) December 1, 1918, 1.
2. *Times* (London) January 27, 1919, 10.
3. *FRUS: The Paris Peace Conference, 1919,* vol. 3, 215. Arthur Walworth, *Woodrow Wilson,* vol. 2 (New York: W.W. Norton, and

Company, 1978), 258.
4. Jean-Baptiste Duroselle, *From Wilson to Roosevelt: Foreign Policy of the United States, 1913-1945* (Cambridge: Harvard University Press, 1963), 94.
5. *Congressional Record*, 65th Congress, 3rd Session, vol. 57, pt. 5, (Washington: U.S. Government Printing Office, 1919) 4520-4530. *New York Times*, March 5, 1919, 1. Knox, *Wilson*, 230-233. William C. Widenor, *Henry Cabot Lodge and the Search for an American Foreign Policy* (Berkeley: University of California Press, 1981), 315-317.
6. Duroselle, *From Wilson to Roosevelt*, 96. Heckscher, *Woodrow Wilson*, 544-545.
7. Paul Mantoux, *Les Délibérations du Conseil des Quatre* (24 mars-28 juin, 1919) (Paris: Editions du Centre national de la recherche scientifique, 1955) 40. Duroselle, *From Wilson to Roosevelt*, 99.
8. Ibid., 101. Knox, *Wilson*, 248-249. Schwabe, *Woodrow Wilson, Revolutionary Germany, and Peacemaking*, 275-285.
9. Ernst Fraenkel, *Wilson's Diplomacy: An International Symposium*, ed. J. Joseph Huthmacher and Warren I. Susman (Cambridge: Schenkman Publishing Co., 1973), 54.
10. Klaus Schwabe, *Woodrow Wilson, Revolutionary Germany, and Peacemaking*, 1918-1919: Missionary Diplomacy and the Realities of Power (Chapel Hill: University of North Carolina Press, 1985), 330-352.
11. *Congressional Record*, 66th Congress, 1st Session, vol. 58, pt. 3, 2336-2339. Knox, *Wilson*, 251-252.
12. *The Papers of Woodrow Wilson*, vol. 53 (Princeton: Princeton University Press, 1990), 511.
13. Knox, *Wilson*, 262-264.
14. Richard Pipes, *Russia Under the Bolshevik Regime* (New York: Alfred A. Knopf, 1993), 116-117.
15. Orlando Figes, *A People's Tragedy: A History of the Russian Revolution* (New York: Viking, 1997), 670-674.
16. John Lewis Gaddis, *The Long Peace: Inquiries Into the History of the Cold War* (New York: Oxford University Press, 1987), 10-11.
17. *Times* (London), July 15, 1920, 9. *Documents on British Foreign Policy, 1919-1939*, ed. Rohan Butler and J.P.T Bury, First Series, vol. 8 (London: Her Majesty's Stationery Office, 1958), 527-530.
18. *Soviet Documents on Foreign Policy*, ed. Jane Degras, vol. 1 (New York: Oxford University Press, 1951), 197.

19. Debo, *Survival and Consolidation,* 280-282.
20. Lenin, *Complete Works,* vol. 31, 17-104.
21. V. I. Lenin, *The Unknown Lenin,* ed. Richard Pipes (New Haven: Yale University Press, 1996), 114.
22. *The Communist International,* vol. 1, 348.
23. Carole Fink, *The Genoa Conference: European Diplomacy, 1921-1922* (Chapel Hill: University of North Carolina Press, 1984), 37-68.
24. *FRUS: 1920,* vol. 3 (Washington, 1935), 468.
25. Lincoln Steffens, *The Autobiography of Lincoln Steffens* (New York: Harcourt, Brace, and World, 1958), 799.
26. Raymond Aron, *The Opium of the Intellectuals,* trans. Terence Kilmartin (New York: Doubleday and Company, 1957). Zbigniew Brzezinski, *The Grand Failure: The Birth and Death of Communism in the Twentieth Century* (New York: Charles Scribner's Sons, 1989)
27. Isaac Deutscher, *The Prophet Unarmed: Trotsky, 1921-1927* (New York: Oxford University Press, 1959), 133.
28. J.V. Stalin, *Works,* vol. 8 (Moscow: Foreign Languages Publishing House, 1954), 13-96. Alan Bullock, *Hitler and Stalin: Parallel Lives* (New York: Alfred A. Knopf, 1992), 190-191.
29. Lenin, *Collected Works,* vol. 36, 595.
30. Isaac Deutscher, *Stalin: A Political Biography* (New York: Oxford University Press, 1967), 327.
31. Bullock, *Parallel Lives,* 256-265.
32. Svetlana Alliluyeva, *Twenty Letters to a Friend,* trans. Priscilla Johnson McMillan (New York: Harper and Row, 1967), 107-108.
33. George F. Kennan, *Russia and the West Under Lenin and Stalin* (Boston: Little, Brown and Company, 1950), 294-295.
34. The Cheka became the United State Political Administration (OGPU) in 1922. It became the NKVD in 1934.
35. Robert Conquest, *The Great Terror: Stalin's Purge of the Thirties,* (New York: Macmillan, 1973) 201-235.
36. Gaddis, *We Now Know,* 9.
37. Stanley G. Payne, *Fascism: Comparison and Definition* (Madison: University of Wisconsin Press, 1980), 3-4.
38. Ivone Kirkpatrick, *Mussolini: A Study in Power* (New York: Hawthorne Books, 1964), 137-148.
39. Gerhard Weinberg, *Germany, Hitler, and World War II: Essays in Modern German and World History* (Cambridge: Cambridge University Press, 1995), 30-53.

40. Klaus Hildebrand, *The Foreign Policy of the Third Reich* trans. Anthony Fothergill (Berkeley: University of California Press, 1973), 12-23.
41. Adolf Hitler, *Mein Kampf,* trans. Ralph Manheim (Boston: Houghton Mifflin, 1943) 204-206, 643-649, 652, 655, 662.
42. Sally Marks, *The Illusion of Peace: International Relations in Europe, 1918-1933* (New York: St. Martin's, 1976), 102-107.
43. Joachim C. Fest, *Hitler,* trans. Richard and Clara Winston (New York: Harcourt Brace Jovanovich, 1965) 271-278. Bullock, *Parallel Lives,* 222.
44. Henry Ashby Turner, Jr., *German Big Business and the Rise of Hitler* (New York: Oxford University Press, 1985), 111-124.
45. Bullock, *Parallel Lives,* 306-316.
46. Bullock, *Parallel Lives,* 562. John W. Wheeler Bennett, *The Nemesis of Power: The German Army in Politics, 1918-1945* (New York: St. Martin's Press, 1964), 340.
47. Peter Rowland, *David Lloyd George: A Biography* (New York: Macmillan Company, 1975), 705.

World War I Peace Settlement in Europe and the Middle East

WESTERN HERITAGE VOL. 2 SINCE 1648 6/E. by KAGAN/OZMENT/TURNER, © 1998. Reprinted by permission of Prentice-Hall, Inc., Upper Saddle River, NJ.

Chapter Three

The Decline of the West

As the Great War was ending, Oswald Spengler published the first volume of *Der Untergang des Abenlandes,* or *The Decline of the West.* Moral strength and values seemed to have declined along with the carnage of war and the crash of empires. The destructiveness of the war itself seemed to verify the irrationality of humanity and the indifference of God, while foretelling the eclipse of Western power and values.

In Britain the end of war brought joy, relief, and then a kind of lethargy. By the summer of 1920 it had become obvious that the American people were not willing to accept the commitments Wilson had made. Collective security was weakened against a nascent Germany without American participation in the League. Clemenceau and Foch had abandoned their claim to the Rhineland in return for a demilitarized zone and an Anglo-American guarantee against another German attack. The American promise had gone the way of the Versailles Treaty, freeing Britain from its obligation and leaving France alone. Many wanted to keep it that way. The victor now began to feel its own form of war guilt. In his *The Economic Consequences of the Peace,* John Maynard Keynes spearheaded a flood of revisionist literature regarding the origins of the war and the harshness of the Versailles Treaty. France was now seen as irrational to the point of sadism in trying to implement the treaty regardless of chivalry or common sense. This change of heart accompanied a general desire to withdraw within the Commonwealth while putting faith in disarmament, pacifism, and the League.[1]

The downfall of the Lloyd George coalition in October of 1920 ended the wartime era. Britain now entered the age of the bland in leadership and drift in foreign policy during what Winston Churchill called "The Baldwin-MacDonald Régime."[2] Peace seemed assured after the Locarno agreements of 1925. Germany had been rendered impotent, France had been severely weakened by the war, and the Soviet Union was preoccupied by internal power struggles and domestic recovery. Stalin's eventual victory and the proclamation of socialism in one country indicated that Communism had made a tactical retreat.

Only Japan and the United States were potentially strong enough to challenge Britain. Japan's appetite for expansion had been demonstrated during the war and later in Siberia. The British and French empires remained intact, and they, along with the United States, were sufficient to keep the peace. Britain terminated the Anglo-Japanese alliance of 1902 in deference to American and Canadian opinion and a desire to reduce foreign commitments. Britain could only chafe at the shift of economic power from London to New York and the continuing arrogance of the Americans over war debts. Beyond that, the Americans had withdrawn from global affairs and offered little threat to British predominance on the seas. British confidence was illustrated by the "Ten Year Rule." Since there would be no war for ten years, military expenditure could be trimmed. In 1919 the idea was sound and continued to be so until the Japanese occupation of Manchuria in 1932.[3]

The Depression forced the creation of a National Coalition of the Conservative and Labour parties. Gradually the difficulties of the Depression were alleviated by a measure of economic recovery. Once again the establishment muddled through with the Conservative Baldwin winning a clear Parliamentary majority in 1935. War clouds were already forming when Neville Chamberlain replaced Baldwin in May of 1937. Baldwin and Chamberlain faced enormous constraints in meeting the challenge. Public opinion continued to believe peace could be preserved by opposing all rearmament while trusting in the League. In the famous "Peace Ballot" of 1935, over eleven million supported the League and general disarmament, with a lesser number favoring a prohibition of heavy military aircraft and the prohibition of private arms manufacturing.

Rearmament had to be taken within limits of the British economy. Chamberlain knew rapid rearmament would strain the economy to the limit and that a year of war would break it. During World War I Britain had avoided bankruptcy by borrowing from the United States. The Johnson Act of 1934 forbade any American loans to countries that had defaulted on their debt, and that included Britain. The American Neutrality Laws forbade the export of war materials to belligerents. The door to American aid, wrote P.M.H. Bell, "was not merely shut; it was locked and bolted."[4] The Dominions too had suffered, and they made it clear that they were not inclined to suffer again for a British involvement on the Continent, especially since they felt more threatened by Japan. Britain could not afford another war against Germany, given the resources of a waning empire.

The search for peace fell primarily upon Chamberlain. To this day he is often seen as a doddering fool who was no match for Hitler. Chamberlain's policy of appeasement, however, was shared by many and grounded in the belief that the Paris Peace Conference had treated Germany too harshly, and that some of the new states in central Europe had been flawed in their creation. Chamberlain believed that reconciliation with Germany offered the best hope of avoiding another war that would surely destroy Europe. Philosophically and politically the appeasers were conservative and sensitive to the Soviet threat. They disliked the brutality of Nazi rule, and tended to rationalize it as the excesses of a young revolution that time and maturity would cure until they realized that noble values are folly against those who hate them.

Britain at least had the security of the channel. France did not, and many feared that Foch had been correct when labeling the Versailles Treaty a twenty-year armistice. The Western Front had ravaged the northern part of the country, and it would take decades to repair destroyed forests and forsaken towns. Eventually they could be regrown and repaired, but the lost men could not. Over a million soldiers had been killed or were missing, or roughly 10.5 for every 100 active men. Another 360,000 men would never return to productive life because of their wounds.[5] French leaders realized that Germany had gained a strategic advantage with the end of Austria-Hungary and Imperial Russia. There now lay a collection of quarrelsome, independent states that could never equal the power of the two empires to check German expansion. France compensated by signing an alliance with Poland in February of 1925. The Polish alliance was supplemented by agreements with the states of the Little Entente: Czechoslovakia (1924), Rumania (1926), and Yugoslavia (1927). Behind the common ground, however, there were lingering animosities. The Entente originally had been formed to guard against the Hungarians as well as the Germans. In addition, the Poles were ready to cooperate with the Hungarians to destroy Czechoslovakia altogether whenever they could get away with it.

French military preparations mirrored those of diplomacy. "Thank God for the French Army," Winston Churchill said in March of 1933.[6] The French army appeared to be the most formidable in Europe when Hitler came to power. Within the Supreme Command, however, there lay complacency and an unwillingness to change the defensive strategy that had saved the country during the Great War.Faith in defense was best illustrated by construction of the most sophisticated series of fortifications in Europe. The "shield of France" was begun in 1930 under War Minister André Maginot. The Maginot Line has been ridiculed since the defeat of 1940, and yet it did deter invasion by allowing a relatively small army to defend a large area of territory running some eighty-seven miles from Basel on the Swiss frontier to Longwy in the north where the borders of Belgium, France, and Luxemburg converge. The line was supplemented in the west by the "impenetrable" Ardennes forest. France lay vulnerable only along the route of the 1914 Schlieffen Plan, and the army was ready. A German move into Belgium would once again bring Britain into war, and that alone would make Berlin hesitate. Also, Belgium was now part of the French defensive plan, although it was increasingly tempted to return to its traditional neutrality.[7]

Deprived of what it was justly entitled to, hated by its enemies, and abandoned by its allies, France faced the challenges of the postwar world divided against itself. The divisions that had plagued the Third Republic prior to the war were compounded by communism and fascism and intensified by the Depression. Tension in France exploded with the arrest of Serge Stavisky in December of 1933. For some time Stavisky had operated in a shady world of financial dealings while keeping friends in high places. Even friends of the Republic were skeptical when it was announced that Stavisky had committed suicide on January 8, 1934. *Action Française* and its allies on the Right viewed Stavisky as the kind of Jewish scoundrel who had plotted the ruin of France with the aid of the corrupt Republic. Prime Minister Camille Chautemp resigned under fire, leaving France without a government until Édouard Daladier consented to form a new ministry on January 29. The Communist *L'Humanité* further inflamed the situation on February 6 by summoning its members to demonstrate against the bourgeois government and fascist leagues alike. The stage was set for the confrontation that nearly toppled the Republic while leaving a legacy of animosity and bloodshed.

The Battle of the Place de la Concorde lasted from six on the night of February 6 until two in the morning. The government survived, but barely. A brave and resourceful soldier who had survived Verdun, Daladier had become the embodiment of the later belief that at Verdun France had won the First World War and lost the Second. Forty thousand demonstrators had taken to the streets against his government. Sixteen had been killed, with nearly seven hundred injured. The guards and police had lost two men, with nearly two thousand injured. The sight of Frenchmen killing each other and the likelihood of more bloodshed were abhorrent to Daladier, and he resigned on February 7.

The Communists celebrated Daladier's resignation as a victory, but some were frightened by how close the Right had come to seizing power. Comintern policy still forbade them from allying with liberal and socialist parties. Stalin also began to rethink his policy. At the end of May *Pravda* dropped the first hint that a change was coming by calling for cooperation between Communists and Socialists against fascism. In October the Communist leader Maurice Thorez called for a broad *front populaire* to combat the forces on the Right. The following April the Popular Front scored an election victory under the Socialist Léon Blum. The new prime minister was a further irritant to those on the Right who resented being governed by a Socialist and a Jew. Some were willing to seek help from abroad. If a choice had to be made, "Better Hitler than Blum."[8]

In the United States the fight over the League and begun the decline of Wilson's reputation and the internationalism he had symbolized. By the time he left office in January of 1921, Wilson was being denounced as an egomaniac and a Machiavellian who "having promised the impossible . . . produced more cynics than any other figure in modern history."[9] Many who supported Wilson's idealism now bitterly denounced him and the Paris settlement. "The peace can not last," wrote Walter Lippmann, for the *New Republic,* and "America should withdraw from all commitments . . . impairing her freedom of action."[10]

The inauguration of Warren G. Harding in March of 1921 was a gala affair. The transition to "reconstruction, readjustment, restoration," as Harding put it, was illustrated by the physical appearance of the two men. Wilson was but a shell of the man he had been four years and countless crises before, with his gaunt face and the cane he needed for his unsteady walk, whereas Harding was exuberant in vowing to return the country to simpler times.[11] Harding announced that the United States would not join the League, while promising to work in harmony with all nations. Neither

Harding nor those who agreed with him thought of themselves as isolationists. They believed peace could be found through a national approach to global diplomacy. Harding's secretary of state, Charles Evans Hughes, would have preferred American entrance into the League, but knew that would never happen as long as a two-thirds vote was required.

Hughes took the lead in organizing the Washington Conference in November of 1921 to pursue international disarmament and to solve some problems left over from the war. The conference accomplished less than some had hoped but more than others expected.[12] Only capital ships were included in naval disarmament, and mainly battleships. The future of the capital ships themselves seemed to be in doubt when the American General William (Billy) Mitchell and his men sank the captured German battleship *Ostfriesland* on the eve of the conference. The French were disappointed that nothing was done about land armaments and were offended when placed on a par with Italy in naval strength. The Japanese did well in terms of naval armament and control of the northern Pacific, but they resented being tutored by the Anglo-Americans and embittered by racial policies restricting Japanese immigration.[13]

The United States continued its policy of being with the League but not of it when Calvin Coolidge became president following Harding's death in August of 1923. In February of 1927, Coolidge invited Britain, France, Italy, and Japan to meet in Geneva for another meeting on naval disarmament. The Washington Conference had represented an idea whose time had come. Geneva represented an idea whose time had passed. France and Italy were still smarting from the Washington Conference and had no interest in reducing other ships. The delegates from Britain, France, and the United States became bogged down in defining offensive and defensive vessels, causing the conference to produce only an agreement to disagree.[14]

The Coolidge administration capped its foreign policy accomplishments with the Kellogg-Briand Pact of 1928. The Pact of Paris was the product of political gamesmanship between Briand and the American Secretary of State Frank Kellogg who had replaced Hughes at the beginning of the second Coolidge administration. Kellogg was under pressure to sign an "American Locarno" with France renouncing war. Kellogg believed the effectiveness of a treaty declined in proportion to the number of signers. He decided to totally emasculate it by making it as nearly global as possible. The great and small powers met in Paris on August 27, 1928 to renounce war in a ceremony as solemn as it was futile.[15]

The prospects for peace were favorable when Herbert Hoover took office in March of 1929. Aside from the smoldering situation in China, there seemed little chance for war among the powers that had recently renounced it. The onset of the Depression spurred Hoover and his Secretary of State, Henry L. Stimson, to call for another conference in London. France and Italy still could not reconcile their differences, although this time they did attend. Aside from some paper progress placating the Japanese, the London Conference did little more than the one in Geneva. Hoover had hoped the conference would lead to meaningful disarmament, but the continuing Depression and economic nationalism increased military and political rivalry. Hoover himself succumbed to economic nationalism by signing the Hawley-Smoot tariff of 1930 calling for higher import duties. He also tried to ease the crisis, however, by proposing a one year moratorium on international debts in June of 1931.[16]

Hoover became increasingly preoccupied with war in Asia while trying to alleviate the situation in Europe. The Nationalist Government of Chiang Kai-shek (Jiang Jieshi) had begun to threaten Japanese power in China. The upsurge in Chinese nationalism coincided with Japanese militarism, especially in the units garrisoned in northern China known as the Kwantung Army. In September of 1931, just as it appeared that Nanking and Tokyo might reach a settlement, the Kwantung conspirators struck near Mukden and used the incident to establish their control over all of Manchuria.[17] The League hoped the crisis would just go away, and some members even supported the Japanese. In December, the League sent the Lytton Commission to investigate the incident. The United States announced in January 1932 that it would not recognize Japanese control in Manchuria. The Stimson Doctrine of non-recognition was probably as far as the United States could go toward halting Japanese aggression without the economic and military resources to actively intervene. The League admitted as much in February when members were instructed to withhold recognition. By the time the Lytton Commission made its report the following October, the Japanese had established their control in Manchuria and intended to keep it. When the League accepted the Lytton report on February 4, 1933, calling for restoration of Manchuria to Chinese sovereignty, the Japanese ambassador, Matsuoka Yosuke, led his delegation out of the assembly. On March 27, Tokyo formally withdrew from the League.[18]

Franklin Roosevelt took office as president of the United States two weeks before Japan left the League. Roosevelt brought the ease of an aristocrat to the presidency. He had become an advocate of America as an arbiter of world power as assistant secretary of the Navy during the Wilson administration. Roosevelt had accompanied the American delegation to Paris in 1919, and championed the League when he ran for vice president. His political career, as well as his life, seemed over when he was stricken with polio the following year. Although he never regained the use of his legs, he returned to political life, and in 1928 he was elected governor of New York and then president in 1932. He also brought a style noted for vagueness that allowed him to control events until the last minute. It was generally successful, but it often confused friends and enemies alike.[19]

Roosevelt said little about foreign affairs in his inaugural address and with good reason. Foreign problems were of little interest to an audience fearful of unemployment, poverty, and impending chaos. Most Americans opposed any active role for the United States in world affairs, and many now believed the United States had been duped into war by British intrigue or by arms makers in search of profits, the merchants of death. Congress responded by passing the neutrality laws of 1935, 1937, and 1939, curtailing the ability of American business to supply war material to belligerents.[20]

It appeared as though the internationalist wing of the Democratic Party had won control of foreign policy when Roosevelt appointed Tennessee senator Cordell Hull as secretary of state. The new secretary had admired Wilson and continued to believe that morality and law must replace the old diplomacy based on national interests and the balance of power. Hull called for a moral regeneration among nations and a renewal of good faith among nations on February 24, 1933.[21] The future looked ominous indeed for anyone who believed in international law and morality. Less than a month before Adolf Hitler had become chancellor of Germany and on the day Hull spoke, Japan walked out of the League. Relations between Roosevelt's new government and Nazi Germany began badly and grew worse. Jewish groups and their sympathizers in the United States retaliated with rallies and a boycott of German goods in the wake of Nazi ideology and the maltreatment of Jews, but neither had much impact. Few Americans saw Hitler as a threat to the Western Hemisphere, and even fewer favored any action leading to another war.

The German threat lay more in the future than in the present for Roosevelt and Hull. Japan posed a more serious problem. Since at least 1900 the United States had pursued the "open door" policy in Asia. Japanese officials were publicly stating their intention to impose a kind

Monroe Doctrine for Asia before Roosevelt took office.[22] When Hull protested, the Japanese ambassador in Washington suggested the two countries divide the Pacific into spheres of influence. Hull responded with a moralistic lecture criticizing Japanese policy for increasing tension. The Japanese threat helped to change American policy toward the Soviet Union. Previous administrations had considered recognition, but had rejected it. Resentment over Comintern intentions to destroy capitalist governments, Soviet policy on religion, and war debts lingered well into the Hoover administration.[23] By 1933 the climate had improved somewhat as the Red Scare of the early twenties faded. Stalin's emphasis on socialism in one country seemed to reduce the threat of international revolution. Soviet need for foreign goods and the Depression offered the chance for increased trade with the Soviets while bringing more employment at home.

The Japanese conquest of Manchuria worried Moscow and Washington, but Roosevelt and Hull remained wary. Following a period of secret talks Stalin sent his commissar for foreign affairs, Maxim Litvinov to Washington in November of 1933. After ten days of amicable negotiations, the two governments jointly announced they would establish formal diplomatic relations. Many of the hopes accompanying recognition did not materialize. Comintern activity in the United States did not abate, nor was there any significant increase in trade. The Soviets soon realized the United States would play no active role in containing Germany or Japan, nor would it provide needed loans and economic assistance. Although the establishment of formal relations disappointed both parties, it indicated that Roosevelt intended to challenge Japanese ambitions in the Pacific as well as those of Hitler in Europe.

By the time Roosevelt campaigned for reelection in 1936, Italian troops had conquered Ethiopia and there was civil war in Spain. The campaign concentrated on domestic recovery, but still the distant thunder could not be ignored. "We must remember," Roosevelt warned in August of 1936, "that so long as war exists on earth there will be some danger that even the Nation which most ardently desires peace may be drawn into war."[24]

NOTES

1. P.M.H. Bell, *The Origins of the Second World War in Europe* (New York: Longman Incorporated, 1986), 101.
2. Winston S. Churchill, *The Gathering Storm* (London: Houghton

Mifflin Company, 1948), 21.
3. Bell, *Origins of the Second World War,* 176.
4. Ibid., 147.
5. Philippe Bernard and Henri Dubief, *The Decline of the Third Republic, 1914-1938,* trans. Anthony Forster (New York: Cambridge University Press, 1985), 78.
6. *Winston S. Churchill, His Complete Speeches, 1897-1963,* ed. Robert R. James. vol 5 (New York: Chelsea House Publishers, 1974), 5236.
7. Paul-Emile Tournou, "Les Origins de la Ligne Maginot," *Revue d'histoire de la deuxième guerre mondiale,* No. 3 (Janvier, 1959), 3-12.
8. William L. Shirer, *Collapse of the Third Republic: An Inquiry into the Fall of France in 1940* (New York: Simon and Schuster, 1969), 232-236, 286-295, 324.
9. Harry Elmer Barnes, "Woodrow Wilson," *American Mercury*, vol. 1 (April, 1924), 490.
10. "The Covenant Now," *New Republic,* vol. 19 (May 24, 1919), 110.
11. *New York Times,* March 5, 1921, 1, 4.
12. Thomas Buckley, *The United States and the Washington Conference, 1921-1922,* (Knoxville: University of Tennessee Press, 1970), 185-190.
13. Meirion and Susie Harries, *Soldiers of the Sun: The Rise and Fall of the Imperial Japanese Army* (New York: Random House, 1991), 132-134.
14. Marks, *Illusion of Peace,* 89-90.
15. L. Ethan Ellis, *Frank B. Kellogg and American Foreign Relations, 1925-1929* (New Brunswick, NJ: Rutgers University Press, 1961), 193-212.
16. *New York Times,* June 20, 1931, 1.
17. Robert J.C. Butow, *Tojo and the Coming of The War* (Princeton: Princeton University Press, 1961), 28-47. Harries, *Soldiers of the Sun,* 145-154.
18. Akira Iriye, *The Origins of the Second World War in Asia and the Pacific* (New York: Longman Incorporated, 1987), 13-18. *New York Times,* March 26, 1933, 1.
19. Arthur M. Schlessinger Jr., *The Age of Roosevelt,* , vol. 1, *The Crisis of the Old Order, 1919-1933* (Boston: Houghton Mifflin Company, 1957), 317-365, 386-407.
20. Robert Dallek, *Franklin D. Roosevelt and America Foreign Policy, 1932-1945* (New York: Oxford University Press, 1979), 85, 117-

121.
21. *New York Times,* February 25, 1933, 1.
22. Iriye, *Second World War in Asia,* 22.
23. Edward M. Bennett, *Recognition of Russia: An American Foreign Policy Dilemma* (Toronto, 1970), 74-78.
24. *New York Times,* August 15, 1936, 4.

CHAPTER FOUR

A Spectacle of Miserable Disagreement

Cordell Hull recalled in his memoirs how poor relations were between Britain, France, and the United States during the period prior to World War II. Instead of forming a united front against the common enemy, Hull noted, "We presented a spectacle of miserable disagreement and recrimination more often than of accord."[1] Hull and many others believed the war might have been prevented had Hitler's enemies only been stronger and wiser. Churchill also helped to set this tone in *The Gathering Storm*, when he condemned British "fatuity and fecklessness, which though devoid of guile, was not devoid of guilt" in bringing about the war.[2] There is much truth in the assertion, but much exaggeration as well.[3]

In his work on the origins of the First World War, Luigi Albertini spoke of the disproportion between the intelligence and morality of leaders in 1914 and the gravity of the task confronting them.[4] To a great extent the same may be said for the origins of the Second World War. Leaders in the West, especially in Britain and France, well knew the gravity of the moment, perhaps in part because the leaders in 1914 had not. Preventing the onset of war in Europe in 1939 may well have been beyond the talent of any leader of Britain or France when confronted with an adversary who preferred expansion and war to containment and peace.

Simmering animosities and divisions among the powers were intensified by the Depression. Each country pursued more and more nationalistic policies toward economic recovery and defense. Some European conservatives saw Roosevelt's New Deal as dangerously close to socialism, while radicals perceived it as a betrayal of the working class. Being unable to form any common front among themselves, the former allies could hardly find one with the Soviet Union. The Soviets did little to allay suspicion until the Popular Front of 1935. The vitriolic language of the Comintern and the constant threat to overthrow the capitalist order were hardly words to engender compromise and cooperation. Soviet Ambassador to Britain Ivan Maisky later recounted that Neville Chamberlain had referred to his country as "the enemy" during their first meeting in 1932. Maisky expressed shock at Chamberlain's attitude without considering that the Soviets had given the British little cause to see them as anything else.[5]

Discord among the Western democracies burst into the open early 1933 over the issues of economic recovery and disarmament. Plans were formulated for a World Economic Conference in London during the closing months of the Hoover administration. Roosevelt initially seemed to take the lead by inviting foreign leaders to Washington for preparatory talks.[6] In a radio address on May 7, he expressed the hope that the conference would make progress toward limiting armaments, lowering trade barriers, and stabilizing international currency. Roosevelt then reversed himself when he realized that the conference might produce agreements more beneficial to other countries than to the United States. The president worsened things by appointing a motley delegation that underwhelmed everyone with its mediocrity and manners upon arriving in London in early June and were widely ridiculed as "Six Delegates in Search of a Chief."[7] Secretary Hull came on June 8 with diminished hope and little chance of success. The Americans and their president continued to give on impression of confusion, if not duplicity. Roosevelt effectively killed the conference on July 3 by publicly chiding other nations for trying to stabilize international currencies before repairing their own economies.

John Maynard Keynes praised Roosevelt for "cutting through the cobwebs" and "forcing the delegations to forge a new path," but he had little company.[8] Georges Bonnet of France left the conference "swearing" at the Americans.[9] Neville Chamberlain was as angry with the French for their intransigence on the gold standard as he was with the Americans. "The worst feature about the whole episode," wrote the *Spectator,* "is that it will intensify the impression all too prevalent in Europe that America is a country it is impossible to work with."[10]

When the World Economic Conference died in London, the World Disarmament Conference was already terminally ill in Geneva. It had opened on February 2, 1932 and had achieved little. It adjourned five months later. Delegates again assembled in Geneva in December, but without Germany. British Prime Minister Ramsey MacDonald managed to hammer out a compromise solution with the help of the impatient Americans. On December 11, the five powers signed a declaration granting equal rights to Germany and other disarmed powers. Germany joined the other delegations but for only a short duration, since the conference adjourned again in January of 1933. Time ran out on January 30 when Hitler became German chancellor.

Mussolini had long doubted that any tangible results would come from the conference. He proposed instead a four power pact among Britain, France, Germany, and Italy. Stability could be best preserved by a return to some form of the old Concert of Europe. France was skeptical. Any revision of the treaties was risky, especially with a more hostile government in Berlin. Such a pact was also contrary to the spirit of the League by shifting political power in Europe from the smaller states to the great powers. Poland and the states of the Little Entente were equally fearful of revision and were resentful of any French attempt to exclude them by joining the Four Power Pact.

The strident rhetoric from Germany and the open persecution of the Jews caused all of Europe to become more wary. Negotiations did continue, however, and finally the treaty was initialed in Rome on June 7, 1933. The final version, however, was considerably removed from Mussolini's original draft. It was little more than a reaffirmation of the powers to respect previous treaties, such as the League Covenant, the Locarno treaties, and the Pact of Paris.[11] The Four Power Pact helped to further undermine the situation in Geneva where it appeared that Germany would leave the conference. Hitler responded to criticism on May 17 with his first speech on foreign policy since becoming chancellor. He offered to renounce offensive weapons, if other countries would do the same. Germany would gladly sign a non-aggression pact, he said, because it "does not think of attacking, but only of acquiring security." Germany had more to fear than anyone else because it was disarmed and at the mercy of its neighbors. This humiliating condition could not go on indefinitely. "It would," he warned, "be difficult for us a constantly defamed nation to continue to belong to the League of Nations."[12] The warning was little noted at home or abroad in the glow of the speech. The Nazi party newspaper, *Völkischer Beobachter,* spoke the truth when it declared that the entire country was behind Hitler.[13] Hatred of the Versailles Treaty had always cut across class and party lines, and Hitler had skillfully exploited it.

The relic of past hopes continued when the weary delegates returned to Geneva in September. American, British, French, and Italian delegates devised a plan calling for disarmament in two stages. First, there would be a period of approximately four years during which Germany could substitute a shorter period of service for its army. Actual disarmament would begin during the second stage, also lasting four years. Differences remained between Britain and France regarding supervision. Hitler would have none of it. He had kept Germany in the conference only to conceal its own rearmament while waiting for the right moment to leave. Now it had come.

On October 14 Hitler announced that Germany would leave both the Disarmament Conference and the League. To support his move, he dissolved the Reichstag and called for new elections on November 12. The twelfth would, he said, mark the day of rebirth of national honor following the day of shame in 1918. There was the slight danger of foreign action but here he assessed the psychology of his foreign adversaries as well as he had previously assessed those within Germany. On November 12, the electorate gave him a mandate of over 90 percent and there was no foreign action.[14]

Hitler's move also allowed him to breach the French alliance system. Poland had begun to pursue a more independent course following Jozef Pilsudski's coup d'état in 1926, and especially after the appointment of Colonel Jozef Beck as foreign minister in 1932. Polish leaders believed that France had virtually left them alone to face Germany as a result of the Locarno settlement, and they were increasingly worried about Hitler's designs on Poland. In early 1933 Pilsudski allowed rumors to spread of a preventive strike against Germany as a way of cooling any ardors Hitler might have about the Polish corridor.

Failure to achieve disarmament and the impotence of the League convinced Pilsudski to seek better relations with Germany. Hitler quickly seized the opportunity. On November 15, he and the Polish Ambassador, Jozef Lipski, stunned the world with a flowery communiqué promising better relations in the future. Two months later Pilsudski gave Hitler his first major victory in foreign policy with a 10 year non-aggression pact.[15] Any move toward Berlin, Pilsudski realized, had to be balanced with a similar step toward Moscow, and in May he extended his current non-aggression pact with the Soviet Union to ten years.

France turned increasingly to Czechoslovakia as reliance on Poland waned. The Czechs were a valuable ally, but they alone could not deter a German attack into the Balkans, and there were no joint military plans for war with Germany. An understanding with the Soviet Union could offer additional security to France and preserve the balance of power in Europe. French policy toward the Soviet Union had begun to change prior to the Popular Front. When Gaston Doumergue became prime minister in February, 1934, he appointed Louis Barthou as his foreign minister. Barthou believed that France must hold firm against Germany, especially now that Hitler was actively pressing rearmament. France must not rely too heavily on Britain for its own security, should strengthen relations with its allies on the Continent, and reach an agreement with the Soviet Union.

Barthou toured the Little Entente in the spring of 1934 to shore up the alliance and possibly to lay a foundation for an eastern Locarno that would include Germany and Poland. The latter, he realized, was remote to say the least, but it would have at least the advantage of improving relations with Poland. In September, Barthou traveled to Geneva for a meeting with Maxim Litvinov, the Soviet foreign minister.

The Soviet Union had denounced the League since its inception in 1919, and had refused to join it. In keeping with the new Popular Front policy, however, the Soviet Union joined the League shortly before Barthou's visit with Litvinov. Barthou hoped the Soviet entrance into the League would serve as a prelude for resurrecting the Franco-Russian alliance that had saved France in the Great War. He did not live to see his work completed. On October 9, King Alexander of Yugoslavia paid a state visit to France as part of Barthou's efforts. As the two men rode in an open car, a Croatian terrorist opened fire, killing the king and mortally wounding Barthou.

Pierre Laval continued Barthou's policy, but with far less enthusiasm for the Soviet pact. He would have scuttled it entirely, but negotiations had gone too far.[16] On May 2, 1935, he and the Soviet ambassador to France, Vladimir Potemkin, signed the treaty in Paris. Laval went to Moscow two weeks later for conversations with Stalin. At the meeting Stalin agreed to publicly state his "complete understanding and approval of the national defense policy pursued by France" and to thereby ease Laval's efforts toward rearmament by removing Communist opposition. The Soviets allied themselves with Czechoslovakia, and it appeared as though France and the Soviet Union were more secure against Germany and that Stalin could now devote more of his resources to meet any Japanese threat in Asia.

Behind the facade of a common front, however, there were many weaknesses. Stalin's agreement to aid the Czechs was conditional on prior action by France, and this became increasingly unlikely as time went on. There was an almost leisurely process involved to determine German aggression. All such acts would have to be certified by the Council of the League of Nations. Such niceties were not in keeping with the emergency of the moment, nor with the importance of time in the event of war. The new agreement had no plans for military action, in contrast to the Franco-Russian military agreement of 1892. The Soviets pressed for one, but Laval managed to avoid it. At this stage in his career, Laval was hardly the man to forge an alliance with the Soviet Union. He had begun his political career as a champion of the extreme Left, but was already moving rightward along the road to Vichy. He did not trust the Soviets and feared they would try to drag France into a war with Germany, while they in turn watched safely from the buffer zone imposed by geography.[17]

Stalin's purge of the military seemed to have rendered the Soviets an enfeebled ally as well as an unreliable one. Laval stalled ratification of the alliance for months on the grounds that it would provoke Hitler. It was not until February of the following year, a month after Laval had fallen from power over the Ethiopian crisis, that the pact was finally ratified by the Chamber and the Senate. Stalin responded in kind. Despite the rhetoric of the Popular Front and the change in Comintern policy, Stalin had no intention of going to war over Czechoslovakia if he could avoid it.[18]

Laval certainly was the man to seek an agreement with Mussolini, and the prospects for getting one were exceedingly good. The meeting between Mussolini and Hitler in Venice in June of 1934 had not gone well. Mussolini clearly viewed his German admirer as an upstart, did not like him personally, and had no intention of allowing Austria to come under German control. Il Duce was genuinely shocked two weeks later by Hitler's Blood Purge of those who had helped him to power. Then, on July 25, Austrian Nazis attempted a putsch in Vienna. The Austrian chancellor, Engelbert Dollfuss, was Mussolini's ally and friend. The Dollfuss family were already waiting for the chancellor to arrive for a visit at Mussolini's estate at the time of the putsch. Mussolini had to personally inform the family that Dollfuss had been killed in Vienna. Mussolini sent armed forces to the Austrian border, and took some credit for the failure of the coup. The Italian press echoed Mussolini's anger with a stream of attacks on Germany, despite disclaimers from Berlin.

Laval seized the opportunity to forge closer ties with Italy. Should he succeed, Hitler could be contained in the West and the Soviet alliance would become expendable. Laval went to Rome in January of 1935. On the seventh, he and Mussolini completed an agreement to preserve Austrian independence by joint military action, if necessary. Laval also agreed to some concessions to Italy in Africa, and in so doing laid the groundwork for the destruction of his own strategy. Mussolini had been planning to attack Ethiopia for some time, and he wanted French consent to forestall any interference from Britain. Laval gave Mussolini his "free hand." Laval insisted later that he added "but a free hand in the path of peace."[19] Laval was a sophisticated statesman, and it is doubtful whether he actually attempted to restrict Mussolini. There is some evidence that he did at least stress a peaceful settlement. Shortly after the conversation, the Italian undersecretary for foreign affairs, Fulvio Suvich, informed the German ambassador to Italy, Ulrich von Hassell, that the agreement between France and Italy "related only to peaceful intentions" regarding the Ethiopian problem.[20] Laval and Suvich, however, were too shrewd to say anything else. Ethiopia was a member of the League, and neither man could consent to its destruction.

Mussolini apparently believed that neither Britain nor France would oppose his conquest of Ethiopia. No attempt had been made to hide the massive arms buildup in Italian Eritrea, nor to disguise the many ships passing through the Suez Canal. Most likely the Duce would have accepted a peaceful solution making Ethiopia an Italian protectorate. He still feared Germany, and he wished to settle the Ethiopian problem as soon as possible. The Duce was also irritated with the limp response to Hitler in London, but he had to support a united front against Germany until the conquest of Ethiopia allowed him to bring much of his army back home.

Mussolini traveled to the Italian resort city of Stresa in April to meet with the prime ministers of Britain and France, Ramsey MacDonald and Pierre Flandin. Ethiopia was never on the official agenda. Mussolini was given only a vague warning that the consequences of an invasion could not be foreseen. Intelligence from Britain, however, told him that Britain would not go to war for Ethiopia. Britain had to choose independence for either Austria or Ethiopia. Austria was the first stop along Hitler's path of expansion. Ethiopia was the necessary payoff for maintaining peace in Europe. On April 14, the three leaders issued a statement affirming their support for Austrian independence and their opposition to any revision of the Versailles Treaty by force.

This Stresa Front, as it became known, marked the zenith of Laval's efforts to contain Hitler by appeasing Mussolini. The British government was not ready for any active involvement on the Continent, despite the bold words of the communiqué. It had grown weary of disarmament conferences that never achieved their goals and fearful of conflict. It decided to make a deal with Hitler, whatever the repercussions for collective security. Less than two months after the Stresa Conference, London and Berlin exchanged notes establishing a "permanent relationship" between their two navies.[21] The agreement appeared to eliminate any German challenge and legitimized German rearmament. Laval viewed it as another case of perfidious Albion seeking to ensure its own well-being at the expense of others. Maxim Litvinov saw the agreement as the first of many dominoes. In a conversation with American Ambassador William C. Bullitt, he referred to the British as "the blacklegs" whose action would lead to disaster in Asia as well as in Europe. Hitler, he said, could be restrained only by a chain of states armed to oppose Germany. Litvinov, Bullitt wrote, was convinced that England had now broken that "chain" and that the defection of Italy and other states was likely to follow.[22]

The naval agreement was popular in Britain and helped the National Coalition remain in power. Baldwin again became prime minister, with Samuel Hoare replacing Simon as foreign secretary. Eden remained at his post as minister to the League. He traveled to Rome in June in hopes of preventing a crisis in Ethiopia by offering Mussolini part of Ethiopia adjacent to Italian Somaliland along with some economic benefits. Britain then would compensate Ethiopia from its own holdings in British Somaliland.[23] The talks were cordial, but Mussolini refused to accept Eden's terms. The Duce believed that concessions to Ethiopia would make it a British protectorate as well as a maritime power, and that Italy's image as a great power would suffer by accepting mediation from a third country. Mussolini had gone too far to accept anything less than total victory. The costly buildup of his forces had been accompanied by bluster and pageantry. To accept mediation and to gain relatively little would tarnish his image. "Even if they offer me everything," he told Baron Pompeo Aloisi, "I would prefer to avenge Adowa."[24]

Hoare and Laval met in Paris in early September to formulate their strategy. Both recognized that they could not defend Ethiopia and the League without losing Italy as an ally. Laval was quite willing to sacrifice the League for French security as were many pragmatists in Britain. But pragmatists could not ignore the formidable strength of idealists who still clung to the League and collective security. Hoare and Laval attempted to keep a foot in each camp and eventually fell between the two. They agreed to support measures against Italy, but not to the point of risking war. Speaking before the League on September 12, Hoare attempted to thread the needle by stressing collective responsibility for enforcing international law. He had intended to shift the burden of any conflict with Italy away from Britain and France, but in the charged atmosphere of Geneva he appeared to be giving a strident plea for collective security in defense of smaller states.[25]

Hoare called for a solution that would preserve Ethiopian sovereignty while satisfying Italy's claims. Most of his audience believed that war would follow the end of the rainy season in Africa. On October 3, Italian troops moved into Ethiopia and within three days they avenged the defeat of 1896 by capturing Adowa. The League condemned Italy as the aggressor on the seventh and authorized sanctions. League action, supported however reluctantly by Britain and France, infuriated Mussolini. British and French sanctimony about international law and respect for smaller states especially galled him. Their empires had been formed by a host of wars no different from the one he was fighting in Africa. The Duce's anger was shared by compatriots who had not forgotten their treatment at Paris in 1919, and who resented foreign attempts to check Italian ambitions in the Mediterranean and North Africa. Italians gave Mussolini adulation and respect, and even opponents of the government supported the war. The sanctions that came in November were enough to inflame relations between Italy and the League without weakening the Ethiopian campaign. Mussolini realized, however, that he was isolated with his armies tied down in Africa, and that he must end the war as soon as possible.

On November 16, Mussolini relieved the cautious Marshal Emilio de Bono as commander of his army in Ethiopia. He appointed Marshal Pietro Badoglio as the new commander and ordered a drive for victory. Italian troops steadily advanced, and it was obvious that the country would fall unless further sanctions were imposed by the League. That, of course, would likely mean war between Italy and Britain and possibly France. A war in the Mediterranean would weaken all three countries to the benefit of Hitler in Europe, while making British and French holdings in Asia more vulnerable to Japanese pressure.

London and Paris had to find some compromise to end the crisis. To that end Hoare stopped in Paris on his way to a Swiss vacation on December 7. The Hoare-Laval plan for ending the war was probably formulated with Mussolini's consent. It gave Italy more of Ethiopia than it had already conquered, but not as much as it soon would. It was to be presented to Mussolini and then to Ethiopia and the League.[26] Terms of the plan were leaked to the press on the night of the eighth by someone who remains unknown. Hoare and Laval were vilified for secretly rewarding aggression while publicly posing as defenders of the League.

Hoare returned from Switzerland to explain his actions and to submit his resignation in hopes of saving the Baldwin government. He defended the Hoare-Laval plan before Parliament as a distasteful but necessary solution to the Ethiopian problem, and certainly preferable to a war between Britain and Italy.[27] Hoare's argument carried little weight in the heat of the moment, but his resignation and replacement by Eden saved the government. Laval was also tarnished by the revelations, and eventually fell from power in January of the following year.

Laval's fall further aggravated the political polarization in France and left the country leaderless and nearly impotent to face the growing menace from across the Rhine. Laval and others on the Right were especially bitter toward Britain for having broken the Stresa Front and endangering France, all for the sake of a barbaric country in Africa. On the Left there were increasing demands for ratification of the Franco-Soviet Pact and for even closer relations with Moscow, which further intensified the fear of Communism on the Right and alarmed those who wished to ally with Hitler against Bolshevism.[28] Britain, on the other hand, believed the French had let them down by leaking the Hoare-Laval agreement. Anglo-French relations were now strained at a time when each country badly needed the other. The Ethiopian war and the Franco-Russian pact provided Hitler with the opportunity to finish the Stresa Front and to remilitarize the Rhineland. His major concern had always been Mussolini. There was little chance Britain and France would use force to keep German troops out of the Rhineland without Italian support. Mussolini, on the other hand, was in no mood to bail out his erstwhile friends, and in no position to do so with his military forces committed in Africa.[29]

As early as October 1934 Jean Dobler, the French consul in Cologne warned Paris that the Germans were preparing to send soldiers into the Rhineland, but he was ignored by the government and the military.[30] In March of 1935 Hitler ordered plans for "Operation Schulung," a quick strike into the Rhineland at the appropriate moment and with a proper pretext. The moment and the pretext came in February of 1936 when the Chamber of Deputies began to consider the Franco-Soviet pact. Hitler used the debate to play the aggrieved before public opinion and to capitalize on anti-Soviet feeling in Britain and France. The pact, he maintained, was hotile toward Germany and a clear violation of the spirit of the Locarno treaties. When the Chamber approved the agreement on the twenty-seventh, the press in Germany warned of the consequences.

On March 6, Berlin announced that the Reichstag would meet on the following day, and few doubted that Hitler would deal with the Rhineland and Germany's relations with the other powers. Early the next morning German troops marched across the Rhine bridges so dear to Marshall Foch in 1919. But Foch had long since vanished from the scene along with the spirit he personified. His successor, General Maurice Gamelin, vastly overestimated German military strength and underestimated his own.[31] There was little to indicate that the civilian leaders of France were heirs of Clemenceau and Poincaré. Prime Minister Albert Sarrant showed an initial determination to resist with force but faltered under pressure from the army and apathy from the public. The French also realized that Britain would not support war over the Rhineland, and that world opinion might well see France as a bully, once again depriving Germany of its legitimate rights.

Hitler skillfully played his role in his speech to the Reichstag. The Franco-Soviet pact, he said, was aimed at Germany and went beyond any defensive commitment to collective security and the League. France in concert with the Soviet Union had altered the balance of power in Europe to the further detriment of Germany. To ensure its own defense Germany had therefore restored "the full and unrestricted sovereignty of Germany in the demilitarized zone in the Rhineland." Despite breaking the Versailles and Locarno treaties, Hitler stressed that he was really a man of peace who had been forced to act in defense of his country. He now offered to create a new demilitarized zone with Belgium and France, which would include the Maginot Line, and to sign twenty-five year non-aggression treaties with the two countries. In addition, he proposed similar agreements with Germany's neighbors to the East.[32]

Hitler knew that many in France had always been uneasy about the Franco-Soviet pact. Blaming it for the crisis would further divide the country. British conservatives had not liked the agreement either. The Baldwin government had to face the fact that few in Britain or in the Dominions believed the Rhineland was worth a war. Remilitarization of the Rhineland was viewed as quite different from the Italian attack on Ethiopia. After all, it was argued, Germany had not attacked France; it had simply occupied its own territory, and neither the British government nor the populace seemed to give "two hoots" about that.

France could rely on the Czechs, but other allies were wavering. Poland, the most important of them, was already playing the double game that would lead to disaster three years later. Colonel Jozef Beck assured France of Poland's loyalty to the alliance. At the same time, however, he assured Berlin that the Polish alliance with France would not come into force because Germany was not planning to attack France itself.[33] Nor would Poland join in any economic sanctions.

Mussolini might have sided with Britain and France a short time before, but now Italy benefitted more than anyone else. Public attention was removed from Ethiopia where Italian forces were completing their conquest, while German troops in the Rhineland weakened France and made Italian friendship more valuable. By the middle of March, it was obvious that Hitler had won a complete victory and the French security system had collapsed. France and its allies had to face a new situation. Germany would now fortify the Rhineland, and France would no longer be able to seize the area in retaliation for a German strike into central Europe. Poland and the states of the Little Entente now had to consider rapprochement with Hitler. As Gerhard Weinberg has noted, the fear was well-founded. The French army virtually wrote off Central Europe following the Rhineland crisis by planning to fight only a defensive war against Germany. "The sight of the French dozing in the Maginot Line," Weinberg wrote, "while Poland was being overrun in 1939 would reveal to all that promises of assistance from Paris had been worthless since 1936, if not before."[34]

The Rhineland crisis was the first of many gambles for Hitler, and it may have provided him with his greatest success because it made his later victories possible. He had feared that the French would force him back, but they had done nothing. His suspicions of French weakness and British unconcern had been confirmed to the point where even bolder moves were possible in the near future. Perhaps even more importantly, his "amazing aplomb" had triumphed over timid advisors in the army and the foreign office who had urged concessions during the height of the crisis.[35] Once the question was settled he would eliminate those who might falter in the future.

As the Rhineland crisis faded during the spring of 1936 it appeared as though Europe would be peaceful at least for awhile. The end of the Ethiopian war in May eased friction between Italy and the Western democracies. Mussolini was willing to consider returning to a modified Stresa

Front. He was grateful for Hitler's support but he recognized the motives behind it, and he still feared Hitler's designs on Austria. Had Britain and France called for an immediate end to sanctions and recognized Italian control of Ethiopia, Mussolini most likely would have responded in kind. In Britain, however, public opinion was still too devoted to the League to permit such a move. In France the situation was complicated by the election of Léon Blum's Popular Front in May. Fascist Italy found it difficult to be friendly to a leftist government reviled by many of its own citizens.[36]

Any chance for returning to Stresa ended in July when a group of army officers attempted to seize power in Spain. By the end of World War I, Spain had become splintered into hostile factions on both the Left and the Right. On the Left, and the term must be used loosely, the nineteenth century struggles between Liberals, Marxists, Syndicalists, and Separatists were intensified by Leninism and then by the hatred between Stalinists and Trotskyists. On the Right, the old royalists' struggles of the Carlist wars were overshadowed by the emergence of fascism.

King Alphonso XIII consented to a military coup by General Miguel Primo de Rivera in September of 1923. Primo de Rivera was a nobleman and a patriot who attempted to build a one-party state modeled on Mussolini's Italy. His government was a relatively benign one which brought a measure of stability to the country. Unlike Mussolini, however, the general never achieved a broad base of support. In January of 1930 Primo de Rivera realized his time had passed. He gracefully resigned and went to Paris to devote the two remaining months of his life to sensual pleasure.[37]

The monarchy now found it dangerous and difficult to restore democracy. In February of 1931 Alphonso called for elections to a Constituent Assembly and found out that the country had grown weary of the monarchy itself as well as of him personally. So had the Army, which did not wish to precipitate a civil war by the new Republican-dominated Assembly. The king left for France in April without officially abdicating.

From its beginning the Second Spanish Republic was plagued by civil strife and increasing violence. The government moved against the ancient privileges of the Church and the nobility, but its methods alarmed many of the middle class who began to fear for their own lives and property. As in France and other countries, Spanish conservatives looked abroad for help. In 1931 Onesimo Redondo founded the *Juntas de Ofensiva Nacional-Sindicalista* (Council of Offensive National Syndicalists) or JONS, a Nazi type of organization advocating national unity but allowing a role for the

Church. Two years later José Antonio Primo de Rivera, son of the old dictator, founded the *Falange Española,* which was molded more on Mussolini's brand of fascism. The two parties merged two years later under the leadership of José Antonio Primo de Rivera, but with most of the original JONS program as well as their symbol of the yoke and the arrow.[38]

The Spanish Army watched events with concern and then alarm. Despite its moderate intentions, the Republic was unable to contain the escalating violence. In August of 1932 General José Sanjurjo attempted a coup in Seville but was foiled by troops loyal to the government. In the fashion of Spanish politics, the general was arrested, sentenced to prison, and later amnestied. Following his release from prison, he left the country to plot anew toward overthrowing the government that had shown him leniency.

Republican strength in Spain was increased by Stalin's Popular Front policy of 1935. The Popular Front gained control of the government in the elections of February of 1936. Victory increased the drive for radical reform and encouraged violence against the Right and Center. They retaliated. The government tried to neutralize Army officers whose loyalty was suspect. Among them was General Francisco Franco who had suppressed a Leftist rebellion in 1934. Shortly after taking office, the government transferred Franco to virtual exile by making him the military governor of the Canary Islands.[39] During his exile Franco consented to join in a plot to overthrow the Republic. As part of the conspiracy he flew to Spanish Morocco on July 16, 1936 to raise the flag of rebellion and to prepare for crossing over the Spanish mainland where he would join with the forces of General Sanjurjo and General Emilio Mola.[40]

The Nationalists, as they became known, believed their coup would require only a few days, but most of the Navy and some of the Army remained loyal to the Republic. For Franco, who moved toward leadership of the movement when Sanjurjo's plane crashed on the first day of the revolt, the action of the Navy was critical. Franco had to transport his men across the Strait of Gibraltar to the mainland. The coup might have failed within a week had it not been for aid from Hitler and Mussolini. The Duce had never liked the Spanish Republic and he was eager to increase the prestige recently won in Africa.[41] Hitler was more calculating in deciding to aid Franco. Raw materials from Spain would aid the coming German rearmament. By aiding Franco, Germany could forge closer ties with Fascist Italy. A Nationalist Spain also would pose a threat to France in any future war with Germany.[42]

Hermann Göring later testified that Spain was useful as a laboratory for testing new military theories and weapons, especially air power.[43] Hitler and Göring decided to send the Condor Legion to Spain to provide Franco with air support. In November the Legion practiced on Madrid and other cities, and in April of the following year it horrified the world by bombing the Basque town of Guernica. Beyond that, however, Hitler was reluctant to make a massive commitment. He preferred that Mussolini take the lead in aiding the Nationalists. The more Mussolini committed himself to Spain the more his ego became involved and the more hostile he became toward those who supported the Republic, such as Blum's Popular Front government in France. For Hitler, the best policy seemed to be simply continuing the war as long as possible in hopes that his enemies would become further divided and that Mussolini would slip even further into his camp.

The Spanish Civil War became one of the great causes of the modern time. Men and women of differing and often hostile ideologies came to Spain from countries throughout the world. They were organized by the Comintern into the famous International Brigades. They were green and ill equipped, but they saved Madrid at great cost and gave the Republic time to raise a new army and prepare for a long war. The Spanish Popular Front soon disintegrated into a civil war within a civil war. The Communists gradually gained control of the Republic and imposed their authority. Stalin's fear of Trotsky also took precedence over the battle against the Nationalists. In December of 1936, the Executive Council of the Communist International approved the policy "aimed at the complete and final destruction of Trotskyism in Spain as essential to the victory over fascism."[44] Stalin also feared political contamination. The idealism generated in the fight against Franco might infect Communists, and especially Russian Communists, with the desire to rejuvenate the idealism of the Russian Revolution now being suffocated by an orgy of confessions and executions of the purges.

Hitler and Stalin had the luxury of distance from Spain and the knowledge that the outcome posed no direct threat to their own national security. For Léon Blum's Popular Front government, however, the outbreak of the civil war posed an immediate danger. The French Republic felt compelled to side with its cousins in Spain, and Blum quickly responded favorably to an appeal from Madrid on July 22. Blum left for London on the following day to attend a previously scheduled meeting with Eden and other members of the British government.

Britons in and out of the government recalled the tangled involvement in the peninsular war against Napoleon and the sorrow that often comes with intervention into distant civil wars.[45] Primarily, however, the government feared that intervention might lead to war with Germany and Italy. Blum was exposed to British coolness toward the Madrid government and the determination not to become involved, but there was no direct pressure on him to change his policy nor a threat to abandon Locarno if France became involved in a war with Germany over Spain. Blum faced a much greater challenge when he returned to France on the twenty-fourth. Word had been leaked to the press on the extent of aid to the Spanish republic. The parties of the Right, and even some moderate elements within the Front itself, exploded in anger.[46] Blum had to face the harsh reality of his situation. Intervention in Spain might well lead to a confrontation with Germany and Italy. At the very least, it would end all chance of a rapprochement with Italy and a restoration of the Stresa Front. France might become identified with the Soviet Union and perhaps fatally estranged from Britain. Supporting the Republic, Blum realized, might also tear the country asunder and bring open civil war. Blum decided to seal the border with Spain and to pursue a policy of nonintervention in cooperation with other countries. On August 2, he invited Britain and Italy to join him in banning the shipment of all war material to Spain. Britain agreed eagerly and Italy gave its guarded consent. Germany, the Soviet Union, and others were steadily added until twenty-seven European countries formally adhered to the agreement by the time the first meeting of the Non-Intervention Committee took place in London on September 6.

The Non-Intervention Committee illustrated the futility of honorable people making agreements with those who are not. By the middle of 1937, Germany and Italy had recognized Franco's government at Burgos and were openly aiding him with men and material. The Western democracies, on the other hand, were fulfilling their pledge not to intervene. Without help from the West, liberal elements within the government were weakened while the Communists were strengthened. As Madrid became more and more dependent on Moscow, the Republic slid more toward a Communist government. Communist control and tales of attacks on other groups confirmed the fears of many in the West and gave credence to those who had supported Franco's fight against communism.

The war in Spain also posed a challenge for Stalin. He wanted no costly foreign involvements during the internal turmoil of the five-year plans and the purges. At the same time, he saw some benefits to be derived by a success of the Popular Front. Communist parties could take credit for leading the crusade to stop fascist aggression. On the other hand, too much Communist success might frighten liberal as well as conservative elements in the West and destroy the Popular Front itself. The rise of Communist strength in Spain was risky to Stalin as well. He had always been uneasy about the war, and he had foreseen the danger of any kind of Communist victory. By June of 1937 it was obvious that Britain and France were not going to intervene, and that many in those countries actually preferred a victory of fascism over communism. A victory for the Republic dominated by Communists might further frighten Stalin's timid associates in the Popular Front, and it might eventually unite them in an alliance with Hitler against the Soviet Union. Stalin decided to limit Soviet intervetion in Spain in order to prolong the war. By so doing, the Soviet could test new weapons and prepare for war.

The only real hope for ending the non-intervention policy lay in Washington. Following his overwhelming reelection, Roosevelt considered measures that would give him more discretionary power in enforcing neutrality legislation. In doing so, however, his effort immediately became entangled in the domestic crisis. The President was already being condemned as a dictator for his struggle with the Supreme Court. Any attempt to acquire more power in foreign policy at the expense of Congress would surely be resisted on that basis alone.[47] Congress could support its position by citing a January 1937 poll in which nearly 70 percent favored Congressional control over policies on neutrality.[48] Despite the help of supporters in Congress, Roosevelt could get only limited discretionary power to withhold raw materials from belligerents and to embargo arms during a civil war in addition to other minor concessions.[49] Supporters of the Republic and members of Congress pressured Roosevelt to apply the neutrality laws to Germany and Italy. On March 16 Senator Gerald Nye introduced legislation to embargo all arms shipments to Berlin and Rome. In addition to punishing Hitler and Mussolini, Nye hoped to end American cooperation with Britain and France and to reduce the chance of any American involvement in any future European war.[50]

The bombing of Guernica in April transformed the indifference of many Americans into a revulsion against the Nationalists and their foreign supporters.[51] In May and June the situation worsened when forces of the Republic came into open warfare with German shipping. After these incidents Roosevelt knew he could move against Germany and Italy with the support of many Americans, but he hesitated to do so without consulting with Britain and France. The response from London itself ended what could have been a turning point in the Spanish Civil War and virtually assured the eventual victory of the Nationalists. Ambassador Robert Bingham reported that Eden did not consider a Nationalist's victory to be a threat, and he noted that action against Germany and Italy would have to be followed by similar action against the Soviet Union and perhaps France.

The military stalemate in Spain began to turn in favor of the Nationalists in the summer of 1937. The Nationalists now had a united command while the divisions within the Republic remained. Stalin, too, sensed that the tide had turned, and he began to remove Communist advisors.[52] Nationalist forces took Barcelona, the great citadel of Republican resistance, in February of 1939. Many who had fought for the Republic fled abroad to escape Franco's final assault as the inevitable defeat came closer. On May 19, 1939, Franco took the salute from his followers in a victory parade through Madrid. After three years of bloody civil war he was master of Spain. He had triumphed only with the help of Hitler and Mussolini and to them he owed a debt of gratitude. It was a debt they expected him to repay and a debt they both resented when he did not.

NOTES

1. Cordell Hull, *The Memoirs of Cordell Hull,* vol 1 (New York: The Macmillan Company, 1948), 378.
2. Winston S. Churchill, *The Gathering Storm* (Boston: Houghton Mifflin Company, 1948), 89.
3. Gordon A. Craig, "Making Way for Hitler," *New York Review of Books,* vol. 36 (October 12, 1989), 11.
4. Luigi Albertini, *The Origins of the War of 1914*, trans. Isabella Massey, vol. 3 (New York: Oxford University Press, 1957), 178.
5. Ivan Maisky, *The Munich Drama* (Moscow: Novosti Press Agency, 1972), 11.
6. Dallek, *Franklin D. Roosevelt and American Foreign Policy,* 42.
7. Roger Nathan, "Histoire désabusée de la Conférence de Londres," *L'Europe Nouvelle,* vol. 16 (1933), 592.
8. R.F. Harrod, *The Life of John Maynard Keynes* (New York: Harcourt, Brace, and Company, 1951), 445.
9. Georges Bonnet, *Quai d'Orsay* (Isle of Man: Times Press and Anthony Gibbs and Phillips, 1965), 110-111.

10. "A Spectator's Notebook," *Spectator,* vol. 151 (July 7, 1933), 6.
11. Kirkpatrick, *Mussolini,* 288.
12. Bullock, *Parallel Lives,* 331-332. *DGFP,* vol 1, 451-455.
13. *Völkischer Beobachter* (Berlin) May 18, 1933, 1.
14. Weinberg, *1933-1936,* 164-166. *DGFP,* 3 Ser, vol 2, 1-12.
15. Bullock, *Parallel Lives,* 334-335. Jozef Lipski, *Diplomat in Berlin, 1933-1939* (New York: Columbia University Press, 1968), 98-99. DGFP, vol. 2, 421-422.
16. Duroselle, *La Décadence,* 139-142.
17. Geoffrey Warner, *Pierre Laval and the Eclipse of France* (New York: Macmillan Company, 1968), 78. *Soviet Documents on Foreign Policy* , vol. 3, 131-132.
18. Jiri Hochman, *The Soviet Union and the Failure of Collective Security, 1934-1938* (Ithaca: Cornell University Press, 1984), 55.
19. William L. Shirer, *The Collapse of the Third Republic,* 244.
20. *DGFP,* vol 3, 791.
21. Telford Taylor, *Munich: The Price of Peace* (Garden City, NY: Doubleday, 1979), 220-223.
22. *FRUS: 1935,* vol. 13 (Washington, 1953), 168.
23. *Documents on British Foreign Policy,* ed. W. N. Medlicott, et al, Second Ser., vol. 14 (London: Her Majesty's Printing Office, 1976), 329-333.
24. Taylor, *Munich,* 162.
25. *Times* (London), September 13, 1935, 12.
26. Henderson B. Braddick, "The Hoare-Laval Plan: A Study in International Politics," *Review of Politics* vol. 24 (July, 1962), 342-364.
27. *Times* (London) December 20, 1935, 14.
28. Shirer, *Collapse of the Third Republic,* 250.
29. Weinberg, *1933-1936,* 256.
30. *Shirer, Collapse of the Third Republic,* 252.
31. Maurice Gamelin, *Servir: Le prologue du drame* (1930-août 1939) vol. 2 (Paris: Plon, 1946), 208-211.
32. *Times,* March 9, 1936, 9.
33. Weinberg, *1933-1936,* 259; *DGFP,* C, vol. 5, 57.
34. Weinberg, *1933-1936,* 262.
35. Adolf Hitler, *Hitler's Table Talk,* trans. Norman Cameron and R. H. Stevens (London: Weidenfeld and Nicolson, 1953) 259.
36. Weinberg, *1933-1936,* 269.

37. Hugh Thomas, *The Spanish Civil War* (New York: Harper and Row, 1961), 15-17.
38. Ibid., 68-71.
39. Ibid., 96-97.
40. Ibid., 108-109.
41. Weinberg, *1933-1936*, 295-296.
42. Ibid., 288-290.
43. International Military Tribunal, *Trial of the Major War Criminals Before the International Military Tribunal,* vol. 9 (Nuremberg: International Military Tribunal, 1947), 281.
44. Degras, *Communist International.* vol. 3, 398.
45. Churchill, *The Gathering Storm,* 214.
46. David W. Pike, *Les Français et la guerre d'Espagne* (Paris: Presses universitaries de France, 1975), 82-93.
47. Dallek, *Roosevelt and American Foreign Policy,* 140.
48. Robert A. Divine, *The Illusion of Neutrality* (Chicago: University of Chicago Press, 1962), 181.
49. Kenneth S. Davis, *FDR: Into the Storm, 1937-1940: A History* (New York: Random House, 1993), 122-123.
50. Wayne S. Cole, *Senator Gerald P. Nye and American Foreign Relations* (Minneapolis: University of Minnesota Press, 1962), 114-115.
51. *New York Times* April 28, 1937, 1-4.
52. Bullock, *Parallel Lives,* 542. Tucker, *Stalin,* 524.

Chapter Five

A New Axis of Power

Fascism stood triumphant in Europe when Franco's forces marched through Madrid. Hitler had used the war in Spain as a launching pad for a string of victories rarely equaled and never surpassed in diplomacy. He had admired Mussolini and had seen Fascist Italy as a natural ally since his early days. The wars in Ethiopia and Spain had isolated Mussolini from the Western democracies and brought him closer to Germany. The Duce signaled a new course in June of 1936 when he dismissed Fulvio Suvich as his chief advisor on foreign policy. He then gave his own position as foreign minister to his son-in-law, Galeazzo Ciano. Suvich had championed Austrian independence, but Ciano now pressured Chancellor Kurt von Schuschnigg to accommodate Hitler as best he could. Schuschnigg responded by signing an agreement with Germany on July 11, 1936. Hitler recognized Austrian independence and agreed not to interfere in Austrian internal affairs. Schuschnigg in return agreed to follow policies similar to those of Germany.[1]

The path was now clear for negotiations between Berlin and Rome. Ciano went to Berchtesgaden in October to meet Hitler for an exchange of views and to make preparations for a later visit by Mussolini himself. Ciano signed a protocol with Foreign Minister Konstantin von Neurath calling for cooperation in a broad area of policy problems. The text itself was not published, but its significance was proclaimed by Mussolini on November 1. Speaking to a large rally in Milan, he called for a "clean sweep of . . . the great shipwreck of Wilsonian ideology," and proclaimed the end of collective security through the League. The new "Rome-Berlin line," he proclaimed, was "an axis around which can revolve all those European states with a will to collaboration and peace."[2]

The Axis appeared stronger than it was, and periodically Mussolini would renew his flirtations with Britain and France. But for all practical purposes, the Berlin protocol marked a giant and fateful step for Mussolini down a road to ruin. His power and his prestige now rode with Hitler. No one appreciated this more than Hitler himself. The appearance of a common front was as valuable to him as the front itself. The very threat of an Italian attack in the south further eroded any willingness in Paris to make war against Germany and brought pressure on the states of eastern Europe to make their own deals with Berlin.

Hitler had altered the balance of power in Europe. He also had altered the balance of power in Asia, although to a much lesser extent. Germany had been more aligned with China than with Japan since the days of the Weimar Republic. This alignment continued into the Nazi era, and was strongly supported by Neurath and most of the foreign office. Closer relations with Japan, they argued, would threaten commercial interests in China and could even ruin any chance of a complete rapprochement with Britain.[3] Neurath, however, was being challenged by Joachim von Ribbentrop, a relatively late comer to the Nazi party, who had impressed Hitler with his knowledge of foreign countries. Hitler appointed him ambassador at large with his own office in the Wilhelmstrasse in 1935. Ribbentrop was resented by the foreign office for several reasons, but mostly because he was an insufferable pompous ass as well as Hitler's toady. In August of 1936, Hitler made Ribbentrop his ambassador to Britain with instructions to gain an alliance. Ribbentrop saw an alliance with Japan as a challenge to Britain in Asia and as an asset in any future war with the Soviet Union. The shift toward Japan was aided when the Japanese military strengthened its control of the government in February of 1936. In July Hitler decided to make a move toward Japan that would not force a breach with China. The Anti-Comintern Pact of October 23 skirted any overt threat to the Soviet government and involved no German recognition of Japan's conquest in Manchuria. The Soviets had always maintained that the Comintern was separate from their government. Turnabout was now fair play. Both countries denied rumors about secret clauses aimed directly at the Soviet government. There were so many reservations that the agreement was little more than an entente of dubious value should there be conflict between either country and the Soviet Union. As with the Axis, however, these reservations remained hidden behind the fanfare of unity and strength.

The Axis and Anti-Comintern Pact elevated Hitler as a statesman. The Germany he ruled was prosperous and unified, and now was becoming a major power. Former prime minister David Lloyd George visited Hitler at Berchtesgaden in September of 1936 and returned home to praise the dynamism of the new Germany and greatness of its leader. There were many more visitors and many more words of praise. Hitler met his most important guest in Munich on September 23, 1937. For five days he spared no effort to make it a lavish tour that would overwhelm Mussolini with the might of Nazi Germany. It did. Mussolini had lost the easy superiority he had displayed toward Hitler at their meeting in Venice three years earlier. The coin had turned. It was now Mussolini who marveled at Hitler's regimented country and the power it represented.[4]

Mussolini's visit added to Hitler's growing self-confidence. With rearmament in full swing, and with the European situation in his favor, the time was fast approaching for action. This he made clear on November 5, 1937, during a lengthy meeting with Field Marshal Werner von Blomberg, commander in chief of the armed forces, General Werner von Fritsch, commander in chief of the army, Admiral Erich Raeder, commander in chief of the navy, General Hermann Göring, commander in chief of the air force, Baron Konstantin von Neurath, foreign minister, and Colonel Friedrich Hossbach, Hitler's military adjutant who recorded the conversation a few days later.[5]

Hitler's views were a declaration of intent in which there lay eventual aggression and the risk of a European war. He had always been both an ideologue and an opportunist. His goals in foreign policy remained unchanged, especially with respect to the expansion of Germany to the East. In tactics, however, he remained flexible, employing a mixture of probe and response, ever ready to seize upon the errors and psychological weakness of his enemies. German policy, he stated, must be "to make secure and to preserve the racial community [*Volksmasse*] and to enlarge it." To attain the eventual goal, Germany must prepare to expand into Eastern Europe within the next few years and by 1943-44 at the latest. By that time, Hitler argued, Germany would lose its current advantage in armaments and he himself would be past his prime.

Hitler's monologue contained nothing he had not said many times before and was similar to what Göring and Nazi leaders were saying to

European and American listeners. Limp opposition came from Blomberg, Fritsch, and Neurath who feared a war that Germany would lose. Their hesitancy may have contributed to their downfall, although Hitler probably would have replaced them anyway.[6] Hitler also centralized his control of the military by eliminating the War Ministry as a barrier between his position as Supreme Commander and OKW. He dismissed or transferred several generals whose zeal for Nazism was questionable. Hitler was less resolute when it came to the foreign office. He appointed the obsequious Ribbentrop as foreign minister, while soothing Neurath's feelings by making him head of the secret cabinet council that never met.

Hitler told General Alfred Jodl that the shakeup of the government would make the Austrian Chancellor Kurt von Schuschnigg "tremble."[7] Schuschnigg might well have trembled had he known the peril awaiting his country and himself, for by February of 1938 the Anschluss, or union of Germany and Austria, was merely a matter of time. Hitler had appointed Franz von Papen as his ambassador to Vienna following the Dollfuss fiasco. As a Catholic and a gentleman of the old school, Papen proved to be an excellent counterpoint to the rebellious Austrian Nazis and their supporters in Germany with whom he did not get along. Papen's goal was the same as the Nazi extremists, except that he believed gradual pressure would eventually bring Anschluss by peaceful means.

Papen had cause to be optimistic. He arrived in Vienna in July of 1934 to find a country seething with internal discord. A year earlier Dollfuss had dissolved all political parties and replaced them with the Fatherland Front. The Front was supposed to have been an organization containing all political creeds united against the German menace. In following February, however, Dollfuss eliminated socialist opposition in a brief but bloody coup. The Front remained essentially a quasi-fascist government supported mainly by the middle class with the blessing of Mussolini. The Duce, however, was ready to accept the inevitable. His resources were strained to the limit by wars in Ethiopia and Spain, and he knew that most Austrians would rather be conquered by Germans than rescued by Italians. Schuschnigg hoped to blunt German pressure by eliminating radical Austrian Nazis and appealing to the patriotism of the moderates. Here he made a major mistake in trusting an old friend, Dr. Arthur Seyss-Inquart, to help mediate with Nazi extremists and Berlin.[8] After two postponements, Papen arranged a meeting between Hitler and Schuschnigg at Berchtesgaden on February 12. He promised Schuschnigg that Hitler would reaffirm the 1936 agreement and make no political demands.[9]

Schuschnigg decided to take the initiative by formulating a new set of concessions designed to remove any pretext for German intervention in Austria. Schuschnigg discussed his plan with Seyss-Inquart on February 11. Seyss-Inquart rewarded Schuschnigg's trust by relaying Schuschnigg's plan to Hitler.[10] Hitler used the meeting to bully the into concessions that would end Austrian independence. Seyss-Inquart was to be appointed minister of public security with unlimited control of the police. All imprisoned Nazis, including the killers of Dollfuss were to be released, and all Nazis were to be admitted to the Fatherland Front.

Schuschnigg compounded his problem upon returning to Vienna by concealing how badly he had been treated as well as the concessions he had made. His claim that the meeting had been friendly was quickly undercut by reports in the press, and even further when he announced Seyss-Inquart's appointment on February 15. The desperation in Austria was highlighted when Schuschnigg appointed a prominent Social Democrat as secretary of state for labor. As minister of justice, Schuschnigg had signed the death warrants for many Socialists executed following the Dolfuss coup four years before. That he would appoint a Socialist to his cabinet spoke volumes for the aura of desperation hanging over Vienna. That a Socialist would accept spoke even more.[11]

As the twilight of independence fell over Austria, Chamberlain renewed his efforts toward a settlement with Germany and Italy. Chamberlain was now ready to recognize the Italian conquest of Ethiopia as the price for lessening the chance of war in the Mediterranean. Foreign Secretary Eden must either accept the move toward Italy or go. He went on February 20 and was immediately replaced by Lord Halifax.[12] Eden's departure gave further evidence that Britain would not intervene to save Austria. Two days later Chamberlain told Parliament, "We must try not to delude small weak nations into thinking that they be protected by the League against aggression."[13]

The events in Austria came like a series of body blows in France until the entire government fell. The weak and ineffectual government of Camille Chautemps had staggered under the weight of economic decline and internal dissension for nearly a year.[14] Fear and panic settled over Paris when the implications of the Berchtesgaden meeting were realized. Foreign Minister Yvon Delbos asked a group of French journalists in desperation, "How can we interfere in a quarrel between a country of 70,000,000 and a country of 7,000,000, and with all the guns on the side of the former?"[15]

Eden's resignation ended all hope Delbos had for support from London. Worse still, the news coincided with Hitler's truculent speech before the Reichstag. Hitler compared his orderly and prosperous Germany to the chaos and weakness he had inherited and criticized the democratic press abroad. He praised Schuschnigg's willingness to bring an understanding between Austria and Germany, while blasting the Paris peacemakers for having caused the problem.[16] The menace and the meaning of his words were clear in London and Paris as well as in Vienna. On the night of the twenty-first, American Ambassador William Bullitt reported that Delbos and the current Minister of National Defense, Édouard Daladier, believed nothing could be done to save Austria.[17] The mood of resignation became public on the twenty-sixth when the Chamber held a long debate on foreign policy. German Ambassador Count Johannes von Welczec reported to Berlin the weariness pervading the Chamber and doubted whether any "energetic" response would come from France over Austria.[18]

Schuschnigg realized that his fragile country was dying. Abroad and at home, people withdrew their holdings in Austrian banks while tourists canceled trips. He considered restoring the monarchy after receiving a letter from Otto von Habsburg in Belgium asking Schuschnigg to appoint him chancellor, if it would save the country. Schuschnigg knew that such a move would anger his neighbors and bring a German invasion. He decided instead to appeal to the patriotism of the Austrian people.[19] Schuschnigg addressed the Austrian Bundestag on February 24. The chancellor was normally a reserved man who found it difficult to display emotion in public, and he was not normally a good orator. On this occasion he melted the barrier that had existed with the Austrian people. Enough concessions had been made. The motto must now be "so far and no farther," and he held Hitler to his promise not to interfere in Austrian affairs. Schuschnigg assured his compatriots that God would protect Austria in the future, and referring to the Austrian flag, he enjoined them to remember "Red, White, Red" to the death.[20]

The speech was viewed in Berlin as an attempt by Schuschnigg to improve his sagging position and to justify his squeamishness at Berchtesgaden. Hitler decided to replace some Nazi party leaders in Vienna with more reliable people to stabilize the situation. Papen was replaced by Wilhelm Keppler, a longtime associate and advisor for economic affairs. Keppler was instructed to pursue an evolutionary policy of cooperation with Schuschnigg and Seyss-Inquart as Hitler's personal representative.[21] Hitler believed the Berchtesgaden agreement ensured the Nazification of Austria and eventually union with Germany. He still wished to settle the Sudeten problem before Austria, and he knew that Mussolini remained touchy about Austria, despite the Axis. The Italian population and world opinion would regard Anschluss as a defeat for Italy, and Mussolini might be compelled to oppose Hitler simply to preserve his own prestige at home and his status as a statesman abroad.

Schuschnigg also sought to build a political base ranging from the socialist Left to the clerical Right. Politics and fear made strange bedfellows as both the Left and the Right fell in behind him, however grudgingly. Schuschnigg sent a special courier to Rome on March 7 to inform Mussolini of his plan to hold a plebiscite. Mussolini replied on the following day. A plebiscite was risky. If Schuschnigg won, the Nazis would denounce it as a fake. If he lost, then Austria was doomed. Göring, he said, had given his word of honor that Germany would not use force, and the future was not as bleak as Schuschnigg might think. It was the last message Schuschnigg received from his former benefactor. Schuschnigg decided to go ahead with the plebiscite. He announced it during a speech at Innsbruck on March 9. Austrian voters would decide on Sunday, March 13, whether they were "For a free and German Austria, an independent and social Austria, a Christian and united Austria; for peace and employment and for the equality of all who stand for their people and their Fatherland." It was Schuschnigg's last great public moment as chancellor. The crowd roared its support when he raised the old Tyrolean battle cry *"Mannder, es isch Zeit!"* ("Men, the time is now!")[22]

Hitler realized that the plebiscite would win easily and delay the Anschluss. At first he had thought of stopping Schuschnigg with internal pressure, but that night he began to consider direct military intervention. Early the next morning he summoned General Wilhelm Keitel and his operations chief, General Max Von Viebahn, to the chancellery and demanded a military move into Austria no later than Saturday, March 12. The stunned generals told Hitler there was no operational plan for such a move, only a vague plan named "Otto" to alert the armed forces in the event of a Habsburg restoration. Hitler ordered OKW to supplement Otto with an operational plan within the next forty-eight hours. Throughout the morning and early afternoon the OKW headquarters at the Bendlerstrasse became a beehive of activity by assorted generals and other staff officers. By mid-afternoon they had formulated a plan to mobilize five infantry divisions from Munich and Nuremberg and join them to an armored division from Würzburg. These ground units would be further augmented by Luftwaffe units based in Bavaria. Hitler approved the troop units, but he hesitated to order mobilization until seven that night because of the repercussions it might have abroad. At 2 a.m on March 11 Hitler ordered German troops into Austria to protect Germans and establish constitutional conditions. His soldiers should act as friends, but tolerate no resistance.[23]

Schuschnigg was awakened at 5:45 by an emergency phone call from State Security. The Germans had closed the border, and there were troop movements in the southern part of the country. Later at the chancellery he received a telegram from the Austrian consul in Munich bearing the cryptic message "Leo is ready to travel." Invasion was imminent.[24] Schuschnigg was unable to reach Seyss-Inquart who had spent the early morning with Keppler. They went to the chancellery at 9:30 to inform Schuschnigg that Hitler was furious and insisting the plebiscite be canceled. Schuschnigg then secluded himself with leaders of the Fatherland Front to consider various compromises. Later in the afternoon Seyss-Inquart again insisted the plebiscite be canceled. Schuschnigg conferred briefly with President Wilhelm Miklas and agreed.

Hitler and Göring now pressed for the final blow. Schuschnigg and his cabinet must resign and be replaced by a new government under Seyss-Inquart. The new chancellor then would ask Hitler to send troops into Austria in order to restore order. Schuschnigg agreed to resign, but President Miklas refused to appoint Seyss-Inquart in his place, and held his ground throughout the day. At 7 p.m. radio Vienna announced that the plebiscite had been canceled and that Schuschnigg had resigned along with the rest of his cabinets. Seyss-Inquart, the announcement continued, would remain as minister of interior.

News of Schuschnigg's fall stunned his allies and emboldened his enemies. A series of putsches took place throughout Austria with the Nazis taking control of local and provincial governments. Rumors began to filter into Vienna that the Germans had already begun their invasion, prompting Schuschnigg to address the Austrian people. At approximately 8 p.m. he told the country of the German ultimatum and the impending invasion. In the President's name Schuschnigg announced that the Austrian Army would offer no resistance. "We are resolved that, on no account, and not even at the grave hour, shall German blood be spilled. . . . God protect Austria!"[25]

Schuschnigg had surrendered but Hitler still hesitated to send troops. He was still unsure about Mussolini. Around noon he had penned a message to the Duce and dispatched his personal courier, Prince Philip of Hesse, to Rome, and there was still no reply. Göring again pressed for the invasion no matter what the risk. Finally Hitler exclaimed, "*Jetzt geht's los!*" (Now we go for it!)[26] Hitler wanted a legal basis for the invasion. Göring again called Vienna with instructions for Seyss-Inquart to request German interventions to restore order.[27] Seyss-Inquart agreed only reluctantly. He did not see any need for the invasion now, and he resented being "a historical telephone girl."[28] Everything was now legal and success was assured, but still there was no word from Rome. Prince Philip finally called Berlin at 10:30 p.m. The prince had just returned from the Venetian palace where Mussolini had "accepted the whole thing in a very friendly manner." Hitler's relief was profound and understandable. Without Mussolini there would be no serious opposition. "I will never forget it," Hitler promised.[29]

Ribbentrop was lunching at 10 Downing Street while Austria was falling. Messages arrived with the news that Schuschnigg had canceled the plebiscite and was under pressure to resign. Chamberlain and Halifax held a private conversation with Ribbentrop to demand an explanation. Chamberlain kept calm despite his irritation.[30] For some time he, as well as Halifax, had accepted the eventual union of Germany and Austria, but they wished Hitler had been more polite about it.

Britain at least had a government to deal with the crisis. France did not. The wobbly Chautemps government had fallen on March 10 without asking for a vote of confidence. It was simply easier to resign than to face the challenge from Berlin.[31] Since then, Léon Blum had frantically searched for some kind of government to deal with the looming crisis. The loss of Austrian independence posed a direct threat to the security of France itself. German troops could attack directly across Czechoslovakia from the north and south to encircle the Czech Maginot Line and destroy the lynchpin of the French alliance system. The politicians and the generals recognized the threat but were unwilling to prevent it at the price of war. Word arrived on the afternoon of March 12 that London would do no more than protest. The rump French government now had the best of all possible worlds: a policy of inaction and someone to blame for it. That evening Blum addressed the Chamber of Deputies to plead for a truly national government. The Left and the Center parties of the Popular Front had already consented to join in a national coalition, and now he needed the conservatives. His appeal was eloquent and futile. Blum patched together a second Popular Front government the following day with full knowledge that it would not last long. Less than a month later it, too, joined the cascade of cabinets.

German troops were already marching through Vienna when Blum addressed the Chamber. Austria's longest day had come to an ominous end for Schuschnigg. He had been driven home by Seyss-Inquart through a howling mob of Austrian Nazis. Seyss-Inquart promised to look after his welfare, but the next morning Schuschnigg awoke to find his house surrounded. He was now a prisoner, and remained so for the next seven years. President Miklas, however, still had some usefulness and no harm came to him for the moment. Shortly before dawn on the twelfth German soldiers crossed into Austria for the first of the *Blumenkriegen,* the flower wars. "The populace saw that we came as friends," wrote General Heinz Guderian, "and we were joyously received everywhere."[32]

Hitler issued a proclamation explaining his actions and pledging his support for Germans outside of the Reich. The great majority of Austrians, he said, had risen to ask his help after years of oppression. He then flew to Munich and proceeded to Austria by car as a tourist visiting the grave of his parents. He was relieved when informed that German soldiers had been welcomed with flowers. Relief turned to ecstacy when he crossed the border at Braunau am Inn into the land of his birth he had not seen for nearly a quarter of a century. After a brief visit to his parents' home, he proceeded on to Linz. The roads were lined with cheering throngs as were the streets of Linz itself. Seyss-Inquart welcomed him at the Town Hall around 8:00 p.m. Addressing Hitler as *Mein Führer,* Seyss-Inquart acknowledged Hitler as the leader of both countries while noting Austrian independence. Hitler, in turn, addressed Seyss-Inquart as *Herr Bundeskanzler* and seemed to accept Austrian independence for at least the near future.

Seyss-Inquart returned to Vienna with the belief that Austria was to remain independent in a strange echo of the old Dual Monarchy of Austria-Hungary. Sometime during the night Hitler decided to incorporate Austria directly into the Reich. His joyous reception and the certainty that there would be no opposition from abroad convinced him that the time had come to annex Austria now instead of waiting for some evolutionary development.[33]

On Sunday, the day Schuschnigg had scheduled for his plebiscite, Hitler called Keppler in Vienna and told him to discuss Anschluss with the Austrian government. Whatever resistance there was in Seyss-Inquart and his cabinet remained hidden. President Miklas was defiant to the end. He resigned rather than sign away Austria's independence. Seyss-Inquart traveled to Linz that evening with the Reunification Law making Austria "a province of the German Reich," and calling for a plebiscite on Sunday, April 10, to ratify the decision.

Hitler left for Vienna the following morning. He was irritated by the delay caused by Himmler's concern for safety and the breakdown of several army vehicles. His spirits revived, however, at the thought of having returned to this city in triumph. Papen, who flew to Vienna for the festivities, described Hitler's mood as one of "ecstasy."[34] It may have been an ecstasy born of exaltation for having united the two countries. It may also have been an ecstasy of revenge for having conquered the city and the people who had rejected him so many years before.

Hitler remained at the Hotel Imperial overnight, taking time to make a short speech to Austrian Nazis from his balcony.[35] The next morning he spoke again at the formal ceremonies, reviewed a parade, and then returned to the hotel to receive some leading dignitaries, some of whom were seeking to atone for their earlier support of Schuschnigg. Having had his triumph, Hitler did not wish to remain in Vienna any longer than necessary. The next morning he flew back to Munich, the city where he had begun his rise to fame, glory, and power.[36]

A wave of barbarism swept over Austria in the wake of Hitler's triumph. Himmler's Gestapo arrested nearly 80,000 in Vienna alone. Official terror was augmented and even surpassed by the terror of the mobs who set upon Jews, their businesses, and their homes.[37] Theodore Cardinal Innitzer, the primate of Austria, angered and embarrassed the Vatican by ordering Austrian Churches to hoist swastikas and toll their bells when Hitler arrived in Vienna. A year earlier Pope Pius XI had issued the encyclical *Mit brennender Sorge* (With Burning Sorrow) condemning National Socialism. Eugenio Cardinal Pacelli, the Vatican secretary of state and future Pope Pius XII, summoned Innitzer to Rome for a strong reprimand. In May Pius XI demonstrated his displeasure by ostentatiously leaving the Vatican for Castelgandolfo, the papal summer reseidence, when Hitler made a state visit to Rome.[38]

Many of those who cheered Hitler's entrance into their country came to regret it. Carpetbaggers came from the north almost immediately to impose their will and to reap profits. Vienna became simply another city within the "Danube and Alpine Gau" of the Third Reich. Austria would eventually share the fate of Germany in war and defeat, destruction and death. These things, however, still lay in the future, on Sunday, April 10, 1938. The plebiscite was part of a general election campaign for the

Reichstag and a vote of confidence in Hitler himself. The voters were asked, "Are you in agreement with the reunion of Austria with the German Reich effected on March 13, 1938, and do you vote for the list of our Führer?" Out of joy, fear, or resignation over 90 percent of the voters in both countries said "yes."[39]

NOTES

1. Weinberg, *1933-1936,* 268.
2. *Times* (London) November 2, 1936, 14.
3. Weinberg, *1933-1936*, 343-344.
4. Bullock, *Parallel Lives,* 543-544.
5. Friedrich Hossbach, *Zwischen Wehrmacht und Hitler, 1934-1938* (Göttingen: Vandenhoeck und Ruprecht, 1965), 164-170.
6. Bullock, *Parallel Lives,* 556-558.
7. Alfred Jodl, *Diary,* January 31, 1938, *TMWC*, vol. 28, 362.
8. Gerhard L. Weinberg, *Foreign Policy of Hitler's Germany: Starting World War II, 1937-1939* (Chicago: University of Chicago Press, 1980), 290.
9. Schuschnigg, *Austrian Requiem*, 10.
10. Gordon Brook-Shepherd, *Anschluss: The Rape of Austria* (Westport, CT: Greenwood Press), 34-37.
11. Ibid., 108-109.
12. Anthony Eden, Earl of Avon, *Facing the Dictators: The Memoirs of Anthony Eden* (Boston: Houghton Mifflin Company, 1962), 665-678.
13. *Times,* February 23, 1938, 8.
14. Shirer, *Collapse of the Third Republic,* 326-327.
15. Brook-Shepherd, *Anschluss,* 107-110; Schuschnigg, *Austrian Requiem,* 34-36.
16. *Times,* February 23, 1938, 8.
17. *FRUS: 1938,* vol. 1, 28-29.
18. *DGFP*, Ser. D., vol. 1, 233.
19. Brook-Shepherd, *Anschluss,* 112-116.
20. Times, February 25, 1938, 15.
21. *DGFP,* Ser. D., vol 1, 548-549.
22. Taylor, *Munich,* 352. *Times,* March 10, 1938, 14.
23. *TMWC*, vol 2, 411.
24. Taylor, *Munich,* 358.

25. *Times* (London), March 12, 1938, 12.
26. Taylor, *Munich,* 363.
27. *TMWC,* vol. 31, 366-367.
28. H. J. Neuman, *Arthur Seyss-Inquart* (Graz: Styria, 1970), 95.
29. Ibid., 368-369.
30. Brook-Shepherd, *Anschluss,* 145.
31. Duroselle, *La Décadence,* 328.
32. Heinz Guderian, *Panzer Leader,* trans. Constantine Fitzgibbon (New York: Ballantine Books, 1961), 32.
33. Brook-Shepherd, *Anschluss,* 192-195. DGFP, Ser D., vol. 1, 591-592.
34. Franz von Papen, *Memoirs,* trans. Brian Connell (New York: E.P. Dutton and Company, 1953), 432.
35. *Times,* March 15, 1938, 15.
36. Taylor, *Munich,* 372. *Times,* March 16, 1938, 14.
37. Brook-Shepherd, *Anschluss,* 216.
38. Weinberg, *1937-1939,* 300-301.
39. Bullock, *Parallel Lives,* 567-569.

CHAPTER SIX

A Faraway Country

Reaction to the Anschluss remained a combination of anger, resignation, and sorrow. On March 14, Chamberlain told Parliament of his displeasure with Hitler's shabby attempt to conceal German pressure. He also warned that Britain would not forget what had happened. But in the end, he admitted, "The hard fact is that nothing could have arrested this action by Germany unless we, and others, had been prepared to use force against it."[1] Very few in Britain were willing to do that, and without Britain, France would do nothing. Roosevelt and Hull condemned the disappearance of Austria while reassuring the American people that the United States had no intention of "policing the world."[2] American equivocation was hardly unexpected in London. Chamberlain, whose dislike and distrust of Roosevelt went back to the London Economic Conference of 1933, considered the United States too unreliable for any concerted action.[3] Chamberlain avoided cooperating with the Soviet Union for entirely different reasons. The Soviets had publicly proposed a conference to prevent any further German aggression following the Anschluss, but Chamberlain rejected any commitment beyond those Britain already had to the League and those of the Locarno Treaty. Any conference, he said, "would aggravate a tendency toward establishments of exclusive groups of nations which must be inimical to the prospects of European peace."[4]

Hitler faced adversaries who were divided, fearful, and guilt-ridden. He could not have chosen a better time, nor a more vulnerable target than

Czechoslovakia, and he was ready with a clear objective, organized propaganda, and knowledge of the anxieties and motives of his adversaries.[5] Czechoslovakia had emerged out of the Great War under the leadership of Thomas Masaryk and Edward Beneš to embrace the opportunity and confront the challenges of national self-determination. It had also inherited the legacy of the Habsburg Empire and six hundred years of history. It was a multi-national state consisting of Poles, Hungarians, and other groups in addition to Czechs and Slovaks. The Sudeten Germans were the most troublesome group. They had enjoyed the privileges of a ruling class within the Austrian Empire. They had been included in the new Czechoslovakia against their will, an act which many people at the time considered to be a crime as well as a blunder.

Beneš and Masaryk had promised to make Czechoslovakia a cantonal state similar to Switzerland, with a great measure of autonomy for each of the cantons. This had never been done. The various national groups, including the Slovaks, resented their subordination to the Czechs and looked to their kinsmen in other countries for protection. The country might have splintered sooner than it did but for World War II and the authoritarian Communist rule that followed. The Sudetens and Weimar Germany had accepted the situation until they could change it. The Depression and the rise of Hitler offered hope. Konrad Henlein founded the *Sudetendeutsche Partei* (SdP) in September of 1933. By 1938 the party had the support of a majority of Sudetens and was subsidized from Berlin. Hitler summoned Henlein to Berlin following the Anschluss to appoint him Viceroy *(Stathalter)* for the Sudetenland with instructions to "demand concessions which are unacceptable to the Czech government."[6]

Henlein addressed the annual meeting of the SdP in Carlsbad on April 24. Czechoslovakia, he said, should be part of a new central Europe dominated by Germany, and should cease cooperating with Germany's enemies. He followed with eight specific demands for political reform. If fulfilled, the Sudetenland would become a state with "full freedom to profess German nationality and the German political philosophy *(Weltanschauung)*.[7] The Prague government could not accept Henlein's demands without laying the foundation for the ultimate secession of the Sudetenland along with similar concessions to other national groups and its own destruction.

Henlein's speech added urgency to the meeting between Chamberlain and French Prime Minister Édouard Daladier on April 28. Daladier had become prime minister for the third time when Léon Blum's second Popular Front government fell on April 9 and had decided to abandon

Blum's commitment to the Czech alliance on the grounds that France was not "strong enough to follow it."⁸ Daladier had served as war minister in Blum's government. As the Anschluss was being completed, General Maurice Gamelin reported that France could do nothing to save Czechoslovakia, nor could France win a war with Germany supported by Francisco Franco's Spain. The Soviet Union could do nothing because Poland and Rumania would never allow Russian troops to cross their territory. Germany, Gamelin argued, aided by Italy, Hungary, and the benevolent neutrality of Poland, would easily defeat the Czechs and then turn its full strength against France.⁹

Daladier and Foreign Minister Georges Bonnet traveled to London on April 28 to seek a definite diplomatic and military commitment for the defense of Czechoslovakia. Daladier, in contrast to Chamberlain, recognized that Hitler's real aim was to "tear up treaties and destroy the equilibrium of Europe." "The ambitions of Napoleon," he felt, "were far inferior to the present aims of the German Reich." Chamberlain refused, however, to make a military commitment to Czechoslovakia. He did not believe Hitler would retreat if confronted by a combined Anglo-French threat, and he did not intend to gamble with the "innumerable families, men, women, and children, of our race." The Anschluss had rendered Czechoslovakia defenseless against a German attack from three sides, regardless of what happened in the West. Russian help would be negligible at best because of Stalin's purges and to the lack of any common border. Public opinion, Chamberlain added, in Britain and the Dominions would oppose any war for the Czechs.¹⁰ Daladier and Bonnet left London with only the assurance of British diplomatic support. Chamberlain refused to risk the British Empire and was resolved to find a peaceful solution to the Sudeten problem, even to the point of dismembering Czechoslovakia and strengthening German hegemony in central Europe.

Less than a month later the Sudeten crisis erupted to produce the greatest war scare since the summer of 1914. Henlein severed all talks with the government on May 9 and left for Germany. The Czech police faced scattered riots throughout the Sudetenland that were portrayed as "Czech Terror" by German radio and cinema. On May 18, Czech intelligence reported concentrations of German troops on the border. Beneš responded two days later by calling for a partial mobilization to defend the frontier.

France rallied to the side of its ally, but Britain gave only ambivalent support to France. On May 20 and again the following day, Lord Halifax instructed his ambassador in Berlin, Sir Neville Henderson, to caution

Germany against any military action. At the same time, however, Halifax instructed his ambassador in Paris, Sir Eric Phipps, to warn Bonnet that it would be "highly dangerous" to assume that Britain would take military action to preserve Czechoslovakia against German aggression."[11]

The May crisis passed when Hitler disclaimed any intent to attack Czechoslovakia. He had been impressed, however, with Czech mobilization and the response of Britain and France. Hitler now decided that Operation Green, an attack on Czechoslovakia by October 1, must be swift enough to counter Czech mobilization and foreign intervention.[12] Chamberlain was angry with the German bullies. He was also alarmed at how close Britain had come to war, an alarm shared in Paris where the Czechs were now blamed for causing the crisis.[13] The moment of truth also had come for those governments upon whom the Czechs and the French had depended. Yugoslavia declared it would not go to war in support of the Czechs. Poland and Rumania refused any aid to the Czechs and said they would resist any Soviet violation of their territory or air space. "The result of a French declaration of war," wrote William Bullitt, "would be therefore that two of France's allies would be at war with the third and France would be fighting Germany alone—with Italy waiting to pounce."[14]

British and French leaders may be forgiven for their policy following the May crisis. It is not, however, so easy to forgive the way they pursued it. Beneš had been premature with his order for mobilization, but he had been correct in his belief that Germany meant to destroy his country. He believed Britain and France also saw Hitler's intent, and that they would support Czechoslovakia, if only for their own selfish interests. Chamberlain also may be forgiven for not relying on opposition to Hitler in Germany. German military leaders had a poor record of decisive action during the Weimar Republic and a worse one in dealing with Hitler. Chamberlain could hardly risk a European war on the hope that a coup against Hitler would be launched by those who had benefitted from his government, accepted his promotions, and would eventually help him conquer Europe.[15]

The May crisis had also demonstrated how much Czechoslovakia depended on France. Czechoslovakia was surrounded by neighbors who would do nothing to save it, not to mention Poland and Hungary who were waiting for their chance to seize Czech lands. At a time when Beneš depended most on Western support, he was being written off as a political liability and a danger to peace. On June 3, the *Times* suggested that a plebiscite be arranged for the Sudeten Germans as well as other dissident national groups in Czechoslovakia, such as the Hungarians and Poles. Such a "drastic remedy," the *Times* conceded, might actually strengthen Czechoslovakia by making it a "more homogeneous state" and removing all cause for intervention by foreign powers.[16] While Great Britain and France sought to save Czechoslovakia by dismembering it, Beneš futilely continued to negotiate with Henlein who wanted only to prolong the crisis while rumors of German troop movements added to the tension. "Prevention," wrote Henderson from Berlin, "is better than cure, and I honestly believe that the moment has come for Prague to get a real twist of the screw."[17]

Beneš realized by the end of August that only surrender would expose Henlein's duplicity. On September 4, he agreed to virtually all of Henlein's Carlsbad demands. Henlein responded by ordering disturbances in the Sudetenland and then used "police brutality" as a pretext for ending all negotiations.[18] On September 7, the *Times* published its famous editorial suggesting that Prague cede the Sudetenland to Germany and thereby secure the advantages of becoming a more "homogenous State."[19] The government disclaimed any connection between the editorial and official policy, but in fact the editorial did not differ in substance from what the paper had said previously, nor from what the government had been hinting for some time.

The question now was whether Hitler would wait for peaceful victory or hold to the timetable of Operation Green. During the first week of September, Hitler added to the tension when he attended *Parteitag* at Nuremberg. Here he had given some of his most passionate speeches, and here many feared he would declare war. On September 12, he heaped abuse on Beneš and vowed that "Germans in Czechoslovakia are neither defenseless nor are they deserted," but he stopped short of war.[20] The Nuremberg rally and the continuing tension in Czechoslovakia broke much of the resistance in Paris. On September 8, Daladier lamented his position to Bullitt. France would have to fight, even though he personally felt the Sudetens had been "badly treated" by the Prague government. He now believed the Sudetens should be allowed to choose their own future, and he had conveyed this to the German ambassador.[21] The next day all hope of American aid ended when President Roosevelt denied speculation that America would become involved in a "stop Hitler" coalition should war break out in Europe.[22] In a mixture of panic and despair, Daladier asked Chamberlain to do whatever was necessary to avoid war, including a proposal to Hitler for a three power conference.[23]

Daladier's distress call coincided with reports to London that Hitler was indeed planning to attack Czechoslovakia at the end of September. A dramatic personal visit might be the only way to avoid it. On the evening of the thirteenth, Chamberlain proposed to "come over at once to see you with a view to trying to find peaceful solution [sic]."[24] Hitler was both surprised and flattered by Chamberlain's offer when he received the message at Berchtesgaden. A visit from Chamberlain was useful to sustain Hitler's image of a man seeking a peaceful solution, but he did not intend to alter the plan of attack. Hitler decided that Chamberlain should fly to Munich and then come to Berchtesgaden for a meeting on the fifteenth. Friends and critics alike acknowledged the nobility of Chamberlain's effort and the personal strain of the trip on a man his age. It was hoped that the prime minister would clarify Britain's position and avoid a repetition of 1914.

Chamberlain arrived at Berchtesgaden at 4 p.m. on September 15. Hitler held the advantage. Reports from London and Paris indicated that France had agreed to Chamberlain's plan for ceding the Sudetenland to Germany. Hitler failed to intimidate Chamberlain with a harangue and then simply asked whether Britain agreed to the cession of the Sudetenland. Chamberlain replied that he personally favored the idea, but that he would have to secure the approval of the cabinet before any final agreement could be reached.[25]

Chamberlain returned home believing he had a settlement. At the Anglo-French meeting of September 18, he easily overrode limp challenges from Daladier and Bonnet who now wanted peace at any price and who knew that Beneš was now willing to concede part of the Sudetenland. The two governments decided to present Beneš with an eight-point proposal calling for transfer of the Sudetenland and the "substitution of a general guarantee against unprovoked aggression in place of existing treaties which involve reciprocal obligations of a military character."[26] Czechoslovakia must now depend on the good will of its neighbors. Beneš was stunned and bitter. Britain had constantly pressured him for concessions. He had expected more from France. France was abandoning him and his country after so many years of friendship. Beneš conferred with his cabinet for a day and a half. He then notified London and Paris of his decision to reject the Anglo-French proposals in favor of arbitration under the terms of the 1925 treaty with Weimar Germany. "At this decisive time," the communiqué concluded, "it is not only the fate of Czechoslovakia which is in the balance but also that of other countries and particularly of France."[27] But the Czechs fell short of threatening to fight rather than accept the British and French plan. It may have been that Beneš wanted foreign pressure as a cover for his actions. Whatever the truth, London and Paris responded with the warning that the Czechs would have to fight Germany alone if they rejected the Anglo-French proposals.[28]

All seemed well when Chamberlain departed for Germany on September 22. He had kept his part of the bargain and was now ready to close the deal like the efficient businessman he was. The meeting had been scheduled at Godesberg, a small town near Bonn on the Rhine. Chamberlain and Hitler met at 5 p.m. at the Hotel Dreesen, the place from which Hitler had launched the famous Blood Purge of June 30, 1934. Chamberlain was prideful at having achieved so much in a short time. He reported to Hitler that France and Czechoslovakia had agreed to cede the Sudetenland to Germany and to abandon the Soviet alliance. After Chamberlain finished his full report, Hitler replied simply, "I am very sorry, but after the events of the last few days, this plan is no longer of any use." Chamberlain was stunned. Hitler now asked for occupation of the Sudetenland at once and refused to guarantee the remainder of Czechoslovakia until the claims of Hungary and Poland were settled.

Hitler kept Chamberlain on the defensive with the repeated demand that only the immediate transfer of the Sudetenland could compensate for the injury done by the Prague government. No agreement was reached except to meet the following day.[29] Chamberlain again came to see Hitler on the afternoon of the twenty-third. Hitler presented him with a memorandum calling for the transfer of the Sudetenland and the evacuation of all Czech forces by 8 a.m. on September 28. Chamberlain reacted heatedly to this "ultimatum." In the midst of the discussion word came that the Czechs had mobilized. After a period of strained silence and recrimination about who mobilized first, the two men continued their discussion into the following morning before Chamberlain ended the talks and left for home.

Chamberlain arrived in London on the afternoon of the twenty-fourth. He immediately tried to convince the cabinet to accept Hitler's new demands. Now, however, there was opposition from Alfred Duff Cooper, first lord of the admiralty, and Lord Halifax. The cabinet decided to reject the Godesberg demands. It appeared as though there would be a united front when the French government met the following morning. The French decided to reject the demands and ordered partial mobilization. That afternoon Daladier and Bonnet again came to London. Instead of bolstering the stand against Hitler, however, Chamberlain and others stressed the horror of war and the inability of Britain and France to prevent Germany from overrunning Czechoslovakia.[30]

Chamberlain sent his special representative, Sir Horace Wilson, to Berlin on the twenty-sixth with a personal letter to Hitler calling for moderation and notifying him that the Czechs would not accept his demands. Hitler responded to Wilson with a diatribe and again demanded fulfillment of the Godesberg memorandum. That night he addressed a rally at the *Sportspalast* where he heaped venom on President Beneš and promised to take the Sudetenland by October 1.[31] Wilson again met with Hitler the following noon before returning home. Hitler remained adamant and restated his intention to seize the Sudetenland. Hitler placed sole blame for the crisis on the Czechs. It was an effective ploy, since many in England and France already believed it. "I will still try to make those Czechos sensible," Wilson replied as he left.[32]

Hitler had lost some of his militancy by the end of the day. Developments were going against him at home and abroad. He attempted to rally the Berliners with a display of armor and soldiers. Instead, wrote William L. Shirer, people "ducked into subways, refused to look on, and the handful that did stood at the curb in utter silence. . . ."[33] Hitler also received a series of dispatches from foreign embassies warning of a long war against a coalition that would eventually include the United States. Hitler again appealed to Chamberlain with the promise to guarantee the remainder of Czechoslovakia and urging the prime minister to "bring the government in Prague to reason at the very last hour."[34]

Chamberlain had already been pressuring Beneš when Hitler's note reached him on the night of the twenty-seventh. If Hitler attacked, however, Britain would support France. Chamberlain had made this clear by mobilizing the fleet and preparing the nation for war. Chamberlain no doubt spoke for most in Britain and the Dominions that night when he referred to the crisis as a "quarrel in a faraway country between people of whom we know nothing. Armed conflict between nations is a nightmare to me, but if I were convinced that any nation had made up its mind to dominate the world by fear of force, I should feel that it must be resisted. . . . But war is a fearful thing, and we must be very clear, before we embark on it, that it is really the great issues that are at stake."[35]

Most Britons went to bed believing they would be at war within a day.[36] Chamberlain had believed it until receiving Hitler's letter. There was, after all, one last hope, and he intended to make the most of it. Chamberlain quickly replied to Hitler with the assurance of getting all essentials without war and without delay. "I am ready," Chamberlain continued, "to come to Berlin at once to discuss arrangements for transfer with you and the representatives of the Czech government together with representatives of France and Italy, if you desire."[37]

Chamberlain also appealed to Mussolini. Mussolini's support of a four-power conference probably tipped the scales in Hitler's mind.[38] The mood of the German people and the news from abroad had already made Hitler lean toward a peaceful solution. He continued to have great admiration for his mentor despite the change in their relationship, and was still grateful for Mussolini's attitude toward the Anschluss. There was no point in offending Mussolini. He could have the Sudetenland now and take the rest of Czechoslovakia later.

Chamberlain received Hitler's invitation from the gallery while speaking before a somber Parliament on the afternoon of the twenty-eighth. Announcement of the Munich conference and one last chance for peace transformed tension into mass hysteria unsurpassed in the history of Parliament. Amid wild shouting and tears an anonymous voice spoke for much of the country as well: "Thank God for the Prime Minister."[39] Chamberlain left for Munich the following morning believing he had secured European peace and defeated his domestic critics. He did not consult with Daladier nor anyone else who might delay agreement. The conference began at 12:45 on the afternoon of the twenty-ninth and lasted until 2:00 the following morning. The agreement stipulated German occupation of "predominantly German areas" in four stages from October 1 through October 7. Remaining areas were to be established by an International Commission consisting of the four powers and the Prague government, with occupation of these areas being completed by October 10. The International Commission would then arrange plebiscites by the end of November in those areas where the ethnic majority was in doubt. New borders were to be drawn and guaranteed by the great powers following transfer of the territory. The Czechs were told either to accept the agreement or face Germany alone. They accepted. On October 5, President Beneš resigned under German pressure, and on October 22, he began an exile lasting until the end of World War II. His successor, General Jan Syrovy, decided to accept German domination. "We have been willing to fight on the side of the angels," he said, "now we shall hunt with the wolves."[40]

Chamberlain and Daladier returned triumphant. Daladier had cut a pathetic figure throughout the conference by meekly acquiescing to a policy he knew to be folly as well as dishonorable, yet not having the courage to oppose it. He feared for his life when he saw the waiting crowd at Le Bourget Field in Paris. "The fools," he thought when he realized they approved of what he had done, "they are cheering me. For what?"[41] Chamberlain, however, was exhilarated by the belief that he had avoided war, and obtained "peace with honor" and "peace for our time." He had also secured Hitler's signature to a joint declaration promising to consult in the future to maintain European peace in addition to the four-power pact.[42] When Ribbentrop complained about the declaration, Hitler assured him that the "scrap of paper is of no significance whatever."[43]

Hitler had insisted prior to Munich that the Soviets be excluded and the other powers complied. Moscow now denounced the conspiracies and weaknesses of the Western powers while asserting the purity of Soviet motives. Promises of Soviet aid to Czechoslovakia were conditioned with the phrase "by the ways open to us." Stalin could gain from a war between Germany and France supported by Britain and he might well have sided with the latter, if it cost him little, drained the other parties, and offered him gains in the future. The Munich settlement seemed to further discredit what faith was left in Anglo-French cooperation. But collective security was better than having to face Hitler alone as long as unfriendly signals came from Berlin. Stalin tried to strengthen his position by curtailing publicity surrounding the purge trials, which had contributed to the image of Soviet weakness and had severely decreased Soviet prestige.

In Britain and the United States the euphoria of the Munich settlement gradually gave way to guilt. In both countries the legacy of appeasement and Munich left a psychological scar on minds of those who believed they had suffered because of it. As political leaders they formulated their policies on a perception of the past and a vision of the future warped by the Munich Syndrome—the failure of appeasement and the terrible war that followed. Recounting his decision to intervene in Korea in June of 1950, Harry S. Truman recalled that "Communism was acting in Korea just as Hitler . . . had acted earlier. . . . If this was allowed to go unchallenged, it would mean a third world war, just as similar incidents had brought on the second world war." Two decades later Richard Nixon cited the failure of appeasement when trying to explain his intervention into Cambodia. "I thought Neville Chamberlain was the greatest man living and Winston Churchill was a madman," he told dissident students. "It was not until years later that I realized that Neville Chamberlain was a good man, but Winston Churchill was right."[44]

The victor at Munich considered it a defeat. Hitler had wanted to destroy Czechoslovakia in a war. Chamberlain, he believed, had maneuvered him into accepting only the Sudetenland, denying him all of Czechoslovakia as well as a military triumph. He quickly regretted his decision to attend the Munich conference and he scorned his generals and others who had urged caution. He was also angry at the faint-hearted Hungarians who had wished to devour the Czechs, but would not join him in a war to do it. He was determined that no "*schweinehund*" would again cheat him out of war as he immediately prepared to destroy the remainder of Czechoslovakia.[45] On October 21, he told OKW to continues preparations for an attack. The jackals had their fill after the lion's kill. The Hungarians forced the Czechs to cede nearly five thousand square miles in the south and in the east. The Czechs would have lost Ruthenia as well if Hitler had not been peeved with the Hungarians for their lack of support prior to Munich. The Poles did not bother to wait for the niceties of negotiations. They seized the Teschen district immediately following Munich and later added some minor border areas in Slovakia.

Hitler tried to strengthen his own position by wooing France away from Britain. French Ambassador André François-Poncet visited Hitler at Berchtesgaden on the way to his new post in Rome. Hitler vented his unhappiness with the Munich agreement and condemned the British for their arrogance in trying to dominate other countries. France, on the other hand, would find Germany reasonable. To prove his point, Hitler offered to sign an agreement guaranteeing present boundaries and abandoning all claims to Alsace-Lorraine.[46]

Ribbentrop went to Paris in December to sign the treaty of friendship. He found the atmosphere more frigid than in the defeatist days following Munich. The French were tense because of Italian pressure on Tunis and Nice, and they wanted German support. Ribbentrop, however, had not come to support France. France must jettison its alliances in eastern Europe and acknowledge it as a German sphere of influence. Bonnet admitted that the situation had "fundamentally altered" since Munich, but he never became more specific. For some reason, which may lay simply in an offhand remark by Bonnet, Ribbentrop left Paris believing that France had indeed conceded all of eastern Europe to Germany.[47]

Ribbentrop's assessment strengthened Hitler's opinion that Britain and France would not fight. In October and November, he made speeches attacking British intervention into Europe and warning the entire outside world to mind its own business. His bellicose words were given emphasis when Nazism showed its fangs on Kristallnacht, the night of November 9-

10. The open brutality against the Jews throughout Germany horrified public opinion in the West, especially in the United States where President Roosevelt responded by recalling Ambassador Hugh Wilson home "for consultation."

Hitler's truculence prompted a guessing game throughout the autumn and winter of 1938-39. One report had him striking in the west as a prelude to an attack in the east. Others had him attacking Danzig, Czechoslovakia, and the Ukraine. The destruction of what was called Czecho-Slovakia remained Hitler's number one priority. The Slovaks had been given a large measure of autonomy following Munich. Hitler saw it as a stepping stone to complete independence which would destroy the entire country and leave the Czech area more dependent on Germany. He and Göring had met with dissident Slovaks to encourage them while the Hungarians fomented a similar drive for independence within Ruthenia. By the spring of 1939, Prague faced the same situation Schuschnigg had faced a year earlier. Either it had to restore its own authority or be destroyed by default.

The new Czech president, Dr. Emil Hácha, decided to act on March 6. He ordered the dismissal of the autonomous government in Bratislavia, the arrest of its leader, Monsignor Josef Tiso, and the imposition of martial law. Three days later similar measures were taken in Ruthenia. Once again Hitler had the opportunity to play the liberator. He sent Seyss-Inquart, five generals, and some storm troopers to Bratislavia to press for independence. He then summoned the dismissed Tiso and his deputy, Ferdinand Durcansky, to Berlin. Tiso and Durcansky arrived at the chancellery on the evening of March 13, and were taken to meet Hitler, Ribbentrop, and generals von Brauchitisch and Keitel. Hitler treated his visitors to a lecture on his own self-restraint over the past few months along with a scolding of the Czechs and the Slovaks for their ingratitude. Tiso was told to decide within a "short time" whether Slovakia wanted to be independent. If it did, Hitler would support it; if not, then he would wash his hands of the entire affair. Ribbentrop flavored the occasion by handing Hitler a fresh report of Hungarian troop movements along the Slovakian border. Hitler read the report to Tiso and admonished him to reach a decision soon. Tiso and Durcansky went through the motions of deliberating and then accepted Hitler's offer.[48]

There was now only a rump Czech state surrounded by enemies. President Hácha had little choice but to see Hitler in hopes of salvaging some measure of independence. On the morning of the thirteenth he asked to come to Berlin. Hácha traveled by train because of his age and a heart condition. He and Foreign Minister František Chvalkovsky were accorded full honors when they arrived in Berlin the next afternoon. The weary men were not allowed to see Hitler until after midnight. Hitler was assisted by Ribbentrop, and by Göring and Keitel who could embellish threats with military details. Hitler's harangue and Göring's sadistic threats to bomb Prague were too much for the old man. After fainting and being revived, he agreed to place what remained of his country under Hitler's protection.

German forces moved into the country without opposition at 0600 on the fifteenth. That evening Hitler had his revenge on Chamberlain for denying him a full victory at Munich. In Prague he proclaimed the Protectorate of Bohemia and Moravia within the Third Reich. The next day Tiso carried out his instructions by asking Hitler to also take Slovakia under his protection. Faced with the choice between bad and worse, the Ruthenians preferred Hitler's "protection" to that of the Hungarians, but their appeal was denied, and the area was formally annexed to Hungary on March 15.

Hitler had kept everything legal, not so much to deceive anyone, but to give his adversaries an "out." At first London seemed to take it. On March 15, Chamberlain and Halifax told Parliament that Britain had no obligation to intervene because "Czecho-Slovakia" was the victim of internal dissolution and not foreign aggression. Chamberlain was disappointed, but did not despair. He still believed that war could be avoided. Chamberlain's restraint was the last reflex of hope as much as policy. He also wanted time to assess things. Britain had done its best to avoid war by conciliation, and now Hitler had ended it. He could not again be trusted. The *Times,* which had tried to put the best face on Hitler for years, now reflected the mood of the country with an editorial condemning Hitler and his duplicity.[49] Chamberlain assessed the changing situation during the next two days. The British public and the Dominions demanded a firm policy toward Germany, and failure to lead it would jeopardize his own position as prime minister. Hitler had mistaken a hatred for war as cowardice. He had no regard for the sanctity of treaties nor for the principle of national self-determination that he had so often invoked prior to Munich. Prague had fallen and now there were rumors that Rumania would soon be next. Appeasement through conciliation had failed, but appeasement through containment and deterrence might still prevent war.

As he traveled to his home town of Birmingham on March 16, Chamberlain decided to discard his prepared text on domestic affairs and to prepare another on foreign policy. On the following day, his seventieth birthday, he denounced the German action and warned that "no greater mistake could be made than to suppose that because it [Britain] believes war to be a senseless and cruel thing, this nation has so lost its fiber that it will not take part to the utmost of its power in resisting such a challenge if it ever were made."[50] Chamberlain's speech sparked a new wave of rumor and speculation on how Britain would respond to Hitler's next move.

Shortly after Munich, Ribbentrop held a friendly discussion at Berchtesgaden with Polish Ambassador Jozef Lipski. Ribbentrop proposed a general settlement that included the return of Danzig to Germany and an extra-territorial road and railway across the Polish Corridor to East Prussia. Poland should then pursue a common policy with Germany based upon the Anti-Comintern Pact and the expulsion of Jews from Poland. Ribbentrop hinted at some concessions for Poland at the expense of Russia along with extending the non-aggression treaty and a guarantee of Polish boundaries. Ribbentop's offer to cooperate with Poland at the expense of Russia was nothing new. The interjection of Danzig was, and there was an immediacy in the German proposal that had not been there before.[51] Despite the friendly tone of Ribbentrop's offer, and subsequent conversations with Beck, Polish leaders believed any concessions would simply invite further demands.

On January 5, 1939, Beck stopped in Berlin on his return from the French Riviera. His meeting with Hitler was cordial as Hitler reviewed the question of Danzig and the Corridor. Beck managed to remain non-committal. Hitler continued the appearance of friendly relations on January 30 by making the customary friendly references to Poland in a speech marking his appointment as chancellor six years earlier. There was no reason to hurry the Polish question until he had finished with Czechoslovakia.

Beck tried to strengthen his position by moving closer to Moscow with a trade agreement and a public statement of Polish-Russian friendship. Hitler's coup in Bohemia had come with no warning, a lapse of protocol that was viewed as deliberate in Warsaw. The Poles were still in shock when Germany pressured Lithuania to cede Memel on March 23. Late that afternoon, Hitler was once again hailed by a grateful city for having liberated it from foreign control. While Hitler visited Memel, his government concluded an economic treaty with Rumania giving Germany access to a considerable amount of agricultural and mineral resources. The agreement put the Balkans under German domination and freed Hitler to devote his full time to Poland. Hitler did not yet want to destroy Poland. It might be of good use to him in a future attack on Russia. One way or the other, however, he was determined to have his way on Danzig and the Corridor—and soon. Angry words in Berlin and Warsaw increased and were accompanied by rumors of German troop movements toward Danzig. Beck now believed a German attack was imminent as did Chamberlain in London. On the evening of March 30, Beck agreed to a mutual assistance with Britain and France. In Parliament the next afternoon Chamberlain stunned all of Europe when he said, "In the event of any action which clearly threatened Polish independence and which the Polish government accordingly considered it vital to resist with their national forces, His Majesty's government would feel themselves bound at once to lend the Polish Government all support in their power."[52]

Chamberlain believed that the prospect of a two-front war would force Hitler into a negotiated settlement. Any war between Germany and the Western democracies would be long, but Chamberlain believed Germany would lose because of inferior resources and Anglo-French naval supremacy. There would be no winner because all of Europe would be destroyed with Germany suffering most. This result was so clear to Chamberlain that he believed that Hitler must see it also.

NOTES

1. *Times* (London) March 15, 1938, 15.
2. *New York Times,* March 18, 1938, 16.
3. Charmley, *Chamberlain*, 43.
4. *Times* (London) March 25, 1938, 16.
5. Bullock, *Parallel Lives,* 571.
6. DGFP, Ser. D, vol. 2, 197-198. Weinberg, *1937-1939,* 334-335.
7. *Times,* (London) April 25, 1938, 14.
8. Joseph Paul-Boncour, *Recollections of the Third Republic*, vol. 3. trans. George Marion Jr. (New York: Robert Speller and Sons, 1957), 96.
9. *DDF,* 2 Ser. vol. 8, 786-789.
10. *DBFP,* 3 Ser. vol. 1, 198-233.
11. Ibid., 346-347.
12. Weinberg, *1937-1939,* 369-370.
13. Charmley, *Chamberlain*, 80-81.
14. *FRUS: 1938,* vol. 1, 500-504.
15. Weinberg, *1937-1939*, 458-459.

16. *Times* (London), June 3, 1938, 15.
17. *DBFP,* 3 Ser. vol. 1, 590.
18. Charmley, *Chamberlain*, p. 95.
19. *Times,* September 7, 1938, 12.
20. *Times,* September 12, 1938, 7.
21. *FRUS: 1938,* vol. 1, 581.
22. *New York Times,* September 10, 1938, 1.
23. *DBFP,* Ser. 3, vol. 2, 312.
24. Ibid., 314.
25. Ibid., 342-351.
26. Ibid., 404-406.
27. *DBFP*, Ser. 3, vol 2, 431-434.
28. Taylor, Munich, 789. Weinberg, *1937-1939,* 444-445.
29. *DBFP,* Ser. 3. vol. 2, 463-473.
30. Charmley, *Chamberlain*, 124-127. Paul Reynaud, *In the Thick of the Fight*, 1930-1945 trans. James D. Lambert (New York: Simon and Schuster, 1955), 190-191. DBFP, Ser. 3, vol. 2, 520-534, 536-541.
31. *Times* (London), September 27, 1938, 12.
32. *DGFP*, Ser. D. vol. 2, 963-995.
33. William L. Shirer, *Berlin Diary: The Journal of a Foreign Correspondent* (New York, 1941), 143.
34. *DGFP,* vol. 2, 966-968.
35. *Times* (London), September 28, 1938, 10.
36. John Wheeler-Bennett, *Munich: Prologue to Tragedy* (New York: Viking Press, 1964), 158-159.
37. *Feiling, Life of Neville Chamberlain,* p. 273.
38. Bullock, *Parallel Lives,* 588.
39. Charmley, *Chamberlain,* 137.
40. Wheeler-Bennett, *Munich,* 191.
41. Ibid., 178.
42. *Times,* October 1, 1938, 12. *DBFP*, vol. 2, 640.
43. Bloch, *Ribbentrop,* 197.
44. Churchill, *Speeches,* vol. 6, 6004. Harry S. Truman, Memoirs, vol. 2 (New York: Doubleday and Company, 1956), 333. *Washington Post*, May 10, 1970, 1.
45. "Son of a bitch" probably conveys the meaning in English as well as any other term.
46. *DDF,* 2 Ser. vol, 19, 339-346.
47. *DGFP,* Ser. D, vol. 4, 470-477.

48. *DGFP,* vol. 4, 243-245, 250.
49. *Times* (London), March 15, 1939, 7. March 16, 1939, 17.
50. Ibid., March 18, 1939, 14. Charmley, *Chamberlain,* 167-172. Donald Cameron Watt, *How war came: the immediate origins of the Second World War,* 1938-1939 (New York: Pantheon Books, 1989), 168-169.
51 *DGFP*, Ser. D, vol. 5, 104-107.
52. *DBFP,* 3 Ser. vol. 9, 548. *Times* (London), April 1, 1939, 8.

Chapter Seven

Speak for England!

Hitler was furious with Chamberlain for meddling in an affair that was none of his business. On April 3, he ordered the Wehrmacht to formulate plans for Operation White, the invasion of Poland by September 1.[1] Hitler misread the feeling in Rome where there was growing fear that Germany would drag Italy into a war it could not win. Mussolini had been furious when Hitler seized the remainder of Czechoslovakia. "Every time Hitler occupies a country," he complained to Ciano, "he sends me a message."[2] Mussolini's ego chafed at German arrogance and the sarcastic barbs of Italians who referred to him as Hitler's *Gauleiter*, or district leader, for Italy, while within the Fascist Grand Council there was open complaint about his subservience to Hitler.

Mussolini presented Hitler with his own fait accompli on April 7 when Italian forces seized Albania. Hitler was delighted. It bound Italy more firmly to him and gave the impression of Fascist solidarity to Britain and France that might make them more hesitant to aid Poland. The Italian move gave the appearance of a coordinated Axis strike into the Balkans, but it did not weaken British resolve. Chamberlain responded by extending the British guarantee to Rumania and Greece, and then to Denmark and Switzerland.

President Roosevelt believed the United States should prepare for war while seeking to prevent it. He asked Congress to modify the Neutrality Law, but it declined. Roosevelt then asked Hitler and Mussolini to guarantee the safety of thirty-one countries ranging from Finland to Iran.

Roosevelt's gesture was well intended, but should have been blocked by the state department. The size of the list and the distance of some countries from Germany and Italy offered Hitler the opportunity to dismiss the President's request with ridicule and sarcasm.

Hitler went before the Reichstag to reply on April 28. The nonaggression pact with Poland, he said, the Anglo-German naval agreement of 1935, and the consultative agreement made with Chamberlain at Munich had been nullified by hostile action on the part of Britain and Poland. One by one he mentioned the countries listed by the president. In mock seriousness he assured Roosevelt that "all assertions which have been circulated in any way concerning an intended German attack or invasion on or in American territory have their origin only in a stupid imagination."[3]

Hitler did not launch his customary attack on the Soviet Union. The Soviets had been a negligible factor in his diplomacy to this point, but Chamberlain's guarantee to Poland and Rumania had altered the situation entirely. For their part the Soviets continued their pose of confident strength. On March 10, 1939, Stalin addressed the Eighteenth Congress of the Communist Party to report on foreign affairs. The second imperialist war had already begun, he said, and a world war would soon follow. Although the fascist powers had been the aggressors, Western capitalists were encouraging them with a policy of non-intervention. Any policy intended to bring war between Germany and the Soviet Union would not work, he said, because the Soviets had no intention of "pulling somebody else's chestnuts out of the fire." They wanted only peace with all countries, but were ready to resist any aggressor.[4]

Stalin knew that Hitler had wanted to attack in the West, but had been forced to change his plans because the Poles would not cooperate. The Soviet Union would soon border on a German satellite or on an expanded Germany. Stalin viewed the coming struggle between Hitler and the Western democracies the same way Lenin had viewed the first imperialist war. He saw little difference between them, and he would ally with whichever side made him the better deal. An agreement with Hitler could give the Soviet Union an opportunity to regain areas lost following the collapse in 1917 and time to strengthen itself. If all went well, the second imperialist war would be as protracted as the first, with the Soviet Union becoming the supreme arbiter over an exhausted Europe.[5]

Stalin had hoped Hitler would continue the Rapallo policy of the Weimar Republic, and that the Bismarckian tradition within the German foreign office would temper Nazi designs on eastern Europe. He had made numerous overtures for harmonious relations, but Hitler had terminated the Rapallo policy and continued to menace the Soviet Union with his rhetoric. Stalin felt there was little to lose by casting his small net into the river Spree while at the same time delivering a warning to the West. The next few weeks, he realized, would require all his diplomatic skill. "For a time," wrote Isaac Deutscher, "he would have to run with the hare and hunt with the hounds, and to take care that the hare should not notice his presence among hounds."[6]

To the end the hares distrusted Stalin as much as the hounds. Four days before his guarantee to Poland, Chamberlain confessed "to a profound distrust of Russia. I have no belief whatever in her ability to maintain an effective offensive, even if she wanted to."[7] Chamberlain never intended a "Polish Munich" that would leave the Soviet Union in the lurch to face Hitler alone, nor did he wish to ally with Stalin. He feared an alliance with Stalin might provoke Hitler into starting a war to escape encirclement. Both Poland and Rumania had informed him that they did not want the Soviets involved. Bringing Stalin in could well wreck his alliance system and might drive the Balkan countries into Hitler's camp. His objective remained to contain Hitler in Europe and to keep Stalin out of it.

Stalin made two important moves on April 17. He rejected a British proposal for a unilateral Russian guarantee to Poland and Rumania that would allow them to decide what kind of help they wanted and when they wanted it. Stalin countered by suggesting a military alliance with Britain and France to guarantee all of the countries from the Baltic to the Black Sea. He also wanted a statement that the British guarantee to Poland referred only to German aggression, which appeared to mean that Britain would not challenge Soviet aggression. A political agreement defining obligations would follow only after the conclusion of the military agreement. A military agreement without specific political obligations was unacceptable in Britain and France. Stalin was also concerned that Hitler might use the kind of indirect aggression against the Baltic States that he had used in Austria and the Sudetenland, with the area being absorbed by Germany in an outwardly legal manner. Moscow had warned Estonia in late March that it would tolerate no impairment of its independence by a foreign government. The Baltic States, like Poland, refused to allow themselves to be occupied by Russian troops whenever Moscow deemed it necessary.[8]

Also on April 17, the Soviet ambassador in Berlin, Alexei Merekalov, dropped by the German foreign office for the first time since his appointment the previous June. He ostensibly inquired about some Soviet orders from the Skoda arms works. State Secretary Ernst von Weizsäcker noted that rumors of a Russian alliance with the West were not creating a favorable climate for the shipment of war material. Merekalov responded with some general questions on political conditions in Europe and then turned to German-Soviet relations. Weizsäker assured his guest that Germany wanted satisfactory commercial relations with the Soviets. Merekalov replied that ideological differences had not prevented normal relations with Fascist Italy, and he could see no reason why Germany and the Soviet Union could not have the same. "And from normal," he added, "the relations might become better and better."[9]

This subtle opening move began a new chess game between Hitler and Stalin. Hitler cast his net into the Volga on April 28 by omitting the customary attack on the Soviet Union. Stalin's reply was dramatic and sudden. All appeared to be normal in Moscow as Foreign Minister Litvinov stood beside Stalin to review the annual May Day parade, but Litvinov sensed that something was wrong. His position of honor was duly noted in *Pravda* the following day without any hint of change. On the morning of May 3, Britain rejected the Soviet alliance proposal and again requested a unilateral declaration. Stalin summoned Litvinov to the Kremlin that afternoon to be relieved of his post.[10]

Stalin knew that time was running out. Litvinov was a man of Western ways who had long been associated with collective security and the Popular Front. This, in addition to his Jewish ancestry, made him unacceptable as a negotiator, should Hitler decide to do business. Berlin duly noted that Litvinov's successor, Vyacheslav Molotov, was not Jewish, had been a close associate of Stalin for many years, and that his appointment indicated Stalin intended to take a more active role in foreign affairs.[11]

Hitler still believed Britain and France would not intervene while he destroyed Poland, and any move toward Stalin might upset the Japanese. His Italian ally was also sulking over Czechoslovakia. On March 25, Hitler sought to repair the damage by sending a laudatory message to Mussolini commemorating the twentieth anniversary of fascism. Once again the siren song from the north did its work. The next day Mussolini responded with a speech firmly linking Italy to Germany.[12] A bilateral alliance would serve both countries for the short run. France would face war on two fronts and Italian naval strength would threaten Suez and the Mediterranean. Mussolini knew an alliance with Germany meant war, and that Italy would not be ready for several years. The Duce must rebuild the army, add additional ships to the fleet, and prepare industry for war. He also planned an international exposition in 1942, which he hoped would expand the Italian treasury. Perhaps by that time, Mussolini reasoned, Japan would have solved its problems with China and be ready to challenge America and Britain in the Pacific.

Hitler was preparing for war within months, but saw no need to inform and frighten Mussolini. Ribbentrop was more moderate than usual when meeting Ciano in Milan on May 6. He listened while Ciano relayed Mussolini's desire for peace and assured his host that Germany also did. Ciano called Mussolini during a reception that evening to report on the situation. Mussolini responded impetuously by ordering Ciano to announce that the two countries had agreed on a formal political and military alliance. Ciano hesitated. He had been to Poland and was sure it would fight with the support of Britain and France. Ciano had no alternative than to relay Mussolini's offer. Ribbentrop then called Hitler in Berlin. The Italian alliance was perfect for Hitler. It was sure to make the West think twice about aiding Poland, and the exclusion of Japan would make any deal with the Soviets much easier to negotiate. Mussolini had trapped himself by publicly agreeing to an alliance without first negotiating specific terms. It would be difficult for him to back out now, no matter how much he might want to. Hitler ordered Ribbentrop to agree without hesitation, and the foreign ministers announced their alliance the following day.[13]

Mussolini's blunder soon became apparent. The terms of the treaty were drafted in Berlin, and they clearly showed it. The preamble referred to a common ideology and a common desire to secure "living space." The heart of the alliance in Article III bound each country to aid the other in case of war, without the customary restriction on whether the initial aggressor was the enemy. Neither country would conclude a separate peace. Mussolini feared war, and yet he had become a party to one of the most aggressive alliances in history and had given Hitler a virtual blank check to make war on Poland. His only leverage against war was stipulated in Article II where both parties agreed to consult with the other should their common interest "be endangered through international events." The provision was supposed to protect Mussolini from another of Hitler's surprises, even though there was ample reason to doubt Hitler's word and his treaties. Nevertheless Mussolini agreed. Ciano and Ribbentrop signed the Pact of Steel in Berlin on May 22 amid great ceremony intended to stress Axis solidarity and to frighten the West.[14]

By the time the Pact of Steel was signed, Germany was moving cautiously toward an agreement with the Soviet Union. Litvinov's dismissal, Admiral Erich Raeder later said, had struck Hitler like a "cannon shot."[15] Anti-Soviet statements and cartoons disappeared in the German press, and on May 7, Hitler asked to be briefed on current relations with Moscow. The German ambassador to Moscow, Count Friedrich Werner von der Schulenburg, was then in Teheran. The task fell to Gustav Hilger, who left for Berchtesgaden the following day to meet with Hitler and Ribbentrop. Hilger informed them that Stalin had wanted a rapprochement with the Axis powers for some time, especially now that there might be war over Poland.[16]

Stalin stalled negotiations with the West through what appeared to be deliberate misunderstandings of British proposals. He concealed his dealings with Hitler by recalling Ambassador Merekalov to Moscow for the entire summer. He turned negotiations over to George Astakov, an obscure councillor in the Russian embassy whose activities could easily be denied and disavowed. On May 5, Astakov made his first move when he stopped at the foreign office to follow up on whether Germany would honor Soviet contracts with the Skoda arms works. Astakov spoke with Privy Councillor Karl Schnurre who told him the contracts would be honored. Astakov also asked whether general economic talks, which the Germans had terminated in February, might be reopened and whether the appointment of Molotov might bring a change in German policy.

A flurry of rumors of a German-Soviet rapprochement surfaced during the next two weeks, some fueled by deliberate leaks from Göring's office to frighten the Poles into submission. On May 17, Astakov again visited Schnurre to inquire about the status of a Soviet trade mission in Prague. The Russian remarked on the friendly tone in the German press. He expressed the hope that it reflected more than just a temporary change in German policy and hinted that cordial relations could be restored similar to those of the Rapallo era.[17]

Ribbentrop instructed Schulenburg to see Molotov about resuming negotiations on an economic treaty. Molotov was courteous during their meeting on the twentieth, but refused to discuss an economic treaty until a "political basis" had been established. Germany was not yet ready to go that far. Since May 11, Japanese and Russian forces had been fighting along the Manchurian and Mongolian borders in the so-called Namonhan Incident. Ribbentrop still hoped to bring Tokyo into a tripartite military alliance against the West. Hopefully Germany might eventually mediate better relations between Tokyo and Moscow, but certainly not now. In fact, any political agreement between Berlin and Moscow would anger the Japanese and delay any tripartite pact for some time.[18]

Hitler, however, was in a hurry. He had to attack Poland by September 1, or the autumn rains would delay an offensive until spring. Russia could give what he wanted now, and hurt feelings in Tokyo were well worth the risk. He was aided by the continuing delay in Anglo-Soviet talks caused by the refusal of the Baltic States and Poland to ally with the Soviets and to allow the Red Army to cross their territory. Hitler must move before Stalin reached any agreement with Britain and France.

Hitler met with his military leaders in the new Reich chancellery on May 23. He remained determined to attack Poland at the earliest possible moment. Danzig was useful for propaganda, but it was incidental in his drive for Lebensraum in the east. Britain was the main enemy to be defeated sooner or later. He preferred later, but he was ready to fight Britain and France along with Poland, if necessary. Hitler hoped the war would be short, but he recognized that it could last as long as ten or even fifteen years. In contrast to 1914, Hitler believed military action against France was only a prelude to the war against Britain, and he spoke about the defeat of France as though it would be relatively easy. Hitler rejected Schlieffen's envelopment of Paris in favor of a drive to the sea that would bring the ports of France, Belgium, and Holland under German control. From these ports, Britain could be defeated by naval and air attacks that would sever its lifeline to the outside world. Hitler was still not sure what Stalin would do, but even if Russia allied with the West, he was determined to attack Poland with or without support from Italy or Japan.

The war clouds hanging over Europe frightened Mussolini. He had committed Italy to Germany under the illusion that there would be no war for several years. He was haunted by Italy's defection from Germany during the first war and feared a loss of prestige if it happened again. Ciano traveled to Germany in early August to propose another international conference to settle the dispute with Poland. He met Ribbentrop at Salzburg on the eleventh, and was coldly informed that Germany wanted neither the Corridor nor Danzig, but war. Ribbentrop was in one of his more arrogant moods, and he breezily dismissed Ciano's warning that an attack on Poland would mean a general European war that Italy did not want. Ciano met with Hitler at the Berghof above Berchtesgaden during the next two days. Hitler was more cordial, but the message was the same: there would be war. Hitler did not totally reject the idea of another conference in feigned deference to Mussolini, but he added that Russia could not be excluded. When Ciano asked for a time limit, Hitler revealed that war would come soon because the autumn rains would make many of the roads in Poland impassable for mechanized equipment. It was obvious that Hitler had decided on war and that nothing would change his mind. His confidence increased at the end of the meeting when word arrived that the Soviet Union had agreed to political negotiations.[19]

Ciano returned to Italy disgusted with the Germans, fearful for the future, and painfully aware that Italian counsel carried no weight in Berlin.[20] Neither did that of anyone else, for in the summer of 1939 Hitler was convinced that the optimum time had come to make war. In April he had celebrated his fiftieth birthday and feared that his health would now decline. It was better to strike while he was still relatively young and healthy than to risk infirmities in the future. Britain and France had begun to rearm and would soon narrow the German lead. The prospect of a deal with Russia offered a political and economic situation that could never be surpassed. Spain offered benevolent neutrality and economic aid, while the countries of central and southern Europe would either do the same or actively join with him. Sweden had remained neutral and supplied Germany with critical iron ore during the first war. Swedish ore was still badly needed, and it appeared as though it would be available. Hitler would like to have the military aid of Hungary, but he realized there was no chance of it. In July, the Hungarians had informed him that they would not make war on their former ally, even though they wished to have good relations with the Axis. The Hungarians irritated Hitler, but he knew they would provide economic aid. Access to Rumanian oil had been achieved by the treaty in March. Axis domination of Europe offered Bulgaria the chance to undo the Paris Peace Conference and to regain the borders and influence it had prior to the Great War. It would also intimidate other countries in the area into neutrality.

Belgium might pose a threat to Germany in the West. The remilitarization of the Rhineland and the growth of German power had convinced Belgium to return to its traditional policy of neutrality. Hitler planned to invade Belgium some day but he wanted to keep it neutral until then. A Belgium allied with France would expose German industrial areas along the Rhine to attack. Hitler skillfully mixed soothing words of good will toward Belgium with threats of consequences should King Leopold abandon neutrality. The Belgians hoped they could spare themselves by proving good intentions. They would find, like others before and after, that their hope was futile.[21]

By June of 1939 Hitler had achieved nearly all of his goals in foreign policy. Poland was isolated and the West was impotent to save it. There was now an increasing chance to secure Soviet cooperation. The Soviets made another sounding in Berlin on June 15, when Astakhov paid an unscheduled visit to the Bulgarian embassy. The Bulgarians assumed that they were being used as a conduit to the Wilhelmstrasse, since there was no apparent reason for the visit. Astakhov stated that the Soviets were considering three possibilities: conclusion of a pact with the West; continuing to delay negotiations; and rapprochement with Germany. Moscow preferred the latter, but feared Hitler's designs on the Soviet Union. "If Germany," the report continued, "would declare she would not attack the Soviet Union, or that she would sign a nonaggression pact with her, the Soviet Union would probably refrain from concluding a treaty with England."[22]

Stalin was aided by British hesitation and what appeared to be dilatory tactics in London. On May 31, Molotov had publicly criticized the West for its hesitancy and called for a guarantee for all states bordering the Soviet Union. Privately he demanded that guarantee be given to the Baltic States, whether they wanted it or not.[23] France agreed, but Britain remained reluctant. London sent William Strang, a competent but minor official, to Moscow to break the impasse. Critics, such as Churchill and Lloyd George, argued that such a mission called for someone of higher rank.[24] Sending a minor official reflected a low opinion of the Soviet Union, especially when the prime minister had made three trips to Germany to accommodate Hitler.

The Soviets preferred rapprochement with Germany, but they remained suspicious and were in no hurry to make major concessions, especially since they were aware of Hitler's timetable. Hitler remained distrustful and irritated by Russian tactics as he, like his counterparts in the West later, found out why many in the Russian government referred to Molotov as "iron ass."[25] Talks between the two countries continued through late June and early July with little results. By the middle of the month, however, both sides realized that the other was really serious, and that some kind of a political agreement might be reached along with an economic treaty.

Hitler now decided to deal with Stalin. Treaties can always be undone and a pretext can always be found. He devised a proposal to partition both Poland and the Baltic States. Schnurre presented the proposal to Astakhov and Eugene Babarin, deputy Soviet trade representative, over dinner at a

Berlin restaurant on July 27. A political agreement between Germany and Russia was desirable, Schnurre said, because "controversial problems of foreign policy . . . did not exist" while both countries had a common "opposition to the capitalist democracies."[26]

Hitler was in more of a hurry on July 31 when Chamberlain announced that an Anglo-French military mission would soon leave for Moscow. Any fear in the Wilhelmstrasse about a quick agreement between Russia and the West was as unwarranted in August as it had been for the past four months. Daladier and Bonnet were ready for any agreement that would make Russia an ally. In London, however, the military mission was undertaken with hesitation and suspicion. Both in and out of the government some questioned whether the Soviets really wanted an agreement, and there was a reasonable concern about revealing military information to the Soviets or any other power without first being sure there would be a political alliance.

Stalin had not yet decided whether to sign with Germany or the West. The events of August 14, however, provided a definite impetus for his final decision. The Anglo-French military mission had arrived in Moscow on August 12. On the fourteenth, Marshal Klimenti Voroshilov, who led the Russian delegation, asked whether Soviet forces would be allowed to move against Germany through Poland and Rumania. The British and French replied that Poland and Rumania were sovereign states and that the Soviets would have to consult with them for an answer. Voroshilov then requested a short recess during which he most likely consulted with Stalin himself. Without specific answers to these questions came the reply, "the Soviet military mission cannot recommend to its government to take part in an enterprise so obviously destined to fail."[27]

The Western delegates recognized the logic of the Soviet position, and they sought help from London and Paris. Poland remained the key, but despite the growing danger and the logic of history, Warsaw refused to submit to the reality of the moment: It could not defeat the Germans without help from the Russians. And yet, it is difficult to condemn them too strongly, for the logic of history was also their tragedy. Help from the Russians would mean conquest by Russians and the end of Poland as an independent state. The answer was still no.

Also on the fourteenth, Schulenburg was instructed to tell Molotov that Ribbentrop was willing to settle "joint territorial questions of Eastern Europe" by coming to Moscow. Molotov agreed to the general tone of Ribbentrop's proposal the next day. He also increased the ante by asking whether Germany would agree to a nonaggression pact along with a joint guarantee of the Baltic States?[28] Molotov was cautious, however, about an early trip by Ribbentrop, and he made it clear to Schulenburg that adequate preparations would have to be made. Hitler was in no mood for delay. He and Ribbentrop formulated a reply on the evening of the sixteenth. Germany would sign a nonaggression pact, guarantee the Baltic States with the Soviet Union, and use its influence with Japan. They ordered Schulenburg to once again stress the need for haste, and to inform Molotov that Ribbentrop was "prepared to come by airplane to Moscow at any time after Friday, August 18, to deal on the basis of full power from the Führer, with the entire complex of German-Russian relations. Molotov responded by reminding Schulenburg of past transgressions, such as the Anti-Comintern Pact, and still refused to be pressured into an early trip by Ribbentrop.

The chilly atmosphere in Moscow contrasted sharply with the charged mood at the Berghof. Schulenburg received another telegram from Ribbentrop early in the morning on the nineteenth. He was to see Molotov again and inform him that relations between Germany and Poland were becoming more "acute" each day, and that war could break out at any time. Negotiations on the economic pact had been completed that day, and it was time to move on to the political questions. Ribbentrop was correct, but the Russians would not sign the agreement until they had received final instructions from Moscow.

Schulenburg saw Molotov again at 2 p.m. Molotov remained opposed to any accelerated negotiations until an economic agreement was signed. Schulenburg left after an hour of fruitless entreaties. Within half an hour he received word that Molotov wanted to see him at 4:30. Sometime around 3 p.m. on the nineteenth, and perhaps not until then, Stalin decided that Hitler would give him the agreement he had sought for some time.[29] Molotov apologized for the inconveniences when Schulenburg returned to the Kremlin, and handed him a draft for a nonaggression pact. Ribbentrop could come to Moscow on the twenty-sixth or the twenty-seventh, if the economic agreement were signed the next day. This was not soon enough for Hitler. He drafted a personal request to Stalin "that you receive my Foreign Minister on Tuesday, August 22, but at the latest on Wednesday, August 23. The Reich Foreign Minister has full powers to draw up and sign the nonaggression pact as well as the protocol." Stalin realized that Hitler wanted to settle any loose ends before starting his war. Hitler waited nervously for the answer, which finally came around 10 p.m. on the twenty-first. "The Soviet Government," Stalin replied, "has instructed me to inform you that they agree to Herr von Ribbentrop arriving in Moscow on August 23."[30] Within the hour, Berlin radio announced that Germany and the Soviet Union had agreed to conclude a nonaggression treaty, and that Ribbentrop would fly to Moscow on the twenty-third.

Hitler's anxiety turned to arrogance after having engineered one of the most dramatic diplomatic coups in history. He summoned his military leaders to the Berghof on the afternoon of the twenty-second to tell them of the pact with Russia and to urge them on to victory in Poland. His generals were to wage war against Poland without mercy. "Poland will be depopulated and settled with Germans," he said, and made it clear that the pact with Russia was only temporary. In due time, he said, "We will break the Soviet Union. Then there will begin the dawn of German rule of the earth." The attack on Poland, he concluded, would begin on Saturday, August 26.[31]

Ribbentrop left Berlin for Moscow while Hitler was speaking at the Berghof. He arrived around noon on August 23, stopped for lunch at the German embassy, then proceeded to the Kremlin. The mood during the negotiations was more befitting historic allies than the bitter enemies who had savaged each other for so long and so recently. The terms of the nonaggression pact and the protocol were negotiated quickly, except for a short delay regarding port cities in Latvia, which Hitler quickly conceded, and most of the business was completed by evening. The remainder of the time was spent in friendly conversation unencumbered by the presence of a polygraph. Stalin and Ribbentrop toasted each other, and noted how their bad language of the past had always been aimed at Britain, and not at each other.[32]

If truth is the first casualty of any war, then the meeting in Moscow marked the beginning of the war that would soon engulf Poland. Germany and the Soviet Union promised not to take hostile action against each other and not to join "any grouping of powers whatsoever that is directly or indirectly aimed at the other party." They agreed to settle any future disputes in a friendly manner, or by arbitration. In theory the pact was to last for ten years with an automatic renewal for five years, unless one of the parties objected. The haste of the moment was conveyed in the last sentence. In contrast to other treaties of this type, "The agreement shall enter into force as soon as it is signed." There was no time for ratification.

The secret protocol was in the best tradition of Prussian kings and Russian tsars. Finland, Estonia, and Latvia were placed in the Soviet sphere while Lithuania was allocated to Germany. "In the event," the protocol stipulated, "of a territorial and political transformation of the territory belonging to the Polish state, the spheres of interest of both Germany and the U.S.S.R. shall be bounded approximately by the line of the rivers Narew, Vistula, and San." The terms dealing with Southeastern Europe were deliberately left vague. For the moment, Germany was prepared to declare its "political disinterestedness" in the area and to acknowledge the Soviet claim to the former Russian province of Bessarabia, which, for the moment, belonged to Rumania.[33]

Hitler returned to Berlin in time to welcome Ribbentrop home on the twenty-fourth. The foreign minister was ecstatic about the deal and boasted that his visit to Moscow had been like a meeting of old party comrades. But the price had been high. Concessions were given to the Soviets, the Japanese were furious, the Italians humiliated, and not all Nazis were as happy as Ribbentrop. Hitler himself may have been troubled by what General Franz Halder called "a pact with Satan to cast out the devil."[34] Still, the gains were great: Poland was isolated and there was a chance Britain and France would now let Hitler have his way.

But the German-Soviet agreement had strengthened British resolve instead of weakening it. It had demonstrated how fraudulent Stalin had been with his anti-fascist rhetoric and his call for collective security. The mood in London was one of sad resignation. Britain must go to war, even though there was little chance of saving Poland and a high probability of destroying Europe. Chamberlain convened the Cabinet on August 22 to discuss the failure of the mission to Moscow, and to chart a clear course for the future. That afternoon, the Cabinet issued a communiqué stating that the German-Soviet agreement would have no impact on the British obligation to Poland, and that Parliament would meet the following day to pass an Emergency Powers Bill. To emphasize his point, Chamberlain wrote a personal note to Hitler warning that the German-Soviet agreement did not alter Britain's obligation to Poland. Some believed, he reminded Hitler, that Britain should have made its position clear in 1914. Whether or not that was true, he said, "His Majesty's Government are resolved that on this occasion there shall be no such tragic misunderstanding."[35]

Hitler responded by haranguing the messenger. Britain, he said, was to blame for Polish intransigence. He then asked Ambassador Henderson to wait while he formulated a written reply to Chamberlain. After a two-hour delay, Henderson saw a different Hitler. He again posed as the aggrieved leader who must do his duty with remorseful determination. He did not wish a war with Britain and had tried to be magnanimous to the Poles. The British guarantee, however, had made them more belligerent toward Germany and more hostile toward Germans in Poland. If Britain came to the aid of Poland, he warned, then Germany would be far more prepared than it had been in 1914. Surely it was quite clear to everyone, he added, that the World War would not have been lost if he had been chancellor.[36]

Hitler also had hoped the pact with Russia would cripple French resolve. To some extent it did. News of it inflamed old hatreds between the Left and the Right. The Daladier government retaliated by suppressing the Communists and all who had supported them. French Communists were bewildered and tried to reconcile their ideology with their patriotism. Some left the party to fight the Germans. The Communist leader, Maurice Thorez, and others fled to the Soviet Union when war came, while comrades left behind aided Germany by sabotaging the French war effort. French conservatives answered the question "Why die for Danzig?" by pressuring Daladier into accepting the inevitable destruction of Poland and making the best deal with Hitler. For the beleaguered prime minister, however, France must support Poland or fight a stronger Germany later.

Hitler also had misjudged Mussolini. Ribbentrop had called Ciano and warned him that war was imminent on the night of the twenty-fourth. The next morning Hitler sent a letter to Mussolini reviewing the negotiations with Russia and stressing how much the treaty had strengthened the Axis. He also reproached Poland for repeated provocations and warned Mussolini that he would act immediately if it continued. He stopped short, however, of telling the Duce that the attack would begin on the twenty-sixth. The Italian ambassador, Bernardo Attolico, delivered Mussolini's answer around six that evening: "If Germany attacks," Mussolini wrote, "and Poland's allies open a counterattack against Germany, I wish to warn you now that it would be better if I did not take the *initiative* in military operations in view of the present situation of Italian war preparations." In his heart the Duce wished nothing more than to move with Hitler, but his wounded ego could not ignore how unprepared Italy was for a major war, nor could he ignore the opposition of nearly everyone in the government. To save some face, Mussolini added that Italy would intervene "at once if Germany delivers to us immediately the military supplies and the raw materials to resist the attack which the French and English would predominately direct against us."[37] Hitler was bitter and disappointed with the news from Rome, despite the cavalier way he had treated his ally. "The Italians are acting just as they did in 1914," he muttered after Attolico left.

Hitler overcame his anger, however, and decided to honor Mussolini's request for a rapid reply. He quickly dispatched a short note to Rome asking what kind of supplies Mussolini needed and when they were needed. Perhaps with a little bribe Mussolini would join him after all.[38]

Earlier in the day Hitler had tried to drive a wege between Britain and France by making Henderson a "large comprehensive offer" in which Germany would guarantee the British Empire and aid it, if necessary. He disclaimed any ambitions in the West and agreed to negotiate agreements for arms reductions. All Britain had to do was allow Germany to settle the Polish problem without interference.[39] Henderson left Berlin by plane soon after meeting with Hitler and arrived in London late the same afternoon. It is not clear how much of Hitler's proposal was known by Chamberlain or others while they deliberated the final stages of the Mutual Defense Treaty with Poland. Most likely it does not matter. Negotiations had been going on for some weeks, and it was signed around 5 p.m. on the twenty-fifth.[40] Hitler was stunned when given the news an hour later. Mussolini had let him down, and he apparently had failed to buy off the British. Operation White was scheduled to begin the following morning, and troops were heading for the Polish border. After checking with OKW, he decided to rescind the order in hopes of buying more time. He was determined to push on, however, regardless of what ally or enemy did. The attack on Poland would begin on September 1. Europe would have five more days of peace. Perhaps in that time, he reasoned, he could give Britain the "out" he still believed it wanted.[41]

The events from August 26 to September 1, 1939, were anti-climatic in retrospect. Hitler had made it clear that he intended to attack Poland. Britain and France had made it equally clear that they would aid Poland. But nothing is inevitable until it happens, and there were still many people in the world who feverishly and fervently tried to prevent war. Hitler had already received appeals from Pope Pius XII; President Roosevelt; Dr. Carl Burckhardt, the League Commissioner for Danzig; and the rulers of Belgium, Denmark, Finland, Luxembourg, the Netherlands, Norway, and Sweden when he ordered Operation White to begin on September 1. One of the most eloquent notes came from Daladier on the twenty-sixth. The prime minister wrote it not only to another statesman, but to another veteran of the trenches during the Great War who had seen the carnage and the devastation. Daladier believed that no one would ever wish to see it again.[42] All appeals possessed the same flaw: They were directed to a sense of compassion, decency, and morality that did not exist, and had no chance of success.

Mussolini also clamored for peace, but for entirely different reasons. The list of supplies he required for war made it clear he would not fight. He did promise to aid Germany with bellicose gestures and proposed to "insist anew . . . on the opportunity for a political solution which I regard as still possible and such a one as will give full moral and material satisfaction to Germany."[43] The last thing Hitler wanted was some "son of a bitch" denying him victory with another Munich, and he was more furious with Mussolini for proposing a "political solution" than for reneging on the Axis alliance.

The twilight chess game continued to the end. Hitler made another offer to Henderson on the night of August 29. He would talk directly with the Poles as a gesture to Britain, but cautioned that no territorial changes could be completed without the approval of the Soviet Union. Then came the trap: London must secure "the dispatch to Berlin of a Polish emissary with full powers. They count on the arrival of this emissary on Wednesday, August 30, 1939."[44]

Hitler's demand had the ring of the old pattern of conciliation followed by increased demands. Neither London nor Warsaw was willing to subject any Polish emissary to the fate of Schuschnigg or Dr. Hácha. On August 30, the situation had not really changed since the British guarantee to Poland on March 31. Either Hitler or the Poles must back down or there would be war, and either Britain and France must abandon Poland or there would be a European war.

Hitler, however, was not finished with offers. He formulated a list of sixteen claims against Poland which included the return of Danzig, a plebiscite on the Corridor to be conducted under international supervision, an extra-territorial line of communication between Germany and East Prussia, a transfer of populations, and a guarantee of minority rights. It was Hitler's "alibi" to the German people for the war he wanted and one last attempt to drive that elusive wedge between Britain and the Poles.[45] Warsaw responded by ordering Ambassador Lipski to see Ribbentrop at 1 p.m. on the thirty-first. Lipski was kept waiting for six hours before Ribbentrop saw him. The meeting was brief and cursory. Ribbentrop said there was no point in meeting at all, since Lipski did not possess the required powers. The meeting was also a bit late. Hitler had already signed the order to attack Poland at 0445 the next morning.

At 10 a.m. on Friday, September 1, Hitler drove to the Kroll Opera House. He saw a far different Berlin than the city of 1914. There was neither jubilation nor optimism, but merely a sullen and thin crowd too stunned to respond. Hitler looked worn and disheveled before the Reichstag as he croaked out a tale of Polish provocations and his own peaceful efforts. He announced war with Poland, made much of the pact with Russia, and was clearly embarrassed in making excuses for Italy. He made one last attempt to isolate the Poles by stressing peaceful intentions toward Britain and France.

In London, Chamberlain prepared to tell Parliament that the situation was grave, but that Britain would honor its commitment to Poland. The prime minister notified Berlin of his resolve and that of his country: "Unless," Chamberlain wrote, "the German government have suspended all aggressive action against Poland and are prepared promptly to withdraw their forces from Polish territory, His Majesty's Government will without hesitation fulfill their obligation to Poland." Britain would not negotiate unless Germany stopped fighting and withdrew from Poland. Parliament was restive and demanded an early time limit to the British ultimatum. Chamberlain believed that a joint declaration with France was critical, but the Daladier government hesitated. There could be no declaration of war without the consent of the Chamber, and its members were still hurrying back to Paris from vacations. Bonnet and others in the cabinet still grasped at any chance to avoid war, while some conservatives in the Chamber cursed Britain and urged a public disavowal of the Polish alliance. The military supported delay. France would bear the brunt of the expected German attack in the West, and French cities would soon share the suffering now being inflicted on Warsaw. Bonnet desperately embraced Mussolini's proposal for a conference that would follow an armistice. But Britain would negotiate only after Hitler withdrew his troops from Poland, and neither Mussolini nor Bonnet would suggest that.

By Saturday evening the mood in Parliament had become so ugly that Halifax warned Paris the government might fall. Chamberlain showed the wear of strain and years. He appeared tentative and out of step with the demand for action born of honor. When Arthur Greenwood, acting leader of the Labour Party, rose to reply, he did so amid a rising storm on both sides of Commons. Greenwood began with "Speaking for Labour," but was cut short by the Conservative Leo Amery. "Speak for England!" Amery shouted. Chamberlain was stunned. The message was clear: He must lead his angry country or be replaced.[46]

During the turmoil in London, Daladier had gone before the Chamber and had received a vote for war credits, but he still shrunk from asking for the official declaration that would give him the legal authority for war. It was a lapse of legality that would haunt the Daladier government later, but the prime minister agreed to coordinate his ultimatum with that of Britain the next day without it.[47]

A somber Henderson arrived at the Wilhelmstrasse promptly at 9 a.m. on September 3. The ambassador read the British ultimatum to Hitler's official interpreter, Dr. Paul Schmidt. He referred to the earlier note of September 1 and the British demand for an end to German attacks on Poland and the withdrawal of German forces. Since the German attacks had continued, Henderson continued, "I have accordingly the honor to inform you that unless not later than 11 a.m. British Summer Time, today, September 3, satisfactory assurances to the above effect have been given. . . a state of war will exist between the two countries as of that hour."[48] Schmidt quickly took the note to the chancellery where Hitler and other Nazi leaders waited. Slowly he read the British ultimatum to Hitler and Ribbentrop. After a period of silence, Hitler glared at his foreign minister as though he had been misled. "Now what?" he snapped. Ribbentrop only replied that "We must assume that the French will hand us a similar ultimatum within the hour."[49]

At 11:15 Chamberlain told the British people that they were at war with Germany. It was a painful moment for the prime minister, and there would be worse to come. "We have a clear conscience," he said, " we have done all that any country could do to establish peace. . . . Now may God bless you all and may He defend the right. For it is evil things that we shall be fighting against, brute force, bad faith, injustice, oppression, and persecution. And against them I am certain that the right will prevail."

The prime minister then went to speak to Parliament. He recounted the circumstances of the last ultimatum and sadly confessed that "everything that I have worked for, everything that I have hoped for, everything that I have believed in during my public life, has crashed in ruins." He closed with the hope for a day he would not see: "I trust I may live to see the day when Hitlerism has been destroyed, and a liberated Europe has been reestablished."[50]

NOTES

1. *DGFP*, Ser. D. vol 6, 186-187, 223-227.
2. Count Gallazzo Ciano, *The Ciano Diaries,* 1939-1943. ed. Hugh Gibson (New York: Doubleday and Company, 1946), 43.
3. Dallek, *Roosevelt and American Foreign Policy*, 182-183. Watt, *How War Came,* 261-263. *Times* (London) April 29, 1939, 8-9.
4. *Soviet Documents on Foreign Policy,* vol. 3, 315-322.
5. Tucker, *Stalin in Power*, 592.
6. Isaac Deutscher, *Stalin,* 428.
7. Feiling, *Chamberlain,* 403.
8. *DBFP,* 3 Ser. vol. 5, 775-776.
9. *Nazi-Soviet Relations, 1939-1941: Documents from the Archives of the German Foreign Office,* ed. Raymond J. Sontag and James Stuart Beddie (Washington: U.S. Government Printing Office, 1948), 1-2.
10. Phillips, *Litvinov,* 166.
11. Anthony Read and David Fisher, *The Deadly Embrace, Hitler, Stalin, and the Nazi-Soviet Pact, 1939-1941* (New York: Norton, 1988), 74-75.
12. *DGFP,* Ser. D. vol. 6, 119-120. *Times* (London), March 27, 1939, 12.
13. Watt, *How War Came*, 240-241.
14. *DGFP,* Ser. 5, vol. 6, 561-563. Watt, *How War Came,* 409-410.
15. *TMWC,* vol. 41, 23.
16. Read and Fisher, *Deadly Embrace,* 77,
17. *Nazi-Soviet Relations,* 5.
18. Ibid., 6-7. Weinberg, *1937-1939,* 575.
19. *Ciano Diaries,* 118-120. *DGFP,* Ser D. vol. 7, 39-49. Watt, *How War Came,* 425-429.
20. Ibid., 429.
21. Weinberg, *1937-1939,* 585-593.
22. *Nazi-Soviet Relations,* 20-21.
23. *DBFP,* 3 Ser. vol. 5, 743-746.
24. Churchill, *The Gathering Storm,* 389-390.
25. Ulam, *Stalin,* 307.
26. *Nazi-Soviet Relations,* 32-36.
27. *Soviet Documents on Foreign Policy,* vol. 2, 210. Read and Fisher, *Deadly Embrace,* 163-164.

28. *Nazi-Soviet Relations,* 50-56.
29. Bullock, *Parallel Lives,* 618. Volkogonov, *Stalin,* 351. Volkogonov says that Stalin's decision came on the morning of the twentieth, but Molotov's instructions to Schulenburg took place on the afternoon of the nineteenth.
30. Ibid., 66-69.
31. Bullock, *Parallel Lives,* 620-623.
32. *Nazi-Soviet Relations,* 71-86.
33. Ibid., 76-78. Read and Fisher, *Deadly Embrace,* 246-259.
34. Franz Halder, *Kriegstagebuch; taglishe Aufzeichnungen des Chefs des Generalstabes des Heeres, 1939-1942,* ed. Hans-Adolf Jacobsen, vol. 1 (Stuttgart: W. Kohlhammer, 1962), 38.
35. *Times* (London), August 23, 1938, 13. August 24, 1938, 14. *DBFP,* 3 Ser. vol. 7, 170-172. Charmley, *Chamberlain,* 200.
36. Sir Neville Henderson, *Failure of a Mission: Berlin, 1937-1939* (New York: G.P. Putnam's Sons, 1940), 269-270.
37. Ibid., 285-286.
38. *DGFP,* Ser. D. vol. 7, 289.
39. Ibid., 279-281.
40. *Times* (London), August 26, 1938, 10.
41. Halder, *Kriegestagebuch,* vol. 1, 31. Weinberg, *1937-1939,* 638-639.
42. *DGFP,* Ser. D. vol. 7, 330-331.
43. Ibid., 323.
44. Bloch, *Ribbentrop,* 255-256.
45. Shirer, *Berlin Diary,* 192-193.
46. *Times,* September 4, 1939, 3. *DBFP,* 3 Ser, vol. 7, 501.
47. Bonnet, *Quai D'Orsay,* 270-272. Shirer, *Collapse of the Third Republic,* 510.
48. *DBFP,* vol. 7, 535.
49. Schmidt, *Hitler's Interpreter,* 464. Watt, *How War Came,* 598.
50. *Times* (London), September 4, 1939, 4, 8. Charmley, *Chamberlain,* 208-209.

Axis Europe, 1941

WESTERN HERITAGE VOL. 2 SINCE 1648 6/E. by KAGAN/OZMENT/TURNER, © 1998. Reprinted by permission of Prentice-Hall, Inc., Upper Saddle River, NJ.

Chapter Eight

We Would Have Been Invincible

"Together with the Germans," Stalin lamented after the war, "we would have been invincible."[1] The course of events from September, 1939 to June, 1941 leaves little doubt that Stalin was correct, as all of Europe fell to the dictators. Had the cooperation continued, as Stalin wished, the course of World War II might have ended with the world dominated by a new Quadruple Alliance of Germany, Italy, Japan, and the Soviet Union.

Division of the spoils began at 0445 on September 1 when the new German Wehrmacht sent over a million and a half men against Poland from Germany in the west and north and from Slovakia in the south. Within hours the world learned of the horror and terror of Blitzkrieg.[2] Göring's Luftwaffe received the first benefit from the pact with Russia before the day was over. The Minsk radio agreed to identify itself often and increase its air time as an aid to German navigation.[3]

The Poles had delayed mobilization during the last days of peace for fear of giving Hitler a pretext to attack. Now they paid dearly for it. Most of the obsolete Polish Air Force was blown away within forty-eight hours without leaving the ground. Entire Polish units at the front were rapidly enveloped and destroyed. The most pitiful symbol of the mismatch came on the fourth day when Polish cavalry launched a counterattack against General Heinz Guderian's tanks. On the morning of September 5, General Franz Halder recorded in his diary that "the enemy is as good as beaten."[4] Cracow fell on the sixth while the government in Warsaw began the flight to Lublin and eventual exile in London. Berlin and Warsaw expected a

French attack against the German Western Wall, but none came. On September 9, the *New York Times* reported, "The Germans are crushing Poland like a soft boiled egg."[5] The Germans finished off isolated Polish units from the ninth until the seventeenth and tightened their grip on Warsaw. The Poles valiantly defended their capital against merciless attack and bombardment for another ten days with no help from abroad and no hope of stopping the Germans.[6]

Some Polish units retreated eastward where they intended to fight until autumn weather slowed German operations. The Soviets also expected the Poles to fight for a few more weeks. They had no plans for immediate intervention and hoped the Germans would bear the casualties as well as the onus for the invasion. Ribbentrop asked the Russians to move on September 3, but Molotov made no commitment. The rapid German advance, however, forced Stalin to act. He feared the Poles might surrender and ally with the Germans and negate the August pact. Hitler might also take all of Poland while the taking was easy.

On September 9, Stalin learned that the Japanese were agreeable to a settlement of their border dispute, and he could now move into Poland without worrying about war in the East.[7] The Kremlin used the fate of the Belorussians and the Ukrainians as the pretext for intervention. *Pravda* carried stories of harsh Polish rule in the area and the total collapse of any authority. The Red Army moved into what now became known as the "liberated Ukraine" on September 17. Berlin and Moscow issued a joint communiqué on the nineteenth stating that their purpose was to "restore peace and order in Poland, which had been destroyed by the collapse of the Polish state, and to help the Polish population to reconstruct the conditions of its political existence."[8] The Soviet invasion surprised what remained of the Polish Army, while some naively and tragically believed the Russians were coming to their aid. The Red Army encountered mainly disorganized units that had escaped the Germans and were without supplies. Stalin easily claimed his share of Poland at the cost of 996 dead and 2,000 wounded.[9]

The war in Poland clearly demonstrated German power and Hitler's intention to honor his pact with Stalin for the moment. Germany was still at war with Britain and France, despite the "Phony War" or "Sitzkrieg" in the West. Hitler hoped the Western leaders would accept his conquest of Poland now that they had demonstrated their honor. Stalin feared they might, and he intended to strengthen his position by renegotiating the August agreement. The pact had left him with parts of ethnic Poland, but he now decided that these areas would be difficult to digest. Hitler was receptive when Stalin suggested on September 25 that there be a final settlement on Poland that would "eliminate anything in the future that might create friction between Germany and the Soviet Union."[10] Hitler was primarily concerned with operations in the West where he intended to strike at Britain and France before the end of the year. A bloated and contented Soviet Union was worth several divisions during the attack westward, and he could settle matters with the Russians once France was defeated. Ribbentrop again flew to Moscow on September 27. Negotiations began the following afternoon with Stalin himself taking an active part. He asked for Lithuania in exchange for the province of Lublin and the areas east of Warsaw that earlier had been allotted to the Soviet Union. Ribbentrop and Molotov signed the "German-Soviet Boundary and Friendship Treaty" early in the morning of the twenty-ninth.

The two countries pledged to "reestablish peace and order" by defining their borders and to respect the national interest of the other. A Confidential Protocol and two Secret Protocols calling for the transfer of nations and specifying the changes in the August agreement and an agreement to tolerate "no Polish agitation which affects the territories of the other two parties." After concluding their agreement the two governments issued a joint declaration condemning Britain and France for continuing the war.[11] It appeared as though Stalin had driven a hard and profitable bargain. He had regained much of what had been lost to Imperial Russia with relatively few casualties, and he now had Hitler's consent to do whatever he wished with Lithuania in addition to Estonia, Latvia, and Finland. Hitler realized the Soviet Union would strengthen itself while Germany was preoccupied in the west, but it was a price he must pay. He could, however, lessen the loss for the moment by ordering plans for evacuating over eighty thousand ethnic Germans from those areas under Russian control. He expected them to return another day.[12]

The second Ribbentrop visit to Moscow marked a shift in Soviet policy from benevolent neutrality to de facto ally. The collapse of Poland had placed Germany and the Soviet Union nose to nose, and even the extension of the Soviet border westward offered little protection if Hitler decided to attack. Schulenburg had always been an advocate of cooperation with Russia, and it appeared as though Ribbentrop now agreed with him. But their opinion counted little if Hitler changed his mind, and everyone in the Kremlin knew it.

The Soviet Union publicly supported Germany in calling for peace on

September 28. There was most likely an audible sigh of relief in the Kremlin when Chamberlain rejected the offer on October 3.[13] Now the world waited for Hitler's answer. On October 6, he demanded peace on his terms and soon. Hitler recited his usual list of grievances and basked in the glory of how his Wehrmacht had undone the injustice of Versailles by liquidating the "ridiculous state" of Poland, while again calling for an end to enmity with Britain and France.[14]

The master psychologist was well aware that many in France, and some in Britain, were more willing to trade Poland for peace than they had been a month earlier. Daladier, however, was still determined to remain in the war until Hitler offered "real guarantees" for a permanent peace. Chamberlain went further on the twelfth by refusing any peace that did not undo "the wrongs done to Czechoslovakia and Poland."[15] The words in London and Paris had little impact on Hitler. His offer had been rejected, and he now had someone to blame for continuing the war. As early as September 27 Hitler had shocked his generals with a plan to attack in the West before the end of the year. On October 9, he ordered OKW to prepare for an attack as soon as possible. The attack, he added, should take place before the end of autumn, and should employ sufficient speed and mobility to destroy the Allied armies and avoid the stalemate of World War I.[16] Hitler's generals, however, held the French army in much higher regard than he did, and they doubted whether Germany had sufficient resources for a long war. None of them had the courage to challenge Hitler directly. They instead stalled by stressing technical difficulties in the operation. Hitler jolted the generals again on October 22 by announcing his intention to attack on November 12. He was also thinking of moving the major force of the German thrust from the north to the south. From this point until June of 1940, Hitler benefitted from the combination of his own imagination, the ideas of others, and the demon of chance. At army headquarters in Zossen, a few miles from Berlin, the army divided its time between developing a better plan and fantasies of overthrowing Hitler. The Zossen Conspiracy, as it was called, like many others before it eventually withered before Hitler's willpower and a considerable lack of it among the generals.[17]

The generals revised Operation Yellow on the twenty-third. Again Hitler was not satisfied. The plan was too limited and its major thrust was still too far to the north. He was now thinking of striking farther to the south at Sedan and was becoming disgusted with his timid generals. Hitler invited the military leaders to the chancellery on November 23 for a pep talk. The attack must come now, he said, because "neither a military nor a civil person could replace me. . . . My decision is unchangeable. I shall attack France and England at the most favorable and quickest moment."[18] Hitler continued to hope for an attack until January of 1940 when he accepted a postponement until spring. He would benefit more than anyone else from the timidity of his generals and the postponement of Yellow. Had he gone ahead with the 1939 version of Yellow, the result might well have been the kind of military stalemate in the West so eagerly anticipated by Ribbentrop's friends in the Kremlin.

The continuing Sitzkrieg in the West offered Stalin the opportunity to seize territory allotted to him by the August and September agreements. In October he demanded the right to establish Soviet bases with Russian personnel in Estonia, Latvia, and Lithuania. The Baltic States were told to accept the Soviet demands when they turned to Berlin for help. They did, knowing full well that their escape from Imperial Russia would soon be over. The Finns, however, had more friends abroad, especially in the United States where their payment of the war debt had always been appreciated.

Negotiations opened in October and were more equal than the virtual ultimatums issued to the other Baltic states. Stalin wanted to extend the Russo-Finnish border up the Karelian Isthmus away from Leningrad and to construct additional naval bases in the Gulf of Finland. In return, he offered largely uninhabited territory in the north. Some in Finland acknowledged that the Russian proposals were as equitable and as reasonable as could be expected. But after the Soviet moves against Poland and the Baltic states the Finns saw any concessions as merely the first steps toward further Soviet aggression.

The Soviets grew weary of Finnish resistance by the middle of November. On the twenty-sixth, they reported that Finnish troops had fired on the Red Army. Moscow then abrogated its nonaggression treaty with Finland, severed diplomatic relations, and launched an attack on November 30. Tass reported the formation of a "People's Government of Finland" on December 2. It was located just across the border in the city of Terijoki and headed by the old Finnish Communist Otto Knudsen, who fulfilled his duty by asking the Soviet Union for help.[19]

The Soviets expected a walkover like Poland. They were jolted by the tenacity of the Finns and the apparent incapacity of the Red Army. Stalin had chosen the worst time of the year to launch an offensive, while Field Marshal Karl von Mannerheim commanded one of the best armies in

Europe in its efficiency, leadership, and ability to utilize the terrain for defensive war. The Mannerheim Line held the Red Army at bay during December, while inflicting heavy casualties. Many in the West, as well as in Berlin, overestimated the impact of the purges while underestimating the overall ability of the Red Army. "The Soviet 'mass,'" concluded the German General Staff, "is no match for an army and superior leadership." The performance of the Red Army confirmed Hitler's view that the Slav could not stand up to the German, and that Russia could be conquered in a quick campaign.[20]

Hitler knew that Stalin was using the stalemate in the West to strengthen himself. He also knew that the Soviet attack on Finland had infuriated many Germans who now wished to aid their racial brothers. Hitler realized, however, that he must first secure victory in the West before moving against the Russians, and that for now the German diplomatic corps and press must stifle any criticism of the Soviet Union. The silence in Berlin contrasted sharply with the barrage of anti-Soviet indignation elsewhere. The moribund League of Nations in Geneva expelled the Soviets in December, an action which by itself was harmless and somewhat contemptuous, had it not been accompanied by anti-Soviet policies by individual governments. President Roosevelt expressed the outrage of many Americans when he condemned the Soviet Union as a "dictatorship as absolute as any other dictatorship in the world."[21] American anger stopped short of risking war with the Soviets. The best Congress would do was to authorize twenty million dollars to Finland for non-military supplies.

Moral indignation in Britain and France was accompanied by hostile intentions. Conservatives in both countries took smug satisfaction in reviling Soviet treachery and the scoffing at the failure of the Red Army, both of which they cited as proof of their own wisdom in opposing any Soviet alliance prior to the war. By January of 1940 General Gamelin and others were thinking of launching attacks on the Soviet Union in the Arctic and in the Black Sea along with strikes into Norway and Sweden. Calmer and wiser minds in London convinced the Daladier government that there was little it could do to aid the Finns as long as Hitler remained poised for a strike in the West. The pretext of aid to Finland, however, could serve as fine concealment for striking against Germany. In February the two countries agreed that an Anglo-French force of "volunteers" would land in Norway and then proceed to Finland by way of Sweden. Politically both Norway and Sweden were neutral, and they wished to remain so. Economically, however, both served Germany, and their loss could cripple the German war effort.[22]

By early 1940 the Finnish war had cost the Red Army nearly 200,000 casualties with over 40,000 dead. Anglo-French plans were no secret, nor were Mussolini's entreaties to Hitler urging an attack on the Soviet Union along with an end to the war in the West. In February the Red Army launched a massive offensive against the Mannerheim Line. The Finns fought valiantly, but were worn down by the overwhelming weight of the Russian forces. On March 12, both countries agreed to peace. Stalin's terms were harsher than prior to the war, but not as harsh as they could have been. The Soviets received their naval bases in the Gulf of Finland and extended their control of the Karelian Isthmus farther north to include the Finnish city of Viborg. The Finnish Communist government in exile was simply forgotten. Even so, the loss of Viborg and the other concessions were resented by the Finns and they would resume the war another day.[23]

Anglo-French intentions prompted Hitler to move against Denmark and Norway. The value of Danish and Norwegian ports had been recognized by the German military for decades. As early as October, 1939, Admiral Raeder, had suggested an operation in the north to insure the flow of Swedish iron and other materials. The onset of winter and Allied plans to aid Finland by way of Norway gave additional urgency to Raeder's view. Germany depended on Norway as a conduit for Swedish iron through the port of Narvik during the winter. From there German ships could take shelter in the territorial waters of Norway and proceed unmolested to Germany. Raeder was aware that during the first war Britain had violated Norwegian neutrality by mining its waters, and he feared it would do so again. He was right. Winston Churchill, once again first lord of the admiralty, had been pressing for it since September.[24]

Raeder was aided by Vidkun Quisling, the leader of the Norwegian Nazi party, the National Union, who urged a coup followed by an appeal for German assistance. Hitler and Raeder liked the idea, since it offered the advantage of surprise and a relatively cheap conquest. Hitler then ordered OKW to develop a plan in consultation with Quisling. He also wanted the plan to include the occupation of Denmark to protect his northern flank and to secure more airfields.[25] A German move against Norway would be hazardous without naval supremacy. Hitler had to risk it, however, because of reports that Britain was planning an invasion and a recent speech by Churchill calling upon neutrals to honor their commitment to the League by opposing Nazi aggression.

When Finland and the Soviet Union agreed to end their war on March 12, the Allies and Germany were deprived of a pretext for invading Norway. The race was postponed but not forgotten. Hitler's main concern was dealing with the nuisance visit of Sumner Welles, Roosevelt's undersecretary of state, and the growing disaffection of Mussolini. Welles had begun his peace mission with a visit to Rome in late February, and had then proceeded to Berlin on March 1. Relations between Nazi Germany and the United States had never been good, and they had taken a turn for the worse following *Kristallnach,* in November of 1938. Roosevelt recalled the American ambassador, Hugh Wilson, from Berlin in protest and Hitler retaliated. In April of 1939 Hitler had publicly mocked Roosevelt's effort for peace. When war came, the president had made no secret whom he held responsible. The House and the Senate had lifted the arms embargo by November, making it possible for the United States to supply arms to Britain and France.

On March 2, Hitler bluntly informed Welles that he had no intention of making any compromise peace. He was aware that Mussolini wanted peace, and that his commitment to the Axis was wavering. The Duce was now fifty-six and showing it. His weight was up, his hair was white, and increasingly he moved about like an old man. The strains of the previous months were taking their toll. In January the Duce had shown a measure of independence in scolding Hitler for his alliance with the Soviets and had urged him to make peace with the West. Most Italians did not like the Germans. Their sympathies had been with the Catholic Poles, and they had supported the Finns against Hitler's friends in Moscow. If Mussolini had broken publicly with Hitler he would have enhanced his standing with the Italians and the West.

Hitler received a break on March 1 when the British announced they would no longer permit the shipment of German coal to Italy by way of Holland. The British move threatened the Italian economy and infuriated Mussolini. Hitler made the most of the opportunity by quickly assuring Rome that some way would be found to send the coal by land. Ribbentrop traveled to Rome on March 10 with a letter from Hitler assuring Mussolini that the Soviets had abandoned Bolshevism in favor of Russian nationalism, while insisting again that the war had been forced upon him by others.

The sorcerer once again played to the wounded vanity of his former mentor. He felt no bitterness about the Italian action, or lack of it, in "August of last year." In fact it was probably best that "Italy was not immediately drawn into the war on our side." He believed, however, that the war would decide the fate of Fascist Italy as well as Germany, and that some day Italy must decide its future in combat. On that day, he said, "Your place will then more than ever be at our side, just as mine will be at yours."[26] Mussolini reacted to Hitler's letter with a certain amount of skepticism and questioned whether the Soviets had really abandoned international revolution. He agreed to consider all of Hitler's points, and conceded that in general Hitler was right. Some time during the next few hours Hitler's balm again had its effect. When Ribbentrop returned the next day he found a truculent Mussolini who assured him that Italy had made great strides toward rearmament, and would join with Hitler at the "proper time."

If the apprentice could do that well, the sorcerer himself could do even better. Hitler was hopeful when Mussolini agreed to meet him at the Brenner conference on March 17. The Duce had last seen Hitler at the Munich conference nearly two years earlier. Mussolini remembered how Italy and much of the world had then hailed him as the savior of peace after the conference. But Hitler was now a conqueror and Mussolini envied him more than ever. Once under Hitler's influence, Ciano feared, the Duce would choose the glory of conquest over the prestige of peace.[27] Hitler deferred to the ego of his senior dictator the following morning by boarding Mussolini's private railroad car. The deference ended when the meeting quickly turned into a Hitler monologue with Mussolini periodically nodding in agreement. Hitler easily gained Mussolini's promise to join with him against Britain and France, but at no specific time. Hitler went out of his way to make it easy for the Italians who only had to intervene after Germany had defeated France in the north. After that, Hitler said, "Italy will be mistress of the Mediterranean and England will have to make peace." Mussolini agreed, but still conditioned Italian action on that of Germany. If Germany became bogged down in France he would stay out. Both men left the Brenner meeting with some cause for satisfaction. Hitler had Mussolini's vague commitment to join him, while Mussolini kept his freedom to avoid war.[28]

The end of the Russo-Finnish war revealed just how far France had declined since the end of the Great War. In 1914 politicians who disliked each other intensely had been willing to join the *Union Sacrée* for the good of France. In 1939 the opponents of Daladier and of the war continued to intrigue against him. Communists now carried out Comintern policy by opposing the government. The main challenge came from the Right. For years Pierre Laval had sat in the Senate biding his time. Shortly before the war he had resumed his collaboration with the aged hero of Verdun, Marshal Henri-Philippe Pétain, who now served as ambassador to Spain. The two men had developed an open contempt for the decadent Republic since the formation of the Popular Front. They also shared a fear of Germany, a dislike and distrust of Britain, and a belief that France could remain independent and secure through friendship with Italy. Pétain had become something of a father figure for many on the Right who saw him as the historical man on horseback who would rise above the odious political squabbles of the Republic to restore internal stability and national greatness.

Laval and the conservative Henry Lemery led the attack against Daladier in the Senate two days after the defeat of Finland. They condemned the war against Germany and the failure of the government to recognize that the primary enemy was the Soviet Union. The attack continued in a secret session of the Chamber of Deputies on March 19. Daladier attempted to defend himself, but he was mentally and physically exhausted. He gained a vote of confidence in both houses, but over half of the deputies had abstained in the Chamber. Technically he could have continued, but chose to resign on March 20.

President Albert Lebrun asked Daladier to form a new government, but the embittered prime minister refused. Lebrun then turned to Daladier's old political enemy, Paul Reynaud. Reynaud represented those in France who had opposed appeasement and the defensive posture of the French army, and was often compared to Churchill. But Reynaud admired Churchill more than he resembled him, and did not have Churchill's feel for leadership. He also tended to become involved in the kind of intrigue that had disabled the Daladier government. Reynaud immediately ran into Daladier's revenge. The former prime minister would not serve in a new government unless he continued as minister of defense as well as foreign minister. Reynaud wanted Defense for himself in order to shake up the French army. He relented, however, because he could not form a government without Daladier's support. The sorry spectacle in the Chamber gave proof to all of how divided France remained in the face of mortal danger. It gave hope to Laval and others who believed that Reynaud would soon fall and Pétain would follow. "As for the mass of the people," Charles de Gaulle later wrote, "it was bewildered and, feeling that nothing and nobody, at the head of the State was capable of dominating events, drifted in doubt and uncertainty."[29]

Confusion in France did little to erode optimism in London. On April 5, Chamberlain addressed the Council of the National Union of Conservatives and Unionists Associations. The prime minister believed that the period of inaction in the West had cost Hitler the military advantage he had possessed the previous September. "Whatever may be the reason," Chamberlain said, "he has missed the bus."[30] Hitler, however, had not missed the bus. Early in the morning of April 9, German ships slipped into the harbor at Copenhagen and along the Norwegian coast from Oslo to Narvik. The surprised Danes realized they were no match for the Wehrmacht. Some in the army wanted to resist, but King Christian X ordered surrender. In Norway the Germans achieved surprise with the first use of airborne troops to secure strategic areas behind enemy lines. German forces trying to land by sea had a more difficult time, especially in the attempt to seize Oslo and to capture King Haakon VII. After taking several hits from Norwegian shore batteries and torpedo boats, the German force limped back to sea. Control of the landing fields, however, enabled the Germans to take Oslo by noon, but not in time to prevent the king and most of his parliament from escaping to Nybersund in the north. The fall of Oslo coincided with similar action at the port of Bergen to the west, Trondheim in the center, and Narvik in the north. Within a day the Germans had crushed all serious resistance by the Norwegian Army. The only sizable force remained with the king north of Oslo where it tried to make its way to the port of Andalsnes to link up with a rumored British landing force.

Aid to Norway depended on the British and to a lesser extent on the French. An Anglo-French force of 60,000 men had been assembled in northern Britain since the outbreak of the Russo-Finnish war. There were plans for landings at Bergen, Narvik, Trondheim, and elsewhere. Most of the men were already on their ships when the Germans struck. The Allies could well have launched a rapid counterattack with superior forces, but swift military moves were not the order of the day in London or Paris. Instead of rushing troops to Norway, the Allies unloaded the men and waited for more information before risking them in any attempt to drive the Germans out of Norway.[31]

The British Navy urged quick and decisive action and was more willing to engage the Germans in direct combat. The army, on the other hand, preferred to land where there were Norwegians still in control, and this hesitancy cost them a chance to retake the vital port of Narvik in the north. Anglo-French troops finally landed one hundred miles north and south of

Trondheim on April 20, but neither force had field or anti-aircraft artillery. They were unable to mount any kind of attack on Trondheim and were bombed mercilessly by German planes. All of southern and central Norway was under German control by the end of April. King Haakon hoped to set up a permanent base for continuing the resistance. For a time it appeared as though he would. On May 28, an army consisting of British, French, Polish, and Norwegians landed at Narvik and drove out the much smaller German force. With Narvik under Allied control the king would be safe and Germany would be deprived of Swedish iron ore. But the move had come too late. Nearly three weeks earlier Hitler had begun his offensive in the West. By the time the Allied forces landed at Narvik the Wehrmacht was smashing through the low countries and into the heart of France itself. In the face of such a danger the war in Norway became irrelevant. King Haakon boarded a ship for Britain to begin five years of exile on June 7. The German conquest of Norway brought little power and no fame to Vidkun Quisling. He had little support in his own country where his name became a synonym for traitor, and few Germans respected him. He was arrested at the end of the war and executed for treason.

The defeat in Norway stunned the British Parliament and increased the growing dissatisfaction with Chamberlain's leadership. Chamberlain's attempt to gloss over the defeat in Parliament on May 4 gave the impression of deceit or stupidity. Jeers and insults mounted during the next few days along with the continual taunts of "missed the bus!" The most telling blow again came from the Leo Amery, a friend of many years, who repeated the words of Oliver Cromwell to the Long Parliament three centuries before. "You have sat too long for any good you have been doing. Depart, I say, and let us be done with you. In the name of God, go!" On the ninth, Parliament voted on an opposition motion to censure the government. A united Conservative Party would have given Chamberlain an overwhelming majority, but over thirty Conservatives voted for the motion and double that abstained. Chamberlain still had a majority of 281 to 200, but the level of the opposition was clear when he left the room to the chant of "Go! Go! Go! Go!"[32]

That night Chamberlain went to see King George VI. He still hoped to remain as prime minister in a new coalition government, but the opposition would have none of it. He must go. For weeks, speculation had been rife about who would replace him. King George VI preferred his old friend Lord Halifax, as did most Conservatives. Chamberlain appeared to agree, but privately he doubted whether Halifax had the resolve to continue the war. Labour and the rebels within the Conservative Party wanted Churchill, and Chamberlain agreed. On the evening of May 10 Churchill went to Buckingham Palace, where the king asked him to form a new government.[33]

At sixty-six, Churchill believed he was a child of destiny and that all of his previous life "had been but a preparation for this hour and this trial." It had already been a full life of many accomplishments and failures. As a member of the Liberal Party Churchill had served as first lord of the admiralty and had been forced from office in the wake of the Gallipoli disaster in 1916. He had been a strident advocate of intervention following the Bolshevik revolution and never lost his dislike of Communism. He returned to the Conservative Party in 1924 and served as chancellor of the exchequer under Stanley Baldwin. He began his decade in the wilderness in 1929 following the victory of Ramsey Mac Donald and the Labour Party. He was regarded as reckless and untrustworthy by many, and continued to earn the enmity of the Conservatives and others for his injudicious support of King Edward VIII, his inflexible policy on India, and then his criticism of Baldwin and Chamberlain's appeasement policy toward Germany. The end of appeasement and the outbreak of war had forced Chamberlain to bring him into the cabinet as first lord of the admiralty. His previous absence from the government may have saved him in the wake of the Norwegian disaster, since the parallel with Gallipoli was mentioned. The full fury of discontent fell instead on Chamberlain and those who had been closely associated with him.

Churchill's appointment took second billing to one of the most successful military operation in history. The Allies had waited for the German attack with a mixture of anxiety and confidence. General Gamelin had little doubt about what the Germans would do or where they would come, and he was prepared to meet them. With eastern and central France protected by the Maginot Line and the "impenetrable" Ardennes, the Germans would again attack through the low countries as they had in 1914. Gamelin planned to advance into Belgium to stop the Germans before they could move into France and repeat the destruction of the First World War. Gamelin's strategy was not accepted by everyone, including his subordinate, General Alphonse Georges, who worried about weakness in the French center. Gamelin's plan was also weakened by the Belgian and Dutch refusal to coordinate their defense with Britain and France for fear of offending the Germans.[34]

Gamelin's plan was further undermined by an act of chance known as the Mechelen Incident. By January of 1940, planning for Operation Yellow had progressed little since the previous November. Bad weather on the ninth forced a German plane to land just inside the Belgium border near the town of Mechelen-sur-Meuse. Major Helmut Reinberger was carrying documents and maps for Yellow. He failed to destroy all of them before being captured. Enough of the material survived to convince Gamelin that he had been right. He issued a new directive strengthening his original plan on March 20.

Hitler was furious at the break of security. He considered an immediate attack, but the weather would not permit it. On January 20, he ordered a hold on Operation Yellow until spring as well as a review of the plan itself. Chance again aided Hitler in late January when he sent his military adjutant, Colonel Rudolf Schmundt, on a tour of the front. Colonel Schmundt met General Erich von Manstein who had criticized the original Yellow as too conservative and warned of another stalemate. He was especially concerned about sending tanks through an area containing so many canals and rivers. Manstein had asked Guderian whether it would be possible to send tanks through the Ardennes for a strike at Sedan in November of 1939. Guderian knew the area well from his service during the first war and agreed that it would be possible. Manstein then urged the General Staff to modify Yellow in favor of a feint through the low countries with the main thrust through the center of the French line. Generals Walther von Brauchitsch and Franz Halder were in no way disposed to make such a gamble, and they resented Manstein's brashness. They decided to transfer him to a corps command in the north where he would have far less access to the minds at Zossen.

Manstein was waiting for reassignment when he met Schmundt. Schmundt was impressed with the similarity between Manstein's ideas and those previously expressed by Hitler. He reported them to Hitler when he returned to Berlin on February 2. Hitler arranged a meeting with Manstein on February 17. He listened intently as Manstein explained his plan. The next day Hitler ordered Brauchitsch and Halder to revise Yellow. The new operation called for a thrust into the Low Countries to draw the Allies into Belgium while the Germans smashed through the Ardennes, and then swept westward across the open terrain of northern France like the slice of a sickle to entrap and destroy the cream of the Allied forces.[35]

The Germans launched their attack on the morning of May 10. They faced an enemy of combined equal strength, except in air power where they had tactical superiority. Gamelin's plan, however, invited disaster by committing his best and most mobile forces to the north while assigning half his forces to the Maginot Line.[36] The Germans also had superior leadership and morale. The officer corps had discarded much of the snobbery associated with the old aristocracy, while Hitler insisted on better relations between the officers and the enlisted ranks. Hitler's assessment of the French army had been correct: it was the mirror of a dispirited and divided country. It also reflected a political leadership in fearing that perfidious Albion might well forsake France for safer shores when the going got tough.

The early thrust of the German attack came in Belgium, Luxemburg, and the Netherlands. The defenders were caught by surprise, and in some cases were overwhelmed before they knew what was happening. The Germans were able to seize key bridges and fortifications before they could be defended or destroyed by using infiltrators in conjunction with airborne troops. Berlin stunned the world on May 11 by announcing the capture of the great fortress of Eben Emael near Liège. The Allies responded to the matador's cloak.[37] The movement of the Allied forces into Belgium brought consternation and joy to OKW. To the south the greatest armored force ever assembled stood in three columns from the German border to over fifty miles beyond the Rhine on May 10. Steadily it made its way through the Ardennes. The caravan could have been an easy target for Allied air power, but it was largely ignored because of the heavy fighting in the north. The Panzers were over the river Meuse at Dinant by the thirteenth and converging on Sedan. They broke through the next day and struck westward. The loss of Sedan, where the Prussians had destroyed the Second Empire of Napoleon III seventy years before, was accompanied by a loss of will as well. The next day a desperate Paul Reynaud phoned Churchill to say, "We have been defeated! We have lost the battle!"[38]

Churchill found things worse than he had feared when he flew to Paris on May 16. The government was burning diplomatic papers and leaving for Bordeaux. Gamelin asked Churchill for more aid, especially air power. Churchill hesitated, but agreed to help. He did not yet see the German thrust to the coast as a major threat, since it was not supported by infantry and supplies. By the seventeenth, however, the devastating impact of mechanized warfare had become apparent. The Dutch had surrendered on the fourteenth and the Belgians were wavering. There was confusion and desperation in London and Paris. Allied forces were ordered to fall back in Belgium, but it was too late. The Panzers continued to advance along the Somme, where during the first war armies had fought for months without gaining ten miles. On the morning of the twentieth, Guderian's force reached the North Sea at Abbeville. Allied armies were now divided, with many of them trapped near Dunkirk. Reynaud attempted to avert disaster on the nineteenth by replacing Gamelin with General Maxime Weygand. Weygand had been a staff officer under Foch during the first war and had helped the Poles save Warsaw from the Russians in 1920. Reynaud also recalled Pétain, the hero of Verdun, from Spain and appointed him vice prime minister in his cabinet. The appointments raised hopes briefly, but did little to stop the rout.

Hitler gave the Allies a respite on May 24 by ordering his armies to halt and prepare for the final thrust into France. Brauchitsch, Halder, and commanders at the front objected, and the order has been subject to various interpretations ever since. Hitler was supported by some of his military advisors, especially Field Marshal Gerd von Rundstedt who feared an Allied counterattack against the thin German line and another battle of the Marne. The attack had been successful beyond expectation, but not without cost. Over half of the tanks had been lost to combat or stress, and many had to be repaired for the assault south of Somme. Hitler still believed that the key to the war in the west was France. If it fell, then Britain would have to accept German hegemony on the Continent.

There was still more defiance than defeatism in London. On May 28, hours after the Belgian surrender had made the fate of the British army even more precarious, Churchill told the Commons that Britain would fight on, regardless of what happened on the Continent. He then met with the war cabinet and other members of Parliament. They rejected any negotiations, lest it lead to a loss of morale, the fleet, and eventually to a Britain dominated by Germany.[39] Neither Hitler nor anyone else thought the British would try to evacuate their men from the Dunkirk pocket. Churchill ordered Operation Dynamo to begin on the twenty-sixth. It was a desperate attempt to rescue the forces at Dunkirk at the cost of abandoning others elsewhere in France and Belgium. The government initially hoped to bring back at least 50,000. The Royal Air Force diverted every plane at its disposal to protect the ships and men from the Luftwaffe. Göring had told Hitler that air power could finish off the Dunkirk pocket. German pilots and their planes, however, were worn from three weeks of war, hampered by bad weather, and bloodied by the large concentration of British aircraft.

Hitler rescinded his order to halt on May 26. By June 3, the Germans had closed to within two miles of the sea at Dunkirk but were still held back by Allied resistance. When the last ship left on the morning of June 3, 338,000 men had been saved, with over 100,000 being French and Belgian. As the last troops arrived in Britain, Churchill reminded Parliament that the "miracle of deliverance" should not be seen as a victory, for what had happened in France and Belgium had been a military disaster. But, he added, "We shall go on to the end . . . . We shall never surrender."[40]

The miracle of deliverance was seen more as desertion by an ally across the channel, despite the number of French troops evacuated. The Germans now struck south of the Somme to finish what remained of a crippled and disorganized army. Hitler gloated over how easy the conquest had been in a series of letters to Mussolini.[41] The Duce now believed the defeat of France would mean the end of the war in the West before he could share in the conquest and glory. On the evening of June 10, Mussolini strutted onto the balcony at the Palazzo Venezia in Rome to announce war against the "plutocratic" democracies of Britain and France, against the wishes of the king and without the approval of the Fascist Grand Council.[42]

Hitler was pleased to have Mussolini in the war, but many were more contemptuous of Mussolini's decision than with his failure to join Germany the previous September. Italians were stunned and fearful. They disliked the Germans, worried that the war would someday involve the United States, and felt shame for what Mussolini had done. The American president spoke for many of them as well as for honorable people in all countries when he told the graduating class at the University of Virginia, "On this 10th day of June, 1940, the hand that held the dagger has struck it into the back of its neighbor."[43]

Reynaud and his new under-secretary for national defense, Charles de Gaulle, left Paris for Tours as Mussolini announced war in Rome. The City of Light would be abandoned to the Germans. Raynaud hoped to continue the war from North Africa where he could draw on the resources of the Empire for a long struggle that would one day avenge the defeat of 1940. Reynaud had little support from those whose opinion counted most. Pétain, Weygand, and eventually Admiral Jean Darlan, who commanded the Navy, favored a separate peace with Germany.[44]

The gloom was evident when Churchill and his staff flew to France on the eleventh and thirteenth in a desperate attempt to infuse some spirit of resistance into what remained of the French government. It was now apparent that France might soon surrender, and that its fleet could fall into

Hitler's hands. The Germans entered Paris on the fourteenth. On the following day they took Verdun, the symbol of French resistance under Pétain so many years before. There was open talk of surrender by the time the government arrived in Bordeaux on the fourteenth. The pressure on Reynaud mounted, and he was weakening. Churchill and Reynaud asked Roosevelt for a promise of war against Germany, a promise Roosevelt could never give and still be reelected in November.[45] Reynaud resigned in favor of Pétain on the night of the sixteenth. The old marshal wanted no victories at the cost of a Verdun. Within hours he asked the Spanish ambassador to contact the Germans about an armistice. Hitler had now accomplished in six weeks what Imperial Germany had failed to do in four years. He would now have his revenge for Versailles.

Hitler met Mussolini in Munich on the eighteenth to decide the coming settlement. The Italians had done little to win the war. They had been stopped by the French. The Duce hoped to gain something from it, but was disappointed. Hitler wanted to end further resistance by giving France a lenient armistice. Britain would be isolated, and might be persuaded to accept German domination of Europe. Italian ambitions were expendable to a quick armistice. Mussolini had to settle for the small area of France already taken. The armistice signed with France on the twenty-fourth was so humiliating that Mussolini ordered the Italian press to make no mention of it.[46]

The world must know, however, that lenient terms came from total conquest. Hitler arrived at the forest at Compiègne on June 22, accompanied by Göring, Keitel, Brauchitsch, Raeder, Ribbentrop, and Hess. Marshal Foch had dictated terms here in 1918. The field marshal's old restaurant car was brought from its Paris museum to complete the setting. Hitler's terms were relatively moderate. The northern part of France and the western part down to the Spanish border were occupied by the Germans. All French prisoners were to remain in captivity until the end of the war, which both the French and the Germans thought would come in a few weeks. The French fleet was to be demobilized and disarmed. On the following day Charles de Gaulle, who had fled to London as France was falling, announced the formation of the Committee of National Liberation and urged continued resistance. De Gaulle, however, was almost unknown to the French people and attracted little support. The Pétain government moved to Vichy on July 10 to abolish the Third Republic and set up a new government.[47]

Hitler was now at the peak of his power and prestige, and even the generals who had scoffed at him behind his back fell silent. Europe from Gibraltar to the Vistula and from the Baltic to the Adriatic was under his control, while the remainder feared him more as a new Genghis Khan. It is not surprising, as Alan Bullock has noted, that "so great a triumph went to his head. . . . Henceforward he was convinced that he was not only a political but a military genius, the equal not only of Bismarck, but of von Moltke and Frederick the Great."[48]

Hitler's major irritation in June of 1940 was directed toward Moscow. Throughout the Finnish war Germany had maintained a benevolent neutrality. The war in Scandinavia and France had given the Soviets an opportunity to expand, and they had made the most of it. The Kremlin had feared the West would make peace with Hitler, and then join Hitler against the Soviet Union. Ambassador Schulenburg reported that Molotov actually seemed relieved when informed of the German attack into Denmark and Norway.[49] It involved Germany more deeply in war with the West and ended the chance for peace. But there was also danger. German success brought the war closer to Russia, and for a time Moscow feared a German occupation of Sweden and Finland.

Hitler's attack in France provided the crucial test for Stalin's foreign policy. If it resulted in another bloody stalemate, then all bade well for the Soviet Union. But there was no miracle of the Marne nor even the Seine. Germany had won a total victory while suffering half the casualties the Russians had suffered against Finland. German concentration of troops in the West prodded Stalin to cash in on his agreement with Hitler while he still could. The Red Army began occupying Latvia, Lithuania, and Estonia on June 15, as a prelude to annexation following "elections" in August. The Kremlin could only put a brave face on a frightening situation when Pétain called for an armistice. Molotov congratulated Schulenburg on the "splendid success" of the Wehrmacht on June 14, while Soviet press releases stressed the continuing harmony of German-Soviet relations.[50]

The Soviets were also nervous about Hitler's growing influence in Rumania, despite the fact that he had stated his "disinterest" in the Balkans. The Soviet Union now laid claim to the Rumanian provinces of Bessarabia, which had belonged to Imperial Russia, and to Bukovina, which had not, but which contained many Ukrainians and was seen as an invasion route into the Soviet Ukraine. Berlin readily acquiesced to the Soviet claim to Bessarabia, but tried to keep Bukovina for the Rumanians. Stalin remained adamant. By the end of June it had become apparent that the war in the West would continue, forcing Hitler to pressure the

Rumanians into accepting the loss of both provinces. Stalin had won a victory, but Rumania now had cause to see Hitler as its protector. Soviet territorial expansion was accompanied by sweeping measures at home to prepare Russia for eventual war, and throughout the summer of 1940 many Russians watched the continuing war in the West with the hope that Britain and Germany would exhaust themselves.

Victory in France left Hitler in the unfamiliar position of wondering what to do next. Germany had won the war for the domination of Europe. On June 18, however, Churchill restated the British determination to fight on, not only for the empire, but for the "survival of Christian civilization," warning that "if we fail, all that we have known and cared for, will sink into the abyss of a new Dark Age, made more sinister and perhaps more protracted, by the light of perverted science. Let us therefore brace ourselves to our duties, and so bear ourselves that, if the British Empire and its Commonwealth last for a thousand years, men will still say, 'This was their finest hour.'"[51]

Churchill quickly sent a dramatic signal to Hitler and to the United States that Britain would fight on. Hitler had given up hope of seizing the French fleet, and the French fully intended to keep it neutral. Neither Churchill nor the Americans could allow even the possibility of it falling into Axis hands. Britain could not afford to keep an eye on it in the Mediterranean with ships needed to guard the channel. The fleet must come under British control or be destroyed. French ships in British ports were seized on July 3, while at Mers-el-Kebir and Oran in North Africa British attacks destroyed the heart of the French Navy in the Mediterranean.[52]

Hitler hoped that Churchill's rhetoric and the action in North Africa were for domestic consumption and an attempt to get better peace terms. Churchill's view of a united Britain in *Their Finest Hour* was probably overstated in part to protect the reputations of those who considered making peace with Hitler.[53] At the same time, John Charmley's *Churchill: The End of Glory* overstates the number who seriously wanted to make peace with Hitler as well as the way in which Churchill cowed the "sheep" among the populace. There were a lot of independent rams in Parliament, and one tough ewe in Nancy Astor.[54]

Hitler now had to consider an invasion. Keitel issued a directive from OKW on July 2, stating that an invasion of Britain was possible, but that Hitler had not yet ordered it. Hitler's indecision was compounded when Admiral Raeder urged a submarine campaign on shipping rather than an invasion. Raeder believed obstacles to an invasion were enormous and would remain so for some time. There would be no surprise as in Norway, and German naval strength was weaker because of the losses suffered during the Norwegian campaign. The Luftwaffe must have overwhelming superiority and the Navy must have the kind of landing craft needed to send a large force across the channel.[55] Hitler concluded that Britain now continued the war in hopes of gaining allies. On July 26, he reluctantly ordered OKW to prepare a plan for invading Britain by "mid August."[56]

Hitler hoped that a combination of threat and reason might convince Britain to surrender. He staged a spectacle in Berlin worthy of a conqueror on July 19. He appeared before the Reichstag with a peace offer to Britain and then crowed the victory against France by ceremoniously promoting twelve of his generals to field marshal. He also awarded Göring a rank to match his ego by promoting him to Reichsmarshall.

Control of the channel remained the key to Operation Sea Lion. On July 10, the Luftwaffe made the first of many sorties in the Battle of Britain. It might have achieved its objective of destroying the Royal Air Force (RAF) had it not been for radar installations and "Ultra," the penetration of the German operations code. London was able to better plan its defenses and husband reserves of manpower and planes.[57] The Luftwaffe seemed well on the way to wearing down the RAF by the middle of August. Göring launched Operation Eagle on the fifteenth, a massive attack on Britain by the largest air fleet ever assembled. British defenses were strained to the limit, but they survived to inflict what Churchill later called "a recognizable disaster for the German Air Force."[58]

Göring continued to send more than a thousand planes a day against the RAF. With the advantage of closer bases and the ability to refuel, the RAF fought bravely and well. German numbers, however, took their toll on airfields, radar installations, and above all, on pilots and planes. Attacks against the airfields were accompanied by strikes against other military targets, such as coastal docks and aircraft factories. Both sides had avoided any direct strike against civilian neighborhoods, but this now changed because of an accident. On the night of August 23, German bombers made a navigational error and hit London instead of their original targets. The attack appeared to be deliberately aim at civilians. It produced a demand to "hit them back."[59] The following night British bombers hit Berlin. Their physical damage was negligible, but the psychological damage was severe. Göring had promised Berliners it would not happen. It had, and it happened again on the night of August 28, and this time there were deaths.

Hitler delivered a vicious speech at the *Sportspalast* on September 4.

He threatened to destroy London and other British cities in retaliation for attacks on Berlin. Hitler had already planned to attack civilian targets in conjunction with an invasion. Now he saw them as a chance to end the war without an invasion, or at least to destroy the RAF. Hitler wanted the war against Britain to end by the end of September when weather over the channel would prevent an invasion.

The Luftwaffe began a long series of heavy air attacks on London on the night of September 7. Hundreds of planes hit the city in waves over a period of several hours. The attacks continued for the next week with devastating impact. Göring decided to strike in daylight as well. He tried to launch a knockout blow on September 15 by sending a combined force of over eight hundred bombers and fighters. The RAF was ready. Some of the German planes reached their target, but many more were dispersed or shot down. Failure of the raid demonstrated that the RAF was still capable of defending its homeland, and that the primary requisite for Sea Lion had not been achieved. It was also obvious that a continued and sustained effort to destroy the RAF could bring an air equivalent of Verdun and cripple the Luftwaffe for some time.

Hitler ordered postponement of Sea Lion "until further notice" after the failure of September 15.[60] Attacks on London and other cities continued with the British retaliating in kind. The warnings of General Giulio Douhet and H. G. Wells about death from the sky along with the fears of Chamberlain and many of the appeasers now came to pass. The destruction of London and Berlin, Hamburg and Liverpool followed in the wake of Warsaw and Rotterdam and were but a terrible prelude to carnage about to be inflicted on the cities of the Soviet Union.

NOTES

1. Svetlana Alliluyeva, *Only One Year,* tr. Paul Chavchvadze (New York: Harper and Row, 1969), 132.
2. Gerhard L. Weinberg, *A World at Arms: A Global History of World War II* (Cambridge: Cambridge University Press, 1994), 51.
3. *DGFP,* D, VII, No. 496, 480.
4. Halder, *Kriegstagebuch,* ed. Hans-Adolf Jacobsen, vol. 1, 61.
5. *New York Times,* September 9, 1939, 1.
6. Horst Rohde, "Der Verlauf des Polenfeldzuges vom 1. September bis 6. Oktober 1939," *Das Deutsche Reich und der Zweite Weltkrieg,* vol. 2 (Stuttgart: Deutsche Verlags-Anstalt, 1979), 111-126.

7. Weinberg, *A World at Arms,* 56.
8. *Nazi-Soviet Relations,,* 100.
9. Glantz and House, *When Titans Clashed,* 17.
10. *Nazi-Soviet Relations,* 102-103.
11. Ibid., 104-107.
12. Bullock, *Parallel Lives,* 678.
13. *Times* (London), October 4, 1939, 8.
14. Ibid., October 7, 1939, 6.
15. Ibid., October 13, 1939, 8.
16. *TMWC,* vol. 34, 266-267; vol. 37, 465-486.
17. Bullock, *Parallel Lives,* 649.
18. *DGFP,* Ser. D. vol. 8, 439-446.
19. Glantz and House, *When Titans Clashed,* 19.
20. Bullock, *Parallel Lives,* 661-662.
21. *New York Times,* February 11, 1940, 1, 43-44.
22. Shirer, *Collapse of the Third Republic,* 539-541. Gamelin, Servir, vol. 3, 190-200.
23. Bullock, *Parallel Lives,* 662-663. Glantz and House, *When Titans Clashed,* 23.
24. Churchill, *The Gathering Storm,* 531-533.
25. Bullock, *Parallel Lives,* 664-665.
26. *DGFP,* Ser. D. vol. 8, 871-880.
27. Ciano, *Diaries,* 220-223.
28. *DGFP,* Ser. D. vol. 9, 1-16. Ciano, Diaries, 223.
29. Shirer, *Collapse of the Third Republic,* 547-551. Charles de Gaulle, *War Memoirs,* vol. 1: *The Call to Honor, 1940-1942.* tr. Jonathan Griffin (New York: The Viking Press, 1955), 38.
30. *Times* (London), April, 5, 1940, 8.
31. Gilbert, *Churchill,* vol. 6, 218-219.
32. *Times* (London), May 6, 1940, 6. May 8, 1940, 3-4, 6. May 9, 1940, 6.
33. Gilbert, Churchill, vol. 6, 301-302.
34. Weinberg, *World at Arms,* 124.
35. Bullock, *Parallel Lives,* 667-668.
36. Weinberg, *World at Arms,* 124-125.
37. B.H. Liddel Hart, *History of the Second World War* (New York: G.P. Putnam's Sons, 1971), 68-69.
38. Winston S. Churchill, *Their Finest Hour* (Boston: Houghton Mifflin Company, 1949), 45-47.
39. Gilbert, *Churchill,* vol. 6, 417-420.

40. Churchill, *Speeches,* vol. 6, 6225-6231.
41. *DGFP,* Ser. D. vol. 9, 299-300, 333-334, 374-375, 436-439.
42. Macgregor Knox, *Mussolini Unleashed, 1939-1941: Politics and Strategy in Fascist Italy's Last War* (New York: Cambridge University Press, 1982), 100-125. *Times* (London), June 11, 1940, 6.
43. *New York Times,* June 11, 1940, 6.
44. Reynaud, *Thick of the Fight,* 460-461. De Gaulle, *Call to Honor,* 69-73.
45. David Reynolds, *Creation of the Anglo-American Alliance, 1937-1941* (Chapel Hill: University of North Carolina Press, 1982), 106-107.
46. *DGFP,* Ser. D. vol. 9, 608-611. Ciano, Diaries, 265-266.
47. *DGFP,* Ser. D. vol. 9, 671-676.
48. Bullock, *Parallel Lives,* 672-673.
49. *Nazi-Soviet Relations,* 138-140.
50. Ibid., 154.
51. Halder, *Kriegstagebuch,* vol. 1, 308. Norman Rich, *Hitler's War Aims: II: The Establishment of the New Order* (New York: W.W. Norton, 1974), 395. Churchill Speeches, vol. 6, 6238.
52. Bern Stegemann, "Politik und Kriegführung in der ersten Phase der deutschen Initiative," *Das Deutsche Reich und Der Zweite Weltkrieg,* vol. 2, 29. Weinberg, *World at Arms,* 145-146.
53. Churchill, *Finest Hour,* 226-227.
54. Charmley, *Churchill,* 399-400.
55. Erich Raeder, *My Life* trans. Henry W. Drexel (Annapolis: United States Naval Institute, 1960), 324.
56. Halder, *Kriegstagebuch,* vol. 2, 21.
57. F.H. Hinsley, *British Intelligence In The Second World War: Its Influence on Strategy and Operations,* vol. 1 (London: Her Majesty's Stationery Office, 1979), 176-183.
58. Churchill, *Finest Hour,* 325.
59. *Times* (London), August 26, 1940, 5.
60. Churchill, *Finest Hour,* 332-336.

CHAPTER NINE

Hitler Looks East

Hitler's attack on the Soviet Union has been viewed as his greatest blunder. It had its own logic, however, especially in terms of Hitler's ideology and psychology. Hitler knew that Stalin hoped for a long war that would exhaust Germany and the Western Allies. Stalin's seizure of the Baltic States and his pressure on Rumania were clear evidence to Hitler that the Soviets intended to strengthen their position against a possible German attack in the future, or perhaps to attack Germany at the appropriate time.

Stalin's hope had been partially realized. Britain had been driven from the Continent, but the battered Old Lion continued to bomb German cities and to check the Axis in North Africa. Prior to the war, Allied leaders believed they could defeat Germany with the help of an economic blockade. Hitler's wartime economy would have soon collapsed if Stalin had joined with the West.[1] However, the non-aggression pact and the economic agreements with Stalin in 1939 and January of 1941 had compensated for the materials lost from Europe and from the Western Hemisphere. Russian shipments of iron ore, precious metals, foodstuffs, and oil had enabled the Wehrmacht to defeat Poland and to launch the great offensive against Britain and France, and in due time they would allow for the attack on the Soviet Union itself. The Soviet Union had also served as an invaluable conduit for materials from the Near and Far East. Soviet benevolence also enabled Hitler to leave his Eastern Front virtually undefended during the campaign in the West, and would allow him to complete the struggle against Britain.

Hitler realized that an immediate Russian attack was remote, unless the Wehrmacht suffered a disastrous defeat with Sea Lion. The longer the war continued, however, the weaker Germany would become relative to the Soviet Union. Germany had become dangerously dependent on the Soviet Union for war materials and had fallen behind in its payments. Stalin might shut off Soviet supplies at any time to prevent a decisive German victory over Britain. Stalin's moves against Rumania in June had added a new fear. Germany drew half of its oil supply from the Rumanian oil fields that were within striking distance of Russian aircraft, giving Stalin the ability to endanger a combined 75 percent of Germany's needed oil supplies.[2]

Hitler had made his pact with Stalin to gain economic aid and to avoid war on two fronts. On July 21, he told his military advisors that Britain was hoping for eventual aid from the United States and the Soviet Union, and that Stalin wanted to keep the war in the West going as long as possible. Hitler wanted to strike against the Soviet Union some time in the fall, but dropped the idea when Generals Jodl and Keitel pointed out that such a large invasion was impossible until the spring of 1941.

Reichsmarshal Göring and Admiral Raeder also opposed an attack on Russia until Britain had been defeated. Continued Russian aid would allow Germany to "deliver the British a decisive blow in the Mediterranean, shove them away from Asia . . . and, consolidate the Reich . . . in Western and Northern Europe."[3] Hitler ended further debate a week later by insisting that the defeat of Russia would force Britain out of the war, destroy the balance of power in Asia, and increase rivalry between the United States and Japan. With Russia defeated, he reasoned, Germany would be master of Europe. He now recognized that it would be better to wait until May of 1941 because, as Halder recorded, "Attack achieves its purpose only if the Russian state can be shattered to its roots with one blow. So it is better to wait a little longer . . . If we start in May 1941, we would have five months to finish it."[4]

Now that Hitler had committed himself to attacking the Soviet Union, he laid the diplomatic foundation for his military strategy. Further Russian encroachment into Rumania had to be checked. Hitler was aided by Rumanians who feared Stalin more than him. First he had to deal with the petty claims of Bulgaria and Hungary who coveted the parts of Rumania they had lost at the Paris Peace Conference. On August 28 he met with Ciano and Ribbentrop at the Berghof to formulate a settlement for the entire area. The two foreign ministers then summoned the Rumanians and

Hungarians to Vienna for a meeting on the thirtieth.

The settlement was a bitter pill for the Rumanians, who lost territory to the Bulgarians as well as the Hungarians. Hitler then "guaranteed" the remainder of the country by sending in Wehrmacht units. The Vienna settlement meant the end for the authoritarian, but somewhat pro-British King Carol II who abdicated on September 8 and fled the country. His son Michael replaced him as king, but real power passed to General Ion Antonescu, head of the Fascist Iron Guard and a long-time admirer and friend of Hitler.

Hitler's coup in the Balkans alarmed and infuriated the Russians. Rumania was clearly within the Soviet sphere of influence. German troops now posed a serious threat to the soft defenses of the Ukraine where bitter memories remained of forced collectivization. On September 1, Molotov lodged a frosty protest with Schulenburg. Molotov recognized the danger of provoking Hitler into war, but to appease without protest might tempt Hitler to make additional moves. Ribbentrop indignantly denied any violation of the pact and accused the Soviets of moving against the Baltic states and Rumania without consulting Germany.[5]

German moves in the north and in Asia added to the tension. Hitler had a role for Finland to play in his war with the Soviet Union. By mid-September he began to implement it by sending reinforcements to Norway by way of Finland. German perfidy seemed to be coming from all directions when Schulenburg informed Molotov that Germany and Italy were going to sign an alliance with Japan.[6] Berlin claimed that the agreement was intended to neutralize "warmongering agitation in America," but Molotov suspected it was aimed more at the Soviet Union. He insisted that the Soviets were entitled to see the text of the agreement and any secret clauses before it was signed.

The request was ignored. The Tripartite Pact was signed amid great fanfare in Berlin on September 27, 1940. It seemed to acknowledge a long war to come and carried a warning for the United States to stay out of it. Article V stipulated that the agreement in no way altered the relationship between the parties and the Soviet Union, but the threat appeared to be there. If the three powers could cooperate against the distant United States, they could also do it more effectively against a more vulnerable Soviet Union.[7]

On October 2, Ribbentrop attempted to allay Soviet suspicions in Moscow by sending copies of the Finnish and Tripartite agreements, along with another disclaimer that there were no secret clauses to either one.

Molotov remained suspicious, however, and adopted a truculent tone not recently used toward the German masters of the continent. Ribbentrop breached protocol and offended Molotov on October 23 with a lengthy letter to Stalin stressing cooperation between the two countries and blaming recent discord on British intrigue.[8] Ribbentrop invited Molotov to Berlin as the best way of settling any differences between the two countries. Stalin replied a week later with a brief but cordial note. He agreed that relations could be improved by a permanent delimitation of interest, adding that Molotov would come to Berlin around the middle of November.

Molotov arrived in Berlin on November 12 to a proper but restrained welcome amid speculation that both the Germans and the Russians were playing for time. "Russia does not want to fight Germany ever," the *Times* correspondent noted. "Hitler does not want to fight Russia yet."[9] Ribbentrop began with a rosy picture of British weakness. The time had come, he said, for the Axis powers and the Soviets to define their spheres of influence. Hitler believed that all four powers should expand to the south. Soviet expansion lay in the "Persian Gulf and the Arabian sea." Molotov listened to Ribbentrop's windy monologue with little comment or question. Hitler made policy. That afternoon Molotov questioned Hitler about Finland and the Balkans. Hitler tried to limit the meeting to vague generalities, but Molotov pressed for specific answers. Hitler was not accustomed to being cross-examined, and he did not like it. He soon ended the meeting under the guise of an air raid warning.

Molotov was no less relentless the next morning. He wanted German troops out of Finland, and he made it clear that the Soviets were considering outright annexation. Hitler insisted that the Germans were only passing through Finland on their way to Norway, and warned of "far reaching consequences" of another Russo-Finnish war. The conversation became more acrimonious when Molotov objected to the German guarantee to Rumania and proposed a similar Russian guarantee to Bulgaria. Hitler noted that Rumania had requested the German guarantee, and he added that he knew of no similar request for a Soviet guarantee from the Bulgarians. By this time Hitler's patience had once again worn thin. He now had a clear idea of what the Russians wanted, and it would be useful to him in securing the aid of Finland and the Balkan countries. He told Molotov there could be no German commitment on the Balkans until he had talked with Mussolini. He again adjourned the meeting on the grounds of an impending Allied bombing attack.

Hitler's displayed his irritation by not attending a reception that night at the Russian embassy. This time there really was a British attack deliberately intended to disrupt the festivities and drive the party goers into their bomb shelters. It was hardly the setting for chortling over the impending demise of the British Empire, but Ribbentrop still insisted that the war was won. He then presented Molotov with the draft of a treaty calling for Russian adherence to the Tripartite Pact. Each of the four powers would respect the sphere of the other three, and none of them would support a combination directed at any of the other members. One secret protocol stipulated the Soviet sphere to be "south of the national territory of the Soviet Union in the direction of the Indian Ocean," while another called for pressure against the Turks and Russian predominance in the straits.

Molotov saw the treaty as an attempt to drive the Soviet Union out of Europe and into an area where it would clash with Britain and strain relations with the United States. Molotov wanted clear commitments on German plans for the Balkans in exchange for such a dangerous step, and he made it clear that the Soviet Union still considered the Balkans to be within its sphere.

Stalin saw advantages in the German offer. On November 26, Molotov informed Schulenburg that the Soviets were interested in joining the Tripartite Pact, but only on the condition that Germany withdraw from Finland, that Bulgaria sign a mutual assistance pact with the Soviet Union, and that Japan renounce rights to coal and oil in northern Sakhalin. In return the Soviet Union accepted the Persian Gulf as the focus of its aspirations.[10] Hitler, however, saw no purpose in further charades. He had intended to march east since the end of the French campaign, regardless of what the Soviets did or no matter how much they might wish to please him. The Soviet attitude made it clear that, for the present, Stalin did not want to please his ally very much when it came to the Balkans and Finland.

Plans for the Russian invasion had been proceeding since July. On December 5, Brauchitsch and Halder brought them to Hitler in Berlin. He issued the directive for Operation Barbarossa on the eighteenth, the strike eastward that would *"crush Soviet Russia in a quick campaign* before the end of the war against England (original emphasis).[11] Admiral Raeder and others still opposed the plan. Britain was the key to winning the war, and the Mediterranean was the key to defeating Britain. Control of the Mediterranean, including the oil fields of the Middle East, would give Germany a repository of badly needed raw materials, while denying them to Britain. It would also check any future British or Anglo-American thrust into Africa as a prelude to an invasion of Europe itself.

Hitler was sympathetic to Raeder's plan, but not to the point of giving the Mediterranean priority over the Russian campaign. The great advantage of the Mediterranean strategy in theory was that Germany could wage war on Britain in cooperation with Italy, Vichy France, and Spain. Hitler was quite willing to leave the major responsibility of the war in the Mediterranean to them. There was nothing wrong with Hitler's strategy. Vichy France and Spain could have closed the straits at Gibraltar, while the Italians continued their pressure on Egypt. Some Arabs in the Middle East hoped to free themselves from British domination through an Axis victory without realizing that a far worse foreign rule would follow.

Hitler overestimated Italian military strength. He was eventually forced to make the kind of massive military commitment to the Mediterranean he had wished to avoid, and at a time when it was far less effective than it would have been in the summer of 1940. He also failed to dominate all of his allies. Hitler had a special mission for Spain in the western Mediterranean, and was confident Franco would carry it out. The Caudillo owed the Axis everything. He had told Hitler in June of 1940 that Spain was ready to enter the war in return for much of French North Africa. Franco did not think the war would last long and was eager to share in the spoils.

But the British continued to fight, and Franco well knew that their navy could inflict severe damage on Spain. He was beginning to hedge by September when he sent his future Foreign Minister Ramón Serrano Suñer to Berlin. Serrano Suñer proclaimed enthusiasm for the Axis and assured his hosts that public opinion in Spain supported war. But, he continued, Spain needed considerable economic and military aid. He also displayed a healthy appetite for gains at the expense of the French, and hinted at the future destruction of Portugal, which "had no right to exist." The Spaniards made themselves an unattractive ally by combining greed with weakness. Hitler was aware that Spain could do little to help him in the near future unless Franco consented to German occupation. He also knew that giving Spain any part of the French Empire would offend Mussolini and drive much of Vichy France into the arms of de Gaulle.[12]

Hitler decided to settle things with France and Spain by personal diplomacy, as he had done so well on many occasions with Mussolini. He met with Franco on October 23 at the small French town of Hendaye on the Spanish border. Hitler attempted to dazzle Franco by recounting the German victory over France and the imminent defeat of Britain. Franco, however, had cooled since June. He knew the weather now precluded any attack across the channel until spring, and that any move against Britain would bring some kind of retaliation from the United States. Hitler found Franco to be boring, demanding, and pretentious. He left Hendaye that evening sharing Ribbentrop's view of Franco as an "ungrateful coward. He owes us everything, and now won't join us."[13]

Hitler traveled north for a meeting with Marshal Pétain and Pierre Laval at Montoire. The aged marshal was neither as senile nor as servile as some have thought. He believed France had bargaining strength by still controlling southeastern France and most of the empire along with a naval and merchant fleet. Pétain and Laval believed the most reasonable course lay in securing the best terms within a German dominated Europe. In time a new France would emerge out of the decadence and defeat of the Third Republic to free itself from German domination. It was a hope shared by many under Vichy control, and it had been strengthened by anti-British feeling following the attack on the French fleet.[14]

Hitler greeted the marshal with the respect he usually gave to those who had been victorious in the first war. He made it clear, however, that the Pétain and Laval had to decide whether France or Britain paid the price for defeat. Pétain agreed to cooperate with Germany against Britain and promised to resist any British attacks on French possessions, but he stopped short of war.[15] Pétain's vague promise was as much as Hitler expected. He might have gotten more by giving more, but that would bring further problems. He had promised Mussolini that all Italian claims against France would be satisfied in any peace settlement. To leave French North Africa intact would infuriate the Duce and end all hopes of gaining Franco's cooperation.

Hitler returned to Berlin in a foul mood. On October 24 he was told that Mussolini intended to invade Greece. The Duce's ego had been bruised by Hitler's Vienna settlement and he intended to get even by invading Greece. Hitler wanted to avoid any turmoil in the Balkans, and hoped to prevent it by meeting with Mussolini on October 28. Two hours before arriving in Florence, however, Hitler learned that the attack had begun. Hitler maintained his composure and pledged his support. Privately, however, as his interpreter Paul Schmidt wrote, Hitler left Mussolini "with bitterness in his heart. He had been frustrated three times — at Hendaye, Montoire, and now in Italy. In the lengthy winter evenings of the next four years these long, exacting journeys were a constantly recurring theme of bitter reproach against ungrateful and unreliable friends, Axis partners and 'deceiving Frenchmen.'"[16]

Hitler was bitter when he met with his military advisors on November 4. He made it clear that he had never approved of the Italian attack on Greece, and he now voiced little confidence in the Italian armed forces to secure a victory. The Italians had given the British a pretext to occupy Crete and Lemnos. They could then bomb the Rumanian oil fields and might land troops in Greece. At this meeting, and later on the fourteenth, Hitler talked of intervening in Greece, taking Gibraltar, occupying the Azores, and securing the entire western Mediterranean. To achieve his goals, however, Hitler had to accept Raeder's view that Britain was the "soul of the resistance" to German domination of Europe. Raeder continued to argue that the defeat of Britain would lay the foundation for the eventual defeat of Russia, but Hitler continued to see it the other way around.

More bad news came from the Mediterranean on November 11. British planes attacked the Italian fleet at Taranto in southeastern Italy and inflicted heavy losses. Two weeks later the Greeks drove the Italians back into Albania. In spite of the deteriorating situation, Hitler issued his directive for Barbarossa on December 18. Raeder again tried to sway Hitler on the twenty-seventh by stressing Italian collapse in the Mediterranean and Greece, but Hitler remained impervious. He would win the war by destroying the Soviet Union in a quick campaign. He had to face the unpleasant reality, however, that Spain would not enter the war in the Mediterranean, and that Italy might well lose it. An Italian defeat in Africa and Greece would encourage Vichy to become more independent. The Italians could be saved only by sending German tank units to Libya and Albania. It was also time to consider occupying all of France.

Hitler called for a meeting with Mussolini as soon as possible. The Duce feared any confrontation with the arrogant Germans, but he had no choice while his armies were being defeated on two continents. Hitler did his best to ignore Italian failures when he met Mussolini and Ciano at the Berghof on January 19, 1941. He also revealed plans for invading Greece and securing the Balkans. He said nothing, however, about invading Russia in the spring. It was obvious, as Ciano noted, that he was in a very "anti-Russian mood." Mussolini and Ciano left the meeting with mixed emotions. Hitler had again projected the image of military expert and grand strategist and had revived Mussolini's flagging confidence. But it was now painfully obvious to everyone that the Duce was now little more than Hitler's *Gauleiter* for the Mediterranean.[17]

Hitler seized control of the Balkans during the next few months. Bulgaria abandoned the pretense of neutrality on March 1, by joining the Axis powers. Hitler needed only Yugoslavia to complete his conduit to Greece and mastery of the Balkans. Pressure on Belgrade began in early February, and on March 5, the regent Prince Paul accepted Hitler's bribe of Salonika in exchange for cooperating with Germany. The decision was not popular in Yugoslavia where sympathy for Russia and dislike of the Germans remained strong. There were rumors of an impending coup by the Serbian Army when the Yugoslavian delegation left for Vienna on the twenty-fifth. On the following night a group of army officers seized power in the name of young King Peter II. Hitler responded with Operation Punishment, the invasion and destruction of Yugoslavia. The Wehrmacht struck in full fury at dawn on Sunday, April 6. Hitler ordered Belgrade to be mercilessly bombed for several days as an example of what happened to those who defied him, even though the city had no anti-aircraft defenses. The country was under complete German control by April 13, while the king and other remnants of the government fled abroad to join others in exile.[18]

The invincible Wehrmacht also crushed a tough Greek army that had humiliated the Italians. The German advance threatened to engulf a British force of over 50,000, forcing an evacuation similar to Dunkirk, but not as successful. The Wehrmacht ruled the Balkan peninsula by the end of the month and was making preparations for a successful airborne assault on Crete in late May. To the victor went the spoils, much to the discomfort of Mussolini who now had to acknowledge Hitler as master of the Adriatic and the Balkans.

Italian subservience extended to North Africa when the German Africa Corps under General Erwin Rommel launched a surprise offensive in Libya on March 31. The British had been confident of stopping any Axis offensive and had weakened their forces by dispatching troops to Greece. They were prepared for neither the tanks of the Africa Corps nor for the brilliant tactics of its commander. Rommel's forces drove the British back to the Egyptian border within two weeks. With the Germans pressing on Egypt and in control of the Balkans, the British were in danger of being driven entirely out of the Mediterranean and the Middle East. The time was right for a knockout blow that might have given the Germans possession of Suez and the oil fields of the Middle East. But Hitler still believed he could win the war in Russia in the same quick way he had won in Poland and France. With the resources of Russia at his disposal, the stubborn British would have to give up.

Hitler had no plans for expansion beyond roughly 200 miles east of the Urals.[19] The remainder of Siberian Russia lay open to the Japanese and was coveted by some in Tokyo. Hitler's racial views precluded any warm relations with Tokyo, and at times he referred to an alliance with the Japanese as one with the Devil to drive out Beelzebub. Yet, for all of his racism, Hitler admired the Japanese for their empire and their militarism.[20]

Following their conquest of Manchuria, the Japanese had looked on warily as the Nationalists under Chiang Kai-shek consolidated their hold on China. As long as Chiang dissipated his military strength against Mao Tse-tung's (Mao Zedong) Communists, Japan's hold on Manchuria was secure. In December of 1936, however, Chiang agreed to a united front with the Communists against Japan. The Kwantung Army struck south into China proper on July 7, 1937. Neither the Nationalists nor the Communists could offer much resistance as the Japanese swept toward the Nationalists' capital at Nanking (Nanjing). Their sack of the city in December horrified the world.[21]

Chiang Kai-shek fought on from his new capital at Chungking (Chongqing). Hitler's victories presented a opportunity for Japan to end the war in China by building an new order in Asia. By moving south Japan could conquer the resources of the British, Dutch, and French empires and force Chiang Kai-shek to surrender by cutting his supply lines. The government of Prime Minister Konoe Fuminaro had formulated plans to join the Axis in July of 1940 as a prelude to marching south, even if that meant war with the United States.[22]

Relations between Moscow and Tokyo had been strained since 1931, and on several occasions border skirmishes had nearly brought war. Tokyo had felt angry and betrayed when Hitler made his pact with Stalin. The Japanese now planned to benefit from Hitler's aggression as he planned to benefit from theirs. Hitler issued instructions in early March "Regarding Collaboration with Japan." [23] While seeking Japanese help against Britain, Hitler continued to insist that they not be told of plans for attacking Russia, which he expected to defeat easily and quickly. In late February Ribbentrop painted a glowing picture to Japanese ambassador Oshima Hiroshi of how a quick strike at Singapore would most likely defeat Britain and frighten the United States. In case the United States declared war, he predicted, the Japanese fleet would be able to defeat the Americans with little effort. Hitler made the same pitch when Foreign Minister Matsuoka Yosuke came to Berlin on April 4. He went much further than

Ribbentrop by promising to join Japan "in case of a conflict between Japan and America."[24]

Matsuoka wanted a settlement with the Russians before any strike southward and possible war with the United States. He had been given hints in Berlin that all was not well between Germany and the Soviet Union, but he was not told of impending war. Matsuoka traveled on to Moscow to sign a non-aggression treaty on April 13. Stalin toasted him as a fellow "Asiatic" and displayed a rare friendliness. Stalin had reason to be pleased with the agreement. The pact called for neutrality in case of aggression by a third power and a pledge of non-aggression for five years.

Japanese problems in China and the Pacific seemed to rule out any threat for a while in the East. Stalin honored Matsuoka with a rare public appearance at the train station to see him off on April 18. While there, Stalin publicly embraced Schulenburg, who had come to pay his respects to Matsuoka. "We must be friends," he said to the stunned Schulenburg, "and you must now do everything to that end."[25]

Schulenburg did, but nothing would change the plans in Berlin where Barbarossa was being supplemented with details for the rape of Russia by Hitler's armies. Barbarossa was to be a war of conquest and annihilation. Hitler's infamous "Commissar Order" to OKW on June 6 stated that Soviet commissars were bearers of ideologies directly opposed to National Socialism. They must be executed as soon as possible. Millions of others, Jews and intellectuals, were to be liquidated or left to starve.[26]

Rumors and warnings of a German attack continued throughout April and May. Luftwaffe penetration of Soviet airspace had become almost a daily occurrence despite protests from Moscow. Hitler said nothing about the Soviet Union in his speeches, and there were no replies to Soviet requests for better relations. To some extent, Stalin was unable to shed his own ideological baggage in seeing warnings from foreign powers as a plot to provoke him into war with Hitler.

On the other hand, Stalin faced a situation more perplexing than that to be faced by the Americans prior to Pearl Harbor. The Germans made clever use of disinformation. It was plausible to believe that the German strike into the Balkans was really aimed at the British. The original attack date of May 15 passed without incident. On May 2, Stalin's agent in Tokyo, Richard Sorge, warned that Hitler was "fully determined" to attack the Soviet Union. On June 15, Sorge updated his warning. The attack would begin on June 22.[27] It too, however, could prove to be false. In July, as the Red Army retreated toward Moscow, Stalin told President

Roosevelt's special advisor, Harry Hopkins, that he had "believed that Hitler would not strike but took all precautions to mobilize his army."[28] Stalin's only recourse was to play for time. Hopefully, he could delay the attack until the next year. If not, then at least until autumn when bad weather would prevent any quick German success. He most likely believed the German troop concentrations on his border were intended to intimidate him into economic or territorial concessions. It seemed illogical that Hitler would attack Russia while his armies were occupying much of Europe and making war in Africa. Stalin expected any German attack to come after a period of demands and overtly worsening relations that would give him time to mobilize his armies.[29]

Stalin continued to put up a brave front. The Russian people were assured of the invincibility of the Red Army and warned that "imperialists" might try to maneuver the Soviet Union into war. On May Day the Russian ambassador to Germany, Vladimir Dekanosov, stood close to Stalin as a sign that relations with Germany were still amicable. They along with other Soviet and foreign dignitaries viewed a massive military display featuring the new KV and T-34 tanks, but parades and the appearance of harmony did little to still rumors of war.

Stalin surprised the world on May 6 by taking the position of chairman of the council of people's commissars. Until now he had been content to rule Russia as general secretary of the Communist Party. The Russian people reacted with a mixture of anxiety and relief. They knew that in normal times Stalin would not have taken the new position, and there was cause for concern. It was reassuring to know, however, that "the boss" had officially taken charge. The change was also a demotion for Molotov, who had served as chairman. This was not lost on Schulenburg, who believed the change meant a more conciliatory Soviet policy in the future. Schulenburg's view appeared to have some validity. Stalin went out of the way to please Berlin by closing many of the embassies and legations representing countries Hitler had conquered, including Yugoslavia, with whom the Kremlin had recently signed a treaty of friendship.

Anxiety in Moscow increased considerably when Hitler's long-time deputy Rudolf Hess flew to Britain on May 10. The Hess mission would have provoked fears in Moscow of capitalist encirclement even in dull times. In the tense days of May, 1941, it was feared to mean peace between Britain and Germany and the prelude to a combined attack on the Soviet Union. To his disappointment, Hess found no peace party to overthrow

Churchill and end the war with Germany. The Hess visit caused a stir for a few days and then faded before the urgency of other events, only to be resurrected to one degree or another during his long imprisonment and eventual death in August of 1987.

Stalin continued to seek better relations with Germany. Tass issued a communiqué on June 14, blaming "rumors" of war between Germany and the Soviet Union on British Ambassador Sir Stafford Cripps and denouncing them as "clumsy propaganda by forces . . . interested in the extension of the war."[30] That same day Hitler met with his commanders to review Barbarossa. Everything was now ready for the largest military operation in history. Hitler and his generals were confident. Plans had been coordinated with the Hungarians, Rumanians, and Finns. Hitler again made it clear that this would be a war between ideologies in which the normal practices of international law had to be measured by "completely different standards."[31]

On the evening of June 21, following a week in which there had been no German response to the Tass communiqué, Molotov met with Schulenburg to discuss the deteriorating situation. He asked Schulenburg about the rumors of impending war and why Germany was dissatisfied with the Soviet Union. Schulenburg, who did not know what was going to happen in a few hours, had no answer. He found it when he returned to the German embassy. A coded message from Berlin instructed him to see Molotov and to read him the enclosed message "without entering into any discussion with him." The message was a collection of lies charging the Soviets with violating the 1939 pact and planning a military attack on Germany in cooperation with the British. "Thereby," Schulenburg continued to read, "the Soviet Government has broken its treaties with Germany. The Führer has therefore ordered the German Armed Forces to oppose this threat with all the means at their disposal." The ambassador had read the message with a heavy heart, and he later would pay with his life for opposing Hitler. Molotov sat in stunned silence until Schulenburg finished. At first he seemed unable to grasp the meaning of the message and asked whether it was a declaration of war. Schulenburg replied with only a helpless gesture of his arms. Molotov then became angry and protested the German perfidy and the falseness of the charges. The Soviet Union had remained loyal to the pact of 1939 and now it was being attacked. With considerable justification he said, "Surely we have not deserved that."[32]

NOTES

1. Klaus Hildebrand, *The Foreign Policy of the Third Reich,* tr. Anthony Fothergill (Berkeley: University of California Press, 1973), 92.
2. Norman Rich, *Hitler's War Aims,* vol. 1 (New York: W.W. Norton and Company, 1973), 204-208.
3. Halder, *Kriegstagebuch,* vol. 2, 30-31.
4. Jürgen Förster, "Die Wendung nach Osten. Hitlers Entschluss vom 31. Juli 1940 und seine Folgen," *Das Deutsche Reich und der zweite Weltkrieg,* vol. 4, (Stuttgart, 1983), 23-28. Bullock, *Parallel Lives,* 682.
5. *Nazi-Soviet Relations,* 180-181.
6. Ibid., 181-183.
7. Ibid., 188-199.
8. Ibid., 207-213.
9. *Times* (London), November 13, 1940, 4.
10. *DGFP,* Ser. D., vol. 11, 714-715. Bullock, *Parallel Lives,* 690-691.
11. *Nazi-Soviet Relations,* 260-264.
12. *DGFP,* Ser. D. vol. 9, 509-511, vol. 11, 83-91. Ramón Serrano Suñer, *Entre les Pyrénées et Gibraltar; notes et réflexions sur la politique espagnole depuis 1936* (Genève: Éditions du Cheval ailé, 1948), 156-165.
13. *DGFP*, Ser. D, vol. 9, 371-379. Dr. Paul Schmidt, *Hitler's Interpreter* (New York: Macmillan Company, 1951), 194-197. Paul Preston, *Franco: A Biography* (New York: Basic Books, 1994), 393-400.
14. Rich, *Hitler's War Aims,* vol. 2, 212-214.
15. *DGFP*, Ser. D. vol. 12, XII, 388-392. Griffiths, *Pétain,* 269-271.
16. Schmidt, *Hitler's Interpreter*, 200.
17. *DGFP,* Ser. D. vol. 11, 1127-1133. Ciano, Diaries, 337-338. Knox, *Mussolini Unleashed,* 280-281.
18. Martin L. Van Creveld, *Hitler's Strategy 1940-1941:The Balkan Clue* (Cambridge: Cambridge University Press, 1973), 144-149.
19. Bullock, *Parallel Lives*, 723.
20. Rich, *Hitler's War Aims,* vol. 1, 224.
21. Iris Chang, *The Rape of Nanking: The Forgotten Holocaust of World War II* (New York: Basic Books, 1997), 81-104.
22. Weinberg, *World at Arms,* 167-168. Hosoya Chihiro, "The Tripartite Pact, 1939-1940," *Deterrent Diplomacy,* ed. James William Morley

(New York: Columbia University Press, 1976), 216-221.
23. *TMWC,* vol. 34, 303-305.
24. *DGFP,* Ser. D., vol. 12, 139-151, 453-458. Bloch, Ribbentrop, 325.
25. Bullock, *Parallel Lives,* 716. *Nazi-Soviet Relations,* 323-324.
26. Jürgen Förster, *"Das unternehmen 'Barbarossa' als Eroberungs-ung Vernichtungskrieg,"* Das Deutschen Reich und der zweite Weltkrieg, vol. 4, 421-440. Bullock, *Parallel Lives,* 701-702.
27. Gordon W. Prange, *Target Tokyo: The Story of the Sorge Spy Ring* (New York: McGraw-Hill, 1984), 347.
28. *FRUS: 1941,* vol 1, 808.
29. Bullock, *Parallel Lives,* 717-718. Glantz and House, *When Titans Clashed,* 41-44.
30. *Nazi-Soviet Relations,* 345-346.
31. *TMWC,* vol. 10, 531-533. Halder, *Kriegstagebuch,* vol. 2, 455-456.
32. Nazi-Soviet Relations, 347-349. 355-356. Gustav Hilger & Alfred G. Mayer, *The Incompatible Allies: A Memoir-History of German-Soviet Relations, 1918-1941* (New York: Macmillan Company, 1953), 356.

Chapter Ten

The World Will Hold Its Breath

Hitler arrived at the *Wolfsschanze* (Wolf's Lair), his new underground headquarters at Rastenburg in East Prussia while the diplomatic, steps were taking place in Berlin and Moscow. He dictated a long letter to Mussolini explaining the attack on Russia and why he had not informed his ally earlier. By eliminating Russia, he said, Britain would lose all hope for eventual victory while giving a "tremendous relief for Japan in East Asia, and thereby the possibility of a much stronger threat to American activities through Japanese intervention." He was relieved to be rid of the "mental agonies" that had accompanied his partnership with the Soviet Union. Its purpose had been served, and it was now time to march eastward and lay the foundation for the thousand year Reich.[1]

Hitler had said, while planning Barbarossa, "the world will hold its breath and make no comment."[2] The world certainly held its breath, but there was comment. The most important came from London. Throughout the day Churchill formulated a speech promising aid to the Soviets. He had been an enemy of Soviet communism since the Bolshevik Revolution, and now he was offering aid to Lenin's heirs. When asked whether his speech compromised his anti-communism, Churchill replied, "Not at all. If Hitler invaded Hell, I would make at least a favorable reference to the Devil in the House of Commons." He acknowledged his previous opposition to communism during the speech, but said, "We have but one aim and one single irrevocable purpose. We are resolved to destroy Hitler and every vestige of the Nazi regime. . . . Any man or state who fights on against Nazidom will have our aid. . . . It follows, therefore, that we shall give whatever help we can to Russia and to the Russian people."[3] The word was more guarded from Washington where Under-Secretary Sumner Welles restated American opposition to both communism and Nazism, but stressed the greater danger from Germany, and made it clear that America would honor any Soviet request for aid.[4] The most curious comment came from Moscow where Molotov denounced the German attack as unprovoked and reminded the nation of previous victories over an invader. "Our cause is just," he closed, "the enemy will be defeated. Victory will be ours."[5] For many Russians Molotov's speech provoked the same question asked by the Soviet ambassador to Britain, Ivan Maisky: "Why Molotov? Why not Stalin?"[6]

Stalin was apparently confident of defeating the Germans within a month, and wanted more information before speaking himself.[7] It soon became clear that the Germans had launched a major attack, and units at the front were being encircled and defeated. Behind the lines the Soviet Air Force was being destroyed. But Stalin seemed unable to grasp the reality. Instead of approving strategic withdrawals and using the vast distances of Russia, he ordered the Red Army to counterattack and then to advance into German occupied Poland. The order compounded the debacle by sending valuable units into battle prematurely and undermanned where they were destroyed by the Germans.[8]

Stalin realized that the entire front had collapsed on the twenty-third when told that Minsk would soon fall. He began shouting, fell silent, and went home in a state of nervous collapse. When members of the Politburo came to see him on June 30, he expected to be arrested and might well have been toppled by a military or party coup. Stalin had purged the Red Army mercilessly, exposed it to defeat, and now seemed to be deserting his post in time of war. Leadership passed to a Stavka, or Supreme Field Headquarters, under the direction of Marshal Semyon Timoshenko. Neither Timoshenko nor his chief aide General Georgi Zhukov thought they were running the country. They were merely waiting for Stalin to recover. The possibility arose that he might not, and they had to prepare for it. Stalin had been the public source of all strength and patriotism in Russia for a decade, and for many Russians there may have been something ominous when his name disappeared from the press during the last week of June. The boss officially returned on July 1. A new State Defense Committee was announced with Stalin as the chair. He spoke to his people for the first time since the invasion. He had none of the eloquence of Churchill and sounded like a tired old man. But he was there, and for many Russians that was enough. There was a curious psychology in the fact that a despot, unsurpassed in the terror he inflicted upon his own people, could now say for the first time "Brothers and sisters, I turn to you my friends" and be loved for it.[9] Stalin told the Soviet people what they already suspected after two weeks of bland official bulletins. The Germans had taken large areas of territory and were still advancing. He cautioned the nation not to see the invader as invincible. Napoleon and the Kaiser had eventually been beaten, and so would Hitler. The pact with Hitler, he said, had given the Soviet Union an additional eighteen months to strengthen its defenses. The country now had to unite in a "life and death struggle" against a "cruel and merciless" enemy while eliminating "deserters and panic-mongers" at home. Those who retreated must not leave anything of use to the enemy, while those in the occupied areas were to form partisan units to continue the struggle. The Soviet struggle, he said, was part of a broader war against fascism in cooperation with the people of Britain and the United States.[10] Stalin had been genuinely relieved by Churchill's promised aid, especially in the wake of the Hess flight to Britain and the suspicions it had generated in the Kremlin. To now have Britain as an ally and America as a friend was as much as he could have hoped for, considering his pact with Hitler and Soviet actions following it.

Stalin's broadcast may have lessened anxiety among some of his people, but it could not stop the German advance. In the North, Field Marshal Wilhelm von Leeb's army group struck through the Baltic States toward Leningrad. In the center, Field Marshal Fedor von Bock's group advanced along the road once taken by Napoleon. In the South, Field Marshal Rundstedt's army group moved toward the grain and oil in the Ukraine. Even the normally cautious General Halder speculated that the Russian campaign would be completed within a few weeks. By the middle of July Hitler's army at Smolensk was only 200 miles from Moscow. Hitler told the Wehrmacht that the campaign was virtually over. It would be necessary to reduce the size of the army to allow for increases in air and sea forces needed to defeat Britain, and possibly the United States.[11]

Stalin's appeal to his brothers and sisters could not undue the hatred felt by those who had suffered through collectivization and the purges. Many in the Baltic States, Belorussia, and Ukraine welcomed the Germans as liberators. Collective farms were abolished by their inhabitants, and churches were reopened at the first opportunity. In some cases, the population turned on their former commissars with the blessing of the invader. Had the Germans emulated the victory of 1918 they might well have established their own empire in eastern Europe consisting of autonomous states dominated from Berlin. But Hitler and the minions of Nazi ideology had come to enslave and exterminate an inferior people. Only near the end of the war when it was clearly too little too late did Hitler consent to the creation of an anti-Soviet Russian Army of Liberation under the command of General Andrei Vlasov. By that time, however, German treatment of civilians and soldiers, and the knowledge that the Soviets would one day return, had eliminated any chance of success.[12]

The continued success of the German advance dazzled the world and produced euphoria in Berlin. Field commanders, however, were beginning to see problems ahead. The vastness of Russia began to strain German supply lines. Mechanized equipment had difficulty along poor Russian roads that slowed vehicles and increased fuel consumption. Red Army casualties were staggering, but new soldiers appeared. The Russian soldier often chose to fight to the death rather than surrender, and to take as many Germans with him as he could. Some German forces went beyond their own air support and paid the price for it when they encountered the new T-34 tank. The Germans had not expected it in such quantities and were unprepared for it.

The Germans were being slowed enough to endanger the original goal of Barbarossa. Success of the plan had been predicated on the collapse of the Red Army and the Soviet government. Both still stood, and would have time to gain strength during the lull imposed by the coming winter. In mid-July, Wehrmacht commanders urged Hitler to sacrifice the northern and southern offensives in favor of a concentrated strike in the center toward Moscow. They believed the Stalin government might fall along with its capital, and that the Red Army would by crippled with the loss of its communication and supply hub for the entire front.

Hitler disagreed. Taking Moscow was secondary to isolating Leningrad, seizing the Ukraine, and capturing Rostov on the Don River, a conquest that would give him grain and oil while denying them to his enemy. Army leaders delayed action on his orders when Hitler fell ill with dysentery. He was furious when he found out. The generals had brought on a costly lull in the German attack with their action. On August 21, Hitler angrily criticized the outmoded thinking of the generals and their failure to comprehend the economic role in warfare.[13]

Hitler's decision has remained controversial. His generals and some historians believed the Wehrmacht could have destroyed any large Russian army defending Moscow and virtually ended the war. It is questionable, however, whether the Germans still had the strength or supplies needed for such an offensive. Moscow would have been defended in the same tenacious manner as Stalingrad a year later. The expected collapse of the Soviet government had not happened, and Stalin was prepared to carry on the war if Moscow fell.[14] Hitler's judgment appeared to be vindicated by the success of the southern offensive. Strengthened by Guderian's panzers from the center, Rundstedt's group struck against Marshal Budenny's army guarding the Ukraine. By mid-September the Germans were 150 miles east of Kiev and driving for Rostov. The easy victory seemed to confirm Hitler's belief that the Russians could be beaten before the end of the year. On September 5 he ordered Halder to prepare for an attack on Moscow. On September 30 in the North and October 2 in the south, Bock's reinforced Army Group Center launched Operation Typhoon for the final assault. Hitler returned to Berlin on October 3 for a public speech to raise sagging morale and to encourage further sacrifice. He again blamed Britain for prolonging the war and the Soviets for forcing him to attack. He lauded German conquests since he had come to power, and he promised that "the enemy in the East has been struck down and will never rise again." Following the capture of Orel on the eighth, Berlin radio proclaimed the end of the Soviet Union as a military power and the failure of Britain's hope for a two-front war.[15] A week later the Germans took Mozhaisk, only 65 miles from Moscow. By this time, however, autumn rains turned roads into mud that slowed vehicles and jammed equipment, while at night the onset of an early winter began to take its toll on an army totally unprepared for it. On October 19 Stalin ordered a state of siege and announced that General Georgi Zhukov would supervise the defense of Moscow. Zhukov's appointment demonstrated how the gravity of the moment forced Stalin to rely more heavily on generals than on the political commanders he preferred. He had been forced to sack the only two marshals who had survived the purge. Neither Semyon Budenny nor Kliment Voroshilov had advanced beyond their military experience during the civil war, and had quickly demonstrated their incompetence.

    Stalin had also received reports that Japan planned to strike south. The Japanese threat had forced the Soviets to maintain their strength in the east. At an imperial conference on July 2, Matsuoka urged war on the Soviet Union, but he failed to convince army and navy leaders. The need for oil and other resources necessitated a move into Southeast Asia. If Hitler destroyed the Soviet government, Siberia could be taken in the near future. Stalin began to transfer men and equipment westward in October. The German advance was now aided by colder weather that hardened the ground. By mid-November, however, snow and sub-zero weather became more intense. Tanks without antifreeze had to be started with fires, and no order could stop men without winter clothing from using precious gasoline to keep themselves warm. The more exact and less tolerant German weapons were vulnerable to the cold and tended to jam in combat. Hitler and some of his generals still believed they could take Moscow with one final drive scheduled to begin on December 1. The attack consisted of a thrust of three armies from the North, West, and South. The Germans advanced slowly with heavy casualties. Some soldiers reached the suburbs of Moscow before being forced back. Men and machines were exhausted and could go no farther.

General Zhukov had been assembling his Siberian units and other forces for an attack at the right moment. His soldiers were well equipped and trained to fight in the snow, in contrast to their weary enemy. They struck hard with total surprise on December 5 along the 200-mile perimeter around Moscow. For a time it looked as though the Germans might panic and flee westward in hopes of avoiding the same fate as the Napoleon's Grand Army had in 1812. Hitler avoided a rout by ordering a halt at all costs, except for local withdrawals. He condemned his men to terrible suffering and additional casualties in a winter campaign, but by January of 1942 the front had stabilized. Hitler did not consider the fact that the order to hold had succeeded mainly because Stalin had tried to attain too much along a broad front. Success this time, however, encouraged him to hold every inch of ground in the future with disastrous results.[16] He dismissed many of the generals who had given him victories, but had failed in Russia. Brauchitsch, Guderian, Rundstedt, and others were either relieved of command or allowed to resign. Hitler then took personal command of the army as well as everything else in Germany.

Hitler also added another country to the list of his official enemies on December 11 by declaring war on the United States. Germany and the United States had maintained a frigid contact with each other at the consular level since November of 1938. Hitler knew that most Americans favored the Allies, but were opposed to war with Germany. In March of 1940 he ordered the German Navy to refrain from any harassment of American shipping and to keep a safe distance from the North American continent.[17] Hitler had ample cause to believe Roosevelt would enter the war against him at the first opportunity. In November of 1939 the President had called a special session of Congress to amend the Neutrality Act of 1937. The law forbade the sale of war materials to belligerents and required cash for all other goods. Roosevelt asked for a repeal of arms sales while requiring all goods be put on a "carry" as well as "cash" basis. The changes obviously favored the Allies and appeared to provide a solution that most Americans wanted. With supplies open to them, the Allies could be expected to win a long war of attrition without any American military help.[18]

Many Americans were shocked by the defeat of France in the spring of 1940. It was doubtful whether Britain could stand alone against the Axis. Hitler might soon control the eastern Atlantic and be in a position to strike against the United States. Britain, however, continued to stand and fight. Hitler and Roosevelt had to prepare for a long war.[19] German victories in Europe and the plight of Britain were major factors in Roosevelt's decision to run for a third term. Wendell Willkie and the Republicans were preferable to Roosevelt, but Berlin had to be cautious with its support. Attacks on Roosevelt or blatant support for Willkie might be resented by the American electorate and aid Roosevelt. The German press remained under orders to be neutral in the campaign and to avoid any attacks on Roosevelt. Instead, attempts were made to influence the campaign through financial support to the America First Committee and other organizations opposing Roosevelt, and to intimidate the American public. The fanfare surrounding the Tripartite Pact in September and the announcement of Molotov's visit to Berlin in November were aimed as much at the American voter as at the Roosevelt administration. They were intended to project the vision of America being at war with the entire world if it continued to aid Britain.

Roosevelt, however, had no intention of being intimidated and believed the American public would support him. He broadened his administration in mid-summer by appointing two Republican internationalists to his cabinet. Frank Knox, who had been the party's vice presidential candidate in 1936, became secretary of the navy, while Hoover's secretary of state, Henry Stimson, became secretary of war. The President and most of the population now believed that the defeat of Britain would put the United States in desperate peril. The best course seem to lie in aiding Britain, even at the risk of war with Germany. Roosevelt clearly stepped beyond the limits of neutrality in September. German attacks had reduced the number of British destroyers to the point where the Royal Navy could not adequately patrol the coastal sea lanes. In July, Churchill appealed to Roosevelt for a loan of forty or fifty American destroyers presently not being used by the American Navy. The president knew Congress would never approve such a provocative act in time to save Britain. Roosevelt decided to act through an executive agreement rather than a treaty requiring Congressional approval. He announced the transfer of fifty destroyers to Britain on September 2 and tried to blunt the expected opposition by presenting the agreement as a trade strengthening the defenses of the United States. Britain in return gave the United States bases in Bermuda and Newfoundland for ninety-nine years as well as shorter leases on bases in the Caribbean. The agreement alarmed and angered opponents of war, despite the advantages for the United States, while in Britain there was grumbling at the Americans for unloading some obsolete tubs for valuable real estate.[20] On September 4, OKW noted that the destroyers were ready for combat when they arrived, and that they would strengthen British coastal defenses. OKW overestimated the impact. Only thirty destroyers were in service by April of 1941. The British lacked experienced crews and the aging ships needed to be refitted for anti-submarine patrol.[21] The real impact of the deal lay in its impression of Anglo-American solidarity. Raeder considered the agreement to be an overtly hostile action toward Germany foreshadowing American entrance into the war.

Roosevelt won reelection by a substantial margin on November 5, 1940. His victory, however, was less than in 1936, primarily due to concern that he would take the country into war. Roosevelt recognized the strength of the opposition, but believed the victory represented a national mandate in favor of aiding Britain. Britain had been unable to survive World War I without borrowing from the United States, and it could not do so now. On December 7, 1940 Churchill informed the president that Britain was nearly bankrupt and could not continue to receive arms on a "cash and carry" basis.[22] Roosevelt now needed the consent of the American people and Congress for greater aid. Roosevelt delivered a "fireside chat" on December 29. He warned that a Nazi victory would threaten the United States and appealed to the moral responsibility of Americans to be "the arsenal of democracy" against the advance of Nazi ideology.[23]

Roosevelt used his annual message to Congress on January 6, 1941, to request increased aid to those nations resisting aggression as the best way to keep "war from our Hemisphere." He again went beyond the defense of British or American security to present the struggle in terms of moral conflict from which there would emerge a better world "founded upon four essential human freedoms. . . . Freedom of speech and expression—everywhere in the world. . . . freedom to worship God in his own way—everywhere in the world . . . freedom from want—everywhere in the world . . . freedom from fear—anywhere in the world."[24] House Democratic leaders introduced "An Act to Further Promote the Defense of the United States and Other Purposes" on the tenth. The bill authorized the president to "sell . . . lease, lend, or otherwise dispose of material" to any country whose defense the President deems vital to the defense of the United States.[25] Congress debated the bill for nearly two months. Ohio Senator Robert A. Taft feared it would "give the President power to carry on a kind of undeclared war in which America would do everything except put soldiers in the front line trenches where the fighting is."[26] Despite the opposition, the bill passed by a comfortable margin, and on March 11, Roosevelt signed it into law.

Churchill described Lend-Lease as an "unsordid act," but behind the public gratitude many Britons, and Churchill himself at times, resented being cast in the role of beggar. They also perceived an attempt by the Americans to get a good deal while undermining the future economic strength of the British Empire.[27] For the moment, however, it bound the United States more closely to Britain. The period of biased neutrality was over. Germany and the United States now entered into the period of the undeclared war. Hitler responded by extending the war zone in the North Atlantic to include the coastal waters off Iceland. Roosevelt countered on April 4 by extending the Pan American Security Zone of 1939 to include Greenland. He then ignored Danish protests and ordered American troops to occupy the island. Hitler realized his action had only resulted in giving the United States an additional base from which to aid Britain, and that his attempt to intimidate Roosevelt had backfired. Preparations for invading Russia and the demands of the African war made it prudent to postpone any confrontation with the United States. Hitler publicly recognized the new American security zone on April 20.[28] Roosevelt increased economic pressure in early June by freezing all Axis assets in the United States and ordering all employees of the German government to leave the country. Tension rose on April 11 when a U-boat mistakenly torpedoed the American freighter *Robin Moor* well outside the war zone. Berlin worried about the repercussions, but neither Roosevelt nor the American public favored retaliation risking war. Roosevelt's reply was angry, but more moderate than expected.

The president was relieved when Hitler invaded the Soviet Union.

Britain was safe as long as the Wehrmacht was tied down in Russia. The attack strengthened anti-war feeling in the United States and led some to favor American mediation to bring peace between Britain and Germany. The Molotov-Ribbentrop Pact, the Soviet attack on Finland, and the neutrality agreement with Japan had disgusted many Americans. Soviet actions were compounded by the American Communist Party's condemnation of Britain more than Germany and its attempt to thwart American rearmament and prevent Lend-Lease aid to Britain.[29] Many who disliked Hitler found it difficult to sympathize with the Soviets and shared Missouri Senator Harry S. Truman's assessment that the world would be well-served if Germany and the Soviets destroyed each other. "If we see that Germany is winning we ought to help Russia, and if Russia is winning, we ought to help Germany, and that way let them kill as many as possible, although I don't want to see Hitler victorious under any circumstances. Neither of them think anything of their pledged word."[30] A more judicious assessment of the situation came from the George Kennan who was then assigned to the American embassy in Berlin. Kennan realized that the United States should extend material aid to the Soviets, but also cautioned the state department to avoid any moral support for the county that had aided Hitler and was now paying a somewhat deserved price for it.[31]

As late as August 5, a poll showed that only 38 percent of the American public favored Lend-Lease aid to the Soviet Union. Most Americans, however, did not want Hitler to win. Congress reluctantly gave Roosevelt permission to extend Lend-Lease to the Soviet Union in September. Roosevelt might have made his task easier by stressing the political and military reality and the self-interest of the United States. He instead tried to minimize the totalitarian nature of the Soviet government and to identify it with the moral and political values of Britain and the United States. His attempt brought him into conflict with American religious leaders and civil libertarians who resented Soviet atheism and the long record of religious and other persecution. The president was determined, however, to wrap the war in ideological garb by presenting a sharp moral contrast between the Allies and the Axis. Stalin was astute enough to appease domestic and foreign constituencies by downplaying communism and emphasizing his role as the national leader of a reforming Soviet Union where things would be far better and more liberal after victory.

Aid to the Soviet Union was accompanied by an even more dramatic act of belligerency against the Axis. The president met Churchill at Placentia Bay, Newfoundland, on August 9. Roosevelt wanted to issue a joint declaration of war aims that would clearly state the moral distinction between themselves and the Axis powers. Beyond that, as he told Sumner Welles, the war afforded Britain and America the opportunity to "bring order out of the resulting chaos and, in particular, to disarm all those powers who in his belief had been the primary cause of so many of the wars of the preceding century."[32]

Churchill and Roosevelt formulated the Atlantic Charter during the next two days. They renounced any territorial ambitions and promised no territorial changes without the "wishes of the peoples concerned." All peoples, the Charter stated, had the right to choose their form of government, and the day would come when economic and political rights were restored to those who had been "forcibly deprived of them."[33]

The Charter implied a partnership between Britain and the United States. Britain was at war, however, and the United States was not. Many Americans feared it would be if Roosevelt had his way. While Roosevelt and Churchill were meeting, the House of Representatives voted by only one vote to renew the Selective Service Act. The news brought a sobering shadow to Placentia Bay and hope to Berlin. The German press ridiculed the Charter and portrayed the Selective Service vote as a defeat for Roosevelt. Roosevelt warned Americans on Labor Day that they must help to conquer the "insane violence" Hitler had set loose. "I know," he said, "that I speak the conscience and determination of the American people when I say we shall do everything in our power to crush Hitler and his Nazi forces."[34] Three days later a U-boat fired torpedoes at the U.S. destroyer *Greer* off the coast of Iceland. The U-boat fired in legitimate self-defense when the *Greer* acted as a spotter for British planes.[35] Roosevelt, however, skirted the truth on April 11 by presenting the incident as an unprovoked attack on an American ship innocently carrying mail to Iceland. "The time for active defense," had come, Roosevelt said. Two days later the President pushed the United States into a de facto war with the order to "shoot on sight" all Axis ships encountered in the American neutrality zone.[36] In October Roosevelt moved to repeal the most important parts of the Neutrality Act. The House and Senate gave the President a narrow victory after a heated debate. It was somewhat anti-climactic in view of Roosevelt's shoot on sight orders, but Berlin believed it represented Roosevelt's desire for war in the near future.

Hitler could take some comfort in deteriorating relations between the United States and Japan. The Rape of Nanking and other Japanese atrocities in China had shocked many Americans. American anger flared again in December of 1937 when Japanese planes attacked the clearly marked U.S.S. *Panay* in daylight near Nanking. Tokyo quickly moved to defuse the issue by apologizing and promising restitution to the American government and the survivors of the slain sailors. The Japanese army also eliminated foreign businesses as they marched down the coast of China. The conquests in China were to be the beginning of the New Order in Asia under the Greater East Asia Co-Prosperity Sphere and the end of the American sponsored Open Door.[37]

Roosevelt had more support applying pressure against the Japanese than against the Germans. He increased economic sanctions against Tokyo in hopes of deterring further aggression and saving China. As the pressure increased, however, it threatened to provoke the kind of aggression it was meant to stop. Japan had to contemplate securing war materials by force in Southeast Asia if deprived of them by the United States. A Japanese move against British and Dutch possessions in Southeast Asia could bring war with the United States at a time when the Roosevelt administration viewed Germany as the primary threat.

The European war offered Tokyo an opportunity to increase its position in Asia. Britain and France wanted no trouble with Japan, and they offered little resistance to Japanese attempts to end the war in China. Britain was on the verge of defeat after the fall of France and the Netherlands. The United States was the only barrier to Japanese conquest of Asia after the non-aggression pact between Japan and the Soviet Union. Tokyo hoped the Tripartite Pact would intimidate the Americans with the prospect of a two-ocean war and force Roosevelt to adopt a more conciliatory policy. Japan prepared to strike south in the summer of 1941. Tokyo forced Vichy to form a joint protectorate of Indochina in July. Japan was now capable of air strikes against British and American bases in Southeast Asia. Roosevelt retaliated swiftly with an executive order freezing Japanese assets in the United States. He also strengthened American defenses in the Philippines with the new B-17 bomber and recalled General Douglas MacArthur to active duty as the commander of American forces.[38]

It was too late for deterrence in Tokyo. On September 6, an Imperial Conference approved continuing negotiations with Washington as well as preparations for war. It was obvious by the middle of October that the United States would not accept Japanese domination of Asia or give Japan the material needed to settle what was still euphemistically called the "China incident." Some also suspected that the Americans were stalling in order to prepare for war. The military wanted a clear decision for war by October 15, but the cautious Japanese Prime Minister Konoe could not bring himself to make it.[39]

War Minister Tojo Hideki called for Konoe's resignation on October 16. Emperor Hirohito surprised Tojo by asking him to head a new government. Tojo's appointment completed a process that had begun following World War I. The military had increasingly dominated the civilian government throughout the 1920s and 1930s, and now it officially controlled it. Tojo himself had risen to power within the government in the same way he had become commander of the Kwantung Army in Manchuria. He had impressed those around him even when they opposed him because of his keen intelligence, great disciple, and hard work. The emperor expected him to deliver Japan from its crisis with the United States, and he intended to do it.[40]

The Tojo government developed two sets of proposals to conceal the march to war. Proposal "A" called for withdrawal of all Japanese troops from China by 1966 in return for a restoration of American trade. Proposal "B" offered a temporary settlement that included a promise not to expand once the China incident was settled in exchange for an end to American aid to China and the restoration of normal trade.[41] An Imperial Conference on November 5 approved the plans along with a negotiating deadline of December 1. Tokyo sent the experienced diplomat, Kurusu Suburu, to Washington to lend credence to the effort. Neither he nor the Japanese ambassador, Admiral Nomura Kichisaburo, knew of the impending military strike.

The United States had already rejected Proposal "A" when Kurusu arrived in Washington. Submission of Proposal "B" was delayed until November 20 while Kurusu and Normura consulted with Tokyo. Secretary of State Hull was aided by American intelligence which had broken the Japanese diplomatic code and was now able through "Magic" to relay critical information before meetings with Kurusu and Nomura.[42] The Japanese prepared to attack the American fleet at Pearl Harbor while negotiations continued in Washington. They also planned to attack American, British, and Dutch possessions in Southeast Asia. The rhetoric in Tokyo demonstrated that the entire country supported the government. "In so far as Diet members speak at all," wrote the *New York Times,* "they are so belligerent that the government appears moderate by comparison."[43]

The Japanese had gone too far. They could not accept less than a free hand in China and the restoration of American trade. Capitulation would destroy the government and might bring assassination for its members. Washington was fully aware of the situation and anticipated the outbreak of hostilities at any moment. Roosevelt would have preferred to postpone any confrontation until Hitler was defeated in Europe. The American public also supported its government. A September poll showed that 67 percent of the public were ready to risk war to stop Japanese expansion.[44] Any appeasement of Japan certainly would have angered influential supporters of Chiang Kai-shek and most likely would have provoked a bitter and lengthy fight in Congress.

The Tojo government was in no mood for any delay lasting more than two weeks. On November 20, Kurusu and Nomura gave Hull a revised version of Plan "B" which still contained the crucial demands for a free hand in China and restoration of trade. Two days later Tokyo informed its envoys that "things are automatically going to happen" unless there was a settlement.[45] Hull knew that the November 20 proposals were Japan's last word and that "things" were going to happen soon. He handed Kurusu and Nomura a note restating the American position on November 26.[46] Tojo and the cabinet asked Emperor Hirohito to approve war with the United States on the afternoon of December 1. The emperor agreed, and instructions went out to Japanese units throughout the Pacific to begin offensive operations on December 8, Japanese time. A special message went out to Vice Admiral Nagumo Chuichi, commander of the strike force heading for Hawaii: "Climb Mount Niitaka, 1208" or, attack the American fleet at Pearl Harbor on December 8 as planned.[47]

The Japanese struck the American fleet on the morning of December 7 in Hawaii. The attack was as much a failure as it was unnecessary. The fleet at Pearl Harbor lacked the tankers and other support ships to stop any Japanese conquest of Southeast Asia. Even as late as December, 1941 it remained questionable whether the American public and Congress would have approved war with Japan as long as American personnel and possessions were not directly attacked. Pearl Harbor was a tactical failure as well. The battleships were grounded but not sunk. With the exception of the *Arizona* and the *Oklahoma,* all were repaired and returned to action, as were most smaller ships. Casualties were heavy, but far less than if the ships had been hit at sea. The three American aircraft carriers were gone, and most of the fuel storage depots were missed.[48]

The Japanese blunder was compounded by the clumsiness of the declaration of war. What was left of international law required the declaration to be delivered prior to hostilities, but there was no stipulation as to how long before. Tokyo intended the declaration to be delivered in Washington just prior to the attack in Hawaii. Japanese officials in Washington, however, delayed the transmission, and it was not delivered until after the attack had occurred and was known to the American government. Nothing could have inflamed and unified the American public more than a "sneak" attack on a Sunday while negotiations were being held in search of a peaceful settlement. Speculation persists about Roosevelt's knowledge of the attack on Pearl Harbor. As David Kahn wrote, "Code-breaking intelligence could not have prevented Pearl Harbor because Japan never sent any message to anybody saying anything like 'We shall attack Pearl Harbor.' The ambassadors in Washington were never told of the plan, nor were any other consular officials. The ships of the strike force never radioed any message mentioning Pearl Harbor."[49]

The president now had to decide whether to ask Congress for war against Germany as well as Japan. Anger against Japan and the desire for revenge threatened the entire Europe first strategy. On December 8 Roosevelt asked for a declaration of war only against Japan, but he made it clear that he considered Germany as guilty as Japan. There would not, he added, be a diversion of American forces to the Pacific.[50] Hitler learned of the Pearl Harbor attack while at his headquarters in East Prussia. At last the Japanese were on the move, and he now had an ally with a powerful navy to fight the Americans and the British. The United States, he believed, must concentrate on Japan for some time to come, regardless of what Roosevelt said. Hitler cannot be faulted too much for underestimating the recuperative and productive potential of the United States. Many Americans also doubted the ability of the United States to fight a two-ocean war on such a massive scale. Hitler still believed he could defeat the Soviet Union within a year and then be ready to throw his full weight against the Anglo-Americans.[51]

Hitler went before the Reichstag to declare war on the United States on December 11. Roosevelt, he said, had provoked Germany into war in order to hide the failure of the New Deal. Germany would now join with Italy and Japan against the United States.[52] Hitler's decision to make war against the United States ranks as a blunder equal to that of his attack on Russia. As with the Russian campaign, however, the immediate results seemed to justify his action. For the first time Germany had an ally whose military prowess equaled that of the Wehrmacht.

Pearl Harbor began a spectacular Japanese advance against American, British, and Dutch possessions in Southeast Asia. Whatever doubts remained about air power were swept away within a week. On December

8, a Japanese strike force caught the Americans by surprise in the Philippines and destroyed most of their planes on the ground. On the tenth, two great British capital ships, H.M.S *Prince of Wales* and H.M.S. *Repulse,* became the first to be sunk at sea by air bombardment. Conquest at sea was accompanied by conquest on land. The Japanese took their first American possession on December 10 when Guam fell after a brief fight, while on the same day they landed forces in the Philippines. Throughout the month and into the new year they advanced against ill-equipped enemies who had no hope of victory and little of surviving. By February of 1942, Japanese forces had moved down the Malay peninsula to converge on the "impregnable" fortress of Singapore. The defenses at Singapore, however, had been designed for attack from the sea and were of little value. On February 15, the Gibraltar of the East, the very symbol of the British Empire in Asia, became what Churchill described as "the worst disaster and largest capitulation in British history."[53] The symbol of American power in Asia also fell. The Americans and their Filipino supporters on Luzon had been driven to defensive positions on the Bataan peninsula and the island fortress of Corregidor by February. Roosevelt symbolically abandoned the defenders when he ordered General MacArthur to Australia to direct its defense and then to command a counterattack. It was obvious that the defenders would soon be worn down by disease and starvation when MacArthur left on March 12. They managed to hold out for nearly two months until the inevitable end came on May 6.[54]

The Japanese acquired an aura of invincibility in Asia similar to that of the Germans in Europe in the five months after Pearl Harbor. As with the Germans, however, they attempted to fight on too many fronts at the same time. By dispersing their forces the Japanese were never able to achieve total victory in any one theater. The Japanese advance was stopped by the Battle of the Coral Sea in May and the Battle of Midway in June, 1942. The Coral Sea was more of a draw than a victory, but it represented an important strategic victory for the Americans by stopping the rapid Japanese advance toward Australia. At Midway the overconfident Japanese suffered a major setback from which they never fully recovered. They lost four fleet carriers along with their planes and trained crews. Japanese dominance in other capital ships counted for little, since they could now be protected only by the limited range of land-based planes.[55] By the end of the year, the tide had already begun to turn as American industry produced ships and planes in a marvel of productivity undreamed of even by optimists in Washington.

NOTES

1. *Nazi-Soviet Relations,* 349-353.
2. *TMWC,* vol. 16, 396.
3. Winston S. Churchill, *The Grand Alliance* (Boston: Houghton Mifflin Company, 1950), 370. Churchill, *Speeches,* vol. 6, 6224.
4. *New York Times,* June 24, 1941, 1, 7.
5. Ibid., June 23, 1941, 10.
6. Maisky, *Memoirs,* 157.
7. Dmitri Volkogonov, *Stalin: Triumph and Tragedy,* trans. Harold Shukman (Rocklin, CA: Prima Publishing, 1992), 407-408.
8. Glantz and House, *When Titans Clashed,* 51-53.
9. Ulam, *Stalin,* 539-541.
10. *Times* (London), July 4, 1941, 5.
11. Halder, *Kriegstagebuch,* vol. 2, 38. TMWC, vol. 34, 298-299.
12. Bell, *Origins of the Second World War,* 286. Bullock, *Parallel Lives,* 745.
13. Bullock, *Parallel Lives,* 732. Halder, *Kriegstagebuch,* vol. 3, 192-193. Glantz and House, *When Titans Clashed,* 74-76.
14. Weinberg, *Germany, Hitler, and World War II,* 297.
15. *Times* (London), October 4, 1941, 3. October 10, 1941, 4.
16. Glantz and House, *When Titans Clashed,* 91.
17. Rich, *Hitler's War Aims,* vol. 1, 238-239. Weinberg, *World At Arms,* 238-239.
18. Dallek, *Roosevelt and American Foreign Policy,* 200-205.
19. Waldo Heinrichs, *Threshold of War: Franklin D. Roosevelt and American Entry into World War II* (New York: Oxford University Press, 1988), 9.
20. *Roosevelt and Churchill: Their Secret Wartime Correspondence,* ed. Francis L. Loewenheim et al. (New York: Saturday Review Press, 1975), 107-108. Charmley, *Churchill,* 438-439.
21. David Reynolds, *The Creation of the Anglo-American Alliance, 1937-1941: A Study in Competitive Co-operation* (Chapel Hill: University of North Carolina Press, 1982), 131.
22. *Roosevelt-Churchill Correspondence,* 122-126.
23. *New York Times,* December 30, 1940, 1, 6.
24. Ibid., January 7, 1941, 1,3.
25. *Congressional Record,* 77th, Congress, 1st Session, vol. 87, Pt. 1, 121.

26. Ibid., Pt. 2, 1588.
27. Churchill, *Their Finest Hour,* 569. Charmley, Churchill, 438.
28. Rich, *Hitler's War Aims,* vol. 1, 243-244. Friedlander, *Prelude to Downfall,* pp. 205-207.
29. Harvey Klehr, *The Heyday of American Communism: The Depression Decade* (New York: Basic Books, 1984), 386-416.
30. *New York Times,* June 24, 1941, 7. David McCullough, Truman (New York: Simon and Schuster, 1992), 262.
31. George F. Kennan, *Memoirs, 1925-1950* (Boston: Little, Brown and Company, 1967), 133.
32. Sumner Welles, *Seven Decisions That Shaped History* (New York: Harper and Brothers, 1951), 177-178.
33. Robin Edmonds, *The Big Three: Churchill, Roosevelt and Stalin in Peace and War* (New York: W.W. Norton, 1991), 223-224.
34. *New York Times,* September 2, 1941, 1, 12.
35. Dallek, *Roosevelt and American Foreign Policy,* 287-288. Heinrichs, *Threshold of War,* 166.
36. *New York Times*, September 12, 1941, 1.
37. Iriye, *Origins of Second World War in the Pacific,* pp. 48-50. Ronald Spector, *The Eagle Against Sun* (New York: The Free Press, 1985), 62-65.
38. Ibid., 68-69. Weinberg, *World at Arms,* 254-255.
39. Robert J.C. Butow, *Tojo and the Coming of the War* (Princeton: Princeton University Press, 1961), 256-259.
40. Ibid., 279-314.
41. Iriye, *Origins of the Second World War in the Pacific,* 161-163.
42. Ibid., 321-327. Gordon W. Prange, *At Dawn We Slept: The Untold Story of Pearl Harbor* (New York: McGraw-Hill, 1981), 118-120.
43. *New York Times,* November 19, 1941, 10.
44. Dallek, *Roosevelt and American Foreign Policy,* 302.
45. John Toland, *The Rising Sun: The Decline and Fall of the Japanese Empire, 1936-1945* (New York: Random House, 1970), 139.
46. *FRUS: 1941* vol. 4, 662-664.
47. Butow, *Tojo and the Coming of the War,* 337-370.
48. Weinberg, *World at Arms,* 261-262. John Mueller, "Pearl Harbor: Military Inconvenience, Political Disaster," *International Security,* vol. 17, no. 3, 172-203.
49. David Kahn, "Why Weren't We Warned?" *MHQ: The Quarterly Journal of Military History,* vol. 5, no. 1 (Autumn, 1991), 59.

50. *New York Times,* December 10, 1941, 1,4.
51. Rich, *Hitler's War Aims,* vol. 1, 245-246. Weinberg, World at Arms, 262.
52. *New York Times,* December 12, 1941, 1, 4.
53. Winston S. Churchill, *The Hinge of Fate* (Boston: Houghton-Mifflin, 1950), 92.
54. Spector, *Eagle Against the Sun,* 109-119.
55. Ibid., 346-352.

CHAPTER ELEVEN

The End of the Beginning

The United States discarded the caution and limited aid of Lend-Lease upon entering the war. Britain and the Soviet Union were now members of the Grand Alliance against the Axis enemy, although the Soviets remained at peace with Japan. Japan's role in the Axis became more tenuous after Pearl Harbor. The appearance of unity continued with the usual congratulatory telegrams and public posturing, but Germany and Japan pursued their separate course. Tokyo realized that any confrontation with the Soviets would weaken the effort against the West and might provoke Stalin into giving the Americans bases from which to bomb Japan. The Japanese Navy did nothing to hamper the flow of valuable American goods to Russia across the Pacific, despite the gnashing of teeth in Berlin.[1]

Strains and suspicions also plagued relations between the Soviet Union and its Western allies. Presidential Assistant Harry Hopkins found a weary Stalin when he went to Moscow in July of 1941. Stalin was obviously glad to see Hopkins and went out of his way to be cordial. Russia needed American aid and was willing to make concessions to get it. Stalin was willing to have Russian pilots trained in the United States. Should the United States enter the war, Hopkins reported, Stalin "would welcome American troops on any part of the Russian front under the command of the American army." Such generosity faded quickly and disappeared by the following year. Stalin would not think of having foreign troops within miles of the front once survival and victory were sure, while those Russians who formed close relations with westerners during the war paid dearly for it.²

Stalin was never desperate enough to give up the Baltic States and eastern Poland. The Poles, however, wanted their lost land returned at the end of the war. General Wladyslaw Sikorski, who had led the Polish government in exile since September 30, 1939, broadcast a hopeful message to his beleaguered compatriots on June 23, 1941. The general hoped that the German attack on the Soviet Union offered hope for a free Poland to emerge from the war. Anthony Eden, who had become Churchill's foreign secretary in December of 1940, restated Britain's pledge for an independent Poland before Parliament the following day.³ The British had understandably identified the Polish cause with their own, and now they equated victory with the return of Polish independence.

Churchill realized, however, that the necessity of war had placed him in a quandary with no solution. To seek the re-establishment of prewar Poland would jeopardize the alliance with the Soviet Union, and Germany could not be defeated without the Soviets. When negotiations between Sikorski and Soviet ambassador Maisky began on July 5, the Soviets made it clear that they would not return to the 1939 boundaries. Churchill believed that defeating Hitler took priority. "There was no way out," he later recalled. The future of Poland would have to wait for "easier times" and the generosity of the Soviet Union. The Soviets conceded a general statement that their agreement with Hitler had "lost its validity," but there were no promises involving future boundaries, and Eden told Parliament that Britain had made no commitment to guarantee any frontiers.⁴

Eden arrived in Moscow in mid-December and quickly learned that Stalin would settle for nothing less than the Curzon Line as the boundary between Russia and Poland. He also demanded the incorporation of the Baltic States into the Soviet Union and the 1941 boundary with Finland. Stalin remained cordial at their first meeting, but he turned ugly at the second. Eden informed him that Britain could not agree to the 1941 boundaries without consulting the Poles, the British Dominions, and the Americans. Stalin replied petulantly, "It now looks as if the [Atlantic] Charter was directed at the U.S.S.R."⁵

Desperation failed to preclude gall. The Soviet Union and its Comintern parties had been a de facto ally of Hitler for nearly two years, and they had done much to aid his earlier victories. Those who had denounced Britain for continuing its "imperialist" war, and had tried to prevent American rearmament now demanded shipments of war material with no concern for the needs of others. They also chanted "Second Front

Now," while ignoring the time needed to gather men and materials for an invasion of France.

Stalin and the Allies realized, however, that they must cooperate as long as the common enemy remained. In July, London and Moscow asked Reza Shah Pahlavi of Iran to allow war material to be sent to Russia through his country. The Shah believed he would invite retaliation from Hitler in doing so, and he favored Germany over the two countries that had divided his country into spheres of influence prior to World War I. On August 25, Russian forces invaded from the north while British troops moved from the south and the west. Resistance was feeble, and once again the country was divided into British and Russian spheres. Rezha Shah Pahlavi abdicated in favor of his more cooperative son Mohammed Reza Pahlavi to maintain the appearance of legality. The occupation of Iran was an unqualified success for the war effort. It also contradicted the spirit of the Atlantic Charter and served as a sobering reminder that the needs of great powers took precedent over the rights of lesser ones.[6]

The war effort prompted Churchill to visit Washington on December 22. The prime minister welcomed the Americans into the war, but was worried that the Pacific theater would divert aid from Europe. Churchill was relieved when Roosevelt and Army Chief of Staff General George C. Marshall reaffirmed their commitment to Europe. Roosevelt ran into trouble when he tried to turn this Arcadia Conference into a broader political crusade. The president presented a declaration calling for the independence of all nations following the war. Roosevelt found, like Wilson before him, that Britons bristled when lofty goals of independence were applied to their empire.

The president also had some trouble with the new Soviet ambassador Maxim Litvinov. Litvinov had remained in political limbo following his dismissal in May of 1939. He was an ideal choice to represent the Soviet Union in Washington. Litvinov objected to a phrase in the Charter calling for freedom of religion. Roosevelt believed the phrase was needed to improve the Soviet image among Americans. He later boasted that he had persuaded Litvinov to accept it, but most likely Stalin made the decision. It was in keeping with Soviet requirements for the present and could always be jettisoned in the future.

The Declaration of the United Nations was published on January 1, 1942. Representatives from twenty-two nations assembled at the State Department the next day to join with the United States, Great Britain, the Soviet Union, and China. The solemn occasion was somewhat marred when delegates claiming to represent various "free" governments of the Baltic States, France, and other occupied areas also asked to sign. That would open the door to any fringe organization seeking some diplomatic recognition and embarrass some of the great powers. Britain and the Soviet Union objected sufficiently to prevent it.[7]

Secretary Hull hoped the Declaration would "bind all nations fighting the Axis to the acceptance of certain principles."[8] Common principles, he believed, would prevent the kind of secret treaties which had proved so debilitating and embarrassing to Wilson at Paris. The victors could then make their final settlement at the end of the war on the basis of accepted principles. The secretary and Roosevelt appear to be more naive than they actually were. The road to Washington was not the road to Damascus, and no conversions were made. Stalin did not intend to dismantle Communism at home and reduce the Russian Empire, nor did Churchill intend to liquidate the British Empire. Hull viewed the Declaration as an "inspiring link" in the war effort. In January of 1942 inspiration was badly needed.[9] News of the Declaration took second billing to the fall of Manila and the resigned loss of the Philippines to come. Further bad news from Asia and Africa threatened to paralyze the will of the Allied nations and break whatever spirit of unity they had mustered.

Churchill returned to Britain in January to encounter a smoldering, "unhappy, embarrassed, baffled public opinion." Parliament was not yet close to condemning him as it had Chamberlain after Norway, but there were rumors that he would fall along with Singapore. The prime minister asked for a vote of confidence on January 27. Debate lasted for three days against the background of calamity at Singapore and further defeats in Africa. Churchill won an overwhelming vote by meeting the opposition head on with the grim fact that there was no one to replace him in such a grave hour.[10]

Roosevelt was equally hard pressed to do something about falling morale. Americans found it difficult to accept a Europe first strategy when the Japanese were seizing American territory and killing their soldiers. A February poll showed that over 60 percent favored an all-out war in Asia at the expense of Britain and the Soviet Union. Roosevelt tried to revive morale with a fireside chat to commemorate George Washington's heroic struggle for independence. His effort was aided somewhat by MacArthur's escape from the Philippines and his "I came through, and I shall return" statement, but the country needed more than stirring words.

On April 18, a group of B-25s led by Lieutenant Colonel James A.

Chapter 11

Doolittle took off from the carrier *Hornet*, seven hundred miles from Japan. The planes hit Tokyo, Kobe, Yokohama, Nagoya, and Yokosuka before heading to China. The raid was hardly a military pinprick, but psychologically it gave the Americans a hero and victory they so needed, while sending a chill through those Japanese who had thought their islands were invincible to attack.[11]

The Allies faced the major task of holding long enough to mount a counteroffensive in the future. This was especially true for the Soviet Union. The Soviets were bearing the brunt of the fighting, and they continued to remind their allies of it. If they collapsed or signed a separate peace, Hitler would be free to consolidate his empire and dominate Europe for years to come. London and Washington also remembered Brest Litovsk as well as the Ribbentrop-Molotov pact. Allied fears increased on February 23, 1942, when Stalin's Order of the Day seemed to hint at a possible deal by stressing no hatred for the German people along with a desire to only liberate Soviet territory. Churchill was so worried that he advised Roosevelt to grant Stalin his 1941 boundaries. "The Atlantic Charter ought not to be construed so as to deny Russia the frontiers she occupied when Germany attacked her. . . . I hope therefore that you will be able to give us a free hand to sign the treaty which Stalin desires as soon as possible."[12]

Roosevelt refused, lest he violate the Atlantic Charter and offend many Americans of Baltic and Polish descent. He did not believe Stalin would leave the war over the frontier issue. He explained his position to Litvinov and promised American support for Soviet security needs following the war. A brutal reality lay behind talk about the Atlantic Charter or American opinion. There was little the Americans or British could do about eastern Europe. Lord Halifax, who now served Churchill as the British ambassador in Washington, reported as much after visiting Roosevelt on March 9. Roosevelt recognized Stalin's need for security, but it was "impossible to put anything on paper now. . . . The future of the Baltic States depended on Russian military progress; if during or after the war Russia reoccupied the Baltic States neither the United States nor Great Britain could turn her out."[13]

Roosevelt believed, however, that Stalin trusted him more than Churchill, and that he could persuade Stalin to be more cooperative by demonstrating his own good intentions. Nothing would be better received in Moscow than the promise of a second front. On April 1, Secretary Stimson and General Marshall gave Roosevelt a plan for an assault on western Europe in April of 1943. If, however, the Soviets were in immediate danger of collapsing or German strength in the west was measurably weakened, then there would be an invasion in the fall of 1942. The president was delighted with the plan and more optimistic about it than he ought to have been. The United States did not have the resources for such an invasion at a time when it was fighting a global war.

Roosevelt sent Hopkins and Marshall to London in mid-April to consult with the British. The meeting may have gone too well for everyone's good. Marshall presented his plan mostly to strangers who felt inhibited in speaking their true feelings. General Sir Hastings Ismay later regretted that he and the others had not "come clean" about their opposition to the plan. They instead concealed their objections by carping at various details. The British were opposed to any cross-Channel invasion while their forces were tied down in Africa. Marshall was fighting the ghosts of Dunkirk as well as the Somme. The British feared any venture that might produce the casualties suffered in the First World War or the humiliation suffered in 1940. Churchill and his advisors were vague enough to prevent Americans from abandoning Europe in favor of the Pacific. They hoped the Americans would soon realize that any cross-channel attack was impractical for some time to come.[14]

Marshall, however, returned to Washington believing the British agreed with him, except for questions on details. His belief was strengthened by Churchill's letter to Roosevelt on April 17. Churchill seemed enthusiastic, but hedged.[15] Roosevelt was impressed more by the enthusiasm, and thought the time was right to discuss it with the Russians. He invited Molotov and a leading Soviet general to Washington for "a very important military proposal involving utilization of our armed forces in a manner to relieve your critical Western Front."[16]

Molotov stopped in London on May 20 to continue negotiations on an Anglo-Soviet alliance treaty and to press for a second front in Europe. Churchill gave nothing more than the promise of a cross-channel attack sometime in the future. He pointed out that Hitler had not been able to invade Britain in the summer of 1940 with overwhelming military superiority. Churchill saw no chance of an attack in 1942, given the current strain on American and British resources in Africa and Asia. Molotov appeared to accept the argument. He also accepted the British position on eastern Europe when Eden proposed a general Anglo-Soviet treaty of alliance for twenty years that made no mention of boundaries.[17]

Molotov traveled to Washington for talks with Roosevelt from May 29 to June 1. The visit went as well as possible, considering the pressures of the time, the language difference, and the great personality difference between the affable president and the slab-faced commissar. Roosevelt was pleased by the Soviet flexibility on the border issue, and he assured Molotov that Soviet security needs could be met by other ways through a new international body dominated by the four "policemen" of the United States, Britain, Russia, and China. Speculation about Soviet security following the war was secondary to surviving the war itself, and Molotov continued to press the president for a military action in 1942. Roosevelt's desire to cheer the Soviets caused him to promise more than the United States could deliver. Despite Marshall's objection to setting any date, Roosevelt approved a joint communiqué stating that "full understanding was reached with regard to the urgent task of creating a second front in Europe in 1942."[18]

When Molotov stopped in London for a second visit with Churchill, however, he found the British irritated about being asked to sign a joint communiqué without being consulted beforehand. Churchill went along for the sake of unity and the hope of deceiving the Germans. He did not want to deceive the Russians as well, and he would not approve an assault on western Europe until certain conditions guaranteed success. Churchill clarified the British position in a private aide memoir recounting the difficulties of a cross-channel attack and the damage to be suffered if it failed. *"We can,"* he stressed, *"therefore give no promise in this matter."*

Molotov praised the Anglo-Soviet treaty and expressed confidence in the impending Anglo-American attack on western Europe, despite Churchill's note. "Let us hope," Molotov said after his return to Moscow, "that our common enemy will soon experience to his cost the results of the ever growing military cooperation of the three great powers." The commissar wanted to pressure his allies as much as he wanted to bolster Russian morale. In early July Stalin acknowledged the difference between "wanting" and "having" a second front in Europe in 1942 to the American ambassador William Standley. Later in the month, Molotov told the British ambassador, Archibald Clark Kerr, that the second front was more foreseen than forecast. The Soviets, Molotov admitted years later, were well aware that Britain and the United States were incapable of launching a cross-channel attack in 1942. By securing its promise in writing, they had won a commitment well-suited for diplomatic leverage and propaganada in the future.[19]

This reality was sad comfort when Churchill came to Moscow in August to tell the Russians that there would be no invasion of Europe in

1942. There would be a landing in Africa instead. Rommel's drive to Egypt had stalled for lack of supplies and stubborn British resistance. In December 1941, British forces under General Claude Auchinleck, drove the Germans westward. Rommel kept his armor intact, and by May of 1942 he was again heading for Suez. His success this time included the capture of the fortress at Tobruk, which had become the symbol of British resistance and strength.[20]

The fall of Tobruk was a heavy blow for Churchill, but it helped him to alter the course of the war in his own favor. He received the news on the evening of June 20, while talking with Roosevelt at the White House. Roosevelt immediately offered assistance. Churchill was grateful, and asked the president for new Sherman tanks. He got them, and in some cases, at the expense of American units. Churchill reviewed American troops before leaving for home. He and his advisors realized how long it would be before these soldiers would be ready to fight the German army. But time was running out for Britain. There had been nothing but disasters for the past few months. Churchill would again face a motion of censure when he returned home. He and his country needed a victory, and the only prospect lay in Africa.[21]

Churchill easily defeated his critics in Parliament. A more difficult struggle came with the Americans. Marshall remained set on a cross-channel invasion, despite Roosevelt's wavering. Marshall showed his resolve by sending General Dwight Eisenhower to London on June 23, as commanding general of the United States Forces, European Theatre. Eisenhower's mission was to prepare for a cross-channel attack. If that were not approved, Marshall believed, the United States should switch to a Pacific-first strategy. Roosevelt, however, rejected any abandonment of Europe first, however popular it might be with the American public and Douglas MacArthur. Marshall knew he had little chance of winning when he traveled to London with Hopkins on July 16. The Americans were divided and the British still held firm. On the twenty-second, on what Eisenhower labeled perhaps the "blackest day in history," Marshall consented to an invasion of North Africa, later christened Torch and commanded by Eisenhower.[22]

Churchill now had to placate Stalin. He knew it would be an unpleasant meeting and was glad to have W. Averell Harriman, Roosevelt's advisor on Lend-Lease, along as a symbol of Anglo-American unity. They met Stalin at the Kremlin on the evening of August 12. The first part of the conversation consisted of a somber review of the Russian military situation.

The mood threatened to turn ugly when Churchill let it be known there would be no Anglo-American landing in France. Stalin angrily suggested that the British were afraid of the Germans and were trying to escape the natural price of war. Churchill countered that war was not blind folly, and he reminded Stalin that Hitler had not dared to cross the channel in the summer of 1940.

There was an "oppressive" silence after Churchill presented his case. Stalin replied that he was not entitled to demand an attack on France, but he still rejected Churchill's arguments. The atmosphere improved somewhat when Churchill promised increased bombing of Germany, which the Russians considered to be a poor substitute for an invasion of France. Churchill then drew his picture of a crocodile to illustrate the importance of Torch. The Anglo-Americans would attack the soft underbelly of the enemy before hitting him on the snout in 1943. For the moment Stalin acknowledged the strategic importance of the move and caused a stir in heaven by asking God to "prosper" the attempt. Churchill and Harriman thought the worst was over, but the following night Stalin again called for a landing in France and accused the British of cowardice. Churchill replied that he had not come several thousand miles to hear accusations and insults and reminded Stalin that Britain had fought Germany alone for nearly two years. Prudence dictated that he not ask Stalin what he had been doing during the same period. Stalin mellowed when Churchill threatened to curtail his trip. Relations improved to the point of friendship until Churchill left on the sixteenth, but both leaders were aware that hard times and angry encounters lay ahead.[23]

After stopping in Cairo and Gibraltar, Churchill returned to Britain with an optimistic view of the future. The situation in Africa was improving and he had been successful with the Americans and Russians. The island fortress of Malta was being reinforced and would soon be ready again for action against the Germans. With each passing day more supplies began to arrive in Egypt from the United States, including those Sherman tanks Roosevelt had promised. Churchill found the generals he had been looking for in August. General Harold Alexander became commander of British forces in the Middle East, while General Bernard Montgomery took command of the Eighth Army guarding Egypt. Rommel made another attempt to break British resistance on August 31. The British were ready, and for nearly four days the battle of Alam el Halfa saw furious fighting in the narrow strip of land between the Mediterranean and the impassable area of the Quattara Depression. The Africa Corps came close to victory, but the British line held.

A deceptive lull descended over the North Africa Front for the next six weeks. Rommel returned to Germany on sick leave, leaving behind a battered and weary army. British air power from Malta repeatedly hit German depots and ships carrying badly needed supplies from Europe. Alexander and Montgomery methodically assembled quantities of men and materials for the coming campaign, while resisting Churchill's prodding for an attack until success was assured. On the night of October 23, British artillery began the battle of El Alamein with a massive artillery barrage. The Germans were surprised and without their commander. They and their Italian allies fought well against a force twice as large. Rommel returned to his command late on the twenty-fifth at Hitler's request. His men were barely holding, and any attempt to maintain the position would fail. Rommel asked for permission to retreat when the British broke through on November 2, but Hitler ordered "victory or death." Two days later Rommel ordered a retreat on his own, and on the fifth Hitler reluctantly agreed. The retreat continued for the next two weeks, with most of the Africa Corps and Italian soldiers being killed, captured, or wounded.

Rommel learned that he had an enemy behind him as well on November 8. The planning and execution of Operation Torch revealed the complexities and difficulties of an amphibious invasion. It also revealed the inexperience of the men who carried it out. Torch took place less than three months after American troops had landed in the Solomon Islands in the South Pacific. The invasion of North Africa remains unique in the great distances involved. Over five hundred ships had sailed from ports in America and Britain toward their objectives in Casablanca, Algiers, and Tangiers. They carried an attacking force dangerously inexperienced and small for its assignment.[24] The United States had been at war for only eleven months. It had to supply Britain and the Soviet Union, sometimes at the expense of its own forces. It faced the enormous task of raising an army of millions, equipping it, training it, and transporting it to theaters thousands of miles apart.

The key to success lay with the French. North Africa was controlled by Vichy officials who had little sympathy for de Gaulle and his Free French, and even less for the British. French leaders knew that the slightest collaboration with the Allies would prompt Hitler to occupy all of mainland France. American representatives had contacted leading French officials in hopes of convincing them to change sides. Their primary target was Admiral Jean Darlan, commander of all French forces. Darlan had remained loyal to Vichy since May of 1940, but he had begun to waver as the balance of war shifted slightly from Hitler to the Allies. Darlan was intensely conservative, if not a fascist, but he wanted to be on the winning side. Early in the year he had let it be known that he would join the Americans if they landed half a million men. Neither he nor others believed an attack was imminent. They were angry and surprised when it came.

Eisenhower had hoped an appeal from the anti-Vichy hero, General Henri Giraud, would bring the French over to his cause. It did not. The French opened fire on land and sea at Algiers, Casablanca, and Oran. At his command post on Gibraltar, Eisenhower had to deal with the reality that his force was too small to defeat the Vichy forces and occupy French North Africa. He also realized only Darlan had the authority to end French resistance. The problem of Darlan became critical when Eisenhower received word that the Germans were sending troops into Tunisia. Eisenhower sent General Mark Clark to Algiers for a meeting with Darlan on the ninth. Clark found the admiral angry about the invasion and adamant against issuing orders without Pétain's approval. He was finally convinced to order a cease fire in Casablanca and Oran in Algeria, but he refused to ask the French troops in Tunisia to resist the Germans. Darlan found the pretext he had been looking for when news arrived that German and Italian troops were occupying the remainder of France. He released himself from all obligations to Vichy and joined the Anglo-American camp.[25]

Eisenhower wanted to push on to Tunisia before the Germans secured it. He flew to Algeria to meet Darlan on the thirteenth. He made Darlan the High Commissioner for North Africa with Giraud as second in command. News of the "Darlan deal" created an uproar in Britain and the United States and was especially resented by de Gaulle's Free French. Making such a deal with a "fascist" collaborator seemed to refute the entire moral purpose of the war and to betray those who had supported the Allied cause. It also raised the question of whether similar deals would be made with Germany and Italy.

Churchill and Roosevelt were surprised by reactions to the Darlan Deal. They too bore responsibility for the mess. Eisenhower had not been prepared for the complexities of French politics nor had he been given enough troops to accomplish his mission alone. Churchill and Roosevelt justified the deal on the grounds of military necessity and emphasized its temporary nature. There would be no permanent settlement in France or

North Africa without the consent of the French people. It was permissible, Roosevelt remarked, "to walk with the devil until you have crossed the bridge." Stalin agreed. On November 24, Churchill assured Stalin "not to be disturbed about the rogue Darlan," and explained the advantages of the successful North African landing. With his own past blemished by deals with rogues, Stalin was in no position to be self-righteous. "As for Darlan," he replied, "I think the Americans have made skillful use of him to facilitate the occupation of North and West Africa. Military diplomacy should know how to use for war aims not only the Darlans, but even the devil and his grandmother."[26]

Torch was a qualified success and an example of how chance can influence war. Different decisions by French leaders could have turned it into an Allied disaster. With nearly 120,000 troops in North Africa the French might have stopped the Allied attack for some time. Franco had 150,000 troops in Spanish Morocco and more on the mainland. Had the French resisted with German support, Franco, who feared an Allied invasion of Spanish territory, might well have joined the Axis.[27] Eisenhower and the British were aware of these possibilities, and one suspects that the soldiers on the beach found it easier to live with the deal than to have died without it. The Darlan Deal brought limited success and saved casualties at the cost of a moral and political compromise that influenced American and British desires for unconditional surrender in the future.

The Darlan deal failed to take Tunisia and secure control of the French fleet anchored in Toulon. Hitler poured over a quarter of a million men into Tunisia to stop the Allied advance from the west and to strengthen Rommel's thin and weary Africa Corps. The fleet in Toulon refused to join Darlan in North Africa. Hitler had feared that someday it might. He ordered German troops to attack Toulon and seize the fleet on November 25. When the attack began two days later, however, the French resisted long enough to scuttle their ships and deny them to the Axis as well as to the Allies. Allied and Axis actions together brought an end to what remained of Vichy's prestige. Although the government remained, the future of France now lay with the new rivals, Darlan, de Gaulle, and Giraud.

For a time it appeared as though Eisenhower's preoccupation with political problems might endanger his military success. The Germans had reinforced their defenses in Tunisia by the middle of November and were launching bombing raids on Allied targets. On the twenty-fifth, Allied armies under the command of British General Kenneth Anderson attacked toward Tunis. The Germans had the advantage of superior armor, firepower, and air cover. After three days the drive was halted fifteen miles from the city. Fighting continued for the next few weeks with neither side being able to break through. Hitler used the standoff to bolster Rommel's forces with a new Fifth Panzer Army under the command of General Hans-Jürgen von Arnim. Hitler feared the loss of North Africa might topple Mussolini and take Italy out of the war. Arnim's mission was to hold Tunisia and use it as a springboard for driving the Americans out of North Africa.

It had become obvious by December that the North African war would continue into 1943. The delay was at least accompanied by an improvement in the political situation. On December 24, an unhappy French royalist assassinated Darlan. The motive for the murder was unclear. Giraud and everyone else thought it should remain that way. The assassin was executed two days later and all records of the case destroyed. The struggle for French power was reduced to a duel between de Gaulle and Giraud and the Allies were rid of an embarrassment.[28]

There was little military action until February of 1943. The Allies used the time far better than the Axis. In the year since Pearl Harbor, American industry had converted to wartime production and was able to more adequately supply its armies and its Allies. The Germans still had better soldiers. Rommel routed the Americans at the Kasserine Pass in early February of 1943. Eisenhower was humiliated by the American performance. He responded by sacking several commanders and appointing General George Patton to command the American armies. Patton turned an undisciplined and inadequately trained group of men into a formidable army within a short time.[29]

Arnim and Rommel knew that time was running out. Montgomery continued to advance from the east and Patton from the west. Supplies were insufficient and the enemy seemed to know their plans in advance. They suspected the Italians of treason, whereas in fact, Ultra enabled the Allies to anticipate coming attacks and turn them into Axis defeats. Rommel had had enough by early March and left Africa for good on sick leave. The Africa Corps had been reduced to a group of hungry, weary men whose goal was merely to prolong defeat. The Allies were exhilarated by the prospect of victory after so many defeats. One more thrust and they could drive the Axis out of Africa and dominate the Mediterranean from Gibraltar to Suez. By early May the Axis perimeter had been reduced to an area around Bizerte and Tunis. Both cities fell on May 7. Two days later Luftwaffe units abandoned their airfields. Arnim and a quarter of a million soldiers had surrendered by May 13, when Alexander reported to Churchill, "All enemy resistance has ceased. We are masters of the North African shores."[30] Churchill believed the victory at El Alamein and the liberation of the North Africa "held its own" with the Russian victory at Stalingrad as a turning point in the war. The Battle of Egypt, he said on November 10, 1942, did not mark "the end" of conflict. "It is not," he continued, "even the beginning of the end. But it is, perhaps, the end of the beginning."[31]

Churchill had cause to be cautious as well as hopeful when he spoke, for the outcome at Stalingrad was very much in doubt. In early 1942 Hitler decided to strike toward the Caspian Sea to secure the oil and other resources that he and Stalin needed to continue the war, and also to close the Allied supply route to the Red Army. Hitler prepared for the offensive by increasing German forces and coercing his allies into paying the bill of conquest. Italian, Hungarian, Romanian, Slovakian, and Spanish soldiers were added to form an army as large as the one that had begun Barbarossa. Its quality, however, had been reduced by including soldiers who had neither the training nor the will for the long fight ahead.

On April 5, Hitler issued directive number 41 to end the war in Russia.[32] Leningrad was to be captured and a common front formed with the Finns. He ordered an offensive in the south that would unfold in four stages to secure the Crimea and then press on to the Caucasus and the Caspian Sea. The opening stage began on May 8 when the Eleventh Army cleared the eastern Crimea and encircled Sevastopol. The defenders had been under siege for months and had fought valiantly. They were running low on ammunition by the middle of June but fought on until July 2.[33]

As Sevastopol was falling, Hitler launched Operation Blue on June 28. The Sixth Army under General Frederick von Paulus crossed the Don River toward Stalingrad on the Volga. By the middle of July the offensive had brought victories rivaling those of Barbarossa, leading Hitler to again believe that one last thrust would end the Russian war. The way would then be open for drive to meet the Africa Corps in the Middle East, and an eventual meeting with the Japanese in the Persian Gulf.

On July 13, Hitler ordered another army to strike toward the Caucasus Mountains and the Caspian Sea.[34] The Germans moved toward the precious Maikop oil fields following the capture of Rostov on July 27. On August 22, they symbolized their conquest of the Caucasus by raising the German flag on the top of Mount Elbrus. The drive to Stalingrad, however, was slowed by stubborn resistance and weakness caused by the dispirited and poorly equipped Hungarian, Italian, and Rumanian forces. The Russians were no more beaten now than a year earlier, and the Germans again relied on inadequate and vulnerable supply lines.

In late September Halder warned Hitler of large concentrations of Russian troops to the north and west of Stalingrad as well as in the Caucasus. These troops, Halder argued, were being well equipped and would soon be ready to hit the German flank. German and satellite forces were not strong enough to continue advancing along both fronts. Halder recommended concentrating strength on one front with defensive measures being taken in the other. Hitler refused to accept Halder's argument or his evidence. Hitler responded by sacking Halder and other officers who lacked the necessary "National Socialist ardor" for victory.[35]

Hitler remained optimistic. By the end of September, the Sixth Army had reached the Volga around Stalingrad and had begun fighting within the city. The German aim could have been served by passing north of the city to secure both sides of the Volga and block all traffic on the river. Hitler, however, became swayed by the mystique of Stalingrad itself. In this Imperial Russian city of Tsaritsyn, Stalin had played a role in defeating the Whites, and from this city he had risen to a position of power rivaling that of Hitler. The world would indeed hold its breath as Hitler's armies captured and destroyed the city of Stalin as the final symbolic act in the destruction of the Soviet Russia. Stalin was also affected by personal prestige, but to a lesser extent than Hitler. Stalin knew that the successful defense of Stalingrad would be a psychological victory equal to that of Moscow the previous December.

Hitler's insistence on taking the city deprived his army of its advantages. The Russian commander at Stalingrad, General V. I. Chuikov, ordered his men to "hug" the enemy so closely that German air and artillery superiority would be minimized.[36] The Russians were determined to fight block by block, building by building, and if necessary, room by room. The two armies attacked and counterattacked throughout October until rubble remained where a city had once stood.

Hitler traveled to Munich on November 8, to observe the anniversary of the 1923 putsch. He told the party faithful that Stalingrad had fallen, although he admitted that some pockets of resistance remained.[37] Nearly all of Stalingrad had indeed fallen and the remaining Russian defenders had been driven to the river. But still they denied Hitler his victory and continued to consume the strength of the Sixth Army while keeping it tied to the banks of the Volga. Axis forces behind the city were also weakening. Hitler himself knew the military history of the Russian Civil war and how the Red Army had attacked across the Don to defeat the Whites. He and his generals expected some kind of a Russian attack, but they continued to believe that the Red Army was incapable of mounting a major offensive.[38] OKW reported "alarming news" on November 19. The Russians had struck along the Don against the Romanians and they were breaking through. They were also attacking German and Romanian forces in the south.[39] Hitler returned to his East Prussian headquarters to review the situation with Halder's successor, General Kurt Zeitzler. It was obvious that the Russians were attempting to encircle Stalingrad and trap the Sixth Army, and they would do it, unless Paulus marched westward as soon as possible.

The intuition which had given Hitler victory on so many occasions had succumbed to hubris. He insisted he could counter the Russian threat by transferring troops from the Caucasian front. Zeitzler pointed out that the Russians had launched their attack in a blizzard, and it would become increasingly more difficult to supply all the forces along the Don front in addition to the Sixth Army. Bad weather and distance precluded any effective relief from the Caucasus for two weeks, and by that time it would be too late to keep Stalingrad from being encircled. Hitler would have none of it. I won't go back from the Volga!" he shouted, "I won't go back from the Volga!"[40]

The Russian armies met forty miles west of Stalingrad in less than a week. It is doubtful that Paulus had the resources to escape, if he had been given permission to try.[41] Hitler promised supplies by air, but even in good weather and peacetime the Luftwaffe had insufficient transports to deliver the tons of material needed to survive. Hitler summoned General Manstein from the Leningrad front to form Army Group Don. Manstein initially believed it was possible for Paulus to hold out until Army Group Don reached his forces. Manstein's army began Operation Winter Gale on December 12 and advanced to within thirty miles of Stalingrad. The Red Army hit the flanks of Manstein's force in late December. Hitler realized that Manstein had to retreat westward or be encircled. Manstein retreat endangered German forces in the Caucasus. Hitler now admitted that Zeitzler was right and grudgingly allowed him to order a strategic withdrawal from the Caucasus as well.[42]

The Sixth Army was abandoned to the Russians. Hitler forbade Paulus to surrender and save what remained of it. The Red Army attacked in full force on January 11 and gradually reduced the German perimeter. Hitler still forbade surrender and even promoted Paulus to field marshal as an incentive to fight to the death. But bribes and the accolades on Berlin radio were not enough. On the thirty-first Paulus and nearly one hundred thousand beaten men surrendered. Only a few thousand saw Germany again.

Stalingrad gave the Soviet Union and its leader a prestige undreamed of a few months before. The Red Army had held and then destroyed the largest army of the invincible Wehrmacht. Hitler had personified the war into a struggle between his armies and those of Stalin by placing so much emphasis on taking Stalin's city. Stalin had won. The glory of the Red Army became identified with its leader throughout the world. The Communist dictator of so many wrongs had become the determined leader of gallant Russia. *Time* magazine spoke for many in naming Stalin "Man of the Year" for 1942, complete with a flattering cover picture of the rugged Soviet leader. "All that Hitler could give," read the caption, "he took—for a second time." The accompanying article glossed over or omitted forced collectivization, the purges, and the pact with Hitler. "Stalin's methods were tough," commented *Time,* "but they paid off."[43]

NOTES

1. Johanna M. Meskill, *Hitler and Japan: The Hollow Alliance* (New York: Atherton Press, 1966), 175.
2. *FRUS: 1941,* vol. 1, 802-814.
3. *Documents on Polish-Soviet Relations, 1939-1945*, vol. 1, 1939-1943. ed. Stanislaw Bieganski, et al. (London: Heinemann, 1967), 108-112
4. Churchill, *Grand Alliance,* 390-393.
5. Anthony Eden, *The Memoirs of Anthony Eden, Earl of Avon: The Reckoning* (Boston: Houghton Mifflin Company, 1965), 334-345.
6. George Lenczowski, *Russia and the West in Iran, 1918-1948: A Study in Big-Power Rivalry* (Ithaca: Cornell University Press, 1949), 167.
7. Dallek, *Roosevelt and American Foreign Policy,* 317-324. *New York Times,* January 3, 1942, 1,4.
8. Hull, *Memoirs,* vol. 2, 116.
9. Ibid., 126.
10. Martin Gilbert, *Winston S. Churchill,* vol. 7 (Boston: Houghton Mifflin Company, 1986), 50-52. *Times* (London) January 30, 1942, 5.
11. *New York Times,* March 18, 1942, 1,4. March 21, 1942, 1.

12. *Roosevelt-Churchill Correspondence,* 186.
13. Dallek, *Roosevelt and American Foreign Policy,* 338. *British Foreign Policy in the Second World War,* ed. Sir Llewellyn Woodward, vol. 2 (London: Her Majesty's Stationery Office, 1971), 239.
14. Hastings Ismay, *The Memoirs of General Lord Ismay* (New York: The Viking Press, 1960), 248-252. Forest C. Pogue, *George C. Marshall: Ordeal and Hope* (New York: The Viking Press, 1966), 319-320.
15. *Churchill & Roosevelt: The Complete Correspondence,* ed. Warren F. Kimball, vol. 1 (Princeton: Princeton University Press, 1984), 458-459.
16. *FRUS: 1942,* vol. 3, 542-543.
17. Eden, *Reckoning,* 380-382. Churchill, *Hinge of Fate,* 335-336. Woodward, *British Foreign Policy,* 251-254.
18. Pogue, *Marshall,* vol. 2, 326-327. *FRUS: 1942,* vol. 3, 576-577.
19. 21.Vyacheslav M. Molotov, *Molotov Remembers: Inside Kremlin Politics,* ed. Albert Resis (Chicago: Ivan R. Dee, 1993), 45-46.
20. Weinberg, *World at Arms,* 350.
21. Churchill, *Hinge of Fate,* 383-408. Charles Moran, *Churchill: Taken from the Diaries of Lord Moran: The Struggle for Survival* (New York: Houghton Mifflin Company, 1966), 51.
22. Pogue, *Marshall,* vol. 2, 341-347.
23. Rudy Abramson, *Spanning The Century: The Life of W. Averell Harriman, 1891-1986* (New York: William Morrow and Company, 1992), 336-339.
24. George F. Howe, *The Mediterranean Theater of Operations: Northwest Africa: Seizing The Initiative in the West* (Washington: U.S. Government Printing Office, 1957), 10-32.
25. Stephen E. Ambrose, *Eisenhower,* vol. 1 (New York: Simon and Schuster, 1983), 203-205.
26. Churchill, *Hinge of Fate,* 631-637. *Correspondence Between The Chairman of the Council of Ministers of the USSR and the Prime Ministers of Great Britain During the Great Patriotic War of 1941-1945,* ed. A.A. Gromyko, et al. (Moscow: Progress Publishers, 1957), 89. (Hereafter cited as Stalin Correspondence.)
27. Preston, *Franco,* 474-481.
28. Ambrose, *Eisenhower,* vol. 1, 215. Lacounture, De Gaulle, vol. 1, 409-413.
29. Carlo D'Este, Patton: *A Genius For War* (New York: HarperCollins, 1995), 457-464.

30. Churchill, *Hinge of Fate,* 772-781.
31. *Times* (London), November, 11, 1942, 5.
32. *Hitlers Weisungen,* 183-188.
33. Weinberg, *World at Arms,* 413.
34. *Hitlers Weisungen,* 196-199.
35. Bullock, *Parallel Lives,* 782. Halder, *Kriegstagebuch,* vol. 3, 528-533.
36. Glantz and House, *When Titans Clashed,* 122.
37. *New York Times,* November 9, 1942, 13.
38. Glantz and House, *When Titans Clashed,* 132.
39. *Kriegstagebuch des Oberkommandos der Wehrmacht,* vol. 2, Zusammengestellt und erlaeutere Andreas Hillgruber (Frankfurt am Main: Bernard und Graefe, 1963), 988.
40. Kurt Zeitzler, "Stalingrad," *The Fatal Decisions,* ed. Seymour Freidin and William Richardson (New York: William Sloane Associates, 1956), 152-153. Bullock, *Parallel Lives,* 787.
41. Glantz and House, *When Titans Clashed,* 134.
42. Ibid., 172-178.
43. *Time,* January 15, 1943, 23.

North African Campaigns, 1942-1945

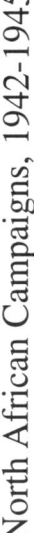

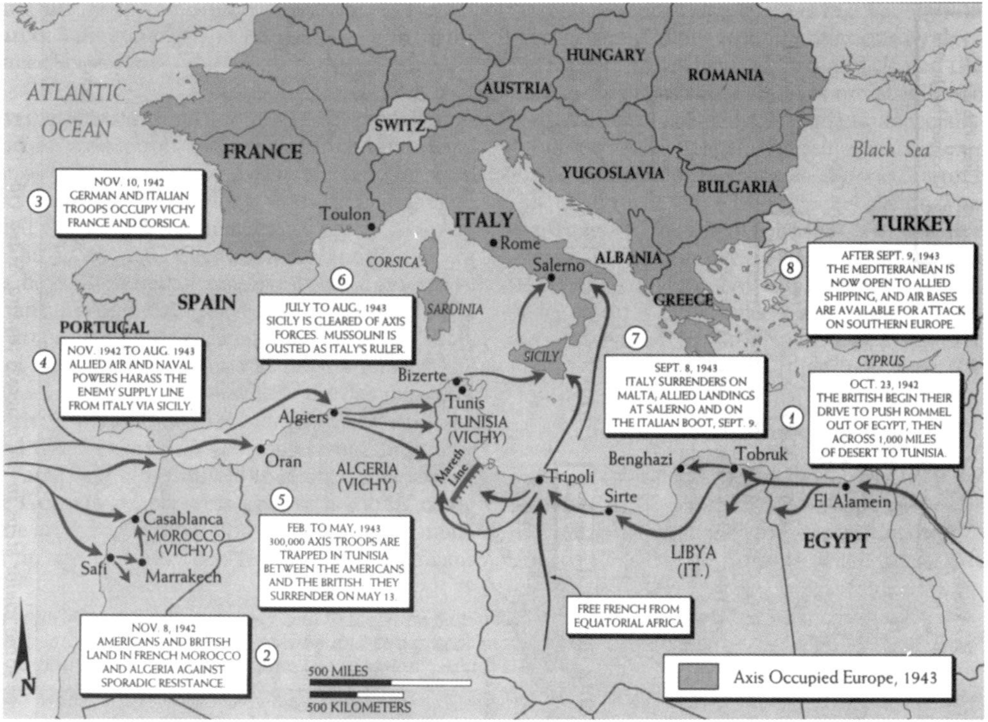

WESTERN HERITAGE VOL. 2 SINCE 1648 6/E. by KAGAN/OZMENT/TURNER, © 1998.
Reprinted by permission of Prentice-Hall, Inc., Upper Saddle River, NJ.

CHAPTER TWELVE

The Road to Teheran

The Allied landing in North Africa laid the foundation for the Casablanca Conference in January of 1943. Churchill and Roosevelt had discussed a possible meeting for some time. They invited Stalin to join them, but he declined because of the continuing battle for Stalingrad. Churchill and Roosevelt were ambivalent about Stalin's refusal. They worried that he might suspect some kind of Anglo-American deal at his expense. They were also somewhat relieved. During November and December Stalin had renewed his pressure for an invasion of western Europe in 1943. Neither Churchill nor Roosevelt looked forward to a personal confrontation while planning for further action in the Mediterranean.[1]

Roosevelt again went against his chief military advisor. Marshall had originally argued against the Mediterranean strategy on the grounds that it would divert the Anglo-American war away from the Atlantic. It had. Any further operations would surely delay a cross-channel invasion of Europe until the spring of 1944, at the earliest. Marshall was also under pressure from MacArthur and Navy Chief Admiral Ernest J. King to divert more resources to the Pacific before the Japanese had time to construct a formidable defense line.[2] Marshall realized that he would probably have to approve an assault on Sicily. In return, however, he demanded increased British action in the Pacific. On January 17, he argued his case so forcefully that the British mistakenly saw a threat to abandon Europe in favor of the Pacific. Marshall had not intended any threat, but the hint of a

Pacific-first strategy alarmed the British. The responded by arguing that Germany was the key to winning the war and that continued action in the Mediterranean was the best way to do it.

The military leaders were able to reach an agreement, despite some testy moments. The British approved offensive action in the Pacific, if it did not endanger the defeat of Germany in 1943. The primary task must be to drive the German U-boats from the seas and to launch an invasion of Sicily. The African war had simply imposed a new reality. "Frankly," Eisenhower wrote on January 28, the invasion of western Europe "could not possibly be staged before August of 1944 because our original conceptions of the strength required were too low. Inaction in 1943 could not be tolerated, and, unfortunately, distances are so great that we could not devote 1943 to one enemy and 1944 to another."[3]

Churchill and Roosevelt were in Casablanca at least in part because of the Darlan Deal, and both were still smarting from the outrage it had provoked. They now felt compelled to state their policy regarding the surrender of Germany, Italy, and Japan, while remaining more flexible with minor Axis countries. They wanted to assure their populace and Stalin that there would be no more deals that left fascists in power. Beyond that, both remembered the armistice of 1918 and how Hitler had later benefitted from the myth that Germany had not been defeated on the battlefield but had been stabbed in the back at home and deceived by Allied duplicity.

These considerations led to the controversial unconditional surrender statement on January 24. Roosevelt made the announcement in a casual manner at a joint press conference with Churchill. The president jokingly attributed the origins of "unconditional surrender" to "a general called . . . 'unconditional surrender' Grant. The elimination of German, Japanese, and Italian war power means the unconditional surrender by Germany, Italy, and Japan." Roosevelt immediately qualified the term by adding "that does not mean the destruction of the population of Germany, Italy, or Japan, but it does mean the destruction of the philosophies in those countries which are based on conquest and the subjugation of other peoples."[4]

Churchill later claimed that he had heard the term "unconditional surrender" for the first time when Roosevelt spoke at Casablanca. He also said he would not have used the term. He corrected himself in his memoirs and acknowledged that he had discussed it with the president. Churchill had hoped to drive a wedge in the Axis by exempting Italy from unconditional surrender, but he had been overruled by the war cabinet. Churchill challenged those who blamed the unconditional surrender policy for prolonging the war. Churchill argued that a vague formula was less frightening than more specific terms would have been, especially since both he and the president repeatedly assured their enemies that unconditional surrender did not mean that murder and rapine would follow their defeat.[5]

Reaction to the Darlan Deal had indicated that many people preferred the cruelty of war to a compromise peace. The war had become a crusade against evil people and systems that were to be eliminated. The Peace of Versailles had called for war crimes trials for the kaiser and many who had served him. Any new peace terms would have to bring Hitler and his government to trial, as they later did, and with far better reason. It remains questionable whether the unconditional surrender formula retarded attempts to remove Hitler. There is no doubt the formula displeased the conspirators, and they continually tried to gain more lenient terms in exchange for action against Hitler. Some of them were handicapped by having helped Hitler to conquer Europe and their desire to keep some of his gains. The unconditional surrender policy did not deter attempts on Hitler's life. In March two army officers attempted to kill Hitler by planting a bomb in his plane. Several more attempts followed, culminating in the unsuccessful one of July 20, 1944.[6]

Churchill and Roosevelt also had to deal with the vexing problems of French politics. Charles de Gaulle had won support in Britain and had brought some of the French Empire under his control. His relations with Washington remained cool, however, although he had been given Lend-Lease in November of 1941. The United States had maintained formal relations with Vichy until November of 1942, but was not ready to recognize de Gaulle. Roosevelt and Hull disliked de Gaulle's authoritarian manner and suspected him of trying to force himself on the French people once victory had been attained. De Gaulle's anger at being excluded from Torch had turned to rage when he learned of the deal with Darlan. Allied action had legitimatized Darlan as the ruler in North Africa, and perhaps eventually all of France. Darlan's switch to the Allied cause also had not altered his harsh treatment of de Gaulle's followers, many of whom had openly helped in the successful completion of Torch.[7]

Darlan's assassination changed the struggle to one between de Gaulle and Giraud. De Gaulle believed he should be recognized as the leader of a new French government in exile. Giraud, however, would never consent to serve under a man he outranked, and the Allies were in no mood to officially recognize any French government. Churchill's relations with de Gaulle had cooled considerably since 1940 and had been stormy at times.

He still favored de Gaulle as the leader of a resurgent France following the war. Roosevelt, however, saw France as a collaborationist country to be dealt with as such. Giraud and de Gaulle were invited to Casablanca to assume joint control. Giraud agreed, but de Gaulle refused until Churchill threatened to abandon him altogether. Once in Casablanca de Gaulle continued to defy the Allies and even berated Giraud for succumbing to the pressure of "foreign powers." For the sake of unity, or the appearance of it, de Gaulle consented to a joint communiqué calling for cooperation in the struggle for victory. The two generals demonstrated their acting ability by shaking hands while standing as far from each other as possible without ruining the show.[8]

De Gaulle's unhappiness was something Churchill and Roosevelt could live with. Stalin's was not. Stalin expected a cross-channel landing in 1943. The Western Allies could not launch one, but they could put the best face on what they planned. Churchill and Roosevelt sent a letter to Stalin on January 25 explaining the decisions at Casablanca. America and Britain would launch operations in the Mediterranean as soon as possible, causing Germany to divert forces to the west and south. There also would be heavy bombing of Germany to destroy material, morale, and fighter defenses. They also added the need for operations against Japan.[9]

Churchill and Roosevelt expected a hostile reply. Stalin, however, took the news calmly, but asked for clarifiction on when the cross-channel attack would come. Churchill and Roosevelt were embarrassed by the massive Soviet effort in contrast to their own. Churchill sent Stalin another letter on February 9 after consulting with Roosevelt. The prime minister stated many conditions, but came dangerously close to promising a cross-channel attack in August or September, even though it was evident that victory in North Africa would not come until April or May. Stalin was not interested in further action in the Mediterranean, and he certainly did not consider an attack on Sicily as equal to one on France.[10]

Churchill confirmed the postponement of the cross-channel attack in a long letter of March 11. The Western Allies further angered Stalin by suspending convoys to Russia because of German naval strength in the North Atlantic. Stalin knew that his victories had increased Soviet leverage as well as its prestige with its Western Allies. He also knew, however, that eventual victory would leave him weak against the rising might of the United States. The Americans still refused to grant him the 1941 boundaries in central Europe, and there was little indication they would change their minds. Those boundaries and more might well be gained, and additional destruction avoided, by a peace with Germany. As early as November 1942, as the Red Army closed around Stalingrad, Stalin had publicly hinted at a settlement with Nazi Germany or whatever military government might replace it.[11] With his own army bearing the brunt of the war and winning the most spectacular victories, Stalin had nothing to lose by sending feelers of a separate peace to the Germans in May of 1943. At the same time, treatment of Allied personnel in Russia went from rudeness to near hostility, while the Soviet press neglected the Americans and the British as much as possible by presenting the war as a German-Russian conflict and ignoring the unconditional surrender formula.[12]

The German military had cooperated with the Soviet Union in the past, and some believed a total commitment should be made to defeat Britain and the United States. Ribbentrop and Goebbels also saw an advantage in ending the Russian war. Mussolini now feared that neither the king nor the Italian people would resist the Allied invasion looming in the future. He wanted Hitler to end the war with Russia, or at the very least shorten his defenses and transfer as many forces as possible to Africa and the Balkans. Hitler, however, saw no point in ending a war that he still expected to win.[13]

Stalin had no intention of accepting anything less than the 1941 boundaries, whether by agreement with the Germans or the Western Allies. Relations with the Polish government in exile had been forced on him by a necessity that no longer existed. In early January of 1943 Stalin told Polish Communists to prepare for a break with the London Poles. On the twenty-third, Tass announced that all residents of eastern Poland "who found themselves" in the Soviet Union in 1939 were to be considered Soviet citizens.[14]

The Poles protested and pressed Churchill for action regarding the fate of Polish prisoners taken in 1939. General Wladyslaw Sikorski, president of the London Poles, told Churchill in early April that he had evidence that the Soviets had murdered nearly 15,000 Polish prisoners near Smolensk during the spring of 1940. Churchill did not doubt the report. But the Devil still had to be defeated, and he must turn his back on the crimes of Beelzebub. He told Sikorski to ignore the report, since nothing could bring the men back.[15] The Germans announced the discovery of over 4,000 bodies in one of four camps in the Katyn Forest on April 13. They charged the Soviets with the murders and offered evidence that the executions had taken place in the early spring of 1940.[16] Churchill and Roosevelt labeled the German charges as propaganda intended to split the Allies. The Poles did not. They asked the International Red Cross to investigate, giving Stalin the pretext he wished.[17] Stalin broke with the London Poles on April 24, despite pleas from Churchill and Roosevelt. The appearance of Allied unity was maintained at the expense of Western conscience. Much of the substance of the Grand Alliance, however, had been lost in the wake of Stalingrad and the Katyn Forest.

As the summer of 1943 approached, Stalin and the Western Allies waited to see whether Hitler would go on the defensive against the Red Army or try again to destroy it. The Wehrmacht was strong enough to hold in the east by adjusting its lines and going on the defensive. The Red Army was now slightly superior in numbers and growing more powerful in air and armored strength. It also had far better morale than the demoralized and badly led force of 1941. Hitler, however, needed a victory to redress Stalingrad and intimidate his wavering allies.

Winter fighting had left a bulge in the German line between Kharkov and Orel in an area known as the Kursk salient. The Red Army strengthened its forces to defend it and possibly use it for future offensive action. Hitler believed he could win a great victory by destroying the salient. OKW began planning Operation Citadel in March with the hope of striking a surprise blow in April. Logistical problems delayed the attack until early May. By this time the Soviets had been given time to strengthen their defenses, but Hitler believed his new Mark V Panther and Mark VI Tiger tanks would make the difference.

On the afternoon of July 4, the Wehrmacht launched its last great offensive in the east. Hitler had over half a million men, including seventeen panzer divisions, and hoped to encircle and destroy the Russians as he had done so often before. The Germans no longer had the overwhelming air power to support their armor. Allied bombing had forced Hitler to move 70 percent of his fighters westward to protect German cities. The offensive made a small gain before being hampered by torrential rainfall and then an unexpected barrage of Russian artillery. By July 9, the Kursk offensive became the greatest battle of armor until the October 1973 Arab-Israeli war. Over a thousand tanks on each side fought in such a small area that air power, artillery, and even infantry were reduced to bystanders. At such close range the newer and more powerful German tanks lost much of their advantage over the proven T-34 while suffering from technical defects inherent in any new model. The Red Army also attacked along other areas of the front, forcing Hitler to divert some of his panzer units from the Kursk fighting.[18] On July 11 Hitler learned of the Anglo-American landing in Sicily. The loss of Italy and its holdings in the Balkans could encourage other countries to desert him. He decided to halt the Kursk offensive on the thirteenth and to send a number of divisions from the Russian front to Italy. A new phase of the war had begun. From now until the end Hitler would have to continually transfer men and armor from one area to another in order to protect his allies and keep his empire.

Operation Husky, the invasion of Sicily, had been approved initially at Casablanca and later in Washington at the May 1943 Trident Conference. Churchill skillfully argued that the collapse of Italy might well shock Nazi Germany as the loss of Bulgaria had shocked Imperial Germany in 1918. At the very least, it would jeopardize German control in the Balkans and divert troops from the Russian front. Neutralizing the Italian Navy could also free British sea power for the Pacific.[19] The Americans, however, were weary of projects that took far more time than originally planned. Marshall was willing to concede that a cross-channel attack in 1942 would have been suicidal. Torch might have been the right move after all. Conquering North Africa had delayed a landing in France until the spring of 1944 at the earliest. It could be delayed further by any operations east of Sicily. The Red Army, Marshall noted, might well advance through central Europe before the Anglo-Americans established their beachhead in France. The Americans would have to consider a Pacific-first policy unless the British were willing to promise a landing in France the next year, and this time Marshal had Roosevelt's support.

Marshall won the British commitment for a cross-channel landing in the spring of 1944, after several conferences, and for greater offensive action in the Pacific.[20] Allied policy in the Mediterranean, however, remained unsettled. Eisenhower's growing importance in the Anglo-American war effort became apparent when Churchill and Marshall traveled to Algiers to state their case. Marshall wanted nothing beyond the conquest of Sicily, and he still suspected the British of trying to find some way to renege on their promise for an invasion of France. Eisenhower made no commitment to either of his superiors; he would make his decision after the campaign in Sicily. The nature of Husky, as well as of the later Italian campaign, was revealed when Eisenhower's forces took the island of Pantelleria on June 11. It was located roughly halfway between North Africa and Sicily, was well fortified, and could have caused problems for the invasion of Sicily. The defenders, however, were sick of a war they had never wanted. Their commander surrendered on the flimsy excuse that his men were short of water. Two days later the island of

Lampedusa also gave up without a fight. It was clear that the Italian people and their army had no stomach for fighting after three years of disastrous war, and that they would rather be prisoners of the Americans and English than the Germans.

German troops were left with the task of defending Sicily when the invasion came on July 10. Hitler and his generals were furious but not surprised by the Italian performance. Hitler hoped to rejuvenate his flagging ally with another conference. Mussolini agreed to meet him on the nineteenth at Feltre near Venice. The despondent Duce now met his lord and keeper. Hitler reproached the Italians for their timidity and threatened to withdraw all aid unless they were ready to fight. Mussolini's humiliation and pain were increased when news arrived that Rome had been bombed, news that Hitler brushed aside without a word of sympathy. The Duce's advisors wanted Hitler's permission for a separate peace. Mussolini knew, however, that Hitler would never consent to it, and that any surrender would mean the end of his own rule in Italy. That evening he returned to Rome with the promise of German help the Italian people did not want.

Hitler was aware of the growing unrest against Mussolini's government. He wanted to keep Mussolini in power and to project the image of Italian independence. He also wanted to take control of Italy and set up a defense line as far from Germany as possible. Neither of the dictators believed a crisis was imminent. For weeks, however, many Italians had decided to make peace with the Allies.

King Victor Emmanuel III had been brooding over the future of his country and the monarchy. On July 22, the king tried to convince Mussolini that the situation was hopeless, and that he had become the major barrier to "internal recovery." The Duce had long ceased to listen to the king or his Fascist colleagues after twenty-one years in power. He did consent to a meeting of the Fascist Grand Council, the first since December 1939, but only because it would give him an opportunity to clarify the situation.

Mussolini had no idea of a plot when he went before the Grand Council on the night of July 24. He began with long and disingenuous defense of his leadership and the conduct of the war, and he took pains to note the amount of aid received from Germany. It was the speech of a man who did not comprehend what was happening around him, and it impressed no one. The conspirators, led by Dino Grandi and including Ciano, condemned the Duce for leading Italy into war and making it a slave of the Germans. After hours of debate the Council voted 19 to 6 to give command of the armed forces to the King and to restore a democratic parliament. Mussolini proceeded on as though nothing had happened. He was partly right. Most conspirators had little more in mind than to voice their displeasure.

The king had other ideas. Plans were already underway to depose and arrest the Duce when he called on the king the following day. Victor Emmanuel told Mussolini that the war was lost and the country was disintegrating. He had to go. Marshal Pietro Badoglio would be the next prime minister. The Duce accepted the king's decision with little more than a murmur. He wanted only to retire to his native Romagna and comfortable obscurity. Victor Emmanuel promised Mussolini personal security, and he intended to provide it whether or not the former Duce wanted it. Mussolini was arrested when he left the palace and taken to the nearby army base in Trastevere, a section of Rome.

General Eisenhower had decided to invade the Italian mainland prior to the fall of Mussolini. Italian exhaustion and the immense buildup of men and material in North Africa offered an opportunity to take Italy out of the war and threaten Germany from the south. An even quicker victory was possible if the new Italian government surrendered. Eisenhower was willing to accept criticism for another "deal" in exchange for Italy by making an immediate radio appeal offering the Italians a conditional surrender leaving the monarchy and the Badoglio government in power.[21]

Roosevelt and Churchill were willing to offer a compromise peace, but feared a repeat of the outrage that had come with the Darlan Deal. Roosevelt made a radio address on July 28 assuring the electorate that "our terms to Italy are the same as our terms to Germany and Japan — unconditional surrender." The new Italian government did little to aid the Allied leaders when it announced loyalty to the Axis alliance and promised to continue the war. A delay of several weeks ensued until the Italians finally signed the unconditional surrender on September 3.[22]

Hitler had considered the possibility of Mussolini's downfall, but was not prepared for it. He had no doubt that Victor Emmanuel and Badoglio would make peace with the Allies as soon as they could but decided to go along with their ruse while planning to seize the country when the armistice came. He ordered the army to secure the critical mountain passes in the north and west of Italy on September 3. On the following day he was ready with four different operations that would rescue Mussolini, restore his government in Rome, occupy the entire Italian peninsula, and destroy the Italian fleet.

Hitler's swift action ended any Allied hope of an easy conquest of Italy. By the time the Anglo-American forces landed at Salerno on September 8, Hitler controlled most of the country and had disarmed much of the Italian Army. German forces under Field Marshal Albert Kesselring launched a series of counterattacks against the Allied beachhead. Within a few days the Allied force of nearly 70,000 men was on the verge of being destroyed. With their backs to the sea and with all the air and sea support available, they managed to barely hang on until September 18 when Kesselring was forced to call off his attack and withdraw to a better position.

Hitler's plans for Italy were unfulfilled as long as Mussolini remained in captivity. He was still fond of the man who had been his mentor and faithful to the promise he had made at the time of the Anschluss to stand by the Duce though the whole world was against him. Hitler received word that Mussolini was being held in a hotel at the top of Gran Sasso Mountain in the Abruzzi region of central Italy. On September 12, German glider troops swept down on the resort and spirited the Duce away with no opposition.

Two days later Mussolini met Hitler at Rastenburg. Mussolini was glad to be free, but he had no desire to lead a new fascist government. He was, however, as much a captive as a guest. Hitler needed him for Italy and to serve as an example for his wavering Balkan allies. Mussolini dutifully proclaimed his Italian Socialist Republic on September 15. The squalid fiction fooled no one. Mussolini was a puppet respected by neither Italians nor Germans. He carried out Hitler's will by ordering the trial and execution of Ciano and others of his old comrades. Hitler completed the humiliation by compelling Mussolini to turn over Trieste and the South Tyrol to Germany, along with the hint that Venetia, the area around Venice, would follow. Hitler continued to hold the valuable industrial north while containing the Allied armies in the south. By the time the Allies took Rome in June of 1944, however, Italy had become a sideshow in the wake of the long-awaited cross-Channel attack on France.

The defeat of Italy again had raised the question of how the victorious allies would administer and occupy a defeated Axis country. Foreign Secretary Eden sent Washington a plan on July 1, proposing that local military commanders initially administer the areas under their control and then turn the area over to a United Nations Commission dominated by Britain, the United States, and the Soviet Union. Eden called for a period of time in which conquered areas would be divided into de facto spheres of influence, and for that reason alone it was coldly received in Washington.

Stalin preferred joint control by the great powers. He complained that Britain and the U.S. were keeping the Soviet Union in a passive role regarding Italian negotiations. He wanted Italy to be governed by an Allied military-political commission that would greatly reduce the authority of local commanders.[23] By the summer of 1943, however, it was becoming apparent that the Red Army might eventually march beyond Berlin. Roosevelt still held to the principles of the Atlantic Charter, but privately he admitted that the Soviets might control eastern Europe for at least twenty years. Roosevelt, and to a lesser extent Churchill, were never able to reconcile their public hopes for a postwar world based on the Charter with their private acceptance of a sphere in eastern Europe controlled by the Soviets. Roosevelt would be charged with "selling out" the principles of the Charter by those who expected their implementation. Others, on the other hand, would condemn Roosevelt's successor, Harry S. Truman, for trying to carry out the principles Roosevelt had embraced.

There was still cause to hope that major problems could be solved in the afterglow of the common struggle. Stalin pleased his allies in June by abolishing the Communist International. Stalin abandoned the Comintern more for his own reasons than to please his allies. With Soviet power growing and peace on the horizon, it was easier to deal with national parties directly than to work through an international organization.[24]

Stalin remained irritated with his Western Allies for delaying the cross-channel attack until the spring of 1944, despite his gesture on the Comintern. He made his anger clear in letters to Churchill and Roosevelt, and publicly underscored it by recalling Ambassador Maisky from London and Litvinov from Washington. Stalin again played his German card. By early July rumors were circulating about German-Soviet meetings in Sweden. Also, the Soviets appealed to potential German resistance by giving public support to the National Committee for a Free Germany, an organization composed of German prisoners.

The Soviet attitude was but one of many things Churchill and Roosevelt had to deal with when they traveled to Quebec in August. Churchill had agreed to the invasion of France, but he continued to put forth conditions, reservations, and even alternatives in the Balkans. As late as August 10, Secretary of War Stimson reported to Roosevelt that the "shadows of Passchendaele and Dunquerque" still hung over British leadership and that any plan for invading France must include an American commander. The president himself had not yet firmly made up his mind. He was committed to the cross-Channel invasion, concerned about Soviet intentions in eastern Europe, and had not ruled out a strike into the Balkans. After reading Stimson's report, however, Roosevelt told the Joint Chiefs that he favored the cross-Channel attack on France, now to be known as Operation Overlord.[25]

Marshall went to Quebec far more confident now that he had Roosevelt's support. But he knew how guileful and persuasive Churchill could be and how reluctant he was to abandon pet projects. The Quadrant conference began on August 14. Victory in Sicily, which came on August 17, strengthened the British drive for the Mediterranean strategy and eventually forced Marshall to approve the invasion of Italy. But Marshall bristled when General Alan Brooke suggested that Overlord be conditioned on the success of operations in Italy. Unless Overlord were given "overriding priority," Marshall threatened, it was doomed and the entire strategic plan of the United States would have to be examined "with a possible readjustment toward the Pacific."

The two staffs confronted their differences on the sixteenth. The British admitted that they had withheld acceptance of Overlord, but they put the blame on Churchill who constantly asked for alternatives. Churchill gave conditional support for Overlord and insisted that it be launched only after a review by the Combined Chiefs of Staff. He then suggested the Allies have a "second string in their bow," which meant resurrecting Operation Jupiter, the invasion of Norway, long a favorite project that made American and British generals wince. The Combined Chiefs recognized that the success of Overlord would be enhanced if the Soviets could divert German forces away from France, and they agreed that the continued advance of the Red Army would require Hitler to keep most of his army in the east.

The Soviet advance raised new problems. Marshall had received reports of a growing "hostile" and "contemptuous" attitude in Russia toward the capitalist countries, and he was concerned whether Moscow would use the chaos in central Europe to spread communism. There was a concern about how far the Red Army would advance if a sudden German collapse left all of central and western Europe open to it. Roosevelt recognized that possession meant power, and on the twenty-third he told the Combined Chiefs that he wanted the Allied forces ready to meet the Russians in Berlin if the opportunity arose.[26]

A new element now entered the picture. The Manhattan Project had already cast the shadow of atomic power over the course of the war and the peace to come. Roosevelt and Churchill had discussed cooperation on developing atomic power since the summer of 1942. On August 19, they signed an agreement calling for joint development of atomic energy and promising not to use atomic weapons against each other nor to inform any other power without mutual consent. There would, as Martin Sherwin has said, be four policemen after the war, "but only two of them would have the bomb."[27] Roosevelt's motives were governed by a well-deserved suspicion of the Soviet Union buttressed by a knowledge of Soviet espionage in Britain and the United States, as well as on a continuing reluctance by the Soviets to share secret information, atomic or otherwise.[28]

It was obvious that the Americans and the British still had opposing ideas on how the world should be organized following the war when Eden and Hull met on August 20. Eden wanted recognition of de Gaulle's French Committee of National Liberation as the legitimate successor to Vichy. Britain wanted a strong France after the war and de Gaulle offered the best chance for it. Eden also undiplomatically said that de Gaulle had been Britain's only friend during the dark days of 1940. The Americans and the British could only agree to disagree on de Gaulle and issue separate statements. They could not do so when discussing the status of colonies following the war. Eden opposed using "independence" on the grounds that it was too vague a word when dealing with the complexities of the Dominion system.[29]

The Quebec conference went as well as possible, aside from the brief rancor between Eden and Hull. Churchill and Roosevelt recognized that any lasting decisions required a meeting with the Russians. Stalin's recent accusations and ill humor caused both Allied leaders to wonder whether a satisfactory settlement could be attained. Previous plans for a three-power conference had foundered on the question of a meeting place. Stalin insisted he could not leave the Soviet Union and Roosevelt shied away from a long and arduous trip to Moscow.

Churchill and Roosevelt proposed a foreign ministers meeting on August 19, if Stalin could not meet with them personally. Stalin repeated his inability to leave Russia, but agreed to a meeting of the foreign ministers. Churchill preferred London, but Stalin held out for Moscow. He did, however, offer to meet with Churchill and Roosevelt sometime in November or December, and suggested Iran as a place both convenient and under Allied control.[30] The Moscow conference marked the first attempt to form a united policy for ending the war and administering the peace. The Americans and British came to Moscow with different goals. Eden wanted a settlement on Poland before it was overrun by the Red Army. Hull knew that Roosevelt had conceded Russian control of eastern Poland and the Baltic States. He was instructed to appeal to the Russians on moral grounds and to suggest plebiscites in the areas following the war.

The conference opened on October 19 with a brief discussion of organizational arrangements. On the following day Molotov surprised the British and shocked the Americans by asking for pressure on Sweden and Turkey to enter the war. The Americans saw this as a dangerous echo of Churchill's Mediterranean and Scandinavian schemes. Bringing Turkey into the war could divert forces from Overlord toward Italy and the Balkans. Eden noted that the Americans and the British were withdrawing their forces from the Mediterranean. Turkey's entrance into the war would bring pressure to return them, but, he added, Britain would be glad to reconsider the matter if its "Soviet friends" wished it to. Hull said the United States shared Eden's views, but he declined any further comment until he heard from Washington. The answer from Washington, however, made it clear that his government did not.[31]

Hull wanted Russian endorsement of his Declaration of Four Nations on General Security. The American desire to include China was not well received by the British or the Russians. The Soviets were not at war with Japan and saw little value in complicating their relations with Tokyo by associating themselves with Nationalist China. Stalin agreed, however, to make war on the Japanese after the defeat of Germany. Russian intervention carried dangers as well as benefits. The Soviets could keep territory they gained or give it to the Chinese Communists. Hull believed, however, the Nationalist government gained prestige and security by being associated with the great powers. The British and the Soviets eventually agreed to accept China as one of the Four Powers, and on October 30, the three foreign ministers signed the document. Hull, the old Wilsonian was "truly thrilled." The Soviet Union had committed itself to joining the resurrected League following the war and had granted Great Power status to a Nationalist China. Hull in turn had consented to revisions that would aid the Soviets in eastern Europe.[32]

Each of the foreign ministers had gained something when the conference ended on October 31. On balance the Americans and the Russians had gained more than the British, and the Russians had gained the most. They had the commitment for a second front in France in the spring of 1944. Creation of the European Advisory Commission and the Advisory Council for Italy gave them more of a voice in western Europe than the Anglo-Americans had in eastern Europe. The Soviets were allowed to present a document on "The Future of Poland and Danubian and Balkan Countries" challenging the right of "émigré governments" to be recognized after the war. Inclusion of the document in the records seemed to imply Anglo-American consent to a free hand for the Soviets in eastern Europe.[33]

Stalin perceived that the Americans were openly ending their previous deference to the British and wanted closer relations with Moscow. It was also clear that the Americans had a different vision of the postwar world and that some of the ideas emanating from Washington threatened the British Empire. Roosevelt believed he could establish closer relations with Stalin with personal diplomacy. Roosevelt and Stalin agreed to meet in early November, but they could not agree on where. Stalin refused to go any farther than Teheran and Roosevelt refused to go that far. Harriman, who had become the American ambassador to Moscow in September, told Roosevelt that communications to Teheran were adequate. Roosevelt agreed then to meet Stalin at the end of the month.[34]

Roosevelt also decided to meet Churchill in Cairo to discuss Anglo-American war plans for the coming year. The prime minister still doubted whether Overlord would be successful in 1944 and requested a meeting of the Combined Chiefs of Staff prior to meeting with Stalin. Roosevelt wanted to avoid the appearance of any Anglo-American front, and annoyed Churchill by suggesting that the Russians send a representative to the Cairo meeting.[35] The question of a Russian presence at Cairo disappeared when Stalin learned that Roosevelt had also invited Chiang Kai-shek. The war had not been going well for the generalissimo. His armies fared poorly in comparison with the Communists, and he had poor relations with the American military advisor, General Joseph Stilwell. The Nationalist government also appeared to be losing popular support. Roosevelt hoped to improve the military situation and bolster Chiang's prestige by presenting him as the leader of a great power.

Roosevelt left for Cairo on the morning of November 12, on the battleship U.S.S. *Iowa*. He looked forward to establishing a rapport with Stalin and building the foundation for a settlement after the war. The *Iowa* docked at Oran on November 20, and from there Rocsevelt traveled to Cairo on the twenty-second. At times the president and his advisors appeared to see the British as more of a barrier to postwar harmony than the Russians. Britain, they suspected, was motivated primarily by the desire to secure its empire in the Mediterranean and the Pacific. "I have not," Churchill had said after El Alamein, "become the King's First Minister in order to preside over the liquidation of the British Empire. . . . Here we are and here we stand, a veritable rock of salvation in this drifting world."[36] The empire was good. The empire was power. Churchill's mind was anchored in the past. It was difficult for him to conceive of Britain without the empire, or to comprehend how fragile the foundation beneath that rock had become and how quickly the world was drifting beyond its control.

Churchill resented the Chinese from the beginning. He thought the Americans made far too much of Chiang Kai-shek and his attractive wife, and he feared that American plans for China would be partly fulfilled at the expense of the British Empire in Asia. It was obvious from Roosevelt's meeting with Chiang on the night of the twenty-third that the president saw China emerging as the dominant power in Asia following the war, and that it would include former British possessions, such as Hong Kong.[37] Churchill was also frustrated by the rejection of his military plans. The Americans wanted to launch an offensive in the Bay of Bengal to clear Burma and increase supplies to Chiang Kai-shek. The prime minister was unimpressed, especially when he realized that needed landing craft would come from the Mediterranean. The most heated exchange came on the night of the twenty-fourth when Churchill once again pressed for an assault on Rhodes. Marshall had had enough. Whatever their argument, he told his Allies, no American was going to die on "that goddamned beach."[38] The three powers agreed on a final draft for the Cairo Declaration at the end of the conference. They pledged to destroy Japanese imperialism, to return Manchuria, Formosa, and the Pescadores to China, and to restore an independent Korea. The Declaration implied that a strong China would dominate Asia after the war, whatever doubts about the military ability of Chiang's government.[39]

Churchill and Roosevelt flew on to Teheran for their long-awaited meeting with Stalin. At Teheran, wrote Herbert Feis, "Matters that are generally thought to have been decided at Yalta in February of 1945 were foreshadowed . . . more than a year before."[40] There was still much hostility toward Britain and Russia in the country, and security was so poor that Roosevelt decided to accept an invitation to stay at the Soviet embassy rather than travel between embassies several times a day. Timing itself worked to the advantage of the Soviets. The Anglo-Americans were feeling guilty because they had done so little to defeat the Germans compared to the Russians. For the Americans, and to a lesser extent the British, there was a respect bordering on intimidation for Stalin and his sinister reputation.

Roosevelt had come partly to prove how well-intended he was toward the Soviet Union, even if he did so at the expense of the British. At their first meeting on November 28, Roosevelt suggested that some of the American and British merchant fleet might be given to the Russians following the war, agreed with Stalin's denigration of de Gaulle's Free French and his plans for a weak France following the war, and made it clear that he foresaw the end of the British and French Empires.[41] Roosevelt and Churchill may have tried Stalin's patience and stomach when they began with high sounding bromides about the future of the world and "God given" opportunities. When his turn came Stalin simply welcomed his guests, agreed the conference was important, and said, "Now let's get down to business."[42] The invasion of France remained the most important "business." The Americans feared Stalin might side with Churchill for more action in the Mediterranean. Churchill based his case on the belief that Rome would be captured by January and that Turkey would be brought into the war. Stalin, however, did not believe the Turks would enter the war, and he questioned the feasibility of striking against Germany through the formidable Alps. A recent German attack on Kiev had given him more cause to expect relief in the west, and he endorsed Overlord as the best way to defeat Germany and suggested that it might be preceded by an invasion of southern France.[43]

Churchill again seemed to be the "odd man out" at dinner that night. Stalin expressed his dislike for France and argued that it should lose its empire and have no power in Europe. He also wanted to ensure that Germany would not recover as it had after the last war. Roosevelt sided with Stalin more than with Churchill, who feared that a weak France and Germany would leave the Soviet Union as master of the Continent. Stalin also insisted on the 1941 boundaries in eastern Europe. Churchill wanted an agreement on boundaries now, while Roosevelt wanted to avoid any public agreement involving Poland. Accepting the 1941 boundaries would infuriate Polish Americans and perhaps cost the Democratic Party in the 1944 election.[44] Churchill and Stalin continued their discussion after Roosevelt became ill. Churchill reminded Stalin that Britain had gone to war to preserve Polish independence in 1939 and wanted to see it emerge again following the war. He verbally accepted the 1941 borders by disclaiming any "attachment" to specific frontiers and then suggested the

Oder as the western boundary for the new Poland.

The conference was not going well for Churchill. For years he had tried to forge a "special relationship" with the United States. That dream was now fading. He and his empire were being viewed as the least among equals.⁴⁵ He had to suffer a personal rebuff from Roosevelt as well. On the morning of the twenty-ninth, Churchill asked for a meeting with the president. Roosevelt refused on the grounds that he did not want to give the impression of any Anglo-American deals behind Stalin's back.

Roosevelt's aloofness after years of friendship and shared tribulation must have hurt Churchill deeply. The president had no reservations about meeting with Stalin nor making fun of Churchill to please Stalin. Stalin needed little encouragement and missed no opportunity to "dig" at Churchill. The most famous encounter came on the night of the twenty-ninth when Stalin accused Churchill of being pro-German and suggested that some fifty to one hundred thousand German officers be liquidated. When Churchill, mindful of what had happened at Katyn, expressed his shock, Roosevelt jokingly suggested "only" forty-nine thousand. If Roosevelt thought Stalin was joking, he either did not know or had forgotten who he was talking to. The man who had liquidated millions of Russians was quite capable of doing the same to "only" one hundred thousand Germans.⁴⁶

Roosevelt presented his plan for the postwar world at a meeting with Stalin on the twenty-ninth. There would be a body of thirty-five nations under the direction of the big four policemen - The United States, Britain, China, and the Soviet Union. Stalin again questioned whether China should be ranked with the other three powers, and he thought European countries might resent being directed by the Chinese. He favored a more regional solution and suggested a European commission overseen by the U.S., Britain, and the Soviet Union in addition to a Far Eastern commission. Roosevelt doubted whether Congress would ever consent to any American participation in an organization that might require sending American troops to Europe. He saw the United States providing only support forces to keep the peace of Europe following the war. Roosevelt's plan, along with his desire to partition and weaken Germany, would clearly leave the Soviet Union as the dominant power in Europe.

Roosevelt conceded de facto control of Poland and the Baltic States to Stalin on December 1. He wanted no agreements prior to the 1944 elections that might anger Polish-American voters or those with ties to the Baltic States. Privately, however, he favored moving the eastern boundary of Poland westward, while at the same time moving the western boundary to the Oder. He jokingly said that he had no intention of going to war over the fate of the Baltic States, but he would like to have some demonstration of public opinion.

Stalin tactfully expressed sympathy for Roosevelt's position. There was no need, he added for a referendum. There were ample opportunities for people to express their will under the Soviet constitution.[47] Acceptance of the new Polish boundaries and the loss of the Baltic States was as close to inevitable as something could be. Churchill believed the new borders gave the Poles a fine place to live. If the London government accepted the settlement, it could return to its new country and once again play a role in central Europe. Stalin was confident that he would determine the fate of central Europe from the Vistula to the Oder. He had no need to mend fences with the London Poles. When Churchill and Roosevelt suggested improving relations at a later meeting on December 1, Stalin accused the Poles of killing partisans and joining the Nazis in spreading "slanderous" propaganda against the Soviet Union and questioned whether the group in London was really fit to lead Poland in a common struggle against Germany.[48]

The Big Three agreed on a harsh peace for Germany, but important differences remained on reconstructing Europe. Roosevelt wanted Germany divided into five parts with other areas, such as the Kiel Canal, under international supervision. Churchill preferred to detach southern Germany and make it part of new Danubian confederation. Stalin had no patience for any British scheme to restore the balance of power in Europe by recreating the Austro-Hungarian Empire. The more division the better, especially when it came to Germany. With these disagreements before them, the Big Three decided to turn the problem over to the European Advisory Commission.[49]

On December 5, the three leaders signed the Teheran Declaration, announcing agreement on coming military operations and promising victory. The Declaration contained only the vague promise to "command good will from the overwhelming masses of the people of the world and banish the scourge and terror of war for many generations" following the war. "We look with confidence," said the three leaders, "to the day when all of the peoples of the world may live free lives untouched by tyranny and according to their varying desires and own consciences." Even the spirit of wartime cooperation could not silence skeptics. "If it can be believed," wrote *Life* magazine, "it solves everything. If it cannot, it is a colossal fraud." The Declaration said nothing about matters of national security, and though the Devil was about to be defeated, it was not by an alliance of saints. It was, after all, difficult to reconcile Soviet Communism, and to a lesser extent the British Empire and the United States, with a family of democratic nations in which individuals lived according to their own conscience.[50]

NOTES

1. Churchill, *Hinge of Fate,* 660-672. Dallek, *Roosevelt and American Foreign Policy,* 366-370.
2. Forest C. Pogue, *George C. Marshall: Organizer of Victory* (New York: The Viking Press, 1973), 3-19.
3. *The Papers of Dwight David Eisenhower: The War Years,* vol. 2, ed. Alfred D. Chandler, Jr. (Baltimore: Johns Hopkins Press, 1970), 929-930.
4. *FRUS: Conferences at Washington, 1941-1942 and Casablanca, 1943* (Washington U.S. Government Printing Office, 1963), 727.
5. Churchill, *Hinge of Fate,* 686-687.
6. Hoffmann, *History of the German Resistance,* 228-232, 282-284.
7. Charles de Gaulle, *The War Memoirs of Charles de Gaulle: Unity, 1942-1944* trans. Richard Howard (New York: Simon and Schuster, 1959), 45-53.
8. Churchill, Hinge of Fate, 695. Lacouture, *De Gaulle,* 427-428.
9. *Stalin Correspondence,* 46-47.
10. Ibid., 49-52.
11. Mastny, *Russia's Road to the Cold War,* 74-75.
12. Woodward, *British Foreign Policy,* vol. 2, 564-574.
13. Weinberg, *World at Arms,* 609-611. Ciano *Diaries,* 556-557.
14. *Documents on Polish-Soviet Relations,* 1939-1945, 473-474. Weinberg, *World at Arms,* 468.
15. Churchill, *Hinge of Fate,* 759-760. Gilbert, *Churchill,* vol. 7, 384-385.
16. *Documents on Polish-Soviet Relations,* 523-524.
17. The Soviet government continued to deny the charge until 1989. Bullock, *Parallel Lives,* 659, 817. On August 25, 1993 Russian President Boris Yeltsin laid flowers at the Katyn cross in Powaski cemetery to honor Stalin's victims. *New York Times,* August 26, 1993, 2.
18. Glantz and House, *When Titans Clashed,* 166-167.
19. *FRUS: 1943: Conferences at Washington and Quebec* (Washington,

Chapter 12   217

   1970), 25-27.
20. Pogue, Marshall: *Organizer of Victory,* 193-199, 211-213.
21. *Eisenhower Papers: The War Years,* vol. 2, 1287-1288.
22. Feis, *Churchill, Roosevelt, Stalin,* 156-158.
23. *FRUS: 1943,* vol. 1, 708-710. Mastny, Russia's Road to the Cold War, 106-107.
24. Bullock, *Parallel Lives,* 798.
25. *FRUS: The Conferences at Washington and Quebec,* 444-452. Henry L. Stimson and McGeorge Bundy, *On Active Service in Peace and War* (New York: Harper and Brothers, 1948), 436-438.
26. *Conferences at Washington and Quebec,* 867, 871-874, 942-944.
27. Ibid., 1117-1119. Martin J. Sherwin, *A World Destroyed: The Atomic Bomb and the Grand Alliance* (New York: Alfred A. Knopf, 1975), 89.
28. Weinberg, *A World at Arms,* 572.
29. *Conferences at Washington and Quebec,* 916-920, 923-928.
30. Winston S. Churchill, *Closing the Ring* (Boston: Houghton-Mifflin, 1951), 277-272.
31. *FRUS: 1943,* vol. 1, 585. Keith Sainsbury, *The Turning Point: Roosevelt, Stalin, Churchill, and Chiang Kai-shek, 1943. The Moscow, Cairo, and Teheran Conferences* (New York: Oxford University Press, 1985), 62-66.
32. *FRUS: 1943,* vol. 1, 542, 755-756. Hull, *Memoirs,* vol. 1, 1307-1309.
33. *FRUS: 1943,* vol. 1, 758-762.
34. *FRUS: Conferences at Cairo and Teheran,* 1943 (Washington U.S. Government Printing Office 1961), 69-72.
35. *Roosevelt and Churchill Correspondence,* 386-389.
36. *Churchill Speeches,* vol. 6, 6695.
37. *Conferences at Cairo and Teheran,* 323-325.
38. Ibid., 329-334. Pogue, *Marshall: Organizer of Victory,* 307.
39. *Conferences at Cairo and Teheran,* 448-449.
40. Feis, *Roosevelt, Churchill, Stalin,* 255.
41. *Conferences at Cairo and Teheran,* 482-484.
42. Ibid., 487.
43. Ibid., 488-497. Weinberg, *World at Arms,* 629.
44. *Conferences at Cairo and Teheran,* 509-512.
45. John Chamrley, *Churchill's Grand Alliance: The Anglo-American Special Relationship, 1940-57* (New York: Harcourt Brace, 1995), 80.
46. Ibid., 553-554. Gilbert, *Churchill,* vol. 7, 580-581.

47. *Conferences at Cairo and Teheran,* 594-595.
48. Ibid., 598-599.
49. Ibid., 601-604.
50. *Life,* vol. 14 (December 20, 1943), 32.

Chapter Thirteen

The Beginning of the End

Churchill and Roosevelt stopped for their Second Cairo on December 5. The decisions at Teheran now forced the Anglo-Americans to alter their own strategy for the coming year. Stalin's promise to enter the war against Japan lessened the need for a strong Chinese contribution and an offensive in Burma. The commitment to the invasion of France now made it necessary to divert resources previously scheduled for other areas. Roosevelt regretfully informed Chiang that the Burma campaign was off. Overlord also put an end to further operations in the Mediterranean and to Churchill's lingering hope for Turkey's entrance into the war. Churchill and Roosevelt met with Turkish President Ismet İnönü on December 5. İnönü stalled on entering the war by asking for a quantity of supplies the Allies could not give without endangering Overlord.

Churchill and Roosevelt also had to agree on a commander for Overlord. American and British leaders had known for some time that the shifting balance of Allied forces now dictated an American commander. Nearly everyone assumed it would be Marshall, and indeed, the general would loved to have it. Prior to leaving Teheran, however, Roosevelt had decided that Marshall was indispensable in Washington. The command would go to Eisenhower.[1]

The president and prime minister were outwardly optimistic when they returned home, but privately doubtful about Stalin and the future course of the war. Roosevelt concealed his concerns when he addressed the country in a Christmas Eve "fireside chat." He spoke of Cairo and

Teheran more like the young man who had accompanied Wilson to Paris than the leader who had allied with the Devil to drive out Beelzebub. The American people, he said, could look forward to the future "with real, substantial confidence that peace on earth and good will toward men" would be realized. He had "got along fine" with Stalin and looked forward to a harmonious relationship when the Big Four, and "all the freedom loving peoples of the world would cooperate to keep the peace."[2]

Roosevelt's words give credence to those who charged him with deception or naiveté. The best that can be said is that Roosevelt, like many of his contemporaries, allowed his hope to cloud his judgment, and that his view of Stalin as "truly representative of the heart and soul of Russia" ignored the history of Lenin's and Stalin's rule. In December of 1943, however, there was a profound admiration for the Russian people and their leader. For many, it was not difficult to believe that, like the road to Damascus for St. Paul, the long and suffering road to Berlin had brought about a deep and lasting change in the Soviet government.

The Red Army continued to advance along the entire front following the battle of Kursk, but mainly in the central and southern sectors. It was now over six million men and was slightly larger than the Wehrmacht, equal in quality, and driven by a consuming hatred for its enemy. The warped German ideology had turned potentially cooperative peoples into partisan units working with the Red Army. But the road to Berlin would be long and difficult. Stalin believed the Soviet Union could defeat Germany even without an Allied landing in France in the spring of 1944.[3] Perhaps, but it would take months or years longer. In their struggle, the Russians benefitted greatly from having to fight only on one front, whereas the Germans had to cover two and eventually three following Overlord.

Hitler sought to keep the enemy as far from Germany as possible, to protect his production centers, and to keep his wavering allies under control. With time, he believed, Germany would develop a new generation of weapons capable of changing the balance of military power while the fragile alliance of its enemies fell apart. The Grand Alliance, however, looked stronger than ever following the Teheran conference and the Russians pressed onward. By early November they had taken Kiev and were crossing the Dnieper into the western Ukraine while isolating German forces remaining in the Crimea.

By January of 1944 the Russians were pressing west to the Rumanian border and south toward the Black Sea. The stalemate along the Volkhov and Baltic Fronts in the north ended on January 14. The long siege of

Leningrad was finally broken on the twenty-seventh, and by March the Red Army stood at Lake Peipus on the Estonian border. Russian advances led to friction between Hitler and his generals. The situation in Ukraine became critical when the Russians threatened to encircle Manstein's Army Group South. Relations between Manstein and Hitler had deteriorated greatly since the victorious days of 1940 and 1941. Manstein's superior military ability came close to intimidating Hitler, and he resented it as much as Manstein's courage to speak his mind. In early January Manstein bluntly told Hitler that his own leadership had brought about the current crisis.[4] Hitler had no intention of relinquishing command of the military and wanted no withdrawals. The German Army must hold in the east until he had defeated the Anglo-Americans in the west. Then he would destroy the Russians.

Hitler's dreams for the future could not alter the crisis of the present. In March Russian armies under Generals Ivan Konev, Rodion Malinovsky, and Georgi Zhukov struck in the Ukraine, forcing the Germans to abandon men and equipment. By early April Konev and Zhukov stood at the Rumanian border while Malinovsky had reached the Black Sea at Odessa. Loss of the Ukraine endangered German forces in the Crimea. Hitler forbade withdrawl for fear that it would cause further anxiety among his Balkan allies and perhaps encourage the Turks to join the war against him or deny him valuable war material. German forces in the Crimea had been aware of their vulnerability for some time. Over 250,000 men had to be supplied by sea from the Rumanian port of Constanta. Any evacuation had to be by sea, and it would take over two weeks just to remove the men. Most Rumanian soldiers had already despaired of the entire war and were ready to surrender after a token resistance.[5]

The Russians began their attack on April 8. They concentrated on Rumanian units in the western part of the peninsula before turning on the city of Simferopol. On April 10, the German commander, General Erwin Jänecke, ordered evacuation of the Crimea to begin, but was overruled by Hitler. By the fifteenth, the Germans were retreating to Sevastopol, and Hitler was forced to consent to the evacuation of all non-essential personnel. He still intended to hold Sevastopol until the Allied invasion had been defeated in the west. The Russians had defended the city for eight months in 1942. Surely, Hitler believed, his army could hold out for three or four. But the Germans had lost most of their weaponry and ammunition in their rapid retreat. They were demoralized and short of supplies when the final Soviet assault came on May 5. Hitler consented to an evacuation on May

9. Nearly 150,000 German and Rumanian troops in the Crimean escaped by sea or air. Approximately 100,000 were dead or missing, with 35,000 in captivity.[6]

Hitler knew that his allies had followed a winner, and that they were preparing to abandon a loser. He had minimized the defection of Italy by swift action and intended to do the same with Hungary and Rumania. The General Staff had formulated plans for Operations Margarethe I and II for occupying Hungary and Rumania in September of 1943. The Rumanians were more reliable. Under the dictatorship of Marshal Ion Antonescu, they had aided Hitler against the Russians more than any other country, and they had the most to fear from a Russian invasion. The Hungarians under Admiral Nicholas Horthy had earlier tried to convince Mussolini to end the war, and they had been much cooler toward the Duce's new government in Italy. They also were openly recalling troops from the Russian front. By March 1944, with the Red Army within 100 miles from the border, Hitler had sufficient evidence of Hungarian intrigues to warrant an invasion. He summoned Horthy to meet with him near Salzburg on March 18. The meeting with the aged regent was reminiscent of the infamous encounters with Schuschnigg and Hácha before the war. Horthy succumbed to a combination of theatrics and threats. Horthy agreed to German occupation, a shakeup in the government, the harnessing of Hungarian industry for the war effort, and measures against Hungarian Jews as part of the Final Solution.[7]

Hitler had once again been able to hold his allies in line and stop the adance of his enemies. He viewed the future with confidence. A lull had settled over The Eastern Front, and it appeared as though the Russians would need time before launching another offensive. The Wehrmacht also had been able to stop Anglo-American advances in Italy. Fighting in Italy received a low priority in Allied strategy following the commitment to Overlord. The situation was made more confusing by a political situation in which a variety of partisan groups existed in addition to the official Italian government and Mussolini's Italian Social Republic at Salò. Field Marshal Kesselring had constructed formidable fortifications across the peninsula north of Naples known as the Gustav Line. The Allies planned to break the deadlock by landing a force thirty miles southwest of Rome at Anzio. The plan was hasty at best, and its execution suffered from bad relations between General Alexander and the American Commander Mark Clark.

The Allies advanced against the Gustav Line in early January 1944 in hopes of moving closer to the Anzio beachhead. Forty thousand men landed on the Anzio beach to begin Operation Shingle on the twenty-second. To their surprise the opposition was light, and they had an opportunity to rapidly strike for Rome. The American commander, Major General John Lucas, believed his job was to establish his position and not to risk defeat with a plunge into the interior. Hitler was determined to hold the Allied line and destroy the Anzio pocket.[8] A victory would help restore German prestige while an American defeat during an election year might frighten Roosevelt into calling off the invasion of France. Kesselring quickly counterattacked against the Anzio beachhead once reinforcements arrived. The Allied advance soon threatened to become a disaster. The assault on the Gustav Line had failed and there would no link up with the Anzio forces. The Germans were close to eliminating the Anzio pocket until they were stopped in early March by Allied air and naval superiority. The front along the Gustav Line became a throwback to the trench warfare of World War I and remained essentially unchanged.

The Italian stalemate brought another confrontation between the Americans and the British. The Allies had planned to supplement the cross-channel attack in France with Operation Anvil, a landing on the Gulf of Lyons that would force the Germans to divert their strength from the west and give them the valuable port of Marseilles. Requirements for the Overlord-Anvil mission precluded further actions in Italy and the Mediterranean. Churchill called for another meeting of the Combined Chiefs in February 1944. Marshall suspected that Churchill had not given up on his penchant for the "underbelly" of Europe. He sent Eisenhower to London instead of going himself. Eisenhower grappled with the British argument that the Germans were diverting troops from the west to Italy. It would be better, they argued, to have one strong and successful assault on France than two weaker ones that might fail. Eisenhower also had to accept the painful fact that needs in the Pacific for landing craft made Anvil an impossibility until after Overlord. Marshall himself reluctantly acknowledged in March that Anvil would have to be postponed.[9]

The Allies sought to cripple the German war effort in Italy by attacking transportation facilities in the north. It was partly successful, but the Germans remained able to deliver minimum supplies by using coastal shipping and by working at night. The Allies were also building up their own forces for Operation Diadem against the Gustav Line on May 11. The offensive coincided with Operation Buffalo in the south to break out of the Anzio pocket northeastward in hopes of cutting off the retreating German forces.

The going was slow for the first three days against stiff resistance, but gradually the Allies advanced. The campaign was undermined when Clark ordered his forces toward Rome instead of eastward on the grounds that the Americans "deserved" to capture the Italian capital. Clark's decision allowed the Germans to hold their escape route at Valmonte. For a time it appeared as though the Germans might hold the Caesar Line south of Rome, but the Americans broke through on May 30. Clark then ordered a general offensive that took Valmonte and fored a German retreat.

Kesselring asked Hitler for permission to withdraw to better defenses north of Rome on June 2, and on the following day Hitler agreed. Clark made the most of the German retreat. The triumphant American Fifth Army entered Rome on June 4, ahead of everyone else.[10] Capture of the Eternal City was a joyous and a solemn moment for the victorious Allies. Rome was one of the cultural and religious rocks of the Western World and the first Axis capital to fall. As President Roosevelt noted in a radio broadcast on the night of June 5, however, much fighting lay ahead.[11] This the president well knew, and it may explain the subdued tone of his talk, for while he was speaking the greatest amphibious invasion force in history was heading for France.

Overlord marked the culmination of American strategic planning tempered by changing conditions. The decisions at Teheran had transformed plans for a cross-channel attack from a probability into a certainty. Eisenhower was determined to make the invaison succeed when he arrived in London in January 1944. He believed that Overlord would decide the European war. Should it fail, no new attempt could be made until the spring of 1945, at the earliest. There was concern that Stalin might come to an agreement with Hitler after regaining the boundaries of 1939, or that the Red Army might march to the Atlantic and bring all of Europe under its domination.

Allied planners had chosen the Normandy coast by a process of elimination combining caution and necessity. The beach had to be firm enough to support tanks and other heavy equipment and there had to be sufficient port facilities to supply a large army once a landing had been successful. The port of Calais was the most obvious place, but it was too close to Germany and too well defended. The Normandy coast had the right beaches and terrain while the port of Cherbourg lay at the end of the Crotentin Peninsula close to the British port of Portsmouth. The attack had to come at low tide in order to avoid protective barriers that would destroy landing craft, and it had to come near dawn with a limited amount of moonlight. It also had to come late enough in the year to allow for adequate assembling of material and the proper training of troops, yet soon enough to allow for at least four months of good weather for the campaign.[12] Churchill was not far wrong when he growled that the fate of two great empires seemed tied to "some goddamned things called LST's."[13] Eisenhower had to delay D-Day from May to June in order to gain 100 landing craft from another month of production. Throughout the spring the buildup continued along with a constant refining of the plan until Eisenhower decided to combine five ground and three airborne divisions for the attack.

The ability of the Germans to transfer troops had nearly caused defeat in Italy, and there was grave concern about it in planning Overlord. With the support of British Air Marshal Arthur Tedder and the Free French General Pierre Koenig, Eisenhower developed the Transportation Plan calling for a steady attack on the rail network in France in the months before D-Day. Such attacks had proven their value during the Italian campaign, but they carried a special risk for France. The German victory in 1940 had been swift and relatively free of destruction. The Transportation Plan would cause more death and destruction than the Germans had inflicted, and Vichy propaganda would make the most of it. Churchill and others initially opposed the plan on the grounds that it might cost the Allies the support of the French people and leave a legacy of hostility. After much arguing, however, Eisenhower got his way. Throughout April and May Allied planes dropped 76,000 tons of bombs on railyards, bridges, and other targets.[14]

German defenses were formidable from France to Norway, and the enemy knew the invasion was coming somewhere and soon. To ensure surprise the Allies imposed civilian, military, and even diplomatic restrictions to separate "one vast military camp," as Eisenhower put it, from the rest of England.[15] "In wartime," Churchill had told Stalin at Teheran, "truth is so precious that she should always be attended by a bodyguard of lies." There was no better example of it than in the preparations for Overlord. To protect the truth of the invasion, the Allies developed "Bodyguard, a scheme that had no less than thirty-six subordinate plans and scores of associated stratagems designed to conceal the time [and place] of the invasion."[16] The bodyguard protected its mistress well, but nothing in the hands of mortals could control the weather or predict it with certainty. The original launching date of June 5 had to be canceled, and it appeared the operation might have to wait until the middle of the month. Then came an unexpected clearing that would allow for the invasion. Eisenhower made the decision to go, although he admitted he did not like it.

Bad weather was reassuring across the channel. The Allies had a record of launching invasions only in good weather, and the Germans doubted whether Eisenhower and Montgomery would take the gamble. Many officers up and down the chain of command were caught unprepared and even out of France. Those who remained faced their enemy with a clumsy command structure and differing views on how best to defeat the invader. In North Africa Rommel had seen how superior enemy air power could destroy mobile armor on the ground. There was no point in keeping armor in reserve for the classical counterattack against an invader on the beaches. Most likely, much of if it would be destroyed by enemy air power before it could be effective. Armor would best be used on the beaches where the battle would be decided. Rommel's views were challenged. The head of Panzer Group West, General Leo Geyr von Schweppenburg, wanted to keep his armor in reserve to counterattack once the enemy had gained the beaches. Rundstedt, the commander in chief, was flexible, but leaned toward the more orthodox Geyr, primarily because he feared exposing his armor to naval fire. A compromise was finally reached dividing allocation as well as command of the armor. When the attack came, the poor coordination between commands at the front was further complicated by the need to secure Hitler's permission in Berchtesgaden to move additional units.[17] Air power presented the greatest example of how the war had changed. In the spring of 1940, Hitler had enjoyed tactical air superiority, but now it could do virtually nothing to stop the invasion, while the Allies continued their assault on German transportation and troop concentrations.

The "longest day" began shortly after 0100 hours on June 6, when the German command received reports of enemy parachutists landing in the area of Troarn, east of Caen. The Germans were confused and surprised. They continued to believe that a large landing would take place northward along the channel coast and hesitated to throw all their available force into the Normandy battle. By the end of the first day, the Allies had landed nearly 175,000 men along the Normandy coast, with some units advancing eight miles inland.[18]

The battle of the hedgerows began on the next day. Rundstedt had wanted to counterattack on June 7, but lacked heavy armor. German forces were weak and unable to prevail against Allied air superiority when they moved on the eighth. The Allies made little progress due in part to German resistance made easier by hedgerows, walls of earth five feet high and several feet thick that surrounded various fields. They continued, however, to consolidate their positions, and by June 9, they had secured a single beachhead.

The Americans took Carentan on June 11, the key city on the road to Cherbourg. The Germans knew that the vast Allied resources in Britain would soon be in France, when Cherbourg fell. They were also having trouble supplying their own forces because of air attacks. Rommel and Rundstedt agreed that the landing had succeeded and that it was nearly impossible to defend positions so far in the west. The field marshals met Hitler at Margival, north of Soissons, on June 17. Hitler blamed his generals for the enemy landings and ordered that Cherbourg be held. Rommel, who spoke for Rundstedt as well, did not believe Cherbourg could be held, nor that there would be a second landing at Calais. Most likely the Allies would build up their forces for a breakout to the south and toward Paris. Rommel's military assessments angered Hitler, who exploded when Rommel recommended ending the war, meaning surrender. Hitler told the marshals to worry about their own immediate fronts and leave politics to him. Germany would be saved by the new generation of weapons, the jet plane, and the *Vergeltungswaffen*, or Reprisal Weapons; specifically, the "V-1" bombs now being launched against London.[19]

The Margival conference began the final stage in the fall of the Third Reich. Hitler bore the physical marks of a man far older than his 55 years. He had learned little from the Russian campaign, and he preferred a flaming *Götterdammerung* to surrender. The conference also marked a turning point in the relations between Hitler and his field marshals. The wizened old Rundstedt always had been contemptuous of Hitler, and had done little to hide it. His command days were numbered. Rommel's relationship with Hitler had deteriorated since the defeat in Africa, and he had begun to listen to conspirators who wanted him to lead Germany out of the war. After leaving Margival he was ready to do more than listen.

The Allies continued to gain during the remainder of the month. Cherbourg fell on the twenty-seventh. Two days later Rommel and Rundstedt traveled to Berchtesgaden to make Hitler accept reality. Hitler's view of the war had more in common with 1940 than the present. He ordered measures far beyond Germany's resources and spoke as though the enemy had inferior air and sea power. Rommel and Rundstedt again raised the issue of ending the war. Again Hitler berated them. Both marshals left Berchtesgaden believing they would be relieved. Rundstedt was right. On July 2, he was replaced, but Rommel stayed on until critically wounded on the seventeenth.

Conspirators in the army attempted to kill Hitler at his East Prussian headquarters on July 20. Hitler retaliated with a reign of murder that included helpless infants who were related in the most distant way to the actual conspirators. The Wehrmacht especially came under attack, and this in turn affected the conduct of the war. "Fear," General Günter Blumentritt later recounted, "permeated and paralyzed the higher commands in the weeks and months that followed."[20] Dislocation and paralysis within the German command came at a time when the Allies launched their breakout from the Normandy perimeter. Groups of B-17 and B-24 bombers began Operation Cobra on July 24, with a carpet of firepower that jarred the Germans mentally as well as physically. The ground attack went slowly at first, but by the twenty-seventh Allied air and mechanized power began to tell. The appearance of George Patton personified the new offensive. Patton had been disciplined for indiscreet words and the improper handling of his troops following brilliant performances in North Africa and Sicily and had been doing penance in Britain as the commander of a nonexistent army that was poised to strike at Calais.

Patton received command of the American Third Army after the beachhead was secured. His presence aided the advance and helped Allied forces stop a German counterattack on August 7. Warned by Ultra, the Allied armies were ready when Hitler attempted to split the American forces at the base of the Crotentin Peninsula. Aided by good weather, Allied air power dealt devastating blows to the German drive. Hitler invited another Stalingrad by throwing so much of his strength into what came to be called the Argentan-Falaise Pocket. Montgomery's Canadian army closed in from the north while part of Patton's Third Army drove from the south to encircle German forces and open the way to the German border. The trap was not closed, however, due to caution, inexperience, and strained relations within the Allied Command, allowing several thousand Germans to escape.

The Allied victory in the west was supplemented on August 15 with the delayed Operation Anvil, now named Dragoon, an invasion of southern France to protect the Allied right flank and open the ports of Marseilles and Toulon. Dragoon was a minor operation compared to Overlord, especially since German strength and morale had been heavily drained by the defeats of the previous week. Hitler realized the futility of trying to make any lasting defense in southern France. On August 17, he reluctantly consented to a withdrawal behind the Saône River to the Vosges Mountains in northeastern France. He issued his directive for "Construction of the German Western Wall" on the twenty-fourth.[21]

The Germans forced what remained of the Vichy government to move north with them, leaving a political vacuum in France and the threat of civil war. Churchill and Roosevelt had tried to forge a shotgun marriage between Generals de Gaulle and Giraud at Casablanca. It was apparent to those on the scene that de Gaulle represented the cause of resistance, and this belief was born out as Giraud gradually faded away. Roosevelt, however, still declined to support the egocentric and sometimes haughty general. Eisenhower originally had planned to encircle Paris and drive on to the German border. He changed his mind because of developments in Paris and de Gaulle's presence in France. On August 19, local groups in the city rose against the German garrison under General Dietrich von Choltitz. The general realized his position was untenable, and he did not not want to be remembered as the man who destroyed Paris. The best solution lay in an honorable surrender after reaching a truce with the insurgents. De Gaulle believed a triumphant entry into Paris would give him control of France and force foreign powers to recognize his committee as the de facto government. He asked Eisenhower to liberate the city on the twenty-first. Eisenhower remained reluctant, but later agreed to send a Free French contingent of the Allied Expeditionary Force into Paris and to give de Gaulle the needed show of force while other units marched to the front. De Gaulle capped his years of lonely resistance on the twenty-sixth with a dramatic walk down the Champs-Elysées. With the help of the Anglo-Americans he was now the dominant figure in France. Soon, and intermittently for the next thirty years, he caused his allies to question their support.[22]

NOTES

1. Stephen E. Ambrose, *D-Day: June 6, 1944: The Climatic Battle Of World War II* (New York: Simon and Schuster, 1994), 69.
2. *New York Times*, December 25, 1943, 8.
3. Georgi Zhukov, *The Memoirs of Marshal Zhukov*, (New York: Delacorte Press, 1971), 493.
4. Seaton, *Russo-German War*, 411-412. Raymond Cartier, *Der Zweite Weltkrieg*, vol. 2 (Munich: Piper, 1967), 697.
5. Seaton, *Russo-German War*, 421-428.
6. Ibid., 430-431. Andreas Hillgruber, *Die Rämung der Krim 1944* (Frankfurt: E.S. Mittler and Sons, 1959), 72-75.
7. Mari Fenyo, *Hitler, Horthy, and Hungary: German-Hungarian Relations, 1941-1944* (New Haven: Yale University Press, 1972),

148-149.
8. Martin Blumenson, *The Mediterranean Theatre of Operation: Salerno to Cassino* (Washington: U.S. Government Printing Office, 1969), 257-363. *Hitlers Weisungen,* 241-242.
9. John Ehrman, *Grand Strategy,* vol. 5 (London: Her Majesty's Stationery Office, 1956), 243-249.
10. Ernest F. Fisher, *The Mediterranean Theatre of Operations: Cassino to the Alps* (Washington: U.S. Government Printing Office, 1977), 36-38, 105, 163-177, 203-223.
11. *New York Times, June 5,* 1944, 1. 5.
12. Stephen E. Ambrose, *The Supreme Commander: The War Years of General Dwight D. Eisenhower* (Garden City: Doubleday and Company, 1970), 329-333.
13. Gordon Harrison, *Cross-Channel Attack* (Washington: U.S. Government printing Office, 1951), 64.
14. Ambrose, *Supreme Commander,* 414-417. Harrison, *Cross-Channel Attack,* 198-230.
15. Ambrose, *D-Day,* 83-84. Dwight D. Eisenhower, *Crusade in Europe* (Garden City: Doubleday, 1948), 248.
16. Anthony Cave Brown, *Bodyguard of Lies* (New York: Harper and Row, 1975) 434.
17. John Keegan, *Six Armies in Normandy: From D-Day to the Liberation of Paris, June 6th-August 25, 1944* (New York: Viking Press, 1982), 64-65.
18. Ambrose, *D-Day,* 576.
19. Hans Speidel, *Invasion 1944: Rommel and the Normandy Campaign* (Westport, CT: Greenwood Press, 1950), 92-98.
20. Hoffmann, *German Resistance, 397-405.* B.H. Liddell Hart, *The German Generals Talk* (New York: William Morrow and Company, 1948), 249.
21. *Hitlers Weisungen,* 272-275.
22. Martin Blumenson, *Breakout and Pursuit* (Washington: U.S. Government Printing Office, 1961), 594-602. De Gaulle, Memoirs, vol. 1, 324, 598-622.

Defeat of the Axis In Europe, 1942–1945

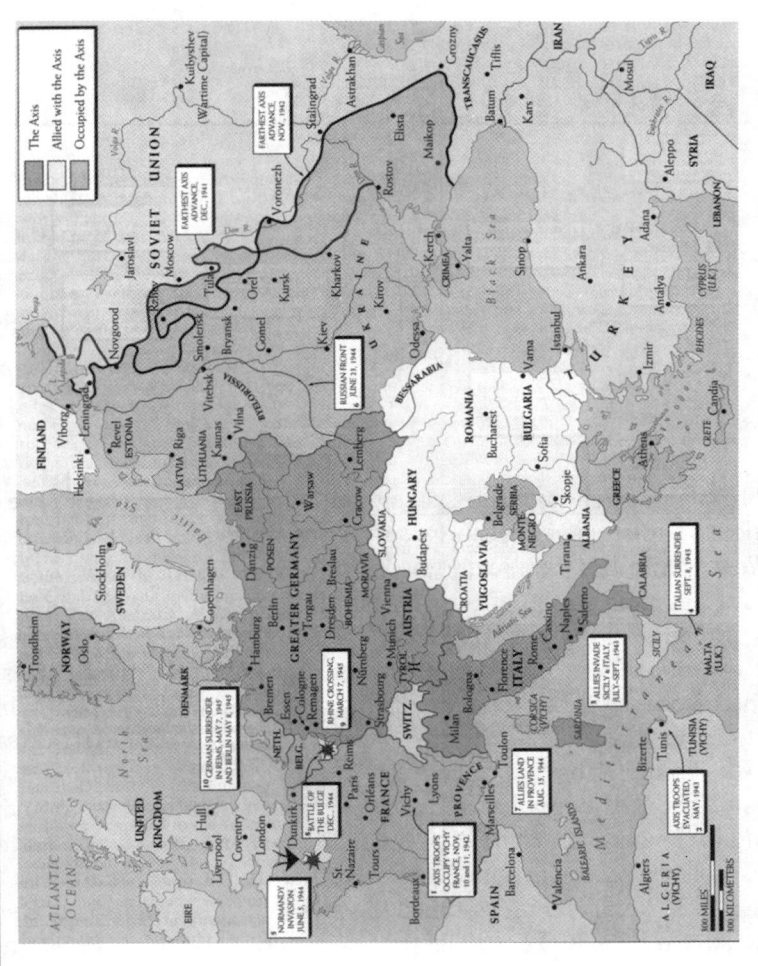

Chapter Fourteen

Victory Disease

The liberation of Paris led to speculation about an early end to the war. American, British, and French forces closed on the German border from the West, while the Red Army made spectacular gains in the East. The Russians appreciated the effort of their allies. Stalin kept his promise to attack in conjunction with Overlord. The Red Army hoped to knock the Finns out of the war with an attack on June 9. The United States had refrained from declaring war on Finland in 1941, but now openly threatened to sever diplomatic relations unless Finland left the war. Surrender, however, could bring a pro-German coup or occupation as it had in Hungary. The Red Army had broken the Finnish line by June 15 and was striking for Vyborg and the 1941 border. The Americans gave an additional twist to the screw on June 30 by severing diplomatic relations.[1] Field Marshal Karl Mannerheim assumed the presidency in August and secured an armistice on September 4. The peace treaty of September 19 was not as harsh as it could have been. Finland lost territory and had to pay reparations, but it remained independent.[2]

Fighting in the north had stabilized in June partly because the Red Army had launched a gigantic offensive against the Germans on the Belorussian front. Operation Bagration coincided with the third anniversary of Hitler's invasion on June 22, 1941, and was aimed at liberating all Soviet territory. It was well prepared and backed by overwhelming Russian superiority in men and weapons. Within two weeks the Russians had reached Minsk and had taken Vilna by the middle of July. By the end of July, troops under Marshal Konstantin Rokossovsky held Brest Litovsk and were striking for Warsaw. The Red Army had advanced nearly four hundred miles in little over a month. It became increasing difficult to maintain supply lines, a problem compounded by the difference in rail gauge as they moved westward. Still, with their momentum going so strongly, it appeared as though Rokossovsky would soon take Warsaw.

The London Poles hoped to increase their leverage with Stalin by controlling Warsaw. Stalin had no intention of dealing with them, nor would he allow them to govern Poland after the war. In late July, Stalin gave official recognition to the Polish Committee of National Liberation, which shortly made its headquarters in Lublin. "We have not found in Poland," Stalin wrote to Churchill, "other forces capable of establishing a Polish administration. The so-called underground organizations, led by the Polish government in London, have turned out to be ephemeral and lacking influence."[3]

Stalin's Committee broadcast an appeal on July 29, calling for an uprising in Warsaw to aid the advancing Russian Army and its Polish contingents. If the underground Home Army did not rebel, the credibility of the London government would be compromised, and its supporters liable to arrest and punishment as German collaborators following the inevitable and apparently imminent Russian victory. The Home Army inside Warsaw rose against the Germans on August 1. The next day Churchill saluted Russians and the Poles alike in Parliament. "Let them come together," he said. "We desire this union, and it would be a marvelous thing if it could be proclaimed . . . at the moment when the famous capital of Poland . . . has been liberated by the bravery of the Russian Armies."[4]

Then there came what Stanislaw Mikolajczyk, who had succeed Sikorski as head of the London Poles, later called "betrayal."[5] The Soviet advance ended as the rebellion began. There was nothing but silence from Moscow radio as the Germans struck back with forces in the city along with the Hermann Göring Division from Italy and special SS reinforcements. On August 4, Churchill asked Stalin to aid the Poles in Warsaw. Stalin's reply, as Churchill put it, was "grim." He dismissed reports of the uprising as "exaggerated and unreliable" and minimized any victories by the resistance.[6] Stalin could not minimize the uprising for long. It became part of the daily news complete with dispatches from General Tadeusz Bor-Komorowski, leader of the Home Army. On August 12, Tass blamed the uprising on the ill-timed responsibility of the émigré government in London.[7] Polish representatives in London and Washington appealed to

Churchill and Roosevelt for help. The two leaders asked Stalin to aid Warsaw directly or to allow American supply planes to land in Soviet territory. The reply was brutal and to the point. Stalin referred to the resistance as a "handful of power-seeking criminals" whose uprising had brought death to innocent civilians and had delayed the progress of the Red Army.[8]

On August 24, the Committee on National Liberation ordered all "secret organizations," meaning the Home Army, to be dissolved. The Home Army continued its hopeless fight with great courage. In retrospect, it might seem that public opinion in America and Britain would have been outraged at what Churchill called "the strange and sinister behavior of the Russians."[9] Stalin's behavior was sinister but not strange. The Germans would complete what he had begun at Katyn. There would be no Polish leaders to oppose him. Churchill and Roosevelt had to put the best face on sordid reality, but their relations with Stalin would never be the same.

Stalin decided to aid the insurgents in mid-September and to make sure the world knew of it. Russian planes had a habit of dropping supplies without using parachutes. After impact much of the equipment was useless, and much of the Russian ammunition was of no help to fighters using weapons captured from the German. American, British, and Polish planes attempting to supply the city from airfields in Italy suffered heavy casualties and were unable to deliver much help. Stalin gave permission for Allied planes to land in Russian controlled territory on September 18. Over a hundred B-17s based in Britain with fighter escorts attempted to supply the rebels, but much of the drops missed the target and fell into German hands. The Poles had lost much ground and were nearly out of ammunition and food by October 1. With no Soviet help coming it was obvious that little could be gained from further struggle. Bor negotiated final surrender terms with the Germans on October 2. Stalin was not content to destroy his enemies — he must ridicule them as well. The Warsaw resistance was now condemned for surrendering. The fighters were to be given rights as prisoners of war, while civilians were to be evacuated from the city. Maltreatment and death were yet to come for many of the survivors. Most who escaped the Germans were captured by the Russians and disappeared into prison camps.[10]

The Warsaw uprising and the surrender of Finland increased the growing feeling that Germany was losing the war, and encouraged Hitler's allies to find a way out. Relations between Germany and Romania had cooled after the disasters at Stalingrad and in the Crimea. The Red Army crossed the Pruth River into Bessarabia on April 2. Molotov made a radio broadcast stating that the Soviet Union had no intention of "acquiring any part of Romanian territory, or of altering the social structure of Romania." Throughout the spring the opposition aided by young King Michael removed army and civilian officials who might be more loyal to Antonescu and the Germans, while at the front there was regular communication between Romanian and Russian military units. The government was surprised, however, when the Red Army launched an offensive on August 20.

King Michael invited Antonescu to the palace on August 23. He arrested the marshal and formed a new government under General Constantin Sanatescu. That night the king announced an end to the war against the Allies. The Soviets agreed to an armistice and pledged to respect Romanian independence.[11] Hitler tried to restore Antonescu to power the next day, but the Romanian Army put up stiff resistance. Stuka dive bombers bombed Bucharest on the afternoon of the twenty-fourth, giving the government an excuse to declare war on Germany. The declaration of war threw the country into chaos and brought a military debacle for the Germans who were now surrounded by a hostile Romanian Army and population. The declaration also gave the Red Army an opportunity to exploit the widest open flank known in modern warfare.[12] Within days it held the Ploesti oil fields as well as the capital. By mid-September it had reached the Yugoslavian border to meet the Communist partisans of Joseph Broz-Tito. The sudden loss of Romania also forced Hitler to pull German forces in Greece and Yugoslavia back to better defensive positions.[13]

Expansionists of various ideologies had dreamed of extending Russian rule to the Dardanelles for centuries. The German collapse offered Stalin the opportunity to fuse these dreams with Leninism to form a Communist Empire under Soviet domination. Bulgaria now stood at the mercy of the Red Army. Bulgaria was at war with Britain and the United States, but not with the Soviet Union, a legality that did not prevent mysterious bombing attacks from the north. The regency for young Tsar Simeon II had lost much of its prestige by 1944, while opposition to the war coalesced in a group of parties known as the Fatherland Front. Churchill warned Bulgaria on August 2 that the day of "redemption" was passing and advised it to make peace through the Soviet Union. The regency withdrew from the war on August 27 and turned authority over to a new pro-western government on September 2. The new liberal prime minister, Constantine Muraviev, announced the restoration of democracy and his desire to end the war with Britain and the United States. Stalin had no intention of allowing a pro-

Western democracy in Sofia. On September 5 the Soviet Union declared war on Bulgaria. Bulgarian and Romanian armies now joined the march across Europe while at home both countries fell under Soviet domination.[14]

The Allied advance in Europe made it clear that the war was ending. Each member of the Grand Alliance looked beyond to the defeat of Japan and the new world to follow. Soviet actions in eastern Europe had sent a chill through London and Washington. The Soviets also seemed to be causing trouble with composition of the United Nations. Negotiations for the new international organization had begun in late August at Dumbarton Oaks Estates in Washington. Within a week the new Soviet ambassador to the United States, Andrei Gromyko, angered the Americans by requesting membership for each of the sixteen Soviet republics. Roosevelt decided to take his case to Stalin. Stalin replied by stressing the rights of the various republics and the Soviet constitution. He was also determined not to give ground on a veto for each of the great powers. "Absurd prejudices," Stalin said, against the Soviet Union made it necessary. The Soviet position threatened to wreck the talks, especially if they became known to Roosevelt's Republican opposition. Roosevelt decided to let the talks end in September with a statement of progress and a note that there were still important issues to be settled.[15]

Churchill and Roosevelt were troubled when they journeyed to Quebec in early September to discuss future plans. The United States had won remarkable victories in the Pacific by the summer of 1944. American forces had moved relentlessly toward Japan with a campaign of "island hopping." Japanese defenders had fought with little or no air support throughout the campaign. In the Battle of the Philippine Sea, or what was called "The "Great Marianas Turkey Shoot" of June 19, superior American aircraft and pilots had effectively destroyed Japanese air strength, and American ground forces had taken Guam and Saipan by the end of the month. The Americans had now breached the inner ring of Japanese defenses and were 1,300 miles from the Home Islands with an excellent base for the new B-29 bombers. The loss of Saipan provided the final jolt to the government of Tojo Hideki. He was forced to resign on July 17 by a coalition of civilian politicians who realized that the war could not be won, and that Japan must seek a compromise peace before being totally conquered. It seemed that nothing less than the total conquest of Japan was possible for the Americans. Japanese soldiers had chosen to die in suicide charges or to kill themselves rather than surrender. Thirty thousand civilians on Saipan also chose or were forced to join in mass suicide.[16]

Chapter 14

One bleak spot remained amid success. The Chinese Nationalist armies were unable to stop a Japanese advance toward American bases and Nationalist capital at Chungking. The impending calamity brought an open break between Chiang Kai-shek and the chief American advisor, General Joseph Stilwell. Stilwell had made little effort to conceal his dislike of Chiang. Burma as well as China might be lost, he argued, unless the Nationalist forces were brought under American control. Chiang refused to humble himself or his government to foreign domination. He asked Roosevelt to relieve Stilwell on September 25. Roosevelt decided that victory in the Marianas and the eventual Russian entry into the Pacific war had made the war in China less important, and he did not want a fight with Chiang's American supporters prior to the November election. Roosevelt notified Chiang on October 19 that Stilwell would be recalled.[17]

The problems of Asia had to await the end of the war in Europe. The Combined Chiefs gave priority to the final assault on Germany. They did not take sides in the continuing struggle between Eisenhower and Montgomery over the proper strategy. Churchill's plan for a drive for Vienna from the south was kept open in case Germany suddenly collapsed. The Americans were convinced there would be a long struggle with Japan after Germany was defeated, and they wondered how long the public would support the war. Japan might be defeated by air bombardment along with a blockade, but such a course would bring an "unacceptable delay." There would have to be, they maintained, an invasion into the "industrial heart of Japan," that would bring terrible casualties.[18]

The scent of victory in Europe helped to produce the blunder known as the Morgenthau Plan. Churchill was surprised when he noticed that Roosevelt had brought Secretary of the Treasury Henry Morgenthau instead of Hopkins or Hull. Roosevelt was in a mood more reminiscent of Clemenceau than Wilson with regard to Germany. Morgenthau believed German industry should be destroyed or given to the victorious Allies, with no concern for the German people. Hull had initially approved the plan, but Secretary of War Stimson vigorously opposed it. Roosevelt stood by Morgenthau. Churchill initially had opposed the plan, and then allowed himself to think it might improve Britain's economy following the war. It might have at first, but Churchill and everyone else should have realized that economic collapse in central Europe would cause a political vacuum and aid Soviet expansion. Details of the plan appeared in the press by late September. The Morgenthau Plan threatened the Germans with economic deprivation and semi-starvation following unconditional surrender. The plan, as one critic noted, was "worth thirty divisions to the Germans," as well as incompatible with the transfer of German territory to Poland. The president privately admitted to Stimson that Morgenthau had "pulled a boner," while publicly stating that only those Germans "directly responsible" for the war would be punished.[19]

It soon became clear that Germany would not collapse soon. Allied armies had won a string of victories similar to those of Marshal Foch in 1918. But Foch had faced a far different Germany than the Allies in 1944. Hitler had eliminated potential opponents following the attempt on his life in July. He and his followers had nothing to lose by fighting to the end. Many fought on simply to defend the Fatherland. Allied diplomats and generals began to suffer from "victory disease," a kind of hubris similar to that experienced earlier by the Axis.[20] The Germans were vulnerable, but by early September the rapid Allied advance had reached its limit. Men were weary, equipment badly needed repair, and supplies were running out.

Hitler did not fully realize the weakness of his Western Wall until British forces captured Antwerp on September 4. The Allies now threatened rocket bases in Holland and had a port from which to strike into Germany. The Germans, however, still held the Scheldt Estuary and were able to deny use of the port to the Allies.[21] Hitler reappointed Rundstedt as commander in the west on September 5. The old field marshal believed the war was lost, but duty compelled him to serve. He well knew the danger in the west and warned Hitler it would take five to six weeks to reorganize the defenses.

Eisenhower believed he could finish the Germans by boldly striking across the Rhine to destroy Hitler's rocket bases and capture German industry in the Ruhr.[22] Operation Market-Garden began on September 17 with good weather and the largest air drop of the war. Successive waves of troops were sent over an area sixty miles behind the German line to secure the vital bridges until ground forces could advance to Eindhoven, on to Nijmegen, and then to Arnhem in the Netherlands. Operation Garden also began well on the ground with the benefit of surprise and good air support.

Rundstedt had considered the possibility of Allied airborne troops north of the Rhine. He was able to respond more quickly when by chance a copy of the Allied plan fell into his hands. The battle began to turn against the Allies by the twentieth. Increased German anti-aircraft fire, fighter defenses, and bad weather delayed reinforcements to the airborne units who lost communication with each other and their commanders. The

Germans hit the narrow Allied ground attack on both flanks as well as in front. Some gains were made, but it was apparent by September 25 that the operation had failed. Montgomery's preoccupation with Arnhem caused him to underestimate the force needed to clear the sixty miles of islands and land along the Scheldt Estuary. He finally agreed to concentrate on the Scheldt after Eisenhower threatened to curtail supplies. Bitter fighting continued into November until the second Canadian Army and British commandos won the area and cleared the Scheldt of mines. The first Allied ships docked at Antwerp on November 28, but by then winter was approaching and the hope for a victory in 1944 was gone.

It was apparent that Eisenhower's armies would not enter Germany in any strength until the coming year. In contrast, the Red Army drove from Warsaw toward the 1939 German border, while in the south it moved closer to Hungary, Greece, and Yugoslavia. Churchill asked for a meeting of the Big Three to deal with the changing situation, but Roosevelt had neither the interest nor the time to interrupt his election campaign. Churchill had cause to be concerned about eastern Europe. Britain had gone to war to preserve Polish independence and had made great sacrifices in Greece. Churchill was also heir to Castlereagh and the long British concern for the balance of power in Europe. The prime minister led an empire that was growing weaker every day. He wanted agreement with the Russians on the Balkans and the Mediterranean as soon as he could get it, whatever Americans might think about it. Stalin originally had thought Churchill was coming to gain his consent to Anglo-American decisions made at Quebec. He was understandably puzzled when Roosevelt informed him that the United States would not be bound by any agreements he made with Churchill dealing with the war.[23] To keep himself informed, however, Roosevelt asked Ambassador Harriman to attend the conference, but to make no commitments.

Churchill and Eden arrived in Moscow on October 9 and had their first meeting with Stalin and Molotov that night. The prime minister began by proving that even great statesmen can do foolish things. Churchill proposed that the Balkans be divided according to a mathematical formula. The Soviets were to have 90 percent influence in Romania, to 10 percent for "others." Britain would have 90 percent, to 10 percent for the Soviets in Greece. In Hungary and Yugoslavia, where Churchill was now having difficulty with Tito, both the British and the Soviets would have 50 percent, while in Bulgaria Churchill conceded a slight edge to the Soviets with 75 percent to 25 percent for "others." Churchill then suggested burning the agreement, but Stalin was content to let him keep it.[24]

Stalin knew that military possession guaranteed 100 percent control. It did no harm to concede Greece where the British had landed troops to check Communist guerrillas. "This war," he later told Milovan Djilas, "is not as in the past; whoever occupies a territory also imposes on it his own social system as far as his armies can reach. It cannot be otherwise."[25] The Soviets took Churchill's percentage figures as a starting point for strengthening their hold in the Balkans. At a later meeting Molotov asked for an increase in Soviet influence. Eden countered with his own horse trading, and the meeting ended on a deadlock. Churchill later maintained that the original percentage figures had been intended only as temporary measures, and he may have been surprised at how seriously the Russians were taking them. That, and Harriman's frown when he heard of the agreements, caused Churchill to back off from the original proposals and to let the entire matter slide into limbo.

Stalin was becoming arbiter for the Balkans and master of Poland. The Soviets and their Lublin toadies continued to eliminate the remnants of the Home Army and to reduce the influence of the London government. Churchill had to deal with Stalin over Poland as Chamberlain had dealt with Hitler over Czechoslovakia. He had threatened to abandon the London Poles unless Mikolajczyk joined him for discussions with Stalin. Poland must accept the Curzon Line in exchange for compensation to the Oder River in the west. The Lublin Poles agreed to Mikolajczyk as leader of the government but with a majority of the cabinet positions in their hands.

Churchill disliked the Lublin Poles, but he believed Mikolajczyk's only hope lay in accepting Stalin's terms. Perhaps Poland could lead an independent existence following the war with support of the two Western democracies. But neither he nor the Americans were going to let the fate of Poland endanger the alliance against Germany or the coming assault of Japan. Mikolajczyk correctly saw it as a ruse to prolong the day when the Lublin Poles took control of the government.[26] Stalin demanded ideological as well as political and military security. The welcome given to the German invaders in 1941 had revealed the unpopularity of Stalin and communism. He could not tolerate the siren song of a liberal and democratic Poland, regardless of its border or how friendly its foreign policy. A pessimistic Mikolajczyk agreed to accept the territorial demands. When he returned to London, however, the more conservative elements in the government remained adamant against the Curzon Line and other territorial concessions. Mikolajczyk resigned on November 24, leaving the London government even more diminished as a factor in the reconstruction of Poland following the war.

The fate of Poland was less important to the Americans and the British than Stalin's intention to enter the war against Japan following the end of the European war. Churchill, Harriman, and their military advisors discussed the coming war with Japan on October 14, and they noted the importance of the Soviet role. Stalin believed the Red Army needed at least three months from the end of the war in Europe to prepare an attack in Manchuria, providing the West could deliver the needed supplies. It was generally agreed that Soviet military operations would involve eliminating Japanese troops on the Asian mainland while the Americans handled air and sea operations against the coastal areas of China and the invasion of Japan. Stalin made it clear that the Red Army would be fighting for specific gains.[27] The weakness of Nationalist China and Communist strength added urgency in the State Department for formulating precise terms for their proposals at the coming meeting of the Big Three.

Churchill left Moscow in a euphoric mood on October 18. A week later he told Parliament that "relations with Soviet Russia were never more close, intimate and cordial than they are at the present time."[28] The prospects did appear promising in October of 1944. The defeat of Germany and the promise of Soviet help against Japan were assured, and there was at least a slender hope that the congeniality of the Moscow meeting might continue. The future looked most promising of all for Stalin. His armies were poised for the final thrust into central Europe and future conquest awaited him in Asia. The day was coming when he would rule an empire worthy of envy by Lenin or Peter the Great.

Hitler, however, continued to believe he would win the war with new weapons and by keeping his allies in line. German armies had occupied Hungary in March to bolster sagging morale and protect needed economic resources. Allied bombers responded by blasting major cities and most of the oil refineries from April to September. Admiral Horthy also resented the deportation of Hungarian Jews, and tried to stop it. The Rumanian surrender in September made the crisis acute. Rumania was now on the Allied side and in a position to gain territory in Transylvania. Horthy wanted to make a separate peace with the Anglo-Americans, but it was soon obvious that the Red Army would occupy the country. Horthy realized he must deal with Stalin, and his agents reached a secret armistice agreement in Moscow on October 11.

Hitler had been warned that the Hungarians were going to defect. In early September he sent Otto Skorzeny, the man who had rescued Mussolini, to strengthen German forces in Hungary. Hitler and Skorzeny were ready on September 14 when news arrived that the moment of defection was near. Skorzeny's men kidnaped Horthy's son the next morning and flew him to Vienna. Faced with the execution of his son and German military superiority in Budapest, Horthy agreed to resign and was taken to Germany for "protection." Hitler held Hungary and delayed the rapid march of the Red Army. For two months the new pro-Nazi "Arrow-Cross" government in Hungary aided their German masters in exterminating the Jews, but by early December the Red Army had crossed the Hungarian plain to begin their siege of Budapest.[29]

Hitler's action in Hungary again demonstrated his ability to move swiftly with sufficient firepower to enforce his will. He planned to do the same in the West. After Market-Garden the Allied advance had been slowed by stiff resistance and bad weather. Hitler knew the Allied armies were spread thinly. He viewed them as being inferior to the Russians in overall fighting quality. A German offensive could break Britain's will to fight with a second Dunkirk and crack the American home front as well. The Anglo-Americans would tremble at the prospect of Russian hordes bringing Bolshevism to western Europe, once their own armies were defeated. They would end the war with Germany, and Stalin too might make peace once deserted by his allies and facing stiff German resistance.

Hitler's plan was daring, but it defied reality. He ordered an offensive along a sixty-mile front that sent one army to capture Antwerp, another toward Brussels, while a commando operation in the south protected the northern thrusts by sabotage and by sowing disarray among the Allied armies. But the Allies were not the hesitant and timidly led force the Germans had routed so easily in 1940. They were battle hardened, well armed, and well led. Above all, they had overwhelming air superiority and knew how to use it. Rundstedt believed the plan was simply too much for German resources. He urged Hitler to pursue a more limited operation against the Allied salient at Aachen.[30] Hitler insisted that surprise and bad weather would bring success. The surprise was not as great as he believed. Allied air reconnaissance and Ultra intercepts indicated that an attack was coming. But Allied intelligence did not perceive that this was an offensive planned by Hitler and not by the traditional Rundstedt, and that Hitler had won his greatest victory in this same area by doing the unorthodox.[31]

The Germans struck on the night of December 15 with an assault that surprised the Allies and drove them back, but not as far as had been hoped. Narrow roads slowed coordination and movement of the two advancing armies, while Skorzeny's Operation Grief to sow disorder behind enemy lines had little impact after the first few days. The key to the German advance lay along the road through Bastogne where the American 101st Airborne Division had taken up its position. The Germans surrounded the town, but the Americans slowed their advance and forced them to divert additional troops for a final attack. The battle turned dramatically on the twenty-second when the sky cleared sufficiently for Allied air power to strike. Hundreds of bombers and fighters devastated German troop concentrations and supply depots. The American Second Armored Division launched a counterattack from the north on the twenty-fourth, while the day after Christmas, Patton's Third Army completed its 100-mile journey to relieve the Bastogne defenders. German forces must now withdraw or be destroyed with the onset of good weather. Hitler, however, ordered the offensive to be renewed on the twenty-eighth. Weary soldiers carried out their orders, and heavy fighting continued into January. Hitler finally agreed to withdraw on January 5 to prevent encirclement. What remained of the Ardennes advance ended on January 12 when the Red Army resumed its offensive, forcing Hitler to quickly transfer men and equipment eastward. The Ardennes failure marked the last great offensive of the once mighty Wehrmacht. Failure in the west helped to quicken its doom in the east. By his actions, however, Hitler had staggered the advancing Western Allies who had to recognize that the Soviets were now in a far better position to administer the final blow to Germany and bring much of the country under its military control.

The Red Army had lain relatively dormant on the Vistula since August of 1944. Stalin had promised to launch an offensive in early January to coincide with the Anglo-American drive on the Rhine. Hitler remained confident about the eastern front and continued to underestimate the strength of the Red Army. Heinz Guderian, who now served as Chief of the General Staff, began to receive reports of a large Soviet buildup in late December. Then, and again in early January, he asked Hitler to transfer troops from the west to stop the Russian advance in Hungary and to meet the expected offensive in Poland. Hitler denounced the intelligence reports as "the greatest imposture since Ghengis Kahn" and insisted the eastern front had enough reserves to hold. Guderian thought not and warned that it would collapse like a "house of cards."[32] Not even Guderian, however, realized what kind of an offensive was coming. Stalin was now looking beyond the Oder to Berlin and perhaps to the Elbe. The Red Army built up its forces throughout the autumn to a five-to-one advantage, stockpiled supplies, and converted needed portions of the Polish rail system to the wider Russian gauge.[33]

On January 12, Marshal Ivan Konev's 1st Ukrainian Front struck from Baranov on the Vistula toward Cracow in southern Poland. As Konev's troops advanced in the south, Zhukov's First Belorussian Front attacked farther north on the fourteenth to encircle Warsaw and advance toward the German frontier. Farther to the north, Rokossovsky's Second Belorussian Front veered northwest toward Danzig to link up with Marshal Ivan Chernyakhovsky's Third Belorussian Front encircling Königsberg. The Russians advanced more quickly after moving into the flatland of western Poland aided by superior firepower, morale, and the large number of American trucks and other vehicles that had poured into the Soviet Union during the previous year. Hitler responded by continuing to rob one front in order to rescue another. He transferred Sepp Dietrich's Sixth SS Panzer Army from the Ardennes to Poland, while other units went to save the vital Hungarian oil supplies. Hitler now relied increasingly on the SS and turned conduct of the war over to unqualified amateurs like Heinrich Himmler, while venting fury on the regular army for failing to hold the line.

The Russians had assembled too much power and the Germans had lost much of their mobility and strength. Konev's forces crossed the Silesian frontier into Germany on January 20, threatening the last industrial area spared by Allied bombing. The magnitude of the Russian advance was symbolized on the following day when Rokossovsky's men swept through historic Tannenberg where the Germans had destroyed the Tsar's armies a generation before. Rokossovsky continued northwest to the Baltic to isolate German forces in East Prussia. Zhukov's First Belorussian Front in the center encircled Poznan on the twenty-fifth, while others pressed on toward the Oder.

Konev and Zhukov had crossed the Oder by the end of the month and now looked westward to the ultimate prize. Zhukov's troops at Küstrin were only forty-eight miles from Berlin. The Red Army now faced its "February Dilemma." Zhukov and the Soviet command in Moscow initially believed they could reach the Elbe by the end of February and then attack Berlin from several directions. But German fortifications and troop concentrations still had to be eliminated. The Red Army also had exposed its flanks to German attacks and there was concern about deteriorating weather and dwindling supplies. Stalin decided to postpone the assault on Berlin. In three weeks the Red Army had made one of the most spectacular advances of the war. He could now meet his Allies at Yalta on February 4 with all of Poland and most of Hungary in his pocket. His armies were little more than a day's march from Berlin, while those of his allies were still fighting to regain the area lost during the Battle of the Bulge. There was no point in taking any risks. In Europe, as well as Asia, his Allies needed him more than he needed them.

NOTES

1. Erickson, *Road to Berlin,* 205. Seaton, *Russo-German War,* 433. *FRUS: 1944*, vol. 3, 605-606.
2. S.C. Leonard Lundin, *Finland and the Second World War* (Bloomington, IN: Indiana University Press, 1957), 222-230.
3. *Stalin Correspondence,* vol. 1, 143.
4. *Times* (London) August 3, 1944, 6. Gilbert, Churchill, vol. 7, 871.
5. Stanislaw Mikolajczyk, *The Rape of Poland: Pattern of Soviet Aggression* (New York: McGraw-Hill Company, Incorporated, 1948), 66.
6. *Stalin Correspondence,* vol. 1, 252-253.
7. *Times* (London) August 13, 1944, p. 4.
8. Woodward, *British Policy in the Second World War,* vol. 2, 207-212. *Stalin Correspondence,* vol. 1, 258.
9. Churchill, *Triumph and Tragedy* (Boston: Houghton Mifflin Company, 1953) 139.
10. Hans von Krannhals, *Warschauer Aufstand 1944* (Frankfurt am Main: Berard and Graefe Verlag für Wehrwessen, 1964) 187-188, 209-212. *Times* (London), October 4, 1944, 4. Weinberg, *World At Arms,* 709-711.
11. *Times* (London) August 24, 1944, 4, August 25, 1944, 4.
12. Glantz and House, *When Titans Clashed,* 219-220.
13. Seaton, *Russo-German* War, 483.
14. Marshall Lee Miller, *Bulgaria During the Second World War* (Stanford: Stanford University Press, 1975), 85.
15. *FRUS: 1944,* vol. 4, 988.
16. Spector, *Eagle Against the Sun,* 307-319.
17. Ibid., 368-369.

18. Ray S. Cline, *Washington Command Post: The Operations Division* (Washington: U.S. Government Printing Office, 1951), 337-338.
19. *New York Times,* September 21, 1944, 1, 11.
20. Ambrose, *Supreme Commander,* 508.
21. Blumenson, *Breakout and Pursuit,* 699-700.
22. Stephen E. Ambrose, *Citizen Soldiers: The U.S. Army from the Normandy Beaches to the Bulge to the Surrender of Germany June 7, 1944 to May 7, 1945* (New York: Simon & Schuster, 1997), 118.
23. *Stalin Correspondence,* vol. 2, 161.
24. Gilbert, *Churchill,* vol. 7, 997-1001.
25. Milovan Djilas, *Conversations with Stalin,* trans. Michael B. Petrovich (New York: Harcourt, Brace and World, Incorporated, 1962), 114.
26. Bullock, *Parallel Lives,* 851.
27. *FRUS: Conferences at Malta and Yalta,* 1945 (Washington: U.S. Government Printing Office, 1955), 368-382.
28. *Times* (London) October 28, 1944, 1, 8.
29. Weinberg, *World at Arms,* 715.
30. Liddell Hart, *The German Generals Talk, 274-276.* Weinberg, *World at Arms,* 765.
31. Charles B. MacDonald, *A Time for Trumpets: The Untold Story of the Battle of the Bulge* (New York: William Morrow and Company, 1985), 79.
32. Bullock, *Parallel Lives,* 867-868. Guderian, *Panzer Leader,* 309-315.
33. Tony Le Tissier, *Zhukov at the Oder: The Decisive Battle for Berlin* (Westport, CT: Praeger, 1996), 13. Earl P. Ziemke, *Stalingrad to Berlin* (Washington: U.S. Government Printing Office, 1968), 419-421.

CHAPTER FIFTEEN

Yalta

The reality of power and need was illustrated at the Yalta Conference. Churchill and Roosevelt had wanted another meeting for months, but there was difficulty finding a site. Roosevelt wanted to meet in the Mediterranean, but Stalin insisted that poor health and the needs of war prevented any long trips. Roosevelt's own health was much worse than most people knew, and he did not want to leave Washington while Congress was in session. He agreed, however, to meet Stalin at Yalta after his inauguration on January 20, 1945.[1] "Ten years of research," Churchill told Hopkins, "could not have found a worse place in the world." The prime minister intended to make the best of it by bringing sufficient whiskey to make the ordeal as bearable as possible.[2]

Divisions within the Grand Alliance were public knowledge. The American people were losing trust in the Soviet Union. Stalin and his Lublin Committee were going to control Poland in their way, whatever the rhetoric of the Atlantic Charter. The United States could not prevent it. Roosevelt privately accepted the reality. He could not do so publicly without endangering relations with the Russians while strengthening isolationism at home.

Relations with the British were also strained. Many Americans continued to suspect Britain of using American blood to gain influence in the Middle East and Asia. Suspicion flared into open condemnation in the autumn of 1944 when Churchill ordered British troops to Greece to check any Communist takeover. British action in Greece appeared to discard the lofty principles of the Atlantic Charter and Teheran Declaration in favor of imperialism and spheres of influence.

The British also had their quarrel with the Americans. In December 1944 the *Economist* lashed out at American bullying and self-righteousness carping. "The ordinary Englishman remembers Woodrow Wilson's statement that the United States is the only idealist country in the world — and he remembers that the only Great Power that made any effort to attain Wilson's ideals in hard practice was Great Britain. The Americans, the article concluded, "have twisted the lion's tail just once too often," and it was time to end Churchill's policy of "appeasement . . . with all its humiliations and abasement . . . ."[3] A week later the *Economist* criticized Churchill for being "universal mediator, go-between, and perpetual aunt" and called for the emergence of a "genuine British foreign policy as opposed to the passive and partial acceptance of other people's policies."[4]

Roosevelt responded at a press conference on January 2, 1945 by minimizing inevitable differences.[5] Four days later he used the State of the Union address to warn against forsaking international responsibilities because of disillusionment with an imperfect world. To do so would only lead to a third world war as it had with the second.[6] Roosevelt had reason to be concerned. On January 10, Senator Arthur Vandenberg of Michigan, the Henry Cabot Lodge of this war, made a powerful speech in defense of the Atlantic Charter. Neither Britain nor the Soviet Union, Vandenberg stated, seemed deterred by the fear of disunity when they made decisions "often repugnant to our ideas and or ideals." It was time, he continued, to ask "What are we fighting for?"[7]

The Americans also challenged Churchill on the division of Germany. Roosevelt and his advisors had first discussed occupation zones in Germany on board the *Iowa* in November of 1943, with the president penciling in his ideas on a *National Geographic* map. He envisioned Berlin as the dividing point between the Russian and Western zones, with the Americans controlling northwestern Germany.[8] In January of 1944 the British proposed to the European Advisory Commission that the Soviets occupy Mecklenburg-Pomerania, Brandenburg, Saxony-Anhalt, Thuringia, and all areas to the east, except for greater Berlin, which was to be occupied by American, British, and Russian forces. They also proposed that the northwestern section of the country, including Brunswick, Hesse-Nassau, The Rhine provinces and the areas north of them come under British occupation. The Americans would receive the Saar, the Bavarian

Palatinate west of the Rhine, Hesse-Darmstadt, Württemburg, Baden, and Bavaria.

Roosevelt and Marshall did not quarrel with the Soviet Zone allocation, but they insisted that the situation in the west be reversed. The United States needed to deploy American forces to the Far East through the ports of northwestern Germany at the end of the European war. Roosevelt agreed to compromise. The Americans accepted a revised southern zone at Quebec in September of 1944. The Saar and the Palatinate west of the Rhine were given to the British in exchange for Hesse-Cassel and Hesse-Nassau. The ports of Bremen and Bremerhaven and staging areas around them were to have an American command to aid American deployment to the Far East.

New disputes rose over the precise areas involved and the amount of American control. Churchill pressed for inclusion of the French Provisional Government on the European Advisory Commission. Bringing the French into the dispute did not appeal to the Americans, but they finally consented at the Malta meetings in late January 1945 after it was pointed out that without specified zones the Soviets could march to the Rhine and occupy all conquered areas for as long as they wished.[9]

Anglo-American animosity had increased during the Battle of the Bulge. Generals Alexander, Brooke, and Montgomery had been in the field when Eisenhower was still an unknown lieutenant colonel with no combat experience. Eisenhower had temporarily placed some American units under Montgomery's command during the emergency in the Ardennes. The British press inflamed matters by implying that Montgomery had saved Eisenhower from defeat. Criticism of Eisenhower and the implied belittling of the American effort in the Ardennes infuriated Omar Bradley, Patton, and Marshall, none of whom had ever liked Montgomery in the first place.

Churchill sought to heal the breach by praising the Americans before Parliament, but it took Marshall's intervention to settle the issue. Eisenhower informed Marshall in late December that either he or Montgomery would have to go. Montgomery knew that Marshall supported Eisenhower, and that he would be replaced by Alexander in any confrontation with the Americans. He accepted defeat in early January by sending Eisenhower a message promising to "go on with your proposals. Your obedient subordinate. Monty." Eisenhower's plan for closing the Rhine in the spring brought renewed opposition from the British who saw it as a continuation of the "broad front" strategy. Marshall agreed with

Eisenhower but intended to bolster the forces in western Europe by transferring British units from Italy and thereby severely limiting any strike into Austria through the Ljubljana Gap.

The Combined Chiefs of Staff clashed again at Malta meeting. Field Marshal Brooke still insisted that all other actions along the western front should be subordinated to Montgomery's attack in the north. He also opposed American plans for transferring heavy bombers from Italy to Britain. Marshall understood the British concern about the bombers, and agreed to make the transfer temporary. According to Marshall, however, "We had a terrible meeting" when the British continued to challenge Eisenhower's plan for victory. Brooke also questioned the influence of Bradley and Patton on Eisenhower. Marshall angrily replied that British worries were "on the wrong foot," and that they should be more concerned about Churchill's interference than any by Bradley and Patton. Marshall was simply fed up with Montgomery's carping and the appearance of open contempt for a superior officer.[10]

Disagreements among the Combined Chiefs were compounded by political and military differences between Churchill and Roosevelt when they arrived at Malta on February 2. Churchill appeared feisty to the outside world, but he was now a man past seventy whose health and strength had to be monitored closely. He also had grown mentally weary and pessimistic about the future when a weakened Britain must face the Soviet threat and he would have to face an election. The prime minister was also saddened by the physical deterioration of Roosevelt. "To a doctor's eye," wrote Churchill's physician, Lord Moran, "the President appears a very sick man. He has all the symptoms of hardening of the arteries of the brain in an advanced stage so that I give him only a few months to live. But men shut their eyes when they do not want to see, and the Americans here can not bring themselves to believe that he is finished."[11]

The president also had a new secretary of state. Hull had resigned the previous November because of poor health. He had been replaced by Edward R. Stettinius, a forty-four-year old former chairman of the board at United States Steel who had entered government service in 1941. As under-secretary of state, Stettinius had presided over the conference at Dumbarton Oaks but had little experience in foreign affairs.

Churchill and Roosevelt met briefly for lunch on February 2 and then that evening for a longer session with the Combined Chiefs. Churchill agreed with the need for a strong assault force in western Europe but remained opposed to withdrawing forces from Italy. When the German surrender came, he maintained, "we should occupy as much of Austria as possible." Churchill noted the inefficiency of the Chinese government. Roosevelt candidly admitted that "three generations of education and training would be required before China could become a serious factor." Roosevelt refused to do anything to help the French regain Indo-China. Marshall expressed more confidence in China when calling for a strategy concentrating on China while essentially bypassing Southeast Asia in the final assault on Japan.[12]

The two leaders and their entourage of seven hundred left for the Crimea later than night. Transports took off in ten-minute intervals on a dangerous journey of 1,500 miles across the Mediterranean to Greece and then toward the Black Sea, flying at times over airfields still occupied by the Germans. The travelers arrived at Saki near Sevastopol the next morning where they were fed and warmly welcomed before covering the last 90 miles by car to Yalta.

The place that was to become so controversial, and even sinister, was virtually unknown to most Americans in February of 1945. The press had to rely on Mark Twain's *The Innocents Abroad* of 1867 for a description of the palaces and villas making up the resort complex constructed for the benefit of the Russian nobility. Roosevelt and the Americans were assigned to Livadia Palace, a fifty-room building built by Nicholas II in 1911. Here the Big Three held their meetings.

The Germans had laid waste to the Crimea in their retreat. The Russians had done their best to refurbish the various buildings, especially Livadia. They had generally succeeded, but the accommodations were poor, with much grumbling about the shortage of bathrooms and an abundance of bedbugs with no respect for rank.[13] Stalin was at his charming best when he visited Churchill and Roosevelt on the afternoon of the fourth, and he was ready to exploit the differences between the two visitors. He told Churchill that bridgeheads had been established on the Oder, and that the Germans were on the verge of collapse. Stalin minimized Russian military strength to Roosevelt and said that there was still heavy fighting for the Oder.

Stalin played to Roosevelt's dislike of de Gaulle by denigrating his ability and the French contribution to the war. Stalin may well have been revealing a lingering bitterness toward the French for ruining his hopes five years earlier. "In 1940," he said, "they had not fought at all." Roosevelt then revealed his disagreements with Churchill over the role for France following the war and his unhappiness with the southern zone of occupation. He did support the idea of a French zone "out of kindness," to which Stalin agreed that it hardly could be for any other reason.[14]

Roosevelt and Stalin left their meeting to join Churchill at the first plenary session of the conference. Marshal Alexei Antonov began by reviewing the Soviet offensive into Germany that had brought the Red Army to within forty miles of Berlin. Marshall had more difficulty reporting for the Anglo-Americans. The Allied armies had regained the area lost during Hitler's Ardennes offensive and had advanced beyond the December battle line in some places. Eisenhower planned to attack in the north on February 8, and to follow it with an attack in the south on the fifteenth. He hoped to cross the Rhine in early March, if all went well. Marshall added that the drive for the Rhine had been slowed by supply problems recently alleviated by opening Antwerp. He mentioned, however, the threat to Antwerp by German rockets and the impact severe damage could have on any offensive. Stalin thought the Anglo-Americans were overcautious and was skeptical of the damage the Germans could inflict on Antwerp. He also pointedly asked about German strength and the numbers of men and equipment Eisenhower could send against them. Stalin asked what his allies wished from the Soviet Union. Churchill and Roosevelt agreed that there should be joint planning among the Allies now that their armies were drawing closer together.

The strains of the meeting continued that evening when Roosevelt hosted a dinner for Churchill and Stalin. Roosevelt offended Stalin by disclosing that he and Churchill referred to him as "Uncle Joe." Stalin seemed to think the familiar term was insulting to a great leader, even after Molotov and Stettinius tried to explain it as a term of endearment similar to "Uncle Sam." The banter became more meaningful when Stalin firmly endorsed great power diplomacy and spheres of influence. Roosevelt, and to a lesser extent Churchill, did little to clarify their position by agreeing with him.

Roosevelt and much of American domestic opinion believed spheres of influence had helped to bring both world wars. A new international order directed by a strong United Nations could best keep the peace. American economic interests in eastern Europe were minimal, but the economy of the east was seen as closely tied to the west. Dividing Europe into political spheres of influence meant economic spheres as well. There was a moral problem as well. The brutality of Stalinism offended the moral values of Western Liberalism, however imperfectly they were practiced. The Darlan Deal had caused many to ask What are we fighting for?

Senator Vandenberg had asked the same question. To say that Stalin was not as evil as Hitler might be sufficient for some, but many people in the West wished for more.

Roosevelt feared that Soviet control in eastern Europe could prevent American participation in the United Nations. As guardian of the British Empire and the man who had the mathematical agreement with Stalin in November, Churchill differed with Stalin only on the degree of Great Power control. Roosevelt failed to challenge Stalin's view of Great Power domination and added that the peace should be written by the "powers at this table." After Stalin left, Eden reminded Churchill and Stettinius that neither smaller powers nor the British public would support an organization dominated by the Great Powers, and later he recorded in his diary that "Stalin's attitude to small countries struck me as grim, not to say sinister."[15]

The powers disagreed on treatment of Germany the following day. They accepted occupation zones but had little idea whether to support two or several autonomous units, or autonomy for some units and international control for others. Stalin had little sympathy for a French occupation zone. The French had "opened the gate to the enemy" and had no right to be elevated equality with those who had sacrificed so much. Churchill noted that every country had made mistakes, but a strong France was necessary to contain Germany in the future. Roosevelt supported Churchill, although he shocked the prime minister by saying the United States would not keep troops in Europe for more than two years following the end of the war. Stalin was willing to conceded a French zone, but it would have to come from the Americans and the British. Roosevelt did not, however, want the French to have a voice in Allied control machinery. That problem, the three agreed, would be left to their foreign ministers to decide.

Stalin was more concerned about reparations than dismemberment and occupation zones. Reparations in goods more than in money would rebuild the Soviet Union and prevent Germany from rebuilding and waging another war. Churchill and Roosevelt considered the Soviet demands too harsh, and reminded Stalin of how the terms of the Versailles Treaty had crippled Germany's ability to pay. This problem, too, remained unresolved until the foreign ministers returned with a recommendation.

Roosevelt had come to Yalta determined to see the creation of a new world organization. Like Wilson at Paris, he was willing to sacrifice many things to make his dream a reality. No organization had a chance to survive without the Soviet Union. Stalin remained wary as long as Britain controlled its Dominions and the United States dominated Latin America and perhaps Western Europe. Stalin demanded veto power in the proposed Security Council and a seat for each of the sixteen Soviet Republics in the General Assembly, an unacceptable demand to American conservatives who disliked international organizations in general and the Soviet Union in particular.

Stalin's suspicions came through at the third plenary session on February 6 when Stettinius presented the American plan. Stalin reminded Churchill and Roosevelt that the League of Nations had expelled the Soviet Union in 1939, and had tried to mobilize a crusade against it. He further implied that the Anglo-Americans were trying to gang up on him. Churchill acknowledged that Britain and France had been angry with the Soviet Union in 1939 but that any similar action was impossible under the new proposal. Roosevelt again stressed the need for unity among the great powers, adding that American policy would continue to work for it. If differences did arise, then the whole world would know of them, regardless of voting formulas.

The question of national sovereignty intersected with the future of Poland. Roosevelt knew that Stalin would concede nothing in Poland. He wanted some cosmetic concessions to assuage American Poles and their supporters. It would have a "salutary effect," he said, if Stalin would cede the city of Lwow and the oil deposits of Lwow Province to Poland along with enlarging the Warsaw government to include members from other parties. Churchill added that he had publicly accepted the Curzon Line. He was more concerned about restoring the independence of Poland that Britain had fought to preserve. Stalin asked for a ten-minute recess before replying. His answer was direct, logical, and uncompromising. The future of Poland was a matter of national survival for the Soviet Union. Twice in thirty years Germany had invaded Russia through Poland. Russia demanded a friendly and strong Poland to protect itself. The Curzon Line, he said, had been created by the Paris Peace Conference and named after the British foreign secretary who recommended it as the boundary between Russia and Poland. He and his government could hardly be expected to be less Russian than Clemenceau and Curzon. Public opinion in Russia would hardly allow him to return home after abandoning the Curzon Line.

Mikolajczyk, Stalin said, had accepted the Curzon Line and he had been dismissed because of it. Agents of the London Poles had killed Russian soldiers. The Warsaw government, Stalin maintained, was equal to de Gaulle. Churchill accepted the Curzon Line. The Lublin government, as he referred to it, represented no more than a third of the people. Britain would not recognize it as it was presently constituted.

At the fourth plenary session on the afternoon of February 7, Molotov reported on the meeting of the three foreign ministers earlier in the day. They had agreed to send the German question to a committee consisting of Eden, John Winant for the U.S., and Fedor Gusev for the Soviet Union. Some progress had been made regarding procedures for determining reparations, but there was no agreement on the amount.[16]

The Soviets eventually suffered a minor defeat on reparations. At the plenary session of February 10, Stettinius later wrote, Stalin "spoke with great emotion, which was in sharp contrast to his usual calm, even manner. On several occasions he arose, stepped behind his chair, and spoke from that position, gesturing to emphasize his point. The terrible German destruction in Russia obviously had moved him deeply." Germany should pay reparations in the amount of twenty billion dollars, half of which should go to the Soviet Union. Stalin offered a compromise when it became apparent that Churchill would not agree to a specific sum. Germany must pay "compensation," with the specific amount being set by a commission meeting later in Moscow.[17] Stalin won a concession in the more informal atmosphere of dinner that evening. Churchill assured him that the Soviets would receive reparations, but not to the extent that Germany would be crippled as after the last war. Churchill tried to prove by promising reparations and setting twenty billion dollars as the basis for discussion.

Without an agreement on Poland it was unlikely there could be any meaningful agreement on much else. Churchill and Roosevelt had to return home with a settlement acceptable to their constituents. The brutal reality remained: Stalin controlled Poland, and there was nothing Churchill and Roosevelt could do about it, short of a war that neither of their constituencies would support. Negotiations had been continuing since February 6. Eden and Stettinius again called for a reorganized government at the meeting of the foreign ministers on February 9. Molotov held to using the current Lublin-Warsaw government as the basis for reorganization. The Red Army needed a friendly government in Poland while it continued operations against the Germans. The Provisional Government would continue only for the short time needed to hold elections. Eden bluntly replied that there would be no free elections if they were supervised by the Lublin government.

Time was running out for Churchill and Roosevelt. It had already passed for Poland. Churchill and Roosevelt at least wanted their constituents to know they had tried to gain some measure of independence. Insistence on free elections was critical for the Anglo-Americans. At the plenary session on the afternoon of February 9, Churchill gained Stalin's agreement to allow Mikolajczyk's participation in the elections, and Roosevelt insisted that the elections be as "pure as Caesar's wife." Stalin cited de Gaulle's government in France as the counterpoint to the Lublin-Warsaw government in Poland, and he pointedly reminded Churchill that he was not challenging British domination in Greece. There is no doubt, however, that the government in Paris had far more popular support than the one in Warsaw, and that Churchill was far more welcome in Greece than Stalin was in Poland. In the end, however, Churchill and Roosevelt had to accept reality.

The final agreement acknowledged that a "new situation" had been created in Poland as a result of its liberation by the Red Army. The Provisional Government would be reorganized to include democratic leaders from within the country and from abroad. The new Provisional Government of National Unity would then hold "free and unfettered elections as soon as possible on the basis of universal suffrage and secret ballot with all democratic and non-Nazi parties having the right to participate. Roosevelt's chief of staff, Admiral William Leahy, complained that the agreement on Poland was "so elastic that the Russians can stretch it all the way from Yalta to Washington without ever technically breaking it." "I know," replied Roosevelt, "but it's the best I can do for Poland at this time."[18]

Great Britain and the United States agreed to recognize the new Polish government after it was formed according to the stated conditions. The agreement specified the Curzon Line as the border in the east, without any plebiscite, which violated the Atlantic Charter. Churchill and Roosevelt held out in the west, however, by giving Stalin only the vague assurance that the new Poland would receive "substantial" territory in the north and the west, with the final borders to await the coming peace conference. The Americans and the British hoped to further guarantee Poland with the Declaration on Liberated Europe. The high-sounding words of the Declaration were also selective. The three powers promised the principles of the Atlantic Charter to those areas conquered by Axis aggression. It did not mention those areas of eastern Europe absorbed by the Soviet Union during its partnership with Hitler, nor did it include those areas of the British Empire where demands for independence had been continuing for some time.[19]

Churchill and Roosevelt had maintained a common front in dealing with Poland. They differed on forming the new United Nations. Stalin openly enjoyed Churchill's testiness when the rights of small nations collided with the continuation of the British Empire. Churchill could understand Stalin's determination to protect Soviet sovereignty within the United Nations. Stalin consented to the American plan for voting on the Security Council, and he may have done so after consulting with Churchill. On the afternoon of February 7, Churchill happily told Roosevelt "Uncle Joe will take Dumbarton Oaks." Each country could veto any motion, except in those matters where it was directly involved, unless the motion included sanctions. Time and politics would reveal how little of a concession it was in practice.

Stalin used his concession on the Security Council to gain three votes in the General Assembly. Stalin dropped his request for one vote for each of the sixteen Soviet republics. Molotov asked for three seats in the Assembly, one for the Soviet Union and one for Belorussia and the Ukraine, both of whom had suffered so much from Nazi aggression and had sacrificed so much to win the war. "This is not so good," Roosevelt noted to Stettinius, but he found it difficult to say no after Stalin's concession on the Security Council.[20] Roosevelt's argument for one-state one-vote collided with the several British votes. "For us," Churchill wrote to his deputy, Clement Attlee, "to have four or five members, six if India is included, when Russia has only one is asking a great deal."[21] Roosevelt eventually accepted the Soviet position after talking with Stettinius, although he was still trying to think of some palatable way of informing the American people.

He found it with the help of Under-Secretary of State James Byrnes. On February 10, Roosevelt wrote to Churchill and Stalin explaining potential opposition to the voting formula in the United States Senate. He hoped to counter the opposition by gaining three votes for the United States as well. Both Churchill and Stalin appreciated the president's position and readily agreed.[22] The president, however, soon cooled on the idea and the Americans did not request two additional votes. Roosevelt and Stalin eventually consented to allow the French to administer their occupation zone. Roosevelt's change of heart on France may have been influenced by the hard Soviet attitude on Poland. Once the President announced his change of mind, however, Stalin merely said he agreed and made no comment.[23]

Roosevelt had achieved his primary goal of creating a United Nations. Some of the terms were kept secret for political reasons. The president wanted to explain the voting formula and the extra seats for the Soviet Union to Congressional leaders before they became public. It was prudent to restrict membership to those nations who had declared war against the "common enemy" by March 1. The powers agreed to hold a United Nations conference on April 25, somewhere in the United States, and they approved the format for the formal invitations.

Agreements on the United Nations and the future of Europe had involved consultation among the Big Three. The future of Asia was largely settled by Roosevelt and Stalin. American forces were now beginning the conquest of Iwo Jima, 700 miles from Tokyo. Beyond lay the Ryukus and the Home Islands. Japanese leaders realized time was running out on the Asian mainland as well as in the Pacific. In May of 1943 the Soviet Union had promised it would adhere to the 1941 non-aggression pact, but Tokyo worried.[24] At best, the agreement would expire in April of 1946; at worst, Stalin would attack Manchuria following the defeat of Germany.

Japan was willing to make concessions to keep the Russian bear at bay, including territory taken during the Russo-Japanese war of 1905.[25] Stalin could remain neutral and be well rewarded for it or he could strike into Manchuria and Korea on his own. He knew the Americans and British would probably have an atomic bomb by the end of the war.[26] The most prudent road lay in securing gains in Asia as an ally of the Americans. Soviet aid in Asia had been a part of American military strategy since early in the war. The Americans faced a long campaign against fanatical Japanese resistance for perhaps two more years. Even the prospect of the atomic bomb offered relatively little hope. By February of 1945 it was as yet untested and its potential power greatly underestimated. The Americans wanted the Red Army to pin down Japanese forces in Manchuria while they invaded the Home Islands.[27]

Stalin had promised to enter the Pacific war at the foreign ministers meeting in Moscow in October 1943 and again at Teheran without specifying what he expected in return. He knew the military situation and the anxieties of his allies. They needed the "second front." He now would decide when it would be launched and how well rewarded he would be. The European war had undone the treaties of Brest Litovsk and Paris. He would now undo the Portsmouth Treaty ending the Russo-Japanese war of 1905.

Roosevelt and Stalin began a series of private meetings on

February 8. Stalin promised to move against Japan "two or three months" following the end of the European war. In return the Americans recognized Soviet predominance in Outer Mongolia. Southern Sakhalin and the islands adjacent to it were to be ceded to the Soviet Union, the Chinese port of Dairen was to be internationalized with safeguards for the preeminent interests of the U.S.S.R. Port Arthur would be restored as a Soviet naval base. Soviet "pre-eminent" interests were recognized in the operation of the Chinese Eastern and Southern Manchurian railways, and the Kurile Islands would be ceded to the Soviet Union.[28]

Most of the territory had been taken from a weak China during the heyday of nineteenth century imperialism. Transfer of it from Japan to the Soviet Union without the consent of the Nationalist government or a plebiscite of the inhabitants violated the Atlantic Charter. Stalin's desire to regain areas lost to Japan contradicted Bolshevik rhetoric denouncing Tsarist imperialism and repudiated Lenin's "no annexations" policy. American concessions involved sacrificing idealistic goals for strategic gain. The agreement was in keeping with Chiang Kai-shek's desire for better relations with Moscow. Stalin reaffirmed Soviet recognition of the Nationalist as the official government of China, a gesture welcomed by a government whose own popularity had waned while that of the Communists increased. Stalin feared that anything known in Chungking would soon be known in Tokyo and provoke a Japanese attack into Siberia. The Roosevelt-Stalin agreement had more in common with the Old Diplomacy than with Wilson's "open covenants openly arrived at." It was excluded from the protocol and made known to only a small circle around the president.

The Yalta conference ended on February 11 with a banquet and good fellowship. Churchill and Roosevelt returned home at a leisurely pace that combined diplomacy with needed rest. Both believed the conference had been a success. Agreement had been reached on the defeat of Germany and occupation zones. The two Western leaders had won as much as they could for Poland and the remainder of eastern Europe. The Soviets were committed, however, vaguely, to free elections. The foundation had been laid for creating a United Nations dominated by three great allies who had won the war and must keep the peace. Russian entrance into the Pacific war would bring victory sooner for the Americans and save lives. Churchill and Roosevelt viewed their agreements as optimistically as they could, despite private doubts and the realization, as Churchill later wrote, that "all now depended upon the spirit in which they were carried out."[29]

Churchill ran into more immediate opposition than Roosevelt. Some in Parliament, especially Conservatives who remembered why Britain had gone to war in 1939, refused to support the settlement on Poland.[30] Opinion in the United States was initially favorable, although some of the terms were not yet known. It would change dramatically in the wake of disclosure and disillusionment following the war. Congress noted primarily that it was a frail and weary man, far older than his sixty-two years, who came before them on March 1 to explain the agreements and ask for their approval. The president acknowledged his exhaustion and infirmity by asking their pardon for sitting before them. "I know," he said, "that you will realize that it makes it a lot easier for me not to have to carry about ten pounds of steel around on the bottom of my legs; and also because of the fact that I have just completed a fourteen thousand mile trip." He believed it had been a fruitful trip, but only Congress could decide. "Unless," he said, "you . . . concur in the general conclusions reached at Yalta, and give them your active support, the meeting will not have produced lasting results." The United States, Roosevelt told Congress, had been thrust into the role of world leadership. The American people must accept their role or "bear the responsibility for another world conflict."[31]

NOTES

1. Dallek, *Roosevelt and American Foreign Policy*, 506-507.
2. *FRUS: The Conferences at Malta and Yalta: 1945* (Washington, 1955), 3-40. Hereafter cited as Yalta Papers.
3. "Noble Negatives," *Economist*, vol. 147 (December 30, 1944), 857-858.
4. "Deadlock in Europe," Ibid., vol. 148 (January 6, 1945), 2.
5. *New York Times,* January 3, 1945, 1, 8.
6. Ibid., January 7, 1945, 1, 32.
7. *Congressional Record, 79th Congress, First Session,* vol. 91, 164-167. C. David Tompkins, *Senator Arthur H. Vandenberg: The Evolution of a Modern Republican, 1884-1945* (Lansing: Michigan State University Press, 1970), 238-240.
8. Maurice Matlof, *Strategic Planning for Coalition Warfare, 1943-1944* (Washington: U.S. Government Printing Office, 1959), 341-342.

9. Philip E. Mosely, "The Occupation of Germany: New Light on How the Zones were Drawn," *Foreign Affairs,* vol. 28 (July, 1950), 589-596.
10. Pogue, *Marshall: Organizer of Victory,* 509-515.
11. Charles Moran, *Churchill: Taken from the Diaries of Lord Moran* (Boston: Houghton Mifflin, 1966), 242.
12. *Yalta Papers,* 543-545. Pogue, *Marshall: Organizer of Victory,* 518.
13. Bullock, *Parallel Lives,* 870. Diane Shaver Clemens, *Yalta* (New York: Oxford University Press, 1970), 113-117.
14. *Yalta Papers,* 570-573.
15. *Ibid,* 589. Gilbert, *Churchill,* vol. 7, 1175.
16. *Yalta Papers,* 589-719.
17. Edward R. Stettinius, *Roosevelt and the Russians: The Yalta Conference,* ed. Walter Johnson (Garden City, NY: Doubleday and Company, 1949), 263-264.
18. William D. Leahy, *I Was There* (New York: McGraw-Hill Book Co., 1950), 315-316.
19. *Yalta Papers,* 921-978.
20. Stettinius, *Roosevelt and the Russians,* 174.
21. Churchill, *Triumph and Tragedy*, 359-360.
22. *Yalta Papers,* 966-968. Weinberg, *World at Arms,* 805.
23. *Yalta Papers,* 899-900. Harriman and Abel, *Special Envoy,* 402.
24. Weinberg, *World at Arms,* 634.
25. Robert J.C. Butow, *Japan's Decision to Surrender* (Stanford: Stanford University Press, 1954), 86-87, 121-122.
26. David Holloway, *Stalin and the Bomb: The Soviet Union and Atomic Energy, 1939-1956* (New Haven: Yale University Press, 1994), 82-83.
27. Dallek, *Roosevelt and American Foreign Policy*, 516.
28. *Yalta Papers,* 984.
29. Churchill, *Triumph and Tragedy,* 392.
30. Gilbert, *Churchill,* vol. 7, 1233-1236.
31. *New York Times,* March 2, 1945, 12-13.

CHAPTER SIXTEEN

Twilight of the Gods

The Soviet Union challenged Roosevelt's hopes for the future. Stalin was determined to rule what he had conquered, regardless of the Declaration on Liberated Europe or the political values of the West. The commissars had come in the baggage of the Red Army in Bulgaria, Hungary, and Romania. Bulgaria remained governed by a coalition of leftist parties known as the National Fatherland Front following conquest by the Red Army. Communists gradually eliminated rivals on the Left, as well as more conservative leaders, through their control of the Ministry of Interior and the courts. By the spring of 1945 the facade of democratic government was fast disappearing while the Communist Party itself was in turn being purged of all "opportunists."[1]

Communist control in Hungary was delayed by fighting against the Germans. A new Provisional Government was formed on December 22 1944, at Debrecen. The National Assembly implemented the Communist program calling for the nationalization of heavy industry and seizure of landed estates. Hungary became "Sovietized" as the Red Army moved westward following the capture of Budapest in February. Leadership of the party fell to those who had spent years in Soviet exile. The Communist Party pursued a policy of "gradualism" as defined in Moscow and was well on its way to controlling the country by the end of the war.[2]

In Rumania, King Michael and the government of General Constantin Sanatescu attempted to hold power in the face of growing animosity within the coalition known as the National Democratic Front. The king appeared to strengthen himself by appointing Nicolae Radescu as prime minister. Communist leaders increased their attack on the government and on other parties within the Front in January 1945. Growing unrest in the country and rumors of a coup caused concern in London and Washington. Churchill had agreed to Soviet predominance in Romania in return for British predominance in Greece. Stalin had kept his word while the British and their supporters defeated Communist partisans. Churchill realized that he could not challenge Stalin in Romania. Washington, however, protested the end of Rumanian democracy and sovereignty through Harriman in Moscow and the American representative Burton Berry in Bucharest.[3] Soviet intervention became as brutal as it was open a few days later. Andrei Vishinsky, Stalin's old hatchet man from the purges, arrived in Bucharest on February 27. Vishinsky demanded the dismissal of Radescu within two hours in a stormy interview with King Michael the next day. King Michael yielded, but he was unable to find a successor. On March 6, Vishinsky ordered the king to appoint a government composed entirely of Communists or their sympathizers. London and Washington reacted with anger and sad resignation. There was little either country could do to enforce the legalities of Yalta, especially since the Soviets justified their actions on military necessity. On March 11, Roosevelt wrote to Churchill, "It is obvious that the Russians have installed a minority government of their own choosing . . . but Rumania is not a good place for a test case."[4]

Poland was the place for a test case. It was soon apparent, however, that the Moscow Commission had little ability to alter Soviet power. The commission first met on February 23, 1945. Harriman joined Molotov and British Ambassador Sir Archibald Clark Kerr. Molotov insisted that the Warsaw group be invited ahead of others for consultation, and that it have veto power on eligibility for the interim government. The prospect of free elections and Polish sovereignty seemed dim amid reports of arrests, imprisonments, and executions currently being carried out inside Poland by the Warsaw faction and its Soviet sponsor. Churchill's support for the London Poles in Parliament and his open dislike of the Warsaw faction increased disharmony in Moscow. Molotov expressed his unhappiness with Churchill on March 1 and made it clear that the Moscow Commission would not be influenced by debates in the House of Commons.

The promise of Russian aid against Japan required Allied unity. Roosevelt accepted Soviet predominance in Poland and was willing to concede some primacy to the Warsaw government. He also opposed the total subjugation of Poland to the Soviet Union and the elimination of democracy.⁵ It had become clear that the Soviets were helping the Warsaw government eliminate rivals. On March 27, after two weeks of negotiation, the Red Army and its NKVD associates agreed to send several representatives of the Home Army in Poland to Britain for consultation with the London government. On the twenty-eighth the Poles boarded a plane ostensibly to meet Red Army commander General Georgi Zhukov before leaving. Their journey ended at Lubianka prison in Moscow.⁶

Military success intensified the chill in Allied relations cast by the shadow of Poland. By the spring of 1945 the industrial resources of Silesia had fallen to the Russians, while those in the Ruhr had been severely crippled by Allied bombing. Most of the antiaircraft guns had been taken from Berlin and other cities to stop the Russian advance. American, British, and Russian bombers roamed at will. Hitler ordered that the eastern front have priority in fuel supplies, despite the fear that Eisenhower's armies were expected to attack soon.

German forces should have withdrawn behind the natural defense of the Rhine. The loss of Silesia, however, made it imperative to hold what industry remained in the Ruhr and to keep the Rhine open. Many Germans still refused to believe the war was lost and were willing to fight ably and tenaciously for what remained of their country. Eisenhower expected a tough fight. On January 15, he told General Marshall that the Germans might well hold his own forces in the West without a strong Russian offensive.⁷

Eisenhower planned to move on the Rhine along a wide front, while remaining flexible enough to cross at the first opportunity. The offensive began on January 20. American and French forces captured Colmar in upper Alsace on the twenty-seventh and eliminated German strength south of Strasbourg by February 9. Other units launched a series of attacks to clear the west bank of the Rhine with Operation Veritable in the north and Operation Undertone in the south. Air and armored superiority gradually weakened German defenses. Allied forces began to advance along the entire front by the middle of February. German defenders were handicapped by supply shortages and roads clogged by refugees and the junk of retreating armies. Soldiers increasingly looked for the chance to surrender in the face of mounting casualties and sagging morale. By the end of the month nearly 250,000 had done so, adding their number to the over 300,000 casualties suffered by the Wehrmacht during the Rhineland campaign.⁸

The Germans faced a new dilemma as the enemy approached the

Rhine. The bridges must be destroyed before the Allies could use them, but they must stand long enough to aid retreating Germans. The delay and indecision involved in waiting long enough but not too long led to one of those "breaks" of military fortune that alter plans, timetables, and the course of war itself. On the morning of March 7 an American pilot spotted the Ludendorff railroad bridge at Remagen still spanning the Rhine intact. He radioed the American Ninth Armored Division headquarters. General William Hoge ordered units near Remagen to take the bridge. The Germans on the other side were surprised by the American infantry and the Pershing tanks supporting them. Their first attempt to blow the bridge failed. The second appeared to be successful. The bridge shook and then settled back on its moorings. American infantry became the first hostile troops to cross the Rhine since Napoleon in 1806. One tank and three infantry companies had established a base on the other side by the end of the day.[9]

The Rhine crossing accelerated the Allied drive on Berlin while the Soviet offensives in the east and south were stalled by heavy resistance. The change in fortune further strained the Grand Alliance. Both the Soviets and the West wondered again whether the other might make a separate peace with Hitler. The Remagen crossing appeared to Moscow as a German attempt to facilitate an Anglo-American advance to Berlin. The Soviets saw additional evidence of another "deal" between Hitler and the West on March 12. Harriman told Molotov of secret contacts between the Allies agents of Field Marshal Kesselring in Bern. Molotov posed no objection to the talks but requested that a Soviet representative be part of actual negotiations. Churchill and Roosevelt declined the Russian request because negotiations involved only the surrender of German troops in northern Italy and not the German government. It was strictly a matter between Kesselring and representatives of Field Marshal Alexander, the Allied commander in Italy. The Western Allies agreed to permit a Soviet representative, but negotiations would remain under Alexander's control. Molotov called the decision "incomprehensible" in a letter to Harriman and demanded that the Bern negotiations be terminated. Roosevelt tried to sooth Soviet suspicions on the twenty-fourth by explaining the Bern talks to Stalin. He reminded Stalin that the Soviet Union had been promptly informed, and that there had been no actual meeting with the Germans. Should the chance for a German surrender in Italy arise, Roosevelt continued, Alexander must be able to move as quickly as possible. "You as a military man will understand the necessity for prompt action. . . . It is in the same category as would be the sending of a flag of truce to your general at Koenigsberg or Danzig." Stalin replied that German troops in the Baltic were surrounded and could go nowhere else. Negotiations in Italy could be used to transfer them to the Russian front.

Roosevelt reminded Stalin on March 31 that the contacts in Bern had been with Himmler's men who might be trying to sow disunity among the Allies. He assured Stalin that the Anglo-Americans would never accept a German surrender allowing the transfer of German troops to the east. Stalin angrily replied on April 3 that Roosevelt had not been "fully informed. An agreement had been reached to allow a rapid advance of the Anglo-Americans in return for more lenient peace terms. Roosevelt scolded Stalin for questioning his "truthfulness and reliability." The Americans and British were advancing, he said, because of military power, not from any deal. "Frankly," Roosevelt said, "I cannot avoid a feeling of bitter resentment toward your informers . . . for such vile misrepresentations of my actions or those of my trusted subordinates."

Stalin found it difficult to believe the Germans were surrendering in the west only because of military defeat. They obviously were not doing so in the east.[10] He was right, but not because of any agreement. No German soldier could expect or hope for good treatment from the Red Army after what the Wehrmacht and the SS had done to Soviet Russia. In the west they could at least hope.

Deteriorating relations spilled over into the coming United Nations conference in San Francisco. On March 23, Moscow announced that Andrei Gromyko would head the Soviet delegation to San Francisco. The absence of Molotov indicated a chilling of relations within the Grand Alliance and a decreasing Soviet interest in the United Nations. Churchill responded by appealing to Roosevelt for a strong stand on Poland. Roosevelt told Churchill on March 29 that he too had been watching the situation in Poland "with anxiety." He conceded that the Warsaw group could be regarded as a kind of first among equals, but it had no right to veto the participation of other individuals. In a letter to Stalin on April 1, Roosevelt warned that disagreement on Poland could destroy Allied unity. A "thinly disguised continuance of the Warsaw regime," he said, "would cause the people of the United States to regard the Yalta agreement as having failed." Stalin replied on the seventh that the Moscow Commission had reached a "dead end" because Harriman and Clark Kerr had tried to alter the Yalta accord. The Warsaw government was to be the "kernel" of any new government, and the Soviet Union had the right to see a "friendly" government in Poland composed of people who publicly accepted the Yalta decisions.

The news from Warm Springs, Georgia on April 12 suddenly overshadowed everything. Roosevelt was dead. "When I received these tiding," Churchill later wrote, "I felt as if I had been struck a physical blow . . . and I was overpowered by a sense of deep and irreparable loss."[11] Molotov came to the American embassy to pay his respects. According to Harriman, he seemed genuinely moved by the news. The following day Stalin greeted Harriman in silence, "holding his hand for perhaps thirty seconds before asking him to sit down." Stalin obviously was concerned about the impact of new President Harry S. Truman on American policy, but he also seemed saddened personally as well. Whether as a gesture to Allied solidarity or to the memory of Roosevelt personally, Stalin agreed when Harriman asked him to send Molotov to San Francisco.[12]

News of Roosevelt's death was fodder for the faithful in Berlin. The advance of the Red Army had forced Hitler to abandon the *Wolfsschanze* in East Prussia and return to Berlin in November. He left in December for Ziegenberg in the West to direct the Ardennes offensive, and there returned to a specially constructed bunker beneath the Reichs chancellery where he continued to direct the war. Hitler and his entourage lived in a twilight world beneath the ground where hope and fantasy combined to cloud the collapse of Germany above them. Hitler still believed that German willpower could delay defeat until the Allied coalition fell into ruin and new weapons were developed. He had identified himself with Frederick the Great since the outbreak of the war. Frederick had been saved in 1762 by "the miracle of the house of Brandenburg," the death of Tsarina Elizabeth, that had ended the coalition with Austria and France. Providence again had intervened. Roosevelt was dead. He and Germany were saved.

But there was only an acceleration of defeat. Hitler had sacked Rundstedt for the last time following the Remagen crossing and replaced him with Kesselring, who had held the Anglo-Americans so long in Italy. Kesselring's mission was to hold the Allies in the west, but they had crossed the Rhine all along the front by the end of March. Montgomery's army swept past the Ruhr toward the Baltic on the left, while to his right American forces passed the Ruhr and then turned left to meet their British allies. The heart of German industry was isolated along with nearly twenty divisions under Field Marshal Walter Model. The Germans held out until April 18. Model chose suicide over surrender, but over 300,000 officers and men did not.[13]

Eisenhower received an intelligence report on March 11 warning of German plans for a last defense in the mountains of southern Bavaria. The existence of "the fortress that never was," as Rodney Minott referred to it, could not be ignored.[14] The Germans had large concentrations of forces in the south, and it was the logical place for soldiers from the Eastern, Italian, and Western Fronts to converge. The Italian campaign had shown how well the Germans used mountainous terrain, and it made much more sense for the Nazi government to make its last stand in the south than in Berlin. Some Nazi leaders had already fled Berlin for Berchtesgaden, and Hitler himself still planned to leave on April 20.[15]

Eisenhower decided to push north to Kassel in Westphalia and then drive east toward Dresden to meet the Russians. The swing to the east would be primarily an American operation to destroy German units while avoiding a collision with the Russians farther north. Marshall advised Eisenhower to push eastward along a broad front on the twenty-seventh. Marshall also raised concern about "unfortunate incidents" involving the "advancing forces." One possible way to minimize the danger, Marshall suggested, was "an agreed line of demarcation."[16] Eisenhower informed Stalin of his plan to strike toward Leipzig and Dresden on March 23. "Could you," he asked, "therefore, tell me your intentions. . . . I regard it as essential that we coordinate our action and make every effort to perfect the liaison between our advancing forces."[17] Eisenhower's message infuriated the British who still wanted to drive for Berlin.[18] Eisenhower also had communicated directly with Stalin without first consulting with the Combined Chiefs. He had changed the primary attack to Dresden while leaving Berlin to the Russians and transferred units from Montgomery's command to General Bradley for the drive on Dresden. The British complained to Marshall and argued for a strong drive north which would secure German ports and submarine bases and open the way to Denmark.[19]

Marshall saw the note as just another episode of endless British carping. The best way to divide Germany and destroy what remained of the Wehrmacht lay in driving for Dresden. Eisenhower held to his plan on military grounds with Marshall's support. On March 30, however, Churchill interjected a political argument for taking Berlin. "If the enemy resistance should weaken . . . why should we not cross the Elbe and advance as far eastward as possible? This has an important political bearing, as the Russian army in the south seems certain to enter Vienna and overrun Austria. If we deliberately leave Berlin to them . . . the double event may strengthen their conviction, already apparent, that they have done everything."[20]

Eisenhower still believed Dresden should be the primary goal. After that, he agreed to give some American units back to Montgomery for a drive to Lübeck in the north to isolate German troops in Denmark and Norway. Eisenhower understood the political and psychological importance of capturing Berlin, just as he understood the importance of occupying Denmark before the Red Army. "I am the first to admit" Eisenhower told Marshall on April 7, "that a war is waged in pursuance of political aims, and if the Combined Chiefs of Staff should decide that the Allied effort to take Berlin outweighs purely military considerations in the theater, I would cheerfully readjust my plans and my thinking so as to carry out such an operation." [21]

There were good political reasons for halting at the Elbe. Berlin was one hundred miles inside the Soviet zone of occupation agreed upon at Yalta. The Americans wanted to defeat Germany quickly with minimum casualties before deploying forces to the Pacific. There was no point in squandering men and material needed for the Pacific nor risking a confrontation with the Soviet Union while expecting to fight Japan for another year or more.

Eisenhower forces were close to outrunning their support and supplies. Any assault across the lakes and streams of northwestern Germany would require some kind of regrouping to be successful, unless the Germans offered no resistance, and that he could not be sure of. Eisenhower also added a human component. When asked to estimate the cost in men of a final drive for Berlin, General Bradley had put the figure at 100,000 casualties, and then explained the situation as plainly and as well as it could be. "A pretty stiff price to pay for a prestige objective, especially when we've got to fall back and let the other fellow take over."[22]

And the other fellow meant to have it. In February the Red Army stood at the Oder in a far better position to reach Berlin before the Anglo-Americans. But the rapid advance of January had left pockets of German forces in the rear and stretched Zhukov's supply and support capabilities. In the southeast, Marshal Rodion Malinovsky's Second and Marshal Feodor Tolbukhin's Third Ukrainian Fronts encountered stronger German resistance than they had expected on their drive to Vienna. German resistance began to weaken in Hungary and Czechoslovakia by the middle of

March. On April 1, the Soviet High Command ordered the Red Army to take Vienna as soon as possible. Defeat in the south and east caused Hitler to rage against his armies and even his most trusted SS units. He replaced the inept Himmler and sent an ailing Guderian on sick leave.[23]

The Red Army slowly broke German resistance along an arc from Vienna northward. The speed of Eisenhower's advance into Germany and the secret peace talks in Bern revived Stalin's distrust of his allies. Eisenhower had tried to allay Soviet concern in his message to Stalin on March 28. Stalin knew that Eisenhower was subject to pressure from above, and he feared that the British would force him to take Berlin with the cooperation of the Germans.[24] Stalin summoned Zhukov and General Ivan Konev to Moscow before replying to Eisenhower. "So who will take Berlin, we or the Allies?" Stalin asked on April 1. "We will take Berlin," Konev answered, "and take it before the Allies."[25] Stalin and his generals now planned to attack on April 16, to capture Berlin by the end of the month, and drive for the Elbe to secure their assigned occupation zone. Stalin then informed Eisenhower that Berlin had lost its military significance and promised that the main blow of the Soviet offensive would begin around the middle of May and aim for a Dresden-Leipzig rendezvous with Eisenhower's forces.[26]

Stalin believed he was in a race for Berlin. On April 9, General William Simpson's American Ninth Army reached the Elbe and was in a position to strike for Berlin. Simpson was eager and remained convinced he could have taken the city, but Eisenhower refused on the grounds that the weight of Simpson's force still lay in the rear. The Red Army had made its swiftest redeployment of the war for the attack. It was an awesome force of 2.5 million men, 20 armies, 150 divisions, 6,000 tanks, 7,500 aircraft, 41,000 artillery pieces and mortars, 3,000 rocket launchers, and nearly 100,000 motor vehicles.[27] In contrast to Anglo-American troops on the Elbe, it was well supplied and "gassed up."

It had an awesome task. Berlin, Zhukov later recounted, had a "total area of almost 350 square miles. Its subway and other widespread underground engineering networks provided ample possibilities for troop movements. The city itself and its suburbs had been carefully prepared for defense."[28] Zhukov relinquished command of the First Belorussian Front to supervise the entire offensive. He appointed General Vasili Sokolovsky to lead the primary drive on Berlin with support from Rokossovski's Second Belorussian Front in the north and Konev's First Ukrainian Front in the south.

Hitler had planned for the coming Russian offensive. He believed the major thrust would come in the center for a linkup with the advancing

Anglo-Americans that would cut Germany in half. He appointed Admiral Karl Dönitz to command forces in the north while assigning the southern command to Kesselring. He, however, would command all forces until the country was divided. Hitler issued his last directive on April 15. With determination, he said, German soldiers could defeat the invader and gain a "turning point in the war."[29]

It was too late for turning points. The forty miles between Berlin and the Red Army was defended by 35 divisions of varied strength and equipment. The Red Army now commanded such overwhelming superiority that even blunders could not prevent its victory. The First Belorussian and First Ukrainian Fronts attacked before dawn on April 16 in an attempt to surprise the Germans while blinding them with searchlights. The initial assault failed, but the Red Army pressed on in spite of terrible casualties.[30] Sokolovsky's Belorussian Front advanced but more slowly than Zhukov had intended. He ordered Rokossovsky to swing southwest instead of northwest to encircle Berlin in case the main drive on the city failed. Progress in the center and the north was also slower than Stalin wanted. Zhukov ordered Konev to accelerate his drive from the southeast across the Spree River. The battle was decided by April 20. Russian soldiers entered Berlin and were fighting their way to the center, street by street, while other forces closed around the city.

The rapid Russian advance threatened to isolate Hitler in Berlin. He had planned to leave for Berchtesgaden on April 20 and to direct the last battle. It was time to celebrate the Führer's fifty-sixth birthday in the unreal world beneath the chancellery. Hitler received congratulations throughout the day from the remnants of the faithful who urged him to leave Berlin before the last escape routes were closed. That night a general exodus began for the southwest.

Hitler ordered SS General Felix Steiner to attack from the southern suburbs of Berlin with all available troops on the twenty-first. "Any commander," Hitler yelled at Luftwaffe General Karl Koller, "who holds back his forces will forfeit his life in five hours."[31] Hitler's decision further confused what remained of German defenses, and the attack was never launched.

Hitler alternated between periods of calm resignation and flashes of rage during the last week of his life. He was bitter toward Göring and Himmler when they presumed to be his successor. Göring wired from Berchtesgaden on the twenty-third asking for instructions if Hitler were unable to leave Berlin. It was a reasonable request in view of the situation.

It was interpreted as an ultimatum in the world of the bunker where illusions and party jealousies still reigned. Hitler had been angry with Göring's self-indulgence and his destructive command of the Luftwaffe for years. He took the opportunity to denounce the Reichsmarshal and order his arrest.

At least Göring had asked permission. Himmler, whose loyalty Hitler always had assumed without question, had not. Himmler and his aid, Walter Schellenberg, made a secret visit to the Swedish Legation in Lübeck for a meeting with Count Folke Bernadotte, Himmler had made exploratory conversations about surrender at a previous meeting, but he remained reluctant to go ahead as long as Hitler lived. He now believed that Hitler was doomed in Berlin, and that it was time to save himself and as much of Germany as possible from the Russians. He offered to surrender to the Western Allies while continuing the war against the Russians. Churchill and the new American president, Harry S. Truman would accept nothing less than unconditional surrender on all fronts, and they properly informed Stalin of Himmler's offer.[32]

Hitler was furious when news of Himmler's contact became known on the twenty-eighth. He retaliated swiftly by stripping Himmler of his position in the party and ordering his arrest. Hitler made final preparations for his death and the disposal of his body as Russian troops closed in on the chancellery on the twenty-ninth. That afternoon Hitler married Eva Braun, his mistress of fourteen years, and set about to justify his existence in a last "Testament."

Hitler had no regrets for the grief he had inflicted as he approached his own death. All the setbacks and suffering were caused by others. The war had been brought on by the Jews and their agents; the Army and the Air Force had let him down; only the Navy had maintained the National Socialist spirit. He rewarded the Navy and made one last gibe at the other services by naming Dönitz to succeed him as president, with Goebbels as chancellor. Other survivors were named to various positions in a government that had no function to perform except unconditional surrender.

News arrived later that Mussolini and his mistress, Clara Petachi, had been captured and executed. Their bodies had then been taken to Milan, hung upside down, and reviled by the crowd. The news had little effect on Hitler's plan. He already knew what would happen if he fell into Russian hands. During the night of the twenty-ninth he made plans to commit suicide along with his wife. He was determined that his body would not be found and put on display. He and his wife were to be cremated in the garden above the bunker.³³

Hitler presided over his last conference the following morning. The Russians were closing to within a block of the chancellery, and soon their advance would prevent survivors from destroying his body. That afternoon he and Eva said goodbye to the others, went to Hitler's suite, and killed themselves. Martin Bormann and Goebbels tried to conceal Hitler's death, although they notified the stunned Admiral Dönitz that he had been named Hitler's successor. Bormann wanted to join Dönitz in the north and take his position in his new government, but he could not as long as the Russians encircled Berlin. Early in the morning of May 1, Bormann and Goebbels sent General Hans Krebs to negotiate a cease fire with Marshal Vasili Chuikov, the defender of Stalingrad, who was directing the final assault. Chuikov and Zhukov were in no mood to grant an armistice or to sign a separate surrender. They sent Krebs back to the bunker with no terms except unconditional surrender.³⁴ Bormann tried unsuccessfully to escape from the city upon hearing the news, while Goebbels and his wife chose to kill themselves and their children. Krebs shot himself. At 0600 hours on May 2, Lieutenant General Helmuth Weidling surrendered along with roughly 100,000 men.³⁵

The Nazi Party had gripped Germany like a belt since 1933, and Hitler had been its buckle. Faith in Hitler and his strength of will had driven the country during the past two years of defeat. All oaths to continue were invalid and all faith in victory gone with his death. German troops in Italy had already surrendered unconditionally, while Kesselring's forces north of the Alps waited until May 4. At Plom in the north Dönitz knew that the war was over. He agreed to surrender German forces in northwest Germany, Denmark, and the Netherlands to Montgomery on May 4 and promised that those in Norway would also surrender when arrangements were made with Eisenhower.

Dönitz sent his naval commander, Admiral Hans von Friedeburg, to Eisenhower's headquarters at Rheims on May 5. His primary aim was to stall long enough to allow additional Germans to flee westward before the final surrender. Friedeburg proposed the final surrender of German forces in the west, but Eisenhower refused. Dönitz then sent General Jodl to Rheims on May 6 to explain why Dönitz did not want to surrender in the east. Eisenhower issued an ultimatum when it became apparent the Germans were stalling. They must surrender immediately on all fronts or he would close the border with the Russian occupation zone to prevent any further movement of German civilians and soldiers to the west. Dönitz labeled Eisenhower's ultimatum "extortion," but there was no alternative. Jodl signed the unconditional surrender at 0241 on May 7.[36] Hitler's war was over.

NOTES

1. Miller, *Bulgaria During the Second World War,* 217-219.
2. Bennett Kovrig, *Communism in Hungary: From Kun to Kadar* (Stanford: Stanford University Press, 1979), 164-172.
3. *FRUS: 1945,* vol. 5, 478-480.
4. *Churchill and Roosevelt Correspondence,* 668.
5. Dallek, *Roosevelt and American Foreign Policy* 524. *FRUS: 1945: Conference of Berlin (The Potsdam Conference),* vol. 1, (Washington: U.S. Government Printing Office, 1960), 714-715.
6. Zbigniew Stypulkowski, *Invitation to Moscow* (New York: Walker and Company, 1962), 223-232.
7. Ambrose, *The Supreme Commander,* 607. *Eisenhower Papers,* vol. 4, 2430-2434.
8. Ambrose, *Supreme Commander,* 615. Cartier, *Zweite Weltkrieg,* 968-971.
9. Cartier, ibid., 971-972. Ambrose, *Citizen Soldiers,* 425.
10. *FRUS: 1945,* vol. 3, 723-751.
11. Churchill, *Triumph and Tragedy,* 471.
12. Abramson, *Harriman,* 394.
13. MacDonald, *Last Offensive,* 344-372.
14. Rodney G. Minott, *The Fortress That Never Was: The Myth of Hitler's Bavarian Stronghold* (New York: Holt, Rinehart, and Winston, 1964), 35-37. Donald E. Shepardson, "The Fall of Berlin and the Rise of a Myth," *Journal of Military History,* vol 62, 140-141.
15. Tony Le Tissier, *The Battle of Berlin* (London: Jonathan Cape, 1988), 80.
16. *Eisenhower Papers: The War Years,* vol. 4, 2364-2365. Ambrose, *Supreme Commander,* 628.
17. *Eisenhower Papers: The War Years,* vol. 4, 2531. David Eisenhower, *Eisenhower at War, 1943-1945* (New York: Random House, 1986), 740-746.
18. Ehrman, *Grand Strategy,* vol. 6, 131.
19. Ambrose, *Supreme Commander,* 633.
20. Churchill, *Triumph and Tragedy,* 463.

21. *Eisenhower Papers: The War Years,* vol. 4, 2592.
22. Stephen E. Ambrose, *Eisenhower and Berlin: The Decision to Halt at the Elbe* (New York: W.W. Norton and Company, 1967), 93. Omar N. Bradley, *A Soldier's Story* (New York: Henry Holt and Company, 1951), 535.
23. Seaton, *Russo-German War,* 556.
24. Zhukov, *Memoirs,* 580-581.
25. O.A. Rzheshevsky, "The Race for Berlin," tr. Col. David M. Glantz, *Journal of Slavic Military Studies,* vol. 8 (September, 1995), 569.
26. *Eisenhower Papers: The War Years,* vol. 4, 2584.
27. Glantz and House, *When Titans Clashed,* 261.
28. Georgi K. Zhukov, *Marshal Zhukov's Greatest Battles,* trans. Theodore Shabad (New York, 1969) p. 284. Zhukov's estimate of Berlin's size is accurate. The metropolitan area was approximately 340 square miles. Its population had fallen from approximately 4,500,000 in 1942 to just under 3,000,000 by the end of the war. Burkhard Hofmeister, *Berlin* (Darmstadt: Weissenschaftliche Buchgessellschaft, 1975), 50. LeTissier, *Battle of Berlin,* 15-24.
29. *Hitler's Weisungen,* 310-311..
30. Glantz and House, *When Titans Clashed,* 263. Le Tissier, *Zhukov at the Oder,* 159.
31. Karl Koller, *Der letzte Monat* (Mannheim: Norbert Wohlgemuth, 1949), 23.
32. Count Folke Bernadotte, *The Curtain Falls: Last Days of the Third Reich,* trans Count Eric L. Lewehnaupt (New York: Alfred A. Knopf, 1945), 106-117. *Stalin Correspondence,* vol. 1, 333-335, vol. 2, 210-211.
33. Bullock, *Parallel Lives,* 892.
34. Le Tissier, *Berlin,* 207-208.
35. The Soviets claimed to have taken 130,000 prisoners, a figure which may have included civilians for labor camps in the Soviet Union. Le Tissier, *Berlin,* 224.
36. Pogue, *The Supreme Command,* 485-490. Walter Lüdde-Neurath, *Regierung-Dönitz. Die letzten Tage des dritten Reiches* (Göttingen: Musterschmidt-Verlag, 1964), 68-70.

World War II in the Pacific

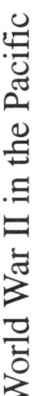

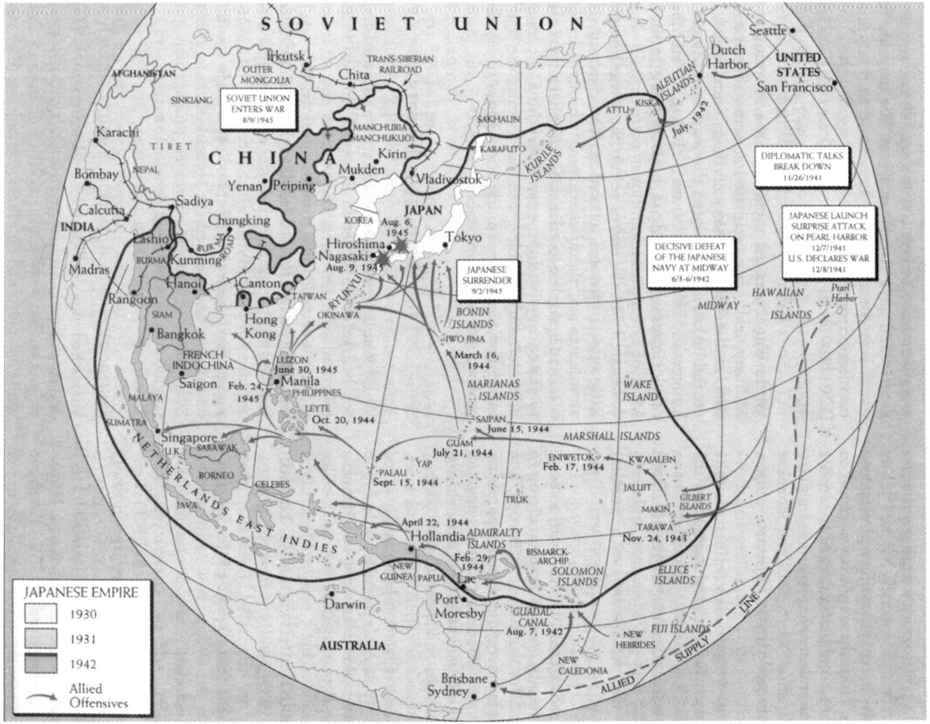

WESTERN HERITAGE VOL. 2 SINCE 1648 6/E. by KAGAN/OZMENT/TURNER, © 1998.
Reprinted by permission of Prentice-Hall, Inc., Upper Saddle River, NJ.

CHAPTER SEVENTEEN

Hell from the Top

The legacy of Hitler, Nazism, and the war continued. Hitler had left a monument to cruelty and destruction. From the Baltic to the Black Sea, from North Africa to the Volga, Europe had been laid waste, with millions dead and millions more condemned to broken bodies, shattered minds, and bitter memories. The Mighty Continent that had dominated the West and conquered the world had been reduced to rubble. "You who have not seen it," George Patton said, "do not know what hell looks like from the top."[1] Hitler had fulfilled the prophecy made a generation before. "It is certain," wrote the Swiss essayist Hermann Kesser in October of 1918, "that mankind must make up its mind either for Wilson or Lenin."[2] Now the heirs of Lenin and Wilson, as well as Alexander I and George Washington, faced each other in Europe.[3] The Grand Alliance had been forged by fear of a common enemy sufficient to transcend mutual animosity and suspicion. The enemy was gone.

The Soviet Union had a large reservoir of good will in the West despite the stresses of the past months. Maxim Litvinov urged reasonable goals providing security for the Soviet Union while tapping Western good will for economic aid. Stalin opted to impose Communist control, under the mistaken assumption that the West needed to aid the Soviet Union in order to maintain its own economy.[4]

The elevation of Harry S. Truman to the presidency altered the course of the confrontation, but it would have come in substance had Roosevelt lived. Roosevelt's political career had been at the top; Truman's had been from the bottom up. He was a machine politician from Kansas City when elected to the Senate in 1934 at the age of fifty. He achieved national prominence by chairing the special Senate Committee to Investigate the National Defense Program in 1941. He had no meaningful experience in foreign affairs and been ignored by Roosevelt as vice president. Truman immediately tried to familiarize himself with the task of winning the war in Asia and establishing world peace. He was troubled by Soviet actions in eastern Europe when he met with Harriman and others on April 20. Harriman believed that Stalin intended to control the internal politics of eastern European countries as well as their foreign policies, whether or not that offended the West. Truman believed the Soviets needed American aid to rebuild their country. "They need us," he said, "more than we need them." He also believed that unfriendly Soviet behavior could cause Congress to veto American participation in the United Nations.[5]

The mood in Washington grew more solemn on the twenty-second when it became known that Stalin had signed a treaty of mutual assistance and friendship with the Lublin-Warsaw government of Poland. Stalin considered the government permanent and not provisional. Stalemate over Poland became more evident when Molotov stopped in Washington on his way to San Francisco. In his initial meeting with Truman the conversation remained cordial. Truman assured his guest that he intended to keep all the agreements made by Roosevelt, and he expected the Soviets to do the same. He reminded Molotov that a fair settlement on Poland was important to the American people and to future relations between the United States and the Soviet Union. Molotov agreed, but noted that Poland bordered on the Soviet Union and was vital to its security. He hoped the meeting later in the day with Eden and Stettinius would bring progress toward a settlement.[6] It did not.

Stalin saw a "friendly" Poland as one totally under his control. He had it and he was determined to keep it. The famous sharp exchange with Truman on April 25 was more one of tone than substance. No argument, whether based on the future of the United Nations or the prospect of economic aid, altered the Soviet position. Nor could Soviet arguments alter the Anglo-American position on free and unfettered elections.

Polish independence had remained a British goal of the war. "We are shocked," Churchill wrote to Stalin on April 29, "that you should think that we would favor a Polish Government hostile to the Soviet Union. . . . It was on account of Poland that we went to war with Germany in 1939. [We] can never feel this war will have ended rightly unless Poland has . . . sovereignty, independence, and freedom on the basis of friendship with Russia."[7]

Differences among the former allies flared into the open at the San Francisco conference. Molotov insisted that representatives from the Warsaw government be recognized as the permanent Polish delegates to the conference. The Americans refused for fear that an aroused American public might turn against the United Nations as they had turned against the League. Molotov, however, persisted even after the other delegations expressed their opposition.

Relations were worsened on May 4, by what Senator Arthur Vandenberg called "a serious shadow."[8] The Soviets admitted that the missing sixteen Polish leaders had been arrested for "diversionist activities against the Red Army." Stalin was not going to allow even the facade of democratic government. There was also grim insight into the Soviet view of jurisprudence when Molotov assured the others that only "the guilty ones will be tried."[9]

The San Francisco conference had been planned to establish the United Nations and open a new era of peace. It revealed instead the split between the United States and the Soviet Union. American officials feared the Soviet veto would prevent the United Nations from keeping the peace. They also feared that an open breach with the Soviets might eventually lead to war. The American public now attributed international danger to the Soviets instead of the British.[10]

Truman had aggravated the situation by ending Lend-Lease to Britain and the Soviet Union on VE Day. A combination of excessive legalism and xenophobia in the government resulted in an immediate cancellation of aid instead of the gradual reduction Truman had intended, with the Soviets seeing the action as an attempt to bully them. When Truman realized the error, he rescinded the order and blamed subordinates. The damage had been done, and neither Britain nor the Soviets would soon let the Americans forget it.[11] Truman appeared to be abandoning Roosevelt's conciliatory polity toward the Soviet Union in favor of a new "get tough" approach. Truman, however, believed he was carrying out Roosevelt's policies, and that Roosevelt himself would have hardened his line in the face of broken agreements.

Truman sought to avoid a breach by sending Harry Hopkins to Moscow on May 26. Hopkins was a link to friendlier days who might be able to ease growing tensions. Hopkins tried his best by explaining the importance of Poland for the future of Soviet-American relations. Stalin again pointed out that Poland had allowed aggressors to invade Russia in the past through its own weakness or dislike of the Russians. In the future, there must be no government that would join another cordon sanitaire like that created following World War I. Hopkins said the United States wished no particular kind of government in Poland, but only one "which was desired by the Polish people and was at the same time friendly to the Soviet Government." The Poles, Stalin knew, would hardly choose a government friendly to the Soviet Union in the way Stalin demanded, and they certainly would not support the Warsaw regime. Stalin dodged Hopkins' request for the blessing of Western civil liberties, saying that they were desirable virtues in peacetime, but not in war. He made it clear that the sixteen Polish leaders would not be released. He did, however, throw a harmless concession as a way of giving the Americans an "out." If the Western Allies would accept the present Warsaw government, representatives from other groups could have four of the eighteen to twenty ministries in the government.

Stalin turned congenial when discussing war against Japan. The Soviet Union would be ready by early August and he supported Roosevelt's policy of unconditional surrender. He had no territorial ambitions in China in addition to the Yalta agreements and saw no rival to Chiang Kai-shek. He also agreed to meet with Churchill and Truman in the vicinity of Berlin around July 15. He had agreed to a request from General Eisenhower that the Allied Control Commission for Germany begin work as soon as possible and had chosen Marshal Zhukov for the position. Stalin felt Churchill was backtracking on dismemberment. Stalin still favored it, but would keep an open mind, and made a conciliatory gesture by accepting the American formula for voting on the United Nations Security Council.[12]

Hopkins left Stalin with at least some hope for better Soviet relations in the future, and even a false glimmer that the arrested Polish leaders might be freed. Truman was also encouraged by the mission, although he remained concerned about the appetite of the old bear in Moscow and the roar of alarm from the old lion in London. Churchill wanted to deal with the Soviet challenge as soon as possible. On May 11, he pressed for a summit in early July and suggested the president stop in London before meeting with Stalin. Churchill wanted to present Stalin with an Anglo-American front to uphold "our rightful interpretations of the Yalta agreements." The Soviets, he believed, were consolidating their control behind an "iron curtain" and were preparing to move westward. "To sum up, this issue of a settlement with Russia before our strength has gone seems to dwarf all others."[13]

For Truman it did not. The Pacific war required withdrawing American troops from Europe. Truman still hoped for an amicable settlement with Stalin and wanted to avoid any appearance of ganging up on him. Truman declined any meeting with Churchill prior to the conference. Truman also sent Joseph Davies to see Churchill. Truman chose Davies because he was a known Russophile whose presence in London would not upset Stalin. Churchill knew Davies by reputation as the former ambassador to the Soviet Union who had achieved a degree of fame as the author of *Mission to Moscow,* a book that so whitewashed the Soviet government that those responsible for the purges roared with laughter when they saw the film version.

Churchill noted the special relationship between Britain and the United States based upon their common heritage and dedication to the moral values of Western liberalism. The great causes," Churchill believed, "and principles for which Britain and the United States have suffered and triumphed are not mere matters of the balance of power. They in fact involve the salvation of the world." Churchill listed concrete examples in eastern Europe and the Balkans where he saw the pattern for Soviet expansionism and domination, a pattern that might well be extended to western Europe should the Americans withdraw. Churchill was also distressed that he had to make a case at all. Davies proved his ignorance of history by lecturing Churchill on Western sins against the Soviet Union since 1918. Davies added stupidity and bad manners by asking whether Britain had made a mistake in not supporting Hitler, since it now appeared Churchill was trying to divide the alliance as Hitler had tried throughout the war.[14]

Truman had demonstrated his desire to carry out Roosevelt's conciliatory policy toward the Soviets with the Davies and Hopkins trips. He followed by transferring troops to the Pacific and withdrawing American forces inside the Soviet occupation zone against Churchill's advice.[15] The Americans and British accepted defeat in Poland on July 5 by officially recognizing the "reorganized" Warsaw government as the government of Poland.[16] The president traveled to San Francisco in late June to help proclaim the United Nations. It was high time for idealism and hope for a new world to come. "Upon our decisive action," he told the closing session, "rests the hopes of those who have fallen, those now living and those yet unborn — and a hope for a world of free countries. . . which will work and cooperate in a friendly civilized community of nations. . . . Let us not fail to grasp this supreme chance to establish a world-wide rule of reason to create an enduring peace under the guidance of God."[17]

Truman had completed preparations for meeting with Churchill and Stalin at Potsdam by July 1. He had immersed himself in a host of problems and dealt with new personalities since Roosevelt's death. Before leaving for Germany he replaced Stettinius with James F. Byrnes who had a long record in public service, in contrast to Stettinius. Byrnes had been in the House and Senate and had served as Director of War Mobilization since 1941. He had accompanied Roosevelt to Yalta and had returned with a higher reputation for expertise in foreign affairs than was warranted. Byrnes was also well qualified to ascend to the presidency should Truman die in office. Truman did not like the prospect of Henry Morgenthau becoming president should Byrnes also die, nor did he favor Morgenthau's plan for Germany. "Morgenthau," Truman said years later, "didn't know shit from apple butter."[18] Morgenthau eased the president's anxieties by resigning after being excluded from the Potsdam delegation. The president had another reason for delay. The conference would not end until after an atomic bomb had been tested.[19]

Truman boarded the USS *Augusta* on July 7. He arrived at Antwerp on the fifteenth and then flew on to Potsdam. He had come to deal with Stalin and to avoid British intrigue. Truman had a physical edge over Churchill and Stalin. He was the youngest at sixty-one and had been spared the accumulated stress of the war years. Churchill had the additional stress of an election campaign. The Labour Party had forced a new election by withdrawing from the coalition that had governed since 1940. Churchill tried to rest in southern France prior to the conference. He was seventy-one years old and haunted by a premonition of losing the election and fearful that the sun was indeed setting on the British Empire. Those around him noticed that something of the old fire had gone, not to be regained during his stay at Potsdam. Stalin also showed the stress of his sixty-six years. He arrived a day late at the conference because of a slight heart attack. Far more than Tsar Alexander I's journey to Vienna in 1814, Stalin traveled over territory under his control. He had all of Poland, half of Germany, and would soon add territory in Asia.

Henry Kissinger described the Potsdam Conference as a "dialogue of the deaf."[20] The men at Potsdam simply rejected what they heard. In a perfect world of reason the stalemate at Potsdam and the return to the Cold War could have been avoided, just as war could have been prevented in 1939, if the perfect world of reason had prevailed over the will of irrational personalities. Realism, like beauty, lies in the eye of the beholder.

Churchill, Stalin, and Truman were the products of their heritage and dedicated to their ideological and national interests. To one degree or another, they were also accountable to constituencies with differing ideologies and differing views on what kind of world should emerge from the war.

Truman opened the first plenary session on the afternoon of July 17 at Cecilienhof Palace. He called for the creation of a Council of Foreign Ministers, including representatives from China and France. Truman also thought the Control Commission established for Germany should begin work as soon as possible. He listed several guiding principles for its operation, such as disarmament, de-Nazification, and economic controls. The United States, Truman noted, was unhappy with implementation of the Declaration of Liberated Europe signed at Yalta, and he suggested how it should be done in Greece, Rumania, Bulgaria, "and possible other countries." Truman's first three items caused little stir, aside from a demur from Stalin on Chinese participation in European problems. Churchill objected when Truman called for Italian admission to the United Nations, noting that Britain had fought Italy several years longer than the Americans and had suffered heavy casualties.

Stalin led off his agenda by including reparations from Germany and Italy as well as the division of their merchant and battle fleets. He then turned to the question of future trusteeships under the United Nations. Stalin argued that Franco's government lacked legitimacy because it had been imposed on the Spanish people by Germany and Italy and was a threat to the United Nations. Stalin wanted to liquidate the "émigré" government in London and transfer its financial assets to the Warsaw regime. Churchill responded by noting Britain's moral and financial obligation to the many soldiers who had fought for the London government. He also hoped the Polish people would be permitted to decide their future in free elections.[21]

The basic issues had been raised, but Truman soon found that in the world of diplomacy there is much talk before the deal. The following day, the Big Three approved the recommendation of their foreign ministers that the future council would comprise only those who had signed instruments of surrender. Truman differed from Churchill and Stalin by proposing that all treaties be submitted to a viable United Nations. Submission of treaties to the United Nations, Stalin said, "would make no difference at all because the three powers represented the interests of all." When it came to the occupation of Germany, they were unable to go any further than deciding that "Germany" excluded Austria and the Sudetenland.

Stalin again urged that the assets of the Polish Army be transferred to Warsaw. Churchill restated that Britain had given refuge to these men when they had been driven out by Germany. The Polish government had little assets beyond those of the Central Bank of Poland that had been frozen at the beginning of the war. Any Pole, Churchill said, who chose not to return would remain as British subjects. Churchill linked the issue to improving conditions in Poland and the promised free elections. Stalin stated his appreciation for the British position, promised to make no difficulties, and agreed to turn the Polish question over to the foreign ministers.[22]

Truman had grown "impatient for more action and fewer words" at the end of the second meeting. He had much more to endure. The Big Three approved the initial plan of the foreign ministers for the treatment of Germany, but little else. Stalin's attempt to get strong action against Franco failed when the Americans and the British refused to initiate measures that might bring another civil war or endanger their investments. Spain would simply be forbidden to join the United Nations.

The western borders of Poland, and fulfillment of the Declaration of Liberated Europe had already been decided by conquest. The Soviets had been employing their right in eastern Europe for months. Those who tried to put the best face on Soviet actions were repulsed by the open and shameless looting of occupied lands along with maltreatment of the population. The Soviets had made the Oder and the western Neisse the border by turning the area over to the Poles. The Americans had protested Soviet action prior to the conference and Truman again challenged it at the July 21 meeting. Stalin claimed the Poles had been guaranteed German territory to the north and west, but no definite boundaries had been set. The German population of the area, he added, had "followed" the German army westward. There was no doubt that many Germans had fled westward, but there was a great likelihood that many had simply been driven out, while others were executed. Stalin, George Kennan noted, seemed to enjoy assuring Churchill and Truman that "no single German" remained in the territory to be given to Poland.[23]

Stalin spoke from strength when dealing with eastern Europe, but he already knew that the balance of global power had shifted to the United States. It shifted more on the morning of July 16 when Truman received word that the first atomic device had been exploded in New Mexico. The president now had to decide whether to use the bomb if Japan refused to surrender. Truman waited several days before informing Stalin about the bomb. Churchill had opposed telling the Soviets anything, and some Americans agreed with him. Truman finally decided to inform Stalin without giving too many details. "On July 24," he wrote, "I casually mentioned that we had a new weapon of unusual destructive force. All he said was that he was glad to hear it and hoped we would make 'good use of it against the Japanese.'"[24] There is some question whether Truman remembered the exchange accurately, but all observers agree that Stalin showed little concern. He had no cause to be impressed or surprised. His agents had been keeping the Kremlin informed on the progress of the Manhattan Project for some time, and he was aware that a test was coming soon.[25]

Truman and the Americans knew that having the bomb gave the United States an advantage it would lose in four to five years. Secretary Byrnes may indeed have had the Soviets in mind when he said the bomb would "put us in a position to dictate our own terms at the end of the war," but most likely he was referring to Japan.[26] Whatever Byrnes may have meant, there was no serious thought of using the bomb against the Soviets as a weapon or as an instrument of intimidation, and the Western Allies scrupulously avoided even the hint of a threat. General Marshall acknowledged that the bomb was of little use in regulating Soviet conduct. He told Stimson that even if America defeated Japan alone, "that would not prevent the Russians from marching into Manchuria anyhow...."[27] In Europe, perhaps in the course of war, it might be used, but certainly not to make the Soviets "behave" in eastern Europe, as demonstrated by the fact that during the period of the American nuclear monopoly Soviet control of eastern Europe increased along with Communist expansion in Asia.[28]

Churchill and Truman decided to warn Japan before using the bomb. China, Great Britain, and the United States issued the Potsdam Declaration on July 26. The Declaration reminded Japanese government of the German defeat and the forces now "poised to strike the final blows upon Japan." The time had come for Japan to reject the "militaristic advisors" who had brought disaster and follow the course of reason. "Following are our terms: We will not deviate from them. There are no alternatives. We shall brook no delay." Japanese sovereignty would be limited to "Honshu, Hokkaido, Kyushu, Shikoku and such minor islands as we determine." Japanese military forces were to be disarmed and allowed to return home. The Declaration also required the Japanese to remove those who had led the country to war and lay the foundation for a democratic government in the future. In turn, the Allies promised the Japanese people would not be enslaved and that one day the country would return to a normal economic and political life among nations. The Declaration did not mention the status of the emperor, but promised that Allied forces would withdraw from Japan when their objectives had been accomplished "and there has been established in accordance with the freely expressed will of the Japanese people a peacefully inclined and responsible government." If, however, Japan failed to surrender its armed forces unconditionally, the alternative would be "prompt and utter destruction."[29]

The Declaration marked Churchill's final act as a wartime leader. The prime minister who had guided Britain through its finest hour had returned home on July 25 to await the results of the general election. And then, as he later said with a tinge of bitterness, "all our enemies having surrendered unconditionally, or about to do so, I was immediately dismissed by the British electorate from all further conduct of their affairs."[30] Britain was exhausted after six years of war. The electorate turned to the Labour Party of Clement Attlee as the best hope for rebuilding the country in peacetime. Attlee and Foreign Secretary Ernest Bevin returned to Potsdam to continue the negotiations on July 28. Attlee had accompanied Churchill as an observer and was familiar with the problems, although he had been virtually ignored by foreign delegations. Bevin was unfamiliar with diplomacy, but had been active for years in government and had much experience as a negotiator. In general, the new team held to the same positions as the old, except for more of a dislike of Franco's Spain. As democratic socialists, they also disliked Soviet methods and policies in eastern Europe. Attlee and Bevin were able and experienced but lacked the stature of their predecessors, and everyone knew it.

Attlee and Bevin found Truman impatient and eager to go home. Stalin probably felt the same way in view of a "cold" that caused him to miss negotiating sessions. Whether the cold was diplomatic or physical, Stalin felt comfortable in allowing Molotov to face the Anglo-Americans while he made the decisions. As the conference drew to a close the irritations and wrangling had produced a change in tone as well as in goals. The Grand Alliance was over and neither the Soviets nor the Anglo-Americans were going to get what they wanted. The military reality of the present was becoming the political reality of the future.

Byrnes attempted to gain the appearance of a settlement by proposing a package deal to Molotov on July 30. The Byrnes proposals set in motion a series of meetings leading to the de facto recognition of Europe into Soviet and American blocks. Stalin gave up his claim for a guaranteed total on reparations and agreed that each country would collect reparations from its own zone. The Soviets also would receive 10 percent "of such capital equipment as is unnecessary for the German peace economy" from the Anglo-American zones, along with another 15 percent of material in exchange for an equivalent commodities from the Soviet zone. The Americans and British agreed to the western Neisse as the Polish border, pending a final peace conference. In return Italy was granted admission to the United Nations, with Stalin dropping his demand for Italian reparations. The three powers also accepted the authority of the Austrian Provisional Government of Karl Renner and clarified their occupation zones.[31] The Anglo-Americans failed in pressing for implementation of the Declaration on Liberated Europe. Stalin always replied by citing Anglo-American control in Greece, Italy, and Western Europe, and he made it clear that he would brook no interference in eastern Europe.

Truman left Potsdam on August 3, determined to block any Soviet influence in the future of Japan following the war he hoped would soon end. He had given his order for using the new atomic bomb on Japan if the war continued. The Potsdam Declaration was Japan's last chance. The situation in the Pacific was grim, and the future looked worse. The Philippine campaign had begun in October 1944 with the Battle of Leyte Gulf and then the invasion of Leyte itself. The Japanese Air Force was now but a shadow of what it had been in 1941. Its planes were inferior and its pilots poorly trained, but they could be used for one-way missions against American ships. The Kamikaze, so named after the Divine Wind that had saved Japan from China in the fourteenth century, now went into action.[32] Fighting on Iwo Jima had begun on February 19. When it ended on March 16, the U.S. Marine Corps had suffered 25,000 casualties with over 6,000 dead.[33] Operation Iceberg, the invasion of Okinawa, began on April 1 and encountered fanatical resistance in the south. At sea Japanese defenders added to the carnage by launching Kamikaze attacks in force against American ships. When the battle finally ended in June, 75,000 American soldiers and sailors had been killed or wounded. Losses in material were staggering, with 38 ships sunk, another 368 damaged, and over 700 aircraft.[34] The War Department formulated plans for the final assault on Japan following the Yalta conference. Operation Olympic, the invasion of Kyushu, was scheduled for December 1945. Operation Coronet, the invasion Honshu, would follow in April 1946. Both operations, and especially Coronet, depended on transferring men and material from Europe. Approximately 400,000 Army Air Forces, Army Ground Forces, and Army Security Forces were scheduled for direct transfer from Europe to the

Pacific from September 1945 to April 1946. Another 400,000 were to have a delay en route in the United States, with all projections subject to available shipping.[35]

Rarely has a victor so anguished over the way victory was attained as the Americans have anguished over the atomic bomb and the defeat of Japan. Truman's decision has to be seen within the context of World War II. No one ever described war more bluntly and clearly than General William Tecumseh Sherman: "War is cruelty," he said to the mayor of Atlanta in September, 1864, "and you can not refine it."[36] This is especially true when war is waged against an enemy perceived as evil. The unthinkable of one day becomes the routine of another through repetition while the moral end justifies the brutal means. "Vengeance against the Japanese," wrote Richard Overy, "was a core element in popular attitudes to the war, fueled by a diet of atrocity stories which helped to dull resistance to indiscriminate destruction of Japanese cities and the eventual use of the atomic bomb."[37] Emphasis on the atomic bomb has overshadowed the cruelty and horror of "conventional" bombing that had laid waste to the cities of Europe and Japan. "It's all well and good to come along later and say the bomb was a horrible thing," Truman's aide George Elsey later recalled. "The whole goddamn war was a horrible thing."[38] President Truman was the commander in chief of the American armed forces. His primary responsibility lay in securing their well-being. Every day of war meant additional American casualties on land and at sea, as well as additional suffering and death in Japanese prison camps.

Truman's decision has often been condemned without adequate consideration for what transpired within the Japanese government.[39] Scholars often cite the 1946 *Japan's Struggle to End the War* as evidence that Japan would have surrendered before an invasion, and that the atomic bomb was therefore unnecessary.[40] The authors of the badly flawed report, however, were not leading Japan in the summer of 1945.[41] They also accepted the view of Emperor Hirohito as a passive bystander unstained by the war. More recent studies give evidence that he played a more bellicose role in the war from the beginning. "Ultimately," wrote Herbert P. Bix, "he also shares with Japan's other war leaders, responsibility for helping to doom Hiroshima and Nagasaki to destruction."[42]

Japan was losing the war by January of 1945, but it was not ready to surrender at the cost of losing the imperial system or sovereignty in the Home Islands. Emperor Hirohito held several interviews with seven senior statesmen between February 7 and February 26. The advisors either did not grasp the real situation or were afraid to tell the truth. General Tojo said that the Americans had fallen short of their objectives and could not continue their current effort. He also believed the Soviet Union could be kept out of the war, and that Soviet intervention would be no major threat. Defeatism was the main enemy. Only Prince Konoe Fuminaro recognized the current situation for what it was. "Japan has already lost the war," he told the emperor. It was time to purge the military of extremist elements as a prerequisite for peace with the Americans, British, and Chinese. Continuing the war, the prince believed, would strain Japan to the point of internal revolution and open the door to Communism. There was no point in seeking help from the Soviet Union.[43]

The emperor and the government declined Konoe's advice. On April 5, as the battle on Okinawa raged, Admiral Suzuki Kantaro became prime minister with a mandate to end the war on favorable terms. Suzuki sought an end to the war as part of the Supreme Council for the Conduct of the War. The Council was usually referred to as the Big Six, since it was comprised of the prime minister, the foreign minister and the four military chiefs.[44] The Council continued to seek Russian help, despite intelligence reports that Moscow was preparing to attack in the near future, instead of pursuing some kind of direct negotiations with the Americans.[45] Stalin's purposes were better served by prolonging the war between America and Japan. The cover of coming to the aid of an ally was preferable to the appearance of unprovoked aggression. Tokyo, however, vainly hoped to reach an agreement with the Soviets before the 1941 pact expired.

The Japanese military intended to bleed the Americans into a compromise peace. "It is characteristic of Americans to hold human lives so dear," Admiral Oikawa Koshiro reported to the emperor in January. "It is necessary that we take advantage of this weakness, and inflict tremendous losses, using all possible methods."[46] Japanese leaders displayed little regard for their own civilian or military losses. On the night of March 9-10, 334 American B-29s hit Tokyo with incendiary bombs. The flames destroyed sixteen square miles of the city and killed between 80,000 and 100,000 people. Approximately 100,000 Japanese soldiers died on Okinawa along with over 150,000 civilians.[47]

In April the Japanese government adopted the "Ketsu-Go" policy for defending the homeland, involving the entire population and relying heavily on Kamikaze, human torpedoes, and other suicide weapons.[48] The Japanese had anticipated the invasion of Kyushu and were ready. There were over 600,000 military and civilian defenders waiting to face an invasion force on a ratio of one to one.[49] The battle for Honshu, would face heavy resistance and heavy casualties. Conquest of the Home Islands might take until the end of 1946, and still leave the Japanese in control of Burma, Formosa (Taiwan), and parts of China. The Kwantung Army in China and Manchuria had lost much of its strength, but still had a million men.

Questions remain whether the war might have been shortened had the Potsdam Declaration stipulated retention of the emperor. Stimson and former Ambassador to Japan Joseph Grew wanted a statement allowing it. Byrnes, Hull, and others thought it smacked of "appeasement," especially since Hirohito was widely regarded as a major war criminal. Such a concession, they also believed, might be interpreted as a confession of war weariness in the United States and encourage the Japanese to fight on. The shadow of Darlan and the armistice of 1918 also influenced Truman's decision on the emperor. Many Americans, especially on the political left, wanted nothing less than a domestic revolution in Japan as the price of peace I. F. Stone, writing in the *Nation,* condemned Grew and "The Pearl Harbor Diplomats" for their gullibility prior to the war and their willingness to accept a "soft" peace. The *Nation* and others wanted a peace "that would be as conclusive as a military victory." There must be an end to the "Emperor system," along with an overhaul of the entire Japanese society.[50]

It is doubtful whether an open offer allowing retention of the emperor would have brought a Japanese surrender.[51] The Suzuki government was aware that the Potsdam Declaration did not forbid retention of the emperor. It continued to pursue the illusory goal of Soviet meditation instead of directly contacting the American government. Japanese ambassador in Moscow, Sato Naotake repeatedly told his government to forget Soviet aid and to end the war as soon as possible, even if it meant accepting the Potsdam terms, a suggestion that was endorsed by other Japanese diplomats. Sato was informed that Japan would not accept unconditional surrender, even if the emperor was maintained. He was ordered to continue seeking Soviet support.[52]

The Suzuki government responded to the Potsdam Declaration with what Robert J.C. Butow described as "one of the most unusual and contradictory actions ever taken by a government against itself."[53] The government chose to *mokusatsu* the Declaration, or to treat it as "unworthy of public notice." At a press conference on July 28, Suzuki said his government did not consider the Declaration "as a thing of any great value; the government will just ignore [*mokusatsu*] it. We will press forward resolutely to carry the war to a successful conclusion."⁵⁴

Suzuki later claimed he meant simply "no comment," but his response was widely interpreted as defiance as well as rejection, leaving no alternative to using the bomb. The Declaration had said the Allies would "brook no delay," and yet Tokyo seemed to think time was on its side. When asked why Suzuki had made such a foolish statement, Navy Minister Yonai Mitsumasa replied, "Churchill had fallen, America is beginning to be isolated. The government will therefore ignore it. There is no need to rush."⁵⁵ This was said at a time when American bombers were blasting Japanese cities every day.

At 0227 on the morning of August 7, on the island of Tinian, Lieutenant Colonel Paul Tibbets started the engines on his B-29, the *Enola Gay*, to begin the bombing run on Hiroshima. The flight was routine after takeoff, and much of the time Tibbets turned control over to "George," the automatic pilot. He climbed and leveled off at 31,000 feet for the final run as he approached the Japanese coast. At 8:16:02 in Japan the first atomic bomb exploded over Hiroshima. "My God," wrote the co-pilot in his log. Nearly 80,000 people were dead by the end of the day.⁵⁶

Truman issued a statement from the *Augusta* to explain the new weapon and why it was being used. "It was to spare the Japanese from utter destruction," he said, "that the ultimatum of July 26, was issued at Potsdam. Their leaders promptly rejected that ultimatum. If they do not now accept our terms they may expect a rain of ruin from the air the like of which has never been seen on this earth."⁵⁷ Not even Hiroshima convinced military leaders to end the war. Truman's warning was dismissed as propaganda in an attempt to deny the existence of an atomic bomb or to minimize its impact. Moscow soon struck another blow. Stalin believed the new weapon might end the war before he could seize the territory promised him at Yalta. He ordered the Red Army to attack as soon as possible. Molotov presented Ambassador Sato with a declaration of war at 5:00 p.m. Moscow time on August 8. The Red Army attacked across the border into Manchuria two hours later at 0100 hours Japanese time. The Russians advanced rapidly to threaten Japan's hold on Manchuria and Korea.⁵⁸ The Japanese government viewed the Russian action as an act of great treachery. Japan had allowed American aid to cross the Pacific to Russia during the war with Germany. Instead of helping Japan end its war, the Soviet Union now violated a non-aggression pact it had promised to honor. The peace faction in the government saw Hiroshima and the Russian attack as a blessing. The government could now say it was forced to leave the war by outside forces, and not by domestic upheaval.[59] The Japanese military, however, continued to resist. The Big Six met again at 11:00 a.m. on August 9. While they were arguing word came that another atomic bomb had hit Nagasaki. The Supreme Council normally presented the emperor with a unanimous decision, but none had been reached at the end of the day. Suzuki and Foreign Minister Togo Shigenori decided to see the emperor. They told him that no decision had been reached to end the war and proposed an Imperial Conference that night.

The emperor convened the Imperial Conference just before midnight. For the next two hours the men present expressed views as opposed as they had been that afternoon. Suzuki stated that the crisis of the moment required a decision from the emperor. Hirohito responded as he should have responded to the Potsdam Declaration. In a soft but sure voice the emperor stated that he could no longer bear to see his innocent people suffer and that peace was the only answer. Those who had promised victory in the past had not delivered it, however good their intentions. It was unbearable for him to see those who had fought for him disarmed and punished as instigators of the war. "Nevertheless," he said, "the time has come when we must bear the unbearable." [60]

The government broadcast its acceptance of the Potsdam Declaration on condition that the Imperial system remain. Hirohito was reviled in China as well as in the United States. A Gallup poll on August 10 indicated that most Americans opposed retaining him, by a wide margin.[61] Truman, however, agreed with Grew and Stimson that keeping Hirohito in power meant giving a little to gain a lot. Refusal could cost the Americans a host of "Iwo Jimas" and "Okinawas" throughout the Japanese Empire. Allowing him to remain would facilitate surrender.[62]

The American reply stipulated that the emperor must be subject to the Supreme Allied Commander who would rule as a foreign shogun while the emperor reigned. The "final form of government," however, "shall be determined by the freely expressed will of the Japanese people."[63] Tokyo heard the context of the American note by way of Allied radio before receiving it officially. The emperor had spoken in favor of peace, but the issue remained unsettled amid the growing danger of assassination by those determined to rid him of bad advisors.

The government was forced to act early on the morning of August 14 when American planes dropped leaflets describing negotiations. Hirohito quickly called another Imperial Council. He listened as he had five days earlier to those who wanted peace or war. "I have studied the terms of the

Allied reply," he said. "I consider the reply to be acceptable."[64] The following day the emperor demonstrated that truth is sometimes the first casualty in peace. He began the recorded speech by ignoring decades of Japanese aggression against other Asians. "We declared war on America and Britain out of our sincere desire to ensure Japan's self-preservation and the stabilization of East Asia, it being far from Our thought either to infringe upon the sovereignty of other nations or to embark upon territorial aggrandizement." He then portrayed Japan as a victim in a war it had begun and had refused to end until forced to do so by atomic weapons. Japan had decided to surrender, he said, because the enemy had now begun to "employ a new and most cruel bomb." [65]

The nation obeyed and accepted its fate, although there were scattered attempts to reverse the will of the emperor along with assassination attempts and suicides. On September 2, General Douglas MacArthur presided over the official surrender ceremony as the Allied Commander and the new shogun of Japan. "Military alliances," he said, "balances of power, leagues of nations, all in turn failed, leaving the only path to be by way of the crucible of war. The utter destructiveness of war now blots out this alternative. We have had our last chance." With him on the deck of the *Missouri* stood Lieutenant General Kuzma Derevyanko who signed for the Soviet Union. The heirs of Lenin and Wilson had slain the common enemy. They now stood victoriously face to face in Asia, Europe, and throughout the world to resume a struggle that had begun a generation earlier. "If we do not devise some greater and more equitable system," MacArthur said, "Armageddon will be at our door."[66]

NOTES

1. McCullough, *Truman*, 406.
2. Arno Mayer, *The Political Origins of the New Diplomacy, 1917-1918* (New Haven: Yale University Press, 1959), 393.
3. André Fontaine, *History of the Cold War*, trans. D. D. Paige, vol. 1 (New York: Pantheon Books, 1968), 12. Gaddis, *We Now Know*, 1.
4. Vojtech Mastny, "The Cassandra in the Foreign Commissariat: Maxim Litvinov and the Cold War," *Foreign Affairs*, vol. 54 (January, 1976), 371-372. Phillips, *Between the Revolution and the West*, 172-173.
5. Alonzo M. Hamby, *Man of the People: A Life of Harry S. Truman* (New York: Oxford University Press, 1995), 316. McCullough,

Truman, 375-376. *FRUS: 1945,* vol. 5, 231-234.
6. *FRUS: 1945,* vol. 5, 235-236.
7. Ibid, 236-262, 265-271.
8. *The Private Papers of Senator Vandenberg,* ed. Arthur H. Vandenberg Jr. (Boston: Houghton Mifflin Company, 1952), 185.
9. Ulam, *Expansion and Coexistence,* 383. *New York Times,* May 6, 1945, 1, 28.
10. John Lewis Gaddis, *The United States and the Origins of the Cold War, 1941-1947* (New York: Oxford University Press, 1972), 228-229.
11. Hamby, *Man of the People,* 319. McCullough, *Truman,* 382, 398.
12. *FRUS: Conference of Berlin* (Potsdam), vol. 1, 24-60. McJimsey, *Hopkins,* 382-385.
13. Martin Gilbert, *Winston S. Churchill,* vol. 8 (Boston: Houghton Mifflin, 1988), 6-7.
14. Gilbert, *Churchill,* vol. 8, 24-26. Potsdam Papers, vol. 1, 64-78.
15. Truman, *Memoirs,* vol. 1, 278-279.
16. Hamby, *Man of the People,* 321.
17. *New York Times,* June 27, 1945, 10.
18. McCullough, *Truman,* 404.
19. J. Samuel Walker, *Prompt and Utter Destruction: Truman and the Use of Atomic Bombs against Japan* (Chapel Hill: The University of North Carolina Press, 1997), 18.
20. Kissinger, *Diplomacy,* 434.
21. *Potsdam Papers,* vol. 2, 52-59.
22. Churchill, *Triumph and Tragedy,* 651-653. *Potsdam Papers,* vol. 2, 91-94.
23. Ibid, vol. 2, 211. Kennan, *Memoirs,* 265.
24. Truman, *Memoirs,* vol. 1, 416.
25. Holloway, *Stalin and the Bomb,* 117.
26. Robert L. Messer, *The End of an Alliance: James F. Byrnes, Roosevelt, Truman, and the Origins of the Cold War* (Chapel Hill: University of North Carolina Press, 1982), 86. Robert J. Maddox, *Weapons for Victory: The Hiroshima Decision Fifty Years Later* (Columbia: University of Missouri Press, 1995), 30.
27. Ibid, 102.
28. Holloway, *Stalin and the Bomb,* 271.
29. *Potsdam Papers,* vol. 2, 1280-1281. Truman, *Memoirs,* vol. 1, 390-392.

30. Churchill, *The Gathering Storm,* 667. Potsdam Papers, vol. 480-483, 533-538. Gaddis, *U.S. and Cold War,* 241.
31. Ibid., 659-685.
32. Weinberg, *World at Arms,* 848.
33. George W. Garand and Truman R. Strobridge, *History of the U.S. Marine Corps Operations in World War II,* vol. 4 (Washington: U.S. Government Printing Office, 1971), 711.
34. Weinberg, *World at Arms,* 882.
35. Robert W. Coakley and Richard M. Leighton, *Global Logistics and Strategy* (Washington: U.S. Government Printing Office, 1968), 585-586. Thomas B. Allen and Norman Polmar, *Code Name Downfall: The Secret Plan to Invade Japan - and Why Truman Dropped the Bomb* (New York: Simon and Schuster, 1995), 145.
36. Charles E. Vetter, *Sherman: Merchant of Terror, Advocate of Peace* (Gretna, LA: Pelican Publishing Company, 1992), 228.
37. Richard Overy, *Why the Allies Won* (New York: W.W. Norton and Company, 1995.), 294.
38. McCullough, *Truman,* 442.
39. Herbert P. Bix, "Japan's Delayed Surrender: A Reinterpretation," *Diplomatic History,* vol. 19 (Spring, 1995), 197.
40. *U.S. Strategic Bombing Survey, Japan's Struggle to End the War* (New York: Garland Publishing, Inc., 1976), 13.
41. Robert P. Newman gives an excellent analysis of the report in *Truman and the Hiroshima Cult* (East Lansing: Michigan State University Press, 1995), 33-56.
42. Bix, "Japan's Delayed Surrender, 203.
43. Butow, *Japan's Decision to Surrender,* 46-49.
44. Toland, *The Rising Sun,* 746.
45. Bix, *"Japan's Delayed Surrender,"* 202.
46. Allen and Polmar, *Downfall,* 169.
47. Bix, "Japan's Delayed Surrender," 212. Weinberg, *World At Arms,* 882.
48. Bix, "Japan's Delayed Surrender," 213.
49. Allen and Polmar, *Downfall,* 238.
50. I.F. Stone, "Pearl Harbor Diplomats," *Nation,* vol. 161 (July 14, 1945), 25-27. T.A. Bisson, "What Program for Japan," (July 14, 1945), 28-29.
51. Stephen E. Ambrose, *Americans at War* (New York: Berkley Books, 1998), 129.

52. Bix, "Japan's Delayed Surrender," 215-216. Butow, *Japan's Decision to Surrender*, 130. Weinberg, World at Arms, 886.
53. Ibid, p. 144.
54. Butow, *Japan's Decision to Surrender*, 148.
55. Bix, "Japan's Delayed Surrender," 206.
56. Rhodes, *Atomic Bomb*, 705-711. Toland, *Rising Sun*, 786.
57. Harries, *Soldiers of the Sun*, 453. *New York Times*, August 7, 1945, 1,4.
58. Butow, *Japan's Decision to Surrender*, 152-154.
59. Bix, "Japan's Delayed Surrender, p. 218.
60. Butow, *Japan's Decision to Surrender*, 168-176.
61. Walker, *Prompt and Utter Destruction*, 85.
62. Stimson and Bundy, *On Active Service*, 626-627.
63. Butow, *Japan's Decision to Surrender*, 243.
64. Ibid, 207.
65. Ibid, 227.
66. Toland, *Rising Sun*, 870.

SELECTED BIBLIOGRAPHY

Documents:

Congressional Record. Washington: U.S. Government Printing Office, 1916-45.

Correspondence Between the Chairman of the Council of Ministers of the USSR and the Presidents of the USA and the Prime Ministers of Great Britain During the Great Patriotic War, 1941-1945. Moscow: Progress Publishers, 1978.

The Communist International, 1919-1943: Documents selected and edited by Jane Degras. 3 vols. New York: Oxford University Press, 1965.

Documents diplomatiques français, 1932-1939. Commission de publications des documents relatifs aux origines de la guerre 1939-1945. Paris: Imprimerie nationale, 1963-1986.

Documents on British Foreign Policy, 1919-1939. ed. E.L. Woodward & Rohan Butler. First Series. 27 vols. London: His Majesty's Stationery Office, 1947-1986.

Documents on British Foreign Policy, 1919-1939. ed. W.N. Medlicott. Second Series. 21 vols. London: Her Majesty's Stationery Office, 1947-1984.

Documents on German Foreign Policy, 1918-1945. ed. Paul R. Sweet, et al, Department of State. Washington: U.S. Government Printing Office, 1957-1964

Documents on Polish-Soviet Relations, 1939-1945, 2 vols. London: Heinemann, 1967.

Foreign Relations of the United States. Annual Volumes, 1911-1945. Washington: U.S. Government Printing Office, 1926-1969.

Foreign Relations of the United States: The Conference at Quebec 1944. Washington: U.S. Government Printing Office, 1972.

Foreign Relations of the United States: The Paris Peace Conference. 13 vols. Washington: U.S. Government Printing Office, 1946.

Foreign Relations of the United States: The Conferences at Washington, 1941 and Casablanca, 1943. Washington: U.S. Government Printing Office, 1963.

Foreign Relations of the United States: The Conferences at Washington and Quebec, 1943. Washington: U.S. Government Printing Office, 1970.

Foreign Relations of the United States: The Conferences at Cairo and Tehran, 1943. Washington: U.S. Government Printing Office, 1943.

Foreign Relations of the United States: The Conferences at Malta and Yalta, 1945. Washington: Washington: U.S. Government Printing Office, 1955.

Foreign Relations of the United States: The Conference of Berlin (The Potsdam Conference), 1945. 2 vols. Washington: U.S. Government Printing Office, 1960.

Hitlers Weisungen für die Kriegführung, 1939-1945: Dokumente des Oberkommandos der Wehrmacht. Herausgegeben von Walther Hubatsch. Frankfurt am Main: Bernard and Graefe, 1962.

International Military Tribunal. *Trial of the Major War Criminals Before the International Military Tribunal, 14 November, 1945-1 October, 1946.* 44 vols. Nuremberg: International Military Tribunal, 1947.

International Military Tribunal for the Far East. *The Tokyo War Crimes Trials.* ed. R. John Pritchard and Sonia M. Zaide. 22 vols. New York: Garland Publishing Co., 1981.

Kriegstagebuch des Oberkommandos der Wehrmacht (Wehrmachtführungsstab) 1940-1945. Geführt von Hemuth Greiner und Percy Ernst Schramm. 5 Vols. Frankfurt am Main: Bernard & Graefe, 1961-1965.

Mantoux, Paul. *Les Délibérations du Conseil du Quartre (24 Mars-Juin 1919).* 2 vols. Paris: Editions du Centre national de la recherche scientifique, 1955.

Nazi-Soviet Relations, 1939-1941: Documents from the Archives of the German Foreign Office. ed. Raymond J. Sontag and James Stuart Beddie. Washington: U.S. Government Printing Office, 1948.

The Papers of Dwight David Eisenhower: The War Years. 5 vols. ed. Alfred D. Chandler, Jr. Baltimore: Johns Hopkins Press, 1970-84.

The Papers of Woodrow Wilson. 69 vols. ed. Arthur S. Link, et. al. Princeton: Princeton University press, 1966-1994.

Roosevelt and Churchill: Their Secret Wartime Correspondence. ed. Francis L. Lowenheim, et al. New York: Saturday Review Press, 1975.

Soviet Documents on Foriegn Policy. Selected and Edited by Jane Degras.

3 vols. New York: Oxford University Press, 1951.

The Speeches of Adolf Hitler, April, 1922-August, 1939. ed. Norman H. Baynes. London: Oxford University Press, 1942.

Books:

Abramson, Rudy. *Spanning the Century: The Life of W. Averell Harriman, 1891-1986.* New York: William Morrow and Company, 1992.

Allen, Thomas B. and Polmar, Norman. *Code Name Downfall: The Secret Plan To Invade Japan — And Why Truman Dropped the Bomb.* New York: Simon and Schuster, 1995.

Alliluyeva, Svetlana. *Only One Year.* trans. Paul Chavchavadza. New York: Harper and Row, 1969.

___. *Twenty Letters to a Friend.* trans. Priscilla Johnson McMillan. New York: Harper and Row, 1967.

Albertini, Luigi. *The Origins of the War of 1914.* ed. and trans. Isabella M. Massey. 3 vols. New York: Oxford University Press, 1952-57.

Ambrose, Stephen E. *Eisenhower: Soldier, General of the Army, President-Elect, 1890-1952.* vol. 1. New York: Simon & Schuster, 1983.

___. *The Supreme Commander: The War Years of Dwight D. Eisenhower.* Garden City, NY: Doubleday and Company, 1970.

___. *Eisenhower and Berlin, 1945.* New York: W.W. Norton and Company, 1967.

___. *D-Day: June 6, 1944: The Climatic Battle of World War II.* New York: Simon and Schuster, 1994.

___. *Citizen Soldiers: The U.S. Army from the Normandy Beaches to the Bulge to the Surrender of Germany, June 7, 1944-May 7, 1945.* New York: Simon & Schuster, 1997

___. *Americans at War.* New York: Berkley Books, 1998.

Aron, Raymond. *The Opium of the Intellectuals.* trans. Terence Kilmartin. New York: Doubleday and Company, 1957.

Balfour, Michael. *The Kaiser and His Times.* New York: W.W. Norton Company, 1972.

Bell, P.M.H. *The Origins of the Second World War in Europe.* New York: Longman Incorporated, 1986.

Bennett, Edward M. *Recognition of Russia: An American Foreign Policy Dilemma.* Waltham, MA: Blaisdell Publishing Company, 1970.

Bernadotte, Count Folke. *The Curtain Falls: Last Days of the Third Reich.* trans. Count Eric L. Lewehnaupt. New York: Alfred A. Knopf, 1945.

Bernard, Philippe and Dubief, Henri. *The Decline of the Third Republic, 1914-1938.* trans. Anthony Forster. New York: Cambridge University Press, 1986.

Bloch, Michael. *Ribbentrop.* New York: Crown Publishers, Incorporated, 1992.

Blumenson, Martin. *The United States Army in World War II, Breakout and Pursuit.* Washington: U.S. Government Printing Office, 1961.

___. *United States Army in World War II, The Mediterranean Theater of Operations: Salerno to Cassino.* Washington: U.S. Government Printing Office, 1969.

Bonnet, Georges. *Quai d'Orsay.* Douglas, Isle of Man: Times Press and Anthony Gibbs and Phillips, 1965.

Bor-Komorowski, Tadeusz. *Secret Army.* New York: Macmillan Company, 1950.

Bradley, Omar N. *A Soldier's Story.* New York: Henry Holt and Company, 1951.

Brook-Shepherd, Gordon. *Anschluss: The Rape of Austria.* Westport, CT: Greenwood Press, 1976.

Brown, Anthony Cave. *Bodyguard of Lies.* New York: Harper and Row, 1975.

Brzezinski, Zbigniew. *The Grand Failure: The Birth and Death of Communism in the Twentieth Century.* New York: Charles Scribner's Sons, 1989.

Buckley, Thomas. *The United States and the Washington Conference, 1921-1922.* Knoxville: University of Tennessee Press, 1970.

Bullock, Alan. *Hitler and Stalin: Parallel Lives.* New York: Alfred A. Knopf, 1992.

Butow, Robert J.C. *Japan's Decision to Surrender.* Stanford: Stanford University Press, 1954.

___. *Tojo and the Coming of the War.* Princeton: Princeton University Press, 1961.

Cartier, Raymond. *Der Zweite Weltkrieg*, 2 vols. München: R. Piper and Company, 1967.

Chang, Iris. *The Rape of Nanking: The Forgotten Holocaust of World War II*. New York: Basic Books, 1997.

Charmley, John. *Chamberlain and the Lost Peace*. Chicago: Ivan R. Dee, 1989.

___. *Churchill: The End of Glory*. London: John Curtis, 1993.

___. *Churchill's Grand Alliance: The Anglo-American Special Relationship, 1940-57*. New York: Harcourt Brace and Company, 1995.

Churchill, Winston S. *The Gathering Storm*. Boston: Houghton Mifflin, 1948.

___. *Their Finest Hour*. Boston: Houghton-Mifflin, 1949.

___. *The Grand Alliance*. Boston: Houghton-Mifflin, 1950.

___. *The Hinge of Fate*. Boston: Houghton-Mifflin, 1950.

___. *Closing The Ring*. Boston: Houghton-Mifflin, 1951.

___. *Triumph and Tragedy*. Boston: Houghton-Mifflin, 1953.

___. *Winston S. Churchill: His Complete Speeches, 1897-1963*. ed. Robert R. James. 5 vols. New York: Chelsea House Publishers, 1974.

Ciano, Count Galeazzo. *The Ciano Diaries, 1939-1943*. ed. Hugh Gibson. New York: Doubleday and Company, 1946.

Clemenceau, Georges. *Grandeur and Misery of Victory*. New York: Harcourt, Brace, and Company, 1930.

Clemens, Diane Shaver, *Yalta*. New York: Oxford University Press, 1970.

Cline, Ray S. *The United States Army in World War II, Washington Command Post: The Operations Division*. Washington: U.S. Government Printing Office, 1951.

Coakley, Robert W. and Leighton, Richard M. *The United States Army in World War II, Global Logistics and Strategy, 1943-1945*. Washington: U.S. Government Printing Office, 1968.

Cole, Hugh M. *The United States Army in World War II, The Ardennes: Battle of the Bulge*. Washington: U.S. Government Printing Office, 1965.

Cole, Wayne, S. *Senator Gerald P. Nye and American Foreign Relations*. Minneapolis: University of Minnesota Press, 1962.

Conquest, Robert. *The Harvest of Sorrow: Soviet Collectivization and the Terror-Famine*. New York: Oxford University Press, 1986.

___. *The Great Terror: Stalin's Purge of the Thirties.* New York: Macmillan Company, 1968.

Crowl, Philip A. *The United States Army in World War II, Campaign in the Marianas.* Washington: U.S. Government Printing Office, 1960.

Dallek, Robert. *Franklin D. Roosevelt and American Foreign Policy.* New York: Oxford University Press, 1979.

Davis, Kenneth S. *FDR: Into the Storm, 1930-1940: A History.* New York: Random House, 1993.

Debo, Richard K. *Survival and Consolidation: The Foreign Policy of Soviet Russia, 1918-1921.* Montreal: McGill-Queen's University Press, 1992.

De Gaulle, Charles. *The War Memoirs of Charles De Gaulle.* 2 vols. trans. Richard Howard. New York: Simon and Schuster, 1955-59.

D'Este, Carlo. *Patton: A Genius For War.* New York: Harper Collins, 1995.

Das Deutsche Reich und der Zweite Weltkrieg. Herausgegeben vom Militärgeschichtlichen Forschungsamt. 6 vols. Stuttgart: Deutsche Verlags-Anstalt, 1979.

Deutscher, Isaac. *The Prophet Unarmed: Trotsky, 1921-1927.* New York: Oxford University Press, 1959.

___. *Stalin: A Political Biography.* New York: Oxford University Press, 1967.

Divine, Robert A. *The Illusion of Neutrality.* Chicago: University of Chicago Press, 1962.

Djilas, Milovan. *Conversations with Stalin.* trans. Michael Petrovich. New York: Harcourt, Brace and World, Incorporated, 1962.

Duroselle, Jean-Baptiste. *From Wilson to Roosevelt: Foreign Policy of the United States, 1913-1945.* Cambridge: Harvard University Press, 1963.

___*La Décadence, 1932-1939.* Paris: Imprimerie nationale, 1979.

Eden, Anthony, The Earl of Avon. *The Reckoning.* Boston: Houghton Mifflin Company, 1965.

Facing the Dictators. London: Cassell, 1962.

Edmonds, Robin. *The Big Three: Churchill, Roosevelt, and Stalin in Peace and War.* New York: W.W. Norton Company, 1991.

Eisenhower, David. *Eisenhower at War: 1943-1945*. New York: Random House, 1986.

Eisenhower, Dwight D. *Crusade in Europe*. Garden City: Doubleday, 1948.

Erickson, John. *The Road to Berlin*. Boulder, CO: Westview Press, 1983.

___. *The Road to Stalingrad: Stalin's War With Germany*. New York: Harper and Row, 1975.

The Fatal Decisions. ed. Seymour Freidin and William Richardson. New York: William Slone Associates, 1956.

Fauvet, Jacques. *Histoire du parti communiste français de 1920 à 1976*. Paris: Fayard, 1977.

Feiling, Keith. *The Life of Neville Chamberlain*. London: Macmillan Company, 1946.

Feis, Herbert. *Churchill, Roosevelt, Stalin: The War They Waged and the Peace They Sought*. Princeton: Princeton University Press, 1957.

Fenyo, Mario D. *Hitler, Horthy, and Hungary: German Hungarian Relations, 1941-1944*. New Haven: Yale University Press, 1972.

Fero, Marc. *Nicholas II: The Last of the Tsars*. trans. Brian Pearce. New York: Viking Press, 1990.

Ferrell, Robert H. *Woodrow Wilson and World War I*. New York: Harper and Row, 1985.

Fest, Joachim C. *Hitler*. trans. Richard and Clara Winston. New York: Harcount Brace Jovanovich, 1965.

Figes, Orlando. *A People's Tragedy: A History of the Russian Revolution*. New York: Viking Press, 1996.

Fink, Carole. *The Genoa Conference: European Diplomacy, 1921-1922*. Chapel Hill: University of North Carolina Press, 1984.

Fisher, Ernest F. Jr. *The United States Army in World War II, Cassino to the Alps*. Washington: U.S. Government Printing Office, 1977.

Fitzgerald, F. Scott. *Tender Is The Night*. New York: Charles Scribner's Sons, 1951.

Fontaine, Andre. *History of the Cold War*, vol. 1: *From the October Revolution to the Korean War, 1917-1950*. trans. D.D. Paige. New York: Pantheon Books, 1968.

Friedlander, Saul. *Prelude to Downfall: Hitler and the United States, 1931-1941*, trans. Aline B. and Alexander Werth. New York: Alfred A. Knopf, 1967.

Gaddis, John Lewis. *The Long Peace: Inquiries into the History of the Cold War*. New York: Oxford University Press, 1987.

___. *The United States and the Origins of the Cold War*. New York: Columbia University Press, 1972.

_____. *We Now Know: Rethinking Cold War History*. New York: Oxford University Press, 1997.

Gamelin, Maurice. *Servir*. 3 vols. Paris: Librairie Plon, 1946.

Garand, George W. and Strobridge, Truman R. *History of the U.S. Marine Corps Operations in World War II*. 4 vols. Washington: U.S. Government Printing Office, 1971.

Gilbert, Martin. *Winston S. Churchill*, vol. 5, *The Prophet of Truth, 1922-1939*. Boston: Houghton Mifflin Company, 1977.

_____. *Winston S. Churchill*, vol. 6, *Their Finest Hour, 1939-1941*. Boston: Houghton Mifflin Company, 1983.

_____. *Winston S. Churchill*, vol. 7, *Road To Victory, 1941-1945*. Boston: Houghton Mifflin Company, 1986.

_____. *Winston S. Churchill*, vol. 8, *Never Despair*. Boston: Houghton Mifflin Company, 1988.

_____. *The First World War: A Complete History*. New York: Henry Holt, 1994.

Glantz, David M. and House, Jonathan M. *When Titans Clashed: How the Red Army Stopped Hitler*. Lawrence: University Kansas Press, 1995.

Grand Strategy. J.M.A. Gwyer and J.R.M. Butler. 6 Vols. London: Her Majesty's Stationery Office, 1956.

Griffiths, Richard. *Pétain: A Biography of Marshal Philippe Pétain of Vichy*. Garden City, N.Y.: Doubleday and Company, 1972.

Guderian, Heinz. *Panzer Leader*. trans. Constantine Fitzgibbon. New York: Ballantine Books, 1961.

Halder, Franz. *Kriegstagebuch: tagliche Aufzeichnungen des Chefs des Generalstabes des Heeres, 1939-1942*. 3 vols. Stuttgart: W. Kohlmanner, 1962-1964.

Hamby, Alonzo M. *Man of the People: A Life of Harry S. Truman*. New

York: Oxford University Press, 1995.

Harries, Merrion and Susie. *Soldiers of the Sun: The Rise and Fall of the Imperial Japanese Army.* New York: Random House, 1991.

Harrison, Gordon A. *The United States Army in World War II, Cross-Channel Attack.* Washington: U.S. Government Printing Office, 1951.

Harrod, R.F. *The Life of John Maynard Keynes.* New York: Harcourt, Brace and Company, 1951.

Heckscher, August. *Woodrow Wilson.* New York: Charles Scribner's Sons, 1991.

Heinrichs, Waldo. *Threshold of War: Franklin D. Roosevelt and American Entry into World War II.* New York: Oxford University Press, 1988.

Henderson, Sir Nevile. *Failure of a Mission: Berlin, 1937-1939.* New York: G.P. Putnam's Sons, 1940.

Hildebrand, Kalus. *The Foreign Policy of the Third Reich.* trans. Anthony Fothergill. Berkeley: University of California Press, 1973.

Hilger, Gustav and Alfred G. Meyer. *The Incompatible Allies: A Memoir-History of German-Soviet Relations, 1918-1941.* New York: Macmillan Company, 1953.

Hillgruber, Andreas. *Die Rämung der Krim 1944: eine Studie zur Entstehung der deutschen Führungsentschlüsse.* Berlin: E.S. Mittler und Sohn, 1959.

Hinsley, F.H. *British Intelligence in the Second World War: Its Influence on Strategy and Operations.* 4 vols. New York: Cambridge University Press, 1979-1990.

Hitchins, Keith. *Rumania, 1866 - 1947.* New York: Oxford University Press, 1994.

Hitler, Adolf. *Mein Kampf.* trans. Ralph Manheim. Boston: Houghton Mifflin Company, 1943.

___. *Hitler's Secret Book.* trans. Salvator Attanasio. New York: Grove Press, 1961.

___. *Hitler's Table Talk, 1941-1944.* trans. Norman Cameron and R.H. Stevens. London: Weidenfeld and Nicolson, 1953.

Hochman, Jiri. *The Soviet Union and the Failure of Collective Security 1934-1938.* Ithaca: Cornell University Press, 1984.

Hoffmann, Peter. *The History of the German Resistance, 1933-1945.* trans.

Richard Barry. Cambridge, Mass: MIT Press, 1977.

Holloway, David. *Stalin and the Bomb: The Soviet Union and Atomic Energy, 1939-1956*. New Haven: Yale University Press, 1994.

Hossbach, Friedrich. *Zwischen Wehrmacht und Hitler, 1934-1938*. Göttingen: Vandenhoeck und Ruprecht, 1965.

Howe, George F. *The United States Army in World War II, Northwest Africa: Seizing The Initiative in the West*. Washington: U.S. Government Printing Office, 1957.

Hull, Cordell. *The Memoirs of Cordell Hull*. 2 vols. New York: Macmillan Company, 1948.

Hutmacher, J. Joseph. *Wilson's Diplomacy: An International Symposium*. Cambridge, MA: Schenkman Publishing Company, 1973.

Iriye, Akira. *The Origins of the Second World War in Asia and the Pacific*. New York: Longman Incorporated, 1987.

Ismay, Hastings L. *The Memoirs of General Lord Ismay*. New York: Viking Press, 1960.

Keegan, John. *Six Armies In Normandy: From D-Day to the Liberation of Paris, June 6th-August 25th, 1944*. New York: Viking Press, 1982.

Kennan, George F. *Memoirs, 1925-1950*. Boston: Little, Brown, and Company, 1967.

___. *Russia and the West Under Lenin and Stalin*. Boston: Little, Brown, and Company, 1950.

Kirby, S. Woodburn et al. *The War Against Japan*. 5 vols. London: Her Majesty's Stationery Office, 1957-1969.

Kirkpatrick, Ivone. *Mussolini: A Study in Power*. New York: Hawthorn Books, Incorporated, 1964.

Kissinger, Henry. *Diplomacy*. New York: Simon and Schuster, 1994.

Klehr, Harvey. *The Heyday of American Communism: The Depression Decade*. New York: Basic Books, 1984.

Knox, MacGregor. *Mussolini Unleashed, 1939-1941: Politics and Strategy in Fascist Italy's Last War*. New York: Cambridge University Press, 1982.

Knox, Thomas J. *To End All Wars: Woodrow Wilson and the Quest for a New World Order*. New York: Oxford University Press, 1992.

Koller, Karl. *Der letze Monat: Die Tagebuchaufzeichnungen des ehema-

ligen Chefs des Generalstabes der deutschen Luftwaffe vom 14 April bis zum 27 Mai 1945. Mannheim: Norbert Wohlgemuth, 1949.

Kovrig, Bennett. *Communism in Hungary: From Kun to Kadar.* Stanford: Stanford Univerity Press, 1979.

Krannhals, Hans von. *Der Warschauer Aufstand 1944.* Frankfurt am Main: Berard und Graefe Verlag für Wehrwesen, 1964.

Kurzman, Dan. *Day of the Bomb: Countdown to Hiroshima.* New York: McGraw- Hill, 1986.

Lacouture, Jean. *De Gaulle.* vol. 1, *The Rebel*, 1890-1944. trans. Patrick O'Brian. vol 2, *The Ruler, 1944-1970.* trans. Alan Sheridan. New York: W.W. Norton Company, 1990-1992.

Leach, Barry A. *German Strategy Against Russia, 1939-1941.* Oxford: Clarendon Press, 1973.

Leahy, William D. *I Was There: The Personal Story of the Chief of Staff to Presidents Roosevelt and Truman Based on His Notes and Diaries Made at the Time.* New York: McGraw-Hill, 1950.

Lenczowski, George. *Russia and the West in Iran, 1918-1948.* Ithaca: Cornell University Press, 1949.

Lenin, V.I. *Collected Works*, 45 vols. trans. Yuri Sdobnikov and George Hanna, ed. George Hanna. Moscow: Progress Publishers, 1964.

___. *The Unknown Lenin: From the Secret Archive.* ed. Richard Pipes. New Haven: Yale University Press, 1996.

Le Tissier, Tony. *The Battle of Berlin.* London: Jonathan Cape, 1988.

___. *Zhukov at the Oder: The Decisive Battle for Berlin.* Westport, CT: Praeger, 1996..

Lincoln, W. Bruce. *Red Victory: A History of the Russian Civil War.* New York: Simon and Schuster, 1989.

Liddell Hart, B.H. *History of the Second World War.* New York: G.P. Putnam's Sons, 1971.

___. *The German Generals Talk.* New York: William Morrow and Company, 1948.

Lewis, W. Roger. *Imperialism at Bay: The United States and the Decolonization of the British Empire, 1941-1945.* New York: Oxford University Press, 1978.

Link, Arthur S. *Wilson: The Struggle for Neutrality, 1914-1915.* Princeton: Princeton University Press, 1960.

___. ed. *Woodrow Wilson and a Revolutionary World*. Chapel Hill: University of North Carolina Press, 1982.

Lloyd George, David. *Memoirs of the Peace Conference*. 3 vols. New York: Howard Fertig, 1972.

___. *War Memoirs of David Lloyd George, 1917-1918*. 5 vols. Boston: Little, Brown, and Company, 1936.

Lüdde-Neurath, Walter. *Regierung Dönitz: Die letzten Tage des Dritten Reiches*. Göttingen: Musterschmidt-Verlag, 1964.

Lundin, C. Leonard. *Finland in the Second World War*. Bloomington: Indiana University Press, 1957.

MacDonald, Charles B. *A Time for Trumpets: The Untold Story of the Battle of the Bulge*. New York: William Morrow and Company, 1985.

___. *The Last Offensive*. Washington: U.S. Government Printing Office, 1973.

___. *The Siegfried Line Campaign*. Washington: U.S. Government Printing Office, 1963.

Macksey, Kenneth. *Guderian: Creator of the Blitzkrieg*. New York: Stein and Day, 1975.

McCullough, David. *Truman*. New York: Simon and Schuster, 1992.

McJimsey, George. *Harry Hopkins: Ally of the Poor and Defender of Democracy*. Cambridge: Harvard University Press, 1987.

Maddox, Robert J. *Weapons for Victory: the Hiroshima Decision Fifty Years Later*. Columbia: University of Missouri Press, 1995.

Maisky, Ivan. *Memoirs of a Soviet Ambassador: The War: 1939-43*. New York: Charles Scribner's Sons, 1967.

___. *The Munich Drama*. Moscow: Novosti Press Agency, 1972.

Marks, Sally. *The Illusion of Peace: International Relations in Europe, 1918-1933*. New York: St. Martin's, 1976.

Mastny, Vojtech. *Russia's Road to the Cold War: Diplomacy, Warfare, and the Politics of Communism, 1941-1945*. New York: Columbia University Press, 1979.

Matloff, Maurice. *The United States Army in World War II, Strategic Planning for Coalition Warfare, 1943-1944*. Washington: U.S. Government Printing Office, 1958.

Matloff, Maurice and Snell, Edward M. *The United States Army in World*

War II, Strategic Planning for Coalition Warfare, 1941-1942. Washington: U.S. Government Printing Office, 1953.

Mayer, Arno J. *Political Origins of the New Diplomacy, 1917-1918.* New Haven: Yale University Press, 1959.

Meehan, Patricia. *The Unnecessary War: Whitehall and the German Resistance to Hitler.* London: Sinclair-Stevenson, 1992.

Meskill, Johanna M. *Hitler and Japan: The Hollow Alliance.* New York: Atherton Press, 1966.

Messer, Robert L. *The End of an Alliance: James F. Byrnes, Roosevelt, Truman, and the Origins of the Cold War.* Chapel Hill: University of North Carolina Press, 1982.

Mikolajczyk, Stainislaw. *The Rape of Poland: Pattern of Soviet Aggression.* New York: McGraw-Hill Company, 1948.

Miller, Marshall Lee. *Bulgaria During the Second World War.* Stanford: Stanford University Press, 1975.

Minott, Rodney G. *The Fortress that Never Was: The Myth of Hitler's Bavarian Stronghold.* New York: Holt, Rinehart, and Winston, 1964.

Montgomery of Alamein, Bernard L. Montgomery. *The Memoirs of Field-Marshal Montgomery of Alamein.* Cleveland: The World Publishing Company, 1958.

Molotov, Viacheslav M. *Molotov Remembers: Inside Kremlin Politics.* ed. Albert Resis. Chicago: Ivan R. Dee, 1993.

Moran, Charles M. *Churchill: Taken from the Diaries of Lord Moran: The Struggle for Survival, 1940-1965.* Boston: Houghton Mifflin Company, 1966.

Morley, James W. ed. *Deterrent Diplomacy: Japan, Germany, and the USSR, 1940.* New York: Columbia University Press, 1976.

___. *The Fateful Choice: Japan's Advance into Southeast Asia, 1939-1941.* New York: Columbia University Press, 1980.

___. *The Final Confrontation: Japan's Negotiations with the United States, 1941.* New York: Columbia University Press, 1994.

Neuman, H.J. *Arthur Seyss-Inquart.* Wien: Verlag Styria, 1970.

Newman, Robert P. *Truman and the Hiroshima Cult.* East Lansing: Michigan State University Press, 1995.

O'Connor, Timothy Edward. *Diplomacy and Revolution: G.V. Chicherin and Soviet Foreign Affairs, 1918-1930.* Ames: Iowa State University Press, 1988.

Overy, Richard. *Why the Allies Won.* New York: W.W. Norton Company, 1995.

Padfield, Peter. *Dönitz: The Last Führer: Portrait of a Nazi War Leader.* New York: Harper and Row, 1984.

Papen, Franz von. *Memoirs.* trans. Brian Connell. New York: E.P. Dutton and Company, 1953.

Paul, Allen. *Katyn: The Untold Story of Stalin's Polish Massacre.* New York: Charles Scribner's Sons, 1991.

Paul-Boncour, Joseph, *Recollections of the Third Republic.* 3 vols. trans. George Marion Jr. New York: Robert Speller and Sons, 1957.

Payne, Stanley. *Fascism: Comparison and Definition.* Madison: University of Wisconsin Press, 1980.

Phillips, Hugh D. *Between the Revolution and the West: a Political Biography of Maxim M. Litvinov.* Boulder: Westview Press, 1992.

Pike, David W. *Les Français et la guerre d'Espagne.* Paris: Presses universitaires de France, 1975.

Pipes, Richard. *The Formation of the Soviet Union.* Cambridge: Harvard University Press, 1964.

___. *The Russian Revolution.* New York: Alfred A. Knopf, 1990.

___. *Russia Under the Bolshevik Regime.* New York: Alfred A. Knopf, 1994.

Pogue, Forrest C. *et al. D Day: The Normandy Invasion in Retrospect.* Lawrence: The University Press of Kansas, 1971.

___. *George C. Marshall*, vol. 2, *Ordeal and Hope, 1939-1942.* New York: Viking Press, 1966.

___. *George C. Marshall*, vol. 3, *Organizer of Victory, 1943-1945.* New York: Viking Press, 1973.

___. *George C. Marshall*, vol. 4, *Statesman, 1945-1959.* New York: Viking Press, 1987.

___. *The Supreme Command.* Washington: U.S. Government Printing Office, 1954.

Prange, Gordon W. *At Dawn We Slept: the Untold Story of Pearl Harbor.* New York: McGraw-Hill, 1981.

___. *Target Tokyo: The Story of the Sorge Spy Ring*. New York: McGraw-Hill, 1984.

Prażmowska, Anita J. *Britain and Poland: The Betrayed Ally*. New York: Cambridge University Press, 1995.

Preston, Paul. *Franco: A Biography*. New York: Basic Books, 1994.

Quinland, Paul D. *Clash Over Romania: British and American Policies toward Romania: 1938-1947*. Los Angeles: American Romanian Academy of Arts and Sciences, 1977.

Read, Anthony and Fisher, David. *The Deadly Embrace, Hitler, Stalin and the Nazi-Soviet Pact, 1939-1941*. New York: W.W. Norton Company, 1988.

Raeder, Erich. *My Life*. trans. Henry W. Drexel. Annapolis: United States Naval Institute, 1960.

Reynaud, Paul. *In the Thick of the Fight, 1930-1945*. trans. James D. Lambert. New York: Simon and Schuster, 1955.

Rhodes, Richard. *The Making of the Atomic Bomb*. New York: Simon and Schuster, 1986.

Rich, Norman. *Hitler's War Aims*. 2 Vols. New York: W.W. Norton Company, 1973.

Rowe, Vivian. *The Great Wall of France: The Triumph of the Maginot Line*. New York: G.P. Putnam's Sons, 1959.

Rowland, Peter. *David Lloyd George: A Biography*. New York: Macmillan Company, 1975.

Rozanov, German. *Hitlers letzte Tage*. Berlin: Dietz, 1963.

Sainsbury, Keith. *The Turning Point: Roosevelt, Stalin, Churchill, and Chiang Kai-shek, 1943, The Moscow, Cairo, and Teheran Conferences*. New York: Oxford University Press, 1985.

Schlessinger, Arthur M. Jr. *The Age of Roosevelt*. vol. 1. Boston: Houghton Mifflin Company, 1957.

Schmidt, Dr. Paul. *Hitler's Interpreter*. ed. R.H.C. Steed. New York: Macmillan Co., 1951.

Schroeter, Heinz. *Stalingrad*. New York: E.P. Dutton, and Company, 1958.

Schuschnigg, Kurt von. *Austrian Requiem.*. trans. Franz von Hildebrand. New York: G.P. Putnam's Sons, 1946.

Schwabe, Klaus. *Woodrow Wilson, Revolutionary Germany, and Peacemaking, 1918-1919: Missionary Diplomacy and the Realities of Power.* Chapel Hill: University of North Carolina Press, 1985.

Seaton, Albert. *The Russo-German War, 1941-45.* New York: Praeger Publishers, 1970.

Serrano Suñer, Ramon. *Entre les Pyrénées et Gibraltar: notes et réflexions sur La politique espagnole depuis 1936.* Genève: Éditions du Cheval ailè, 1948.

Sherwin, Martin J. *A World Destroyed: The Atomic Bomb and the Grand Alliance.* New York: Alfred A. Knopf, 1975.

Shirer, William L. *The Collapse of the Third Republic: An Inquiry into the Fall of France in 1940.* New York: Simon and Schuster, 1969.

___. *The Rise and Fall of the Third Reich: A History of Nazi Germany.* New York: Simon and Schuster, 1960.

___. *Berlin Diary: The Journal of a Foreign Correspondent.* New York: Alfred A. Knopf, 1941.

Spector, Ronald H. *The Eagle Against the Sun.* New York: Free Press, 1985.

Stalin, Joseph V. *Works.* 13 vols. Moscow: Foreign Language Publishing House, 1953-55.

Starr, Chester G. *From Salerno to the Alps: A History of the Fifth Army, 1943-1945.* Washington, D.C.: Infantry Journal Press, 1948.

Steffens, Lincoln. *The Autobiography of Lincoln Steffens.* New York: Harcourt, Brace, and World, 1931.

Stettinius, Edward R. *Roosevelt and the Russians: The Yalta Conference.* ed. Walter Johnson. Garden City, NY: Doubleday and Company, 1949.

Stimson, Henry L. and Bundy, McGeorge. *On Active Service in Peace and War.* New York: Harper and Brothers, 1948.

Stolfi, R.H.S. *Hitler's Panzers East: World War II Reinterpreted.* Norman: University of Oklahoma Press, 1991.

Stoler, Mark A. *The Politics of the Second Front: American Military Planning and Diplomacy in Coalition Warfare, 1941-1945.* Westport, CT: Greenwood Press, 1977.

Stypulskowski, Zbigniew. *Invitation to Moscow.* New York: Walker and Company, 1962.

Taylor, Telford. *Munich: The Price of Peace.* Garden City, NY: Doubleday and Company, 1978.

Tedder, Arthur. *With Prejudice: The War Memoirs of Marshal of the Royal Air Force Lord Tedder G.G.B.* London: Cassell and Company Limited, 1956.

Templewood, Samuel John Gurney Hoare, 1st Viscount. *Nine Troubled Years.* London: Collins, 1954.

Thomas, Hugh. *The Spanish Civil War.* New York: Harper and Row, 1961.

Toland, John. *The Rising Sun: The Decline and Fall of the Japanese Empire, 1936-1945.* New York: Random House, 1970.

Tompkins, C. David. *Senator Arthur H. Vandenberg: The Evolution of a Modern Republican, 1884-1945.* Lansing: Michigan State University Press, 1970.

Thorne, Christopher. *Allies of a Kind: The United States, Britain, and the War Against Japan, 1941-1945.* New York: Oxford University Press, 1978.

Truman, Harry S. *Memoirs.* 2 vols. Garden City, NY: Doubleday and Company, 1956.

Tuchman, Barbara W. *The Guns of August.* New York: Macmillan Company, 1962.

Tucker, Robert. *Stalin as Revolutionary, 1879-1929.* New York: W.W. Norton Company, 1973.

___. *Stalin In Power: The Revolution from Above, 1928-1941.* New York: W.W. Norton Company, 1990.

Turner, Henry Ashby Jr. *German Big Business and the Rise of Hitler.* New York: Oxford University Press, 1985.

Ulam, Adam B. *Expansion and Coexistence: Soviet Foreign Policy, 1917-1973*, 2nd ed. New York: Praeger, 1974.

___. *Stalin: The Man and His Era.* New York: Viking Press, 1973.

U.S. Strategic Bombing Survey. *Japan's Struggle to End the War.* New York: Garland Publishing, Inc., 1976.

Van Creveld, Martin L. *Hitler's Strategy 1940-1941: The Balkan Clue.* London: Cambridge University Press, 1973.

The Private Papers of Senator Vandenberg. ed. Arthur H. Vandenberg Jr. New York: Houghton Mifflin Company, 1952.

Vetter, Charles E. *Sherman: Merchant of Terror, Advocate of Peace.* Gretna, LA: Pelican Publishing Co., 1992.

Volkogonov, Dmitri. *Stalin: Triumph and Tragedy.* trans. Harold Shukman. Rocklin, CA.: Prima Publishing, 1992.

Walker, J. Samuel. *Prompt and Utter Destruction: Truman and the Use of Atomic Bombs against Japan.* Chapel Hill: The University of North Carolina Press, 1997.

Waller, John H. *The Unseen War in Europe.* New York: Random House, 1996.

Walworth, Arthur. *Woodrow Wilson.* 2 vols. New York: Longmans, Green, and Company, 1958.

Warner, Geoffrey. *Pierre Laval and the Eclipse of France.* New York: Macmillan Company, 1968.

Watt, Donald. *How War Came: The Immediate Origins of the Second World War, 1938-1939.* New York: Pantheon Books, 1989.

Weinberg, Gerhard L., *The Foreign Policy of Hitler's Germany: Diplomatic Revolution in Europe, 1933-1936.* Chicago: University of Chicago Press, 1970.

___. *The Foreign Policy of Hitler's Germany: Starting World War II, 1937-1939.* Chicago: University of Chicago Press, 1980.

___. *Germany and the Soviet Union, 1939-1941.* Leiden: E.J. Brill, 1954.

___. *A World at Arms: A Global History of World War II.* New York: Cambridge University Press, 1994.

___. *Germany, Hitler, and World War II: Essays in Modern German and World History.* New York: Cambridge University Press, 1995.

Welles, Sumner. *Seven Decisions that Shaped History.* New York: Harper and Brothers, 1951.

Wheeler-Bennett, John W. *Munich: Prologue to Tragedy.* New York: Viking Press.

___. *The Nemesis of Power: The German Army in Politics, 1918-1945.* New York: Viking Press, 1964.

Widenor, William C. *Henry Cabot Lodge and the Search for an American Foreign Policy.* Berkeley: University of California Press, 1980.

Wilt, Alan F. *The Atlantic Wall: Hitler's Defenses in the West, 1941-1944.* Ames: Iowa State University Press, 1975.

Woodward, Sir Llewellyn. *British Foreign Policy in the Second World War.*. 5 vols. London: Her Majesty's Stationery Office, 1970-1976.

Zhukov, Georgii. *Marshall Zhukov's Greatest Battles.* trans. Theodore Shabad. New York: Harper and Row, 1969.

___. *The Memoirs of Marshal Zhukov.* New York: Delacorte Press, 1971.

Ziemke, Earl P. *Stalingrad to Berlin: The German Defeat in the East.* Washington: U.S. Government Printing Office, 1968.

Ziemke, Earl P. and Bauer, Magna E. *Moscow To Stalingrad: Decisions in the East.* Washington: U.S. Government Printing Office, 1987.

Articles:

Barnes, Harry E. "Woodrow Wilson." *The American Mercury.* 1 (April, 1924): 490.

Bisson, T.A. "What Program for Japan?" *Nation.* vol. 161 (July 14, 1945): 28-29.

Bix, Herbert P. "Japan's Delayed Surrender: A Reinterpretation." *Diplomatic History.* 19 (Spring, 1995): 197-225.

___. "The Showa Emperor's 'Monologue" and the Problem of War Responsibility." *Journal of Japanese Studies.* 18 (Summer, 1992): 295-363.

Braddick, Henderson. "The Hoare-Laval Plan: A Study in International Politics." *Review of Politics.* 14 (July, 1962): 342-364.

"The Covenant Now." *The New Republic.* 19 (May 24, 1919): 108-110.

Craig, Gordon A. "Making Way for Hitler." *New York Review of Books.* 36 (October 12, 1989): 11-13.

Dilnot, Frank. "What Will the Europeans Think of Wilson?" *New York Times* (Supplement), December 1, 1918.

Draper, Theodore, "Eisenhower's War: The Final Crisis," *New York Review of Books.* 33 (October 23, 1986): 61-67.

Fink, Carole. "European Politics and Security at the Genoa Conference." *German Nationalism and the European Response, 1890-1945.* ed. Carole Fink, et al. Norman: University of Oklahoma Press, 1985.

Kahn, David. "Why Weren't We Warned?" *MHQ: The Quarterly Journal of Military History.* 4, no. 1 (Autumn, 1991): 50-59.

Lippmann, Walter. "The Political Scene." *New Republic.* 18 (March, 22, 1919, (Supplement): 1-14.

___. "The A.B.C. of Alliances." *New Republic*. 19 (May, 22, 1919): 106-110.

Mosley, Philip E. "The Occupation of Germany: New Light on How the Zones Were Drawn." *Foreign Affairs*. 28 (July, 1950): 580-604.

Mueller, John. "Pearl Harbor: Military Inconvenience, Political Disaster." *International Security*. 16, no. 3 (Winter, 1991-92): 172-203.

Nathan, Roger. "Histoire désabusée de la Conférence de Londres," *L'Europe Nouvelle*. vol. 16 (1933): 592.

"Noble Negatives," *Economist*. vol. 147 (December 30, 1944): 857-858.

Shepardson, Donald E. "The Fall of Berlin and the Rise of a Myth," *The Journal of Military History*. vol. 62 (January, 1998): 135-154.

"A Spectator's Notebook," *Spectator*. vol. 151 (July 7, 1933): 6.

Stone, I.F. "Pearl Harbor Diplomats." *Nation*. vol 161 (July 14, 1945): 25-27.

Tournow, General Paul-Emile. "Les origines de La Ligne Maginot." *Revue d'historie de la deuxième guerre mondiale*. No. 3 (January, 1959): 3-14.

Newspapers:

New York Times: 1914-1945.

Times (London): 1914-1945.

INDEX

A

Action Française, 40
Albania, invasion of, 98
Alexander, Harold, 185, 186, 190, 222, 249, 265
Alexander of Yugoslavia, 52
Allied Control Commission, for Germany, 280, 283
Alphonso XIII, 60
America First Committee, 164
Amery, Leo, 115, 130
Anderson, Kenneth, 188-189
Anglo-French force, World War II, 124, 129-130
Anschluss, 71-78
  reaction to, 81, 83
Anti-Comintern Pact, 69, 70
anti-Semitism, 28, 50, 78, 91-92
Antonescu, Ion, 145, 222, 235
Antonov, Alexei, 252
appeasement, policy of, 39, 90, 93
Arcadia Conference, 179
Arnim, Hans-Jürgen von, 189-190
Astakov, George, 103, 106-107
Atlantic Charter, 167-168, 179, 181, 248, 256, 259

atomic bomb, 258
  Japan, informing of, 285
  Soviet Union, informing of, 284-285
  testing of, 282, 284-285
  use of, 287, 288
Attlee, Clement, 257
  at Potsdam conference, 286
Attolico, Bernardo, 111
Auchinleck, Claude, 184
Austria
  Anschluss, 71-78
  inter war years, 53-54
Austria-Hungary, in World War I, 7, 11, 13

B

Badoglio, Pietro, 56, 205
Baldwin, Stanley, 38, 55, 131
Bararin, Eugene, 106-107
Barcelona, Spanish Civil War, 65
Barthou, Louis, 52
Battle of the Marne, 1
Beck, Josef, 51, 94, 95
"Beer Hall Putsch," 29
Belgium
  inter war years, 105, 112

in World War I, 1
World War II, 131, 133, 134
Bell, Johannes, 18
Benes, Edward, 82-88
Berchtesgaden, 68, 70, 71, 74, 86, 91, 94, 103, 104, 226, 227, 268
Berlin Treaty, 19
Bernadotte, Folke, 272
Berry, Burton, 263
Bevin, Ernest, at Potsdam conference, 286
Bingham, Robert, 65
Blomberg, Werner von, 70, 71
Blood purge, of Sturmabteilungen (SA), 31-32, 53, 87
Blum, Léon, 41, 62, 76-77, 82-83
Blumenkriegen, 77
Blumentritt, Günter, 228
Bock, Fedor von, 160, 162
Bolshevik Party, 6, 8-9
Bonnet, Georges, 49, 83, 84, 86, 87, 91, 107
Bono, Emilio, 56
Bor-Komorowski, Tadeusz, 233, 234
Bormann, Martin, 273
Bradley, Omar, 249, 268, 269
Brauchitsch, Walther von, 92, 132, 134, 136, 147, 163
Braun, Eva, 272, 273
Brest Litovsk, Treaty of, 7-8, 9
Briand, Aristide, 42
Brockdorff-Rantzau, Ulrich von, 18
Brooke, Alan, 208, 249, 250
Broz-Tito, Joseph, 235

Budenny, Semyon, 162
Bukharin, Nicholas, 24-25
Bulgaria
  communism established in, 262
  inter war years, 105, 106
  post-war plans for, 283
  in World War I, 11
  World War II, 144-146, 151, 235-236
Bullitt, William C., 55, 73, 84, 85
Burckhardt, Carl, 112
Byrnes, James, 257
  at Potsdam conference, 282, 285, 286-287, 290

C

Caesar Line, 224
Cairo Conference, first, 211-212
Cairo Conference, second, 219-220
Carol II, 145
Casablanca Conference, 197-198, 200
Chamberlain, Neville, 38, 39, 49, 72, 76, 81, 83-91, 93-94, 95, 98, 99, 100, 107, 114, 115, 122, 129, 130, 131, 140
Chautemps, Camille, 40, 72, 76
Chernyakhovsky, Ivan, 244
Chiang Kai-shek (Jiang Jieshi), 43, 152, 211, 212, 219, 237, 259, 280
Chicherin, George, 8, 21, 22
China
  inter war years, 43
  Japanese invasion of, 168-169, 237

post-war plans for, 210, 259, 280
World War II, 219, 241, 251
Chotlitz, Dietrich von, 229
Christian X, 129
Chuikov, Vassily I., 191, 273
Churchill, Winston S.
   American war aid, 165, 166
   Atlantic Charter, 167-168, 181
   at Cairo conferences, 211-212, 219-220
   at Casablanca conference, 198-200
   early years, 38, 40, 48, 125
   on Eastern Europe occupation, 263
   France, support for, 133, 135-136, 225
   Germany, war against, 138, 190, 223, 250-251, 268-269
   on Greece, 247-248
   Italy, war against, 205, 250
   Operation Dynamo, 134
   post-war plans, 178, 207, 211-215, 248-249
   at Potsdam conference, 282-286
   as Prime Minister, 130-131, 179-180, 187, 188, 229, 286
   at Quebec conference, 207-208, 209, 236-237
   Soviet policy
      post-war, 280-281
      pre-war, 106
      war time, 158, 159, 182-184, 200, 233-234, 239-241, 265, 278-279
   Truman administration, relations with, 281
   at Yalta, 247, 251-257, 259-260
Churchill: The End of Glory, 138
Chvalkovsky, Frantisek, 93
Ciano, Galeazzo, 68, 102, 104, 105, 111, 127, 150, 204
Clark Kerr, Archibald, 183, 263, 266
Clark, Mark, 187, 222, 224
Clemenceau, Georges, 9, 20
   at Paris Peace Conference, 16, 18
Colby, Bainbridge, 23
Combined Chiefs, allied forces, 208, 211, 223, 237, 250, 268, 269
Comintern, 6, 22, 23, 25, 41, 45, 49, 62, 69, 178-179
   abolition of, 207
Commissar Order, 153
Committee of National Liberation, 136
Condor Legion, in Spain, 62
Coolidge, Calvin, 42
Cripps, Sir Stafford, 155
Curzon, George, 21
"Curzon Line," 21-22, 178, 240-241, 254, 256
Czech Legion, 10
Czechoslovakia
   dismemberment of, 81-93
   inter war years, 39, 51-52, 59

D

Daladier, Édouard, 40-41, 73, 82, 83, 85-87, 89-90, 107, 111, 112-113, 114-115, 122, 124, 128
Darlan, Jean, 135, 186-189, 199
Davies, Joseph, 281
Dawes Plan, 30
Decline of the West, The, 37
de Gaulle, Charles, 127, 135, 136, 187, 188, 189, 199, 200, 209, 229
Dekanosov, Vladimir, 154
Delbos, Yvon, 72-73
"democratic centralism," 6
Deniken, Anton, 20
Denmark
   inter war years, 98, 112
   World War II, 125, 129
Derevyanko, Kuzma, 293
Deutsche Arbeiter Partei, 29
Die Deutsche Katastrophe, 28
Dietrich, Sepp, 244
Diktat, 18
disarmament, desire for, 37-38
Disarmament Conference, 49-51
Djilas, Milovan, 240
Dobler, Jean, 57
Dolchstoss, myth of, 29
Dollfuss, Engelbert, 53, 71
Dönitz, Karl, 271, 272, 273-274
Doolittle, James A., 180-181
Douhet, Giulio, 140
Doumergue, Gaston, 52
Duff Cooper, Alfred, 87
Dumbarton Oakes, 236, 250
Durcansky, Ferdinand, 92

E

Ebert, Frederick, 12, 19
Economic Consequences of the Peace, The, 37
Eden, Anthony, 55, 72, 73, 178, 182, 206-207, 209, 239-240, 278
   at Yalta, 253, 255
Eisenhower, Dwight D., 184, 187, 188, 189, 198, 203, 205, 223, 237-239, 249, 264, 273
   Dresden campaign, 268-269
   Operation Overlord, 219, 224-226
   post-war role, 280
   Rhineland campaign, 264
El Alamein, battle of, 186, 190
Elsey, George, 288
Enabling Act, in Germany, 31
Erzberger, Matthias, 12
Estonia, 9, 109-110, 123, 137
Ethiopia, 45, 54, 55, 56, 59
European Advisory Commission, 210-211, 215, 248, 249

F

Facta, Luigi, 27
Falange Española, 61
Falkenhayn, Erich von, 2
Fasci di Combattimento, 26
fascism
   in Italy, 26-27
   in Spain, 60-61
Fatherland Front, 71, 72, 75, 235
"February dilemma," 244

Final Solution, 222
Finland
  inter war years, 109-110, 112
  World War II, 123-124, 126, 127, 145, 146, 232
"Fireside chat," Franklin D. Roosevelt, 165, 180, 219-220
Flandin, Pierre, 54
Foch, Ferdinand, 10, 11, 12, 18, 20, 39
Four Power Pact, 50, 90
Fourteen Points Plan, 10, 11, 12, 16, 18
France
  allied invasion plans, 207-208
  Free French, 199, 229. *See also* de Gaulle
  German invasion of, 122, 124-125, 127-128, 131-134, 135-136
  inter war years, 38, 39-41, 51-54, 59, 72-73, 76-77, 81, 82-83, 83-91, 106, 107, 111, 112-113, 114
  Paris Peace Conference, 16, 18
  post-war plans for, 251-252, 253, 257
  Spanish Civil War, 62, 63
  Vichy government, 136, 149, 169, 186-188, 229
  in World War I, 2-3, 13
Franco, Francisco, 61, 65, 148-149, 284
François-Poncet, André, 91
Franco-Soviet Pact, 57-58
Free Corps, Weimar Republic, 19

Friedeburg, Hans von, 273
Fritsch, Werner von, 70, 71
front populaire. See Popular Front

G

Gamelin, Maurice, 58, 83, 124, 131-133
Geneva conference (1927), 42
Genoa conference (1922), 22
George VI, 130-131
Georges, Alphonse, 131
German-Soviet Pact (1939), 30, 99-101, 102-103, 106-110, 120-121
Germany
  Eastern front, 143-152, 155, 158, 160-162, 220-222, 232-233, 242-243
  Norway/Denmark, attacks on, 125
  post-war plans for, 215, 237-238, 239-240, 248-249, 253, 255, 280, 283, 284
  Soviet Union, relations with, 120-122, 124
  Spanish Civil War, 61-62, 63
  Third Reich, 51, 57-59, 69, 73-76, 93-94, 98, 99, 102-114
  United States, war with, 163-164, 172
  Weimar Republic, 19, 30-31
  Western front, 132-136, 227
  in World War I, 1-3, 4, 7, 8, 9, 11-13
  World War II, last days of, 199, 201-206, 220-224, 226-228, 235, 238, 241-243, 264, 267-

268
Geyr von Schweppenburg, Leo, 226
Giraud, Henri, 187, 188, 189, 199, 200, 229
Goebbels, Joseph, 201, 272, 273
Göring, Hermann, 62, 70, 74, 76, 92, 93, 134, 136, 139, 140, 144, 271-272
Grand Alliance, 177, 202, 220, 236, 247, 265, 277
Grandi, Dino, 204
Great Britain
  Anglo-German naval agreement, 55
  and Anschluss, 76, 81
  Cairo conference, 211-212
  Czechoslovakian crisis, 84-94
  Dunkirk, 134-135
  on Eastern Europe, Soviet occupation of, 263
  Ethiopian policy, 72
  Greece, role in, 247-248
  guarantor role, 98, 111, 112, 114-115
  Hess visit, 154-155, 180
  interwar years, 37-39
  in North Africa, 151, 184
  Paris Peace Conference, 16, 18
  post-war plans, 248-249
  Rhineland crisis, 58-59
  Soviet Union, relations with, 106, 107, 110, 122, 124, 158-159, 182, 265, 278-279
  Spanish Civil War, 63, 65
  in World War I, 2-3, 13

World War II, 125, 126, 129-130, 138-140
Great Depression, impact of, 27-28, 31, 38, 40, 43, 45, 48-49
"Great Marianas Turkey Shoot," 236
Greece, 98, 149-150, 239, 247-248, 283
Greenwood, Arthur, 114
Grew, Joseph, 290
Gromyko, Andrei, 236, 266
Gröner, William, 12, 19
Guderian, Heinz, 77, 119, 132, 134, 162, 163, 243, 270
Guernica, bombing of, 62, 64
Gusev, Fedor, 255
Gustav Line, 222-223

H

Haakon VII, 129, 130
Habsburg, Otto von, 73
Hácha, Emil, 92-93
Haig, Sir Douglas, 12
Halder, Franz, 110, 119, 132, 134, 144, 147, 160, 162, 191
Halifax, Lord, 72, 76, 83-84, 87, 93, 114, 130-131, 181
Harding, Warren G., 41-42
Harriman, W. Averell, 184, 239-240, 241, 263, 265, 266, 267, 278
Hassell, Ulrich von, 54
Henderson, Neville, 83-84, 85, 110-111, 112, 113, 115
Henlein, Konrad, 82, 83, 84
Hess, Rudolf, 136, 154-155
Hilger, Gustav, 103

Himmler, Heinrich, 78, 244, 270, 271, 272
Hindenburg, Paul von
  in Weimar Republic, 30, 31
  in World War I, 2, 4, 11, 12
Hirohito, 170, 175, 288-289, 292-293
  Chinese view of, 292
  U. S. view of, 290, 292
Hiroshima, bombing of, 291
Hitler, Adolf
  Anschluss, 70-78
  consolidation in Europe, 143-153, 155
  conspiracies against, 122, 227-228
  Danzig/Corridor, 94-95
  dismemberment of Czechoslovakia, 81-82, 84-93
  inter war years, 50-51, 53, 57-58, 69
  legacy of, 277
  last days of, 270-272, 273
  rise of, 28-32
  Soviet Union, invasion of, 158, 161-164, 166, 168, 172, 190-193
  Spanish Civil War, 61, 65, 68
  North Africa, war in, 186, 189
  West, invasion of, 121-127, 132, 134-140
  World War II
    last stages of, 199, 201-206, 220-224, 226-228, 235, 238, 241-243, 264, 267
    preparation for war, 98, 99, 102, 104, 105, 106, 107, 108-109, 110-114
Hoare, Sir Samuel, 55-57
Hoare-Laval plan, 56-57
Hoffmann, Max von, 8
Hoge, William, 265
Home Army, Poland, 233, 234, 240, 264
Hoover, Herbert C., 43
Hopkins, Harry, 153-154, 177, 182, 184, 279-280
Horthy, Nicholas, 222, 241-242
Hossbach, Friedrich, 70
House, Edward, 16, 17-18
Hughes, Charles Evans, 42
Hull, Cordell, 44-45, 48, 49, 81, 170, 171, 180, 199, 209, 210, 237, 250, 290
Hungary
  communism established in, 262
  inter war years, 91, 92, 93, 98, 101-102, 104-105, 110, 111, 113, 105
  post-war plans for, 239, 245
  World War II, 144, 145, 222, 241

I

Innitzer, Theodore Cardinal, 78
Inönü, Ismet, 219
International Brigades, in Spain, 62
International Women's Day march, 5
Iran, 179
Ismay, Sir Hastings, 182
Italy

324 *Index*

allied post-war plans, 213-215, 283
fascism, rise of, 26-27
inter war years, 45, 53-54, 56, 59-60
invasion of, 197-198, 200, 202-206, 208, 222-223
Paris Peace Conference, 16
Spanish Civil War, 61, 63
World War II, 126-127, 135, 136, 148-150

J

Jänecke, Erwin, 221
Japan
    inter war years, 38, 43, 44-45, 69, 103
    Siberia, penetration into, 9, 21, 38
    Soviet declaration of war, 291
    surrender terms for, 280, 285-286, 292-293
    war causalities, 289
    World War II, 120, 145, 152, 152-153, 162-163, 168-173, 177, 236, 237, 241, 258, 287, 288-290
Japan's Struggle to End the War, 288
Jiang Jieshi. *See* Chiang Kai-shek
Jodl, Alfred, 71, 144, 273-274
Juntas de Ofensiva Nacional-Sindicalista (JONS), 60-61

K

Kamenev, Lev, 23, 24-25
Katyn Forest, 201-202, 234

Keitel, Wilhelm, 74, 92, 93, 136, 138, 144
Kellogg, Frank B., 42
Kellogg-Briand pact, 30, 42
Kennan, George F., 25, 167, 284
Keppler, Wilhelm, 73-74, 75, 77
Kerensky, Alexander, 6-7
Kesselring, Albert, 206, 222, 223, 224, 265, 267, 271, 273
Ketsu-Go policy, 289-290
Keynes, John Maynard, 37, 49
Kienthal conference, 6
King, Ernest J., 197
Kirov, Sergei, 26
Kissinger, Henry, 282
"Kitchener's Army," 2-3
Knox, Frank, 164
Knudsen, Otto, 123
Koenig, Pierre, 225
Kolchak, Alexander, 20
Koller, Karl, 271
Konev, Ivan S., 221, 244, 270, 271
Konoe Fuminaro, 152, 170, 289
Krebs, Hans, 273
Kristallnacht, 91-92, 126
kulaks, Soviet policies toward, 24, 25
Kurusu Suburu, 170, 171
Kwantung Army, 43, 152, 170, 290

L

Latvia, 109-110, 123, 137
Laval, Pierre, 52, 53-55, 57, 127-128, 149
League of Nations, 17-18, 37-38,

Index 325

41, 43, 44, 51, 52, 53, 55, 112, 124
Leahy, William, 256
Lebensraum, 29-30, 104
Lebrun, Albert, 128
Lemery, Henry, 128
Lend-Lease Act, 166, 167, 199, 279
Lenin, Vladimir I., 5-6, 7, 8-9, 19, 20, 22, 23
Liebknecht, Karl, 19
Lipski, Joseph, 51, 94, 113
Lithuania, 94, 123, 137
Little Entente, 39-40, 50, 52, 59
Litvinov, Maxim, 45, 52, 55, 101, 179, 181, 277
Lloyd George, David, 32, 70, 106
  defeat of, 38
  Genoa Conference, 22
  Paris Peace Conference, 16, 18, 20
Locarno conference, 30, 38
Lodge, Henry Cabot, 17
London Poles, 201-202, 215, 233, 240, 254, 263
Lublin Poles, 233, 240, 254-255, 256, 278
Lucas, John, 223
Ludendorff, Erich, 2, 4, 11-12
Lusitania, sinking of, 4
Luxemburg, 112, 133
Luxemburg, Rosa, 19
Lvov, George, 5

M

MacArthur, Douglas, 169, 173, 180, 197, 293
MacDonald, Ramsey, 50, 54, 131
Madrid, Spanish Civil War, 62, 63, 65
Maginot Line, 40, 58, 76, 131, 132-133
Maisky, Ivan, 49, 159, 178
Malinovsky, Rodion I., 221, 269
Malta conference, 249, 250
Manchuria
  Japanese control of, 43, 45, 152
  Soviet attacks on, 103, 291
Manhattan Project, 208-209
  Soviet knowledge of, 285
Mannerheim, Karl von, 123, 232
Mannerheim Line, 124, 125
Manstein, Erich von, 132, 192, 221
Mao Tse-tung (Mao Zedong), 152
Margival conference, 227
Marshall, George C., 179, 181, 182, 184, 197-198, 203, 208, 212, 219, 223, 249-250, 251, 264, 268, 285
  at Yalta, 252
Masaryk, Thomas, 82
Masurian Lakes, battle of, 2
Matsuoka Yosuke, 43, 152-153, 162
Max of Baden, 11, 12
Mechelen Incident, 131-132
Mein Kampf, 29
Meinecke, Friedrich, 28
Merekalov, Alexei, 100-101, 103
Mexico, 4, 25
Midway, battle of, 173
Miklas, Wilhelm, 75, 77

Mikolajczyk, Stanislaw, 233, 240, 254, 256
Mission to Moscow, 281
Mit brennender Sorge, 78
Model, Walter, 267-268
mokusatsu policy, 290-291
Mola, Emilio, 61
Molotov, Vyacheslav
   end-of-war negotiations, 265
   Germany, negotiations with, 103, 106, 107-108, 120, 121, 137, 145-147, 155
   Japan, war with, 291
   at Moscow conference, 210
   post-war demands, 239-240
   at Potsdam conference, 286
   at San Francisco conference, 267, 279
   selection of, 101
   on Soviet East European policy, 263
   United States, negotiations with, 182-183, 278
   on World War II, 159
   at Yalta, 252, 255, 257
Moltke, Helmuth von, 1
Montgomery, Bernard, 185, 186, 189, 226, 228, 237, 239, 249, 267, 268, 269
Morgenthau, Henry, 237-238, 282
Morgenthau Plan, 237-238
Moscow conference, 209-210, 258
Müller, Hermann, 18
Munich Syndrome, 90
Muraviev, Constantine, 235
Mussolini, Benito
   Albania, war with, 98
   death of, 272
   downfall of, 204-205, 206
   Ethiopia, war with, 56, 57, 59
   inter war years, 53, 68-69, 70, 89, 101-102, 104, 111, 113
   rise of, 13, 26-28,
   Spanish Civil War, 61, 65
   Stresa Front, 54-55, 59-60
   at World Disarmament Conference, 49-50
   World War II, 125, 126, 127, 135, 136, 149-150

N

Nagasaki, bombing of, 292
Nagumo Chuichi, 171
Namonhan Incident, 103
Nanking (Nanjing), China, 152, 168-169
National Coalition, Great Britain, 38, 55
National Socialist German Worker's Party. *See* Nazi Party
Nationalists, in Spain, 61, 64-65
Nazi Party, 29, 31-32, 50
Netherlands
   inter war years, 112
   World War II, 131, 133
Neurath, Konstantine von, 68, 69, 70, 71
New Deal, 48-49
New Economic Policy (NEP), 23, 24
Nicholas II, abdication of, 5
Nixon, Richard M., 90
Nomura Kichisaburo, 170, 171

Norway
    inter war years, 112
    World War II, 125, 129-130
Nuremberg Laws, 32
Nye, Gerald, 64

O

occupation zones, post-war
    Germany, 248, 253
Oikawa Koshiro, 289
Old Diplomacy, 16-17, 18
Olympic Games (1936), 32
Operation Anvil, 223, 228
Operation Bagration, 232-233
Operation Barbarossa, 158, 161
    preparations for, 147-148, 150, 153, 155
Operation Blue, 190
Operation Buffalo, 223-224
Operation Cobra, 228
Operation Coronet, 287-288
Operation Diadem, 223
Operation Dragoon, 228
Operation Dynamo, 134-135
Operation Eagle, 139
Operation Green, 84, 85
Operation Grief, 243
Operation Husky, 203-204
Operation Iceberg, 287
Operation Jupiter, 208
Operation Margarethe I and II, 222
Operation Market-Garden, 238-239, 242
Operation Olympic, 287-288
Operation Overlord, 224-228
Operation Overlord, preparation for, 208, 210, 211, 213, 219
Operation Punishment, 151
Operation Schulung, 57
Operation Sea Lion, 139-140
Operation Shingle, 223
Operation Torch, 184, 185, 186, 188, 199, 203
Operation Typhoon, 162
Operation Undertone, 264
Operation, Veritable, 264
Operation White, 98, 112
Operation Yellow, 122-123, 132
Orlando, Vittorio, Paris Peace
    Conference, 16-20
Ostfriesland, sinking of, 42

P

Pact of Steel, 101-102
Pahlavi, Mohammed Reza, 179
Papen, Franz von, 31, 71, 78
Paris Peace Conference, 17-18, 27, 39
Patton, George, 189, 228, 243, 249, 277
Paulus, Friedrich von, 190, 192-193
"Peace Ballot," 38
Pearl Harbor, attack on, 170, 171, 172-173
"permanent revolution," 24
Pershing, John J., 12
Petachi, Clara, 272
Pétain, Henri-Philippe
    France, invasion of, 128, 134, 135, 136
    in World War I, 2
    Vichy, 136, 149

Petrograd, 5, 6
Petrograd Soviet of Workers and Soldiers, 5, 7
Phipps, Sir Eric, 84
"Phony War," 120, 123
Pilsudski, Joseph (Jozef), 21
Pius XI, 78
Pius XII (Eugenio Pacelli), 78, 112
plebicite, in Austria, 74-76, 78-79
Poland, communism established in, 263-264
Poland
    Germany, invasion by, 119-120
    inter war years, 39-40, 51-52, 59, 84, 91, 94-95, 107, 110, 112
    post-war plans for, 240, 245, 254-256, 257, 266-267, 283, 284
    Soviet Union
        conditions for, 278, 279-280, 283, 284
        invasion by, 120
        invasion of, 21, 233-234
Polish War, 21-22
Popular Front, 41, 49, 52, 61
Potemkin, Vladimir, 52
Potsdam conference, 282–287
Potsdam Declaration, 285-286, 287, 290, 291, 292
Primo de Rivera, José Antonio, 61
Primo de Rivera, Miguel, 60
Pritwitz, Max von, 2

Q

Quebec conference, 208-209, 236, 239
Questions of Leninism, 24
Quisling, Vidkun, 125, 130

R

Radescu, Nicolae, 262-263
Raeder, Erich, 70, 103, 125, 136, 138-139, 147-148, 150, 165
Rapallo Treaty, 22
Rathenau, Walter, 22
Red Army
    Berlin, drive to, 269-270, 271
    Eastern Europe, advance in, 208, 220-222, 232-235, 242-245
    Manchuria, attack on, 291
    early role of, 20, 21
    occupation of Eastern Europe, 262, 264
    purge of, 26
    World War II, 123-124, 125, 153, 159, 161, 192- 193, 201, 202
Redondo, Onesimo, 60
Reichswehr (German army)
    replacement of, 32
    Soviet training of, 23
Renner, Karl, 287
Reunification Law, in Austria, 77-78
Reynaud, Paul, 128, 133, 134, 135
Rhineland Crisis (1936), 58-59
Ribbentrop, Joachim von, 69, 76, 90-94, 102, 104, 108-111, 120-121, 126-127, 136, 144-147, 201
Robin Moor, sinking of, 166

Rokossovsky, Konstantin K., 244, 270, 271
Rome-Berlin axis, 69, 70
Rommel, Erwin, 151, 184, 185-186, 189, 226-227
Roosevelt, Franklin D.
  on Anschluss, 81
  at Arcadia conference, 179
  Atlantic Charter, 168
  background of, 43-44
  at Casablanca conference, 197-202, 229
  death of, 267
  on Eastern Europe occupation by Soviet Union, 263-264
  Lend-Lease, 164-166, 167
  post-war plans, 207, 211-215, 237-238, 248-249
  pre-war policies for war, 64, 85, 92, 98-99, 126, 136
  at Quebec conference, 208-209, 236, 339
  Soviet Union, relations with 124, 181-182, 219-220, 233-234, 265-266
  at Teheran conference, 211, 212-215, 219-220, 224
  World War II, 112, 171-172, 180-181, 187-188, 205, 207-208, 236
  at Yalta conference, 247, 251-260
Romania
  communism established in, 262-263
  inter war years, 39, 84, 94, 98, 105
  post-war plans for, 239, 283
  during World War II, 137-138, 144-145, 146, 178, 220-221, 222, 234-235, 241-242
  in World War I, 9
Rundstedt, Gerd von, 134, 160, 162, 163, 226-227, 238-239, 242, 267
Russia. *See also* Soviet Union
  Provisional government in, 4, 5, 7
  World War I, 2, 3, 7, 13

S

San Francisco conference, 266, 279
Sanatescu, Constantin, 235, 262
Sanjurjo, José, 61
Sarrant, Albert, 58
Sato Naotake, 290, 291
Scheidemann, Philipp, 12
Schellenberg, Walter, 272
Schlieffen Plan, 40
Schmundt, Rudolf, 132
Schnurre, Karl, 103, 106-107
Schulenburg, Friedrich Werner von, 103, 107, 108, 121, 137, 145, 153, 154, 155
Schuschnigg, Kurt von, 68, 72, 73-77
Second Book of 1928, 29
Seyss-Inquart, Arthur, 71-72, 73-78, 92
Sikorski, Wladyslaw, 178, 201
Simeon II, 235
Simpson, William, 270

Sitzkrieg (Phony War), 120, 123
Skorzeny, Otto, 242-243
"socialism in one country," 24, 45
Sokolovsky, Vasili, 270, 271
Somme (1916), battle of the, 2-3
Sorge, Richard, 153
Soviet Union. *See also* Russia
  in Asian theater, 259, 289
  civil war in, 8, 9, 10, 20-21
  establishment of, 7, 8-9
  Eastern Europe, policy in, 262, 263, 278, 279, 284
  German invasion of, 153-155, 158, 160-163, 177-178, 181, 190-193, 202-203
  inter war years, 45, 49, 52-53, 90, 99-101, 103-104, 106-110
  post Stalingrad, 210, 232-235, 242-245, 252
  Spanish Civil War, 62, 63-64
  during war in West, 120-122, 123-124, 125, 126, 137-138, 143, 146-147
Spain, 105, 110, 383
  civil war in, 45, 60-65
Spartakusbund, 19
Spengler, Oswald, 37
Stalin, Joseph, 23
  at Casablanca conference, 197
  Eastern European policy, post-war, 262, 263, 279-280, 284
  fear of separate Western peace, 266, 270
  inter war years, 38, 52, 53, 65, 90, 99-100, 106, 107, 109
  Japan, war with, 291

Polish policy, 120-121, 123-124, 201-202, 233-234, 240, 266-267, 278
  post-war plans, 207, 210, 213-215, 236, 240, 245
  at Potsdam conference, 282-287
  relations with West, post-war, 277
  pre-war policies, 147, 153-155
  purges of, 25-26, 53
  rise of, 24-25
  Spanish Civil War, 62, 63-64, 65
  United States, relations with, 177-178, 211, 267
  World War II, 119, 143, 159-161, 162-163, 183, 184-185, 188, 191, 193, 200-201, 232-233, 243-244, 245
  at Yalta conference, 247, 251-259
Stalingrad, battle of, 190-193, 201
Standley, William, 183
Stavisky Affair, 40
Steffens, Lincoln, 23
Steiner, Felix, 271
Stettinius, Edward, 278
  at Yalta, 250, 252, 253, 254, 255, 257
Stilwell, Joseph W., 211, 239
Stimson Doctrine, 43
Stimson, Henry L., 43, 164, 181, 207, 237-238, 285, 290
Stone, I. F., 290
Strang, William, 106

Stresa Front, 54-55, 57, 59-60
Stresemann, Gustav, 30
submarine warfare, in World War I, 4
Suedetenland, crisis in the, 82, 83-86, 88-89, 91
Suñer, Raymond Serrano, 148
Suvich, Fulvio, 54, 68
Suzuki Kantaro, 289, 290-292
Sweden, 105, 112
Switzerland, 98
Syrovy, Jan, 89

T

Taft, Robert A., 166
Tannenberg (1914), battle of, 2, 3
Tedder, Arthur, 225
Teheran conference, 211, 212-216, 219-220, 224, 258
Third International, Lenin's call for, 6. *See also* Comintern
Thorez, Maurice, 41, 111
Tibbets, Paul, 291
Timoshenko, Semyon, 159
Tiso, Monsignor Josef, 92, 93
Togo, Shigenori, 292
Tojo Hideki, 170, 171, 236
Tolbukhin, Feodor, 269
Transportation Plan, Operation Overlord, 225
Tripartite Pact, 145, 147, 164, 169
Trotsky, Leon, 7, 24-25
Truman, Harry S., 90, 167, 207, 272
  atomic bomb, 291
  background of, 277-278
  Pacific, war in, 281
  at Potsdam conference, 282-287
  Soviet policy of, 277, 278, 279-280
  on United Nations, 281-282
Tunisia, 187-190
Turkey, 11, 210, 219

U

"Ultra," 139, 189, 228, 242
United Nations, negotiations to create a, 236, 252, 253-254, 257, 258, 280, 283
  San Francisco conference, 279, 281
United States
  Anschluss, reaction to, 81
  inter war years, 38, 41-44, 45, 81, 85, 90, 92, 98-99, 112
  Japan, planned invasion of, 287-288
  Paris Peace Conference, 16-19
  post-war Japanese government, 292-293
  on Soviet occupation of Eastern Europe, 263-264
  Spanish Civil War, 64-65
  in World War I, 4
  World War II, 159, 163-165, 166-169, 171, 172, 199, 236, 258
U.S.S. Greer, sinking of, 168

V

Vandenberg, Arthur, 248, 253, 279
Verdun (1916), battle of, 2, 3

Versailles, Peace of, 17, 18, 19, 37, 50-51, 58, 199
Victor Emmanuel III, 27, 204-205
"victory disease," 238
Viebahn, Max Von, 74
Vlasov, Andrei, 161
Voroshilov, Klimenti, 107, 162

W

Warsaw Uprising (1944), 233-234
Washington conference (1921), 42
Washington conference (1943), 203
Wehrmacht (German army), 32, 98, 119-120, 122, 129, 145, 151, 161-162, 202, 222, 228, 243
  casualties of, 264
Wehrmacht Law, 32
Weidling, Helmuth, 273
Weizsäcker, Ernst von, 101
Welczec, Johannes von, 73
Welles, Sumner, 126, 159
Wells, H. G., 140
Western Front, World War I, 1, 2, 3, 39
Weygand, Maxime, 21, 134, 135
Whites, in Soviet Union, 8, 9, 20-21
William II, 11, 12
Willkie, Wendell, 164
Wilson, Hugh, 92, 126
Wilson, Sir Horace, 88
Wilson, Woodrow
  attacks on, 41
  Paris Peace Conference, 16-19
  views of, 3-4, 9-11

Winant, John, 255
World Economic Conference, 49

Y

Yalta conference, 245, 251-259
Yezhov, Nicholas, 26
Young Plan, 30
Yudenich, Nicholas, 20
Yugoslavia
  inter war years, 84
  post-war plans for, 239
  World War II, 151, 235

Z

Zeitzler, Kurt, 192
Zhukov, Georgi K., 159, 162, 163, 221, 244, 264, 269, 270, 271, 273
  Allied Control Commission, 280
Zimmerwald conference, 6
Zinoviev, Gregory, 23, 24-25
Zossen Conspiracy, 122

Studies in Modern European History

The monographs in this series focus upon aspects of the political, social, economic, cultural, and religious history of Europe from the Renaissance to the present. Emphasis is placed on the states of Western Europe, especially Great Britain, France, Italy, and Germany. While some of the volumes treat internal developments, others deal with movements such as liberalism, socialism, and industrialization, which transcend a particular country.

The series editor is:

>Frank J. Coppa
>Director, Doctor of Arts Program
>in Modern World History
>Department of History
>St. John's University
>Jamaica, New York 11439

To order other books in this series, please contact our Customer Service Department:

>800-770-LANG (within the U.S.)
>(212) 647-7706 (outside the U.S.)
>(212) 647-7707 FAX

or browse online by series at:
>WWW.PETERLANG.COM